Law and sustainable development since Rio

Legal trends in agriculture and natural resource management

FAO
LEGISLATIVE
STUDY

73

FAO Legal Office

FOOD AND AGRICULTURE ORGANIZATION OF THE UNITED NATIONS
Rome, 2002

ISBN 92-5-104788-X

FOREWORD

The United Nations Conference on the Environment and Development (Rio de Janeiro, 1992), known as UNCED and more familiarly as Rio, has been a legal landmark. It produced the Convention on Biological Diversity (CBD), which in turn has been complemented by the Cartagena Protocol on Biosafety and followed by the International Treaty on Plant Genetic Resources for Food and Agriculture (ITPGR).

Rio also produced several soft law instruments, especially Agenda 21, which contains extensive prescriptions for the "further development of international law on sustainable development" and for the establishment of effective national legal frameworks. Both of these have been acted upon. The Rotterdam Convention on the Prior Informed Consent Procedure for Hazardous Chemicals, the Stockholm Convention on Persistent Organic Pollutants and the UN Fish Stocks Agreement are only examples of a busy period in international law. These and other hard and soft law instruments are in turn influencing national legislation.

Not everything that has happened since Rio is due to Rio. As this book demonstrates, there has hardly been an area untouched by law reform in the last ten years. While Rio catalysed or influenced much of this activity, much of it is also due to the World Trade Organization agreements of 1994, as well as to the collapse of communism, which led to wholesale law reform in the affected countries. Thus the same decade has seen a burst of activity in the drafting of seed, plant variety and food safety legislation as well as laws concerning land reform and every sort of privatization.

The Legal Office of FAO has one of the largest programmes of legal technical assistance of any international organization. This has given its officers a unique vantage point from which to observe the legislative changes in food, agriculture and natural resource management, subjects at the core of sustainable development law. In many cases we have participated directly as advisers to governments developing new legislation. The Legal Office has also been directly involved in the preparation of important international agreements, including the Convention to Combat Desertification, the CBD, the ITPGR, the Rotterdam Convention, the revised International Plant Protection

Convention, the Fisheries Compliance Agreement and several regional fisheries agreements. A number of non-binding international legal instruments were also developed. The officers and non-staff collaborators of the Legal Office have written this book in order to commemorate the ten years since Rio, and also to share our collective experience in development law over an even longer period.

The book consists of 12 chapters, for the most part divided into categories such as water or fisheries that correspond with administrative departments in many governments. These chapters reflect very considerably our experience in advising governments, usually through such departments, on legislation dealing with these subjects. To some extent, the organization of this book is a matter of convenience. As will be evident, none of these subjects stands alone, and they are linked together in often intricate ways. Good lawmaking is almost inevitably a multisectoral affair. Any law on forestry, for example, will reverberate through the land, wildlife, plant protection and water sectors, and will in turn be shaped by the legal frameworks governing each of these. We hope that a collection of this sort, bringing together legal analyses on such a wide range of specific topics, will help build a better appreciation of the interrelationships that hold them together.

Two chapters, on mountains and on gender, are specifically organized around cross-sectoral themes. Both of these have emerged as significant issues for sustainable development law. The year 2002 is the International Year of Mountains, and the theme is likely to be given a lot of attention at the World Summit on Sustainable Development in Johannesburg (Rio plus 10). Gender issues cut across virtually all aspects of agriculture and natural resource management, and ways of enhancing the rights of women have received renewed attention in recent years.

Many people have contributed to the book in different ways through their regular advisory work, their discussions with national counterparts in member countries and with each other and through their collaboration in conceptualizing, writing and reviewing the chapters that make up the book.

I wish to take this occasion to mention particularly those who contributed directly to the writing of the different chapters: Alexander Behrens (animals), Stefano Burchi (water), Claudia Cantarella (agrobiodiversity), Astrid Castelein (mountains), Maria Teresa Cirelli (wildlife), Lorenzo Cotula (gender, wildlife), William Edeson (fisheries), Laurence Helfer (plants), Blaise Kuemlangan (fisheries), Jonathan Lindsay (introduction, land), Ali Mekouar (agrobiodiversity, forestry, mountains), Steve Neves (food), Marta Pardo Leal (animals, food, plants), Laura Pasetto (reports and publications), Melvin Sprey (fisheries, food), Patrice Talla (introduction, mountains), Annick Van Houtte (fisheries), Jessica Vapnek (afterword, animals, food, plants), Margret Vidar (food) and Annie Villeneuve (mountains). I would also like to thank Barbara Moauro, who was responsible for the layout and printing of the book, and Jonathan Lindsay, who assisted greatly with everything from conceptualizing the book to checking formatting and references in the final stages.

Finally, I wish to extend special thanks to Jessica Vapnek and Ali Mekouar for their outstanding contributions. They edited every chapter of the book, dedicating evenings and weekends to its style and accuracy. In addition, Ali conceived the idea of the book, prepared the first plan for producing it, established the deadlines that few of us met and prodded us to keep going in order to meet the final deadline that would allow the book to appear at Rio plus 10. Without him we would not have done it.

Lawrence Christy
Chief
Development Law Service
Legal Office

TABLE OF CONTENTS

1

INTRODUCTION

Contents

I.   RIO AND THE LAW OF SUSTAINABLE DEVELOPMENT

The United Nations Conference on Environment and Development (UNCED, Rio de Janeiro, 1992) did not invent the term "sustainable development", but it was very much the occasion that gave it formal, general acceptance. The term itself was defined in the report of the World Commission on Environment and Development (the Brundtland Report) in 1987 as "development that meets the needs of the present without compromising the ability of future generations to meet their own needs".

Sustainable development law can similarly find antecedents prior to Rio, but it was only there that the world community subscribed to its essential principles. It is not just environmental law, but an integrated approach in which environmental protection and its legal instruments are incorporated into the development process. How this is to be done in practice is still being worked out, but several general principles seem well accepted. One is that policies must be designed to meet development needs, especially those of the poor. The "sustainable" corollary is that the environmental effects of development must be taken into consideration before acting. Another principle, which has been particularly influential since Rio, is that in the absence of scientific certainty, any action that risks serious or irreversible harm should not be undertaken (the precautionary principle). Two further related principles are those of access to information and participation in decisionmaking.

Rio was not a legal conference, but it had a particularly marked effect on law. The Conference adopted the Convention on Biological Diversity, the Rio Declaration on Environment and Development, the Non-binding Forest Principles and the extremely influential Agenda 21. Besides giving some systematic content to sustainable development law, the Rio Declaration and Agenda 21 place law in a central position among the means of achieving the goals of the Conference. Chapter 19 of Agenda 21 is devoted to international law and recognizes first of all the importance of the "further development of international law on sustainable development". Chapter 8B states that "an effective legal and regulatory framework" is essential to the effective integration of the environment and development in national policies.

The outputs of Rio did not end with the Conference. The Convention on Biological Diversity has since come into force (as has the Framework Convention on Climate Change) and is now being incorporated into national legislation. The Forest Principles have continued to be developed and to influence thinking on forestry and forestry law. Agenda 21 continues to guide the further development of sustainable development law, both internationally and nationally.

Ten years after Rio, the World Summit on Sustainable Development (Rio plus 10) provides an appropriate occasion for taking stock of what has been accomplished in the law of sustainable development. This book reports and reflects on the changes that have taken place, on emerging trends and on interesting experiments in the legal frameworks governing agriculture and natural resource management, subjects that are at the centre of the sustainable development agenda. Since it has been a very active decade in the legal world, there is much to report on.

II.   FACTORS INFLUENCING THE DIRECTION OF LEGAL CHANGE SINCE RIO

The role of law in development has been perceived differently over time, ranging from a belief that good laws lead directly to development, to great skepticism that law matters at all. Generalizations in this area are dangerous. In the first place there are many different legal systems, some of which accept change more easily than others. Each country has its own traditions regarding administrative law, the use of litigation and the role of the judiciary and other legal institutions. Moreover, the role of law in society varies enormously: in some countries legislation seems generally effective, while in others it appears to have little impact. Other sources of variation are almost infinite.

Nonetheless, as legal professionals working in development worldwide, the authors have come to believe that law is essential to creating suitable enabling environments for government action and private initiative. Good laws and functioning legal institutions contribute to the predictability, security and flexibility needed to foster development. Conversely, poorly designed and implemented laws can inhibit effective action, by distorting incentives and discouraging appropriate interventions by government and civil society. Good law, of course, is only one among a number of elements that need to be in place for meaningful change to occur, but it is an important one – and judging from the amount of new legislation the past decade has produced, law's central importance is widely recognized.

There are often quite specific reasons for a given legal reform, but there are also some overarching factors that have influenced the pace, nature and direction of legal reform more generally over the last ten years. Some of these factors have taken the form of tangible events, others have emerged as shifts in thinking, priorities and strategies. They include greatly expanded environmental awareness at global and national levels; the collapse of communism; the movement towards privatization of many government functions; the acceleration of globalization; the strengthening of regional cooperation in many parts of the world; heightened international appreciation of the importance of good governance; and an increasing emphasis on devolution and decentralization strategies across all sectors of government. These factors, in various combinations, have influenced virtually every one of the areas addressed in this book, resulting in some striking similarities among innovations in very different legal systems.

Environmental awareness. In the wake of the Rio Conference and a host of other international environmental conferences, many developing countries are seeking to design basic legal instruments for environmental protection and the sustainable management of natural resources. Many countries have adopted national framework environmental laws, creating new environmental agencies and establishing environmental impact assessment procedures. Sectoral laws governing the exploitation of natural resources have been or are being revised to reflect the imperatives of sustainable development and the specific national obligations set forth in the Rio agreements, as well as in such international instruments as the Basel Convention on the Control of Transboundary Movements of Hazardous Wastes and their Disposal, the Convention on International Trade in Endangered Species of Flora and Fauna, the Montreal Protocol on Substances that Deplete the Ozone Layer and others.

Collapse of communism. With the collapse of communist systems, many countries (including a number of entirely new countries) have been faced with the need to create new legal institutions and bodies of market-friendly, democratic law almost from scratch, without even the benefit – dubious as it may be in some contexts – of the colonial legal traditions from which many new countries in other parts of the world were able to start. These countries have needed to create laws that:

- define the universe of property rights in the system;
- set a framework for exchanging these rights;
- set the rules for the entry and exit of actors into and out of productive activities;

- oversee market structure and behaviour to promote competition. (Gray, 1993)

Towards this end, many countries have been engaged in writing everything from constitutions and civil codes to laws on taxation, banking, companies, bankruptcy, competition, commercial transactions, local government, land, housing, elections – in short, the whole panoply of laws perceived as essential for creating a modern national legal framework appropriate for a market economy and for the functioning of democratic institutions.

Privatization. In Central and Eastern Europe and other countries in transition to market economies, privatization is obviously related to the dismantling of socialist governing structures. But it is a worldwide phenomenon. Whether through domestically inspired reform, or under pressure from outside in the form of structural adjustment programmes and the like, countries around the world are facing the need to revise legal structures in a direction that is more favourable to private investment and the disentanglement of government from the market and from the provision of services.

However ambivalent a particular government may feel about it, and however inconsistently it might be applied, the philosophy of privatization has seeped into virtually all sectoral policies, with corresponding adjustments both to general and sector-specific legislation. Thus, in agriculture and natural resource management, there has been increasing legislative attention to issues such as deregulating agricultural cooperatives; introducing cost recovery in irrigation; reducing the role of government in commercial forestry; creating tradeable fishing quotas; facilitating the exchange of private rights in land; and improving the legal environment for private trade.

Globalization. Providing additional impetus to the foregoing trends is the inexorable integration of national economies into the world economy. As a result of this phenomenon, many nations are increasingly looking for domestic legal models with which foreign partners feel comfortable. Sharing of international experience plays a particularly important role in highly specialized, rapidly growing fields such as intellectual property rights, communication and trade, where the meshing of domestic laws with complex international instruments is especially complicated, and where domestic legal experience may be especially absent.

The growth in the number of countries joining the World Trade Organization and therefore bound by its agreements has created a flurry of interest in revising legislation to meet international obligations and to capture the principles of these agreements, such as harmonization, equivalence and non-discrimination. Within the areas covered by this book, the Agreement on the Application of Sanitary and Phytosanitary Measures has had wide-ranging effects on national legal frameworks and policies, due to its identification of the Codex Alimentarius, the *Office international des épizooties* and the International Plant Protection Convention as the sources of international consensus on food safety, animal and plant health measures. The Agreement on Trade-Related Intellectual Property Rights, which imposes specific obligations on WTO member countries to provide protection for plant varieties and to provide reciprocal protection to one another, is another undeniable step toward globalization.

Regionalization. The dynamics referred to in connection with globalization often apply on a regional basis as well. Countries eager to join the European Union (EU), for example, are faced with the task of conforming laws on a wide range of subjects to EU requirements, touching on virtually all areas of agriculture and natural resources law. MERCOSUR, CARICOM and NAFTA, amongst others, have also influenced the legislation of their members, especially although not exclusively on trade matters. Regional standard-setting organizations have also been busy building on international models while tailoring standards and measures to regional interests, in particular in such fields as plant protection. The creation of new regional economic groupings such as the African Union confirms the expectation that regionalization will continue to grow in importance alongside globalization.

Good governance. The goal of good governance is a theme that has increasingly influenced legal and institutional reforms, even if its realization in practice remains elusive in many parts of the world. Concepts such as participation in decisionmaking, access to information, transparency and accountability, have affected law design in every sector, and have begun to change the way governments do business and interact with civil society on matters ranging from awarding forestry concessions to setting food control standards to monitoring environmental compliance. The Declaration of the World Food Summit: five years later gave special emphasis to the importance of strengthening the rule of law and good governance to solve socio-economic problems and to achieve food security. The Aarhus Convention on Access to Information, Public

Participation in Decision-Making and Access to Justice in Environmental Matters was an important step in capturing an international consensus on these concepts, in the context of environmental governance.

Devolution and decentralization. In the face of globalization and other examples of convergence, there are a number of trends that appear to celebrate the potential of *divergence* – namely, the growing emphasis on decentralization and devolution of government powers and responsibilities. Legal frameworks are being changed to reflect policies promoting local decisionmaking and community-based initiatives in a wide variety of fields. Decentralization is a strategy that is widely embraced in principle by governments and international agencies, and is one that finds expression in numerous legal instruments. The promotion of "community" is another theme that figures especially prominently in current thinking about environmental and natural resource management. In forestry, water, fisheries, land use, wildlife and other areas, the emphasis is on moving away from state monopolies, and towards a stronger vesting of management responsibilities and property rights in local governments or communities.

A mixture of forces drives these trends. The reliance on local and community capabilities may be promoted as a pragmatic way of accomplishing more effective management of resources than central governments alone have been able to provide. Devolution is also seen as a better way of meeting the basic needs of resource-dependent populations, and in some contexts, of recognizing indigenous peoples' rights to self-determination. Rio documents, in particular Agenda 21, the Convention on Biological Diversity and the Forest Principles, exhort governments to review legislation and property regimes in order to provide a better legal framework for community management. The challenge is to design legislation that both enables and guides such activities, a task that often requires a significant reorientation of legal texts and institutions.

III. THE PROCESS OF LEGAL CHANGE

The amount of legal activity in the last ten years has made it a good period from which to draw some lessons about the process of legal change. Despite the variations in national strategies and legal traditions, it is possible to suggest a framework for analysing existing legal frameworks and assessing possible reforms. Although it should be obvious, it is worth emphasizing that the analysis needs to begin with existing laws, both the letter and application, before countries can turn to considering what to change. Starting from what is already there is important for several reasons. If the current law is good enough, time may be better spent on other matters. Alternatively, if the reasons the current law is not satisfactory are not changed, the new law is unlikely to work any better. After analysis of the current legal framework comes an assessment of the feasibility of changing the existing constraints – along with an identification of the priority order for legal change, followed finally by the choice of legal solutions.

3.1. Analysing the Substance of the Law

An analysis of the existing written law involves asking some broad questions which are relevant in quite different circumstances. The answers to these questions will provide policymakers with a window onto the strengths, weaknesses, overlaps and gaps in the current legal framework.

- *Does the law provide an appropriate positive regulatory environment for activities in support of sustainable development?* Sustainable development requires a body of predictable, understandable and enforceable rules. Issues that frequently come up in connection with the promotion of sustainable development include whether there are appropriate rules:
    - governing access to and management of public goods, such as water and other natural resources;
    - addressing the externalities of public and private actions, including environmental, land use and public safety implications;
    - regulating the behaviour of government officials, to ensure basic limits on the exercise of discretion, and to support transparency and accountability; and
    - ensuring a right of meaningful participation, including access to information.

- *Is the law relatively free of unnecessary regulatory constraints that could inhibit activities that are essential for achieving the goals of sustainable development?* Regulatory obstacles may hinder development by increasing costs and creating undesirable incentives. Constraints may take the form of bureaucratic procedures that increase the transaction costs of a particular activity, without a corresponding public benefit. Or they may unintentionally create incentives for unwanted behaviour, as when restrictions on logging discourage forest owners from planting trees. Every legal system contains examples of such provisions. A legal framework analysis can help lay the groundwork for weeding these out.

- *Are the mandates for different institutional actors clear, coordinated and desirable?* The laws establishing and empowering institutions may make sustainable development easier or harder to achieve. Laws may leave it unclear, for example, which agency has the power to make certain decisions. The result could be that a key government stakeholder whose action is critical to the success of a particular strategy might find that its authority to undertake that action is open to challenge. In other contexts, the legal allocation of authority may be clear, but sub-optimal – for example, where authority is fragmented among different sub-agencies which do not function well together. Thus, an uncoordinated series of laws may authorize inspection of the same business, resulting in repeated and, in the end, harassing visits.

- *Does the legal framework provide mechanisms by which people can obtain meaningful and secure rights to the assets essential for their pursuit of sustainable livelihoods?* The assets referred to here can, of course, take many different forms, depending on the context. For example, secure rights in land, trees, water and other resources are essential to fostering investment, conservation and development. Many national legal frameworks fall far short of supporting sustainable access to – and providing secure rights over – such resources for rural people, and in fact may criminalize the exercise of traditional rights.

- *Does the law enable the formation and empowerment of appropriate stakeholder organizations?* The implementation of many actions in support of sustainable development depends on effective organization of stakeholders. Examples include local groups for the promotion of community-based management initiatives. The question is whether there is a legal basis for the creation or recognition of such institutions, and for vesting them with real rights, powers and responsibilities. If the law treats them as essentially nonentities, their capacity and incentive to shape and undertake action may be significantly constrained.

3.2. Analysing the Law in Action

The substantive content of law is, of course, only part of the story. It is also important to try to assess the actual effect that relevant laws have on the ground: in what ways do they influence the behaviour of individuals and institutions? A law nominally in force may fall short of its intended purpose or have quite unintended secondary effects, for a number of reasons, such as:

- *lack of political will:* The effectiveness of a law is often undercut by the failure of government to devote sufficient resources or energy to its implementation. Many good laws are simply not implemented.

- *failure to anticipate the modes and costs of effective implementation:* Many ambitious laws, internally coherent and technically well-drafted, have been enacted without sufficient prior attention to the costs of implementation. The result is laws that lie unimplemented or under-implemented.

- *failure to recognize the limitations of legal reform in bringing about social and economic change:* There is no magic to legal reform, and to pursue it effectively means being realistic about its potential for effecting real change on the ground. Laws that require sudden changes in deeply ingrained behaviour, or that require dramatic upheavals in institutional set-ups without laying the groundwork for such change, may prove difficult to implement.

- *lack of understanding or acceptance of the law by regulators and regulated:* Government officials may be ignorant about the content and the procedures of a law, with the result that they implement it improperly. Governments also frequently fail to engage civil society in the design of important laws, and to educate people about the contents of a law once it has been passed. As a result, they fail to build up support for the law amongst those stakeholders most directly affected, and many stakeholders may resist implementation of the law, or may remain ignorant of how to comply with the law or to take advantage of opportunities that it offers.

- *weak judicial institutions:* In many countries, the resolution of legal disputes is the responsibility of a court system that is overburdened and under-financed. Alternatives to traditional court systems may be few or non-existent. As a result, even good laws may not be enforced for lack of judicial mechanisms.

The importance of understanding the law in action has methodological implications. It means that a thorough analysis of the legal framework cannot rely entirely on a review of written instruments and cannot be undertaken only by legal experts. Such a review needs to be nested within a multidisciplinary effort to assess the perceptions, activities and interactions of the main stakeholders.

3.3. Weighing the Importance of Legal Change

Once the constraining features in the legal framework have been identified, the next step is to analyse how easy or hard it may be to correct those features, or at least to mitigate their impact. It is essential to identify what concrete technical and political steps are required to make the necessary changes, and what obstacles stand in the way. If the problems have arisen from the law in action, how can the defects in implementation be cured?

A related question is how high a priority to assign to any potential legal change. To what extent can existing legal deficiencies be, or will they have to be, "lived with"? To what extent are they such fundamental threats to policy goals that they will need to be addressed in a forthright fashion if the policy is to succeed? Here, two somewhat countervailing considerations should be kept in mind:

- On the one hand, it is important to be realistic in analysing the importance of a law. No legal system is flawless, and it is often possible to achieve promising development results in a less than ideal legal environment. Just as good laws do not in themselves ensure good results on the ground, so poor laws do not always lead to bad results, if there is sufficient will on the part of government and others to find ways of mitigating their weaknesses.

- On the other hand, however tempting it may be to find temporary or stop-gap solutions to legal flaws, it is also important to keep the longer view in mind. It may be possible to side-step legal problems for the time being, especially where there is a lot of powerful, high-profile support for a particular activity. But unless the more significant legal problems are dealt with head-on, there may well be difficulties in sustaining early successes. A basic rule is that when the initial wave of enthusiasm for a particular activity begins to wane, legal weaknesses are more likely to come to light and to be exploited.

3.4. Finding an Appropriate Solution

The authors of this study believe that creating a sufficient legal basis for sustainable development, or removing crippling constraints, requires more than technical solutions. It needs the genuine involvement of all categories of stakeholders – government and non-governmental institutions, central and local actors, communities, local resource-dependent people and private sector organizations. This recommendation does not flow only from a belief that people should have the right to be involved. Instead, the authors of this study are making a practical point: without this involvement, there is simply little hope of passing laws that reflect reality – including the real needs and priorities of affected people – and that are capable of being effectively used and implemented.

This recommendation goes beyond simply holding a few seminars or workshops at the end of the drafting process. It requires a true commitment to listening to and understanding the needs, objectives, insights and capacities of the intended users and others potentially affected by the law, and finding ways to accommodate the multiple interests at stake. It requires the determination to prevent the process being driven by the preconceptions of lawyers, donors and other outsiders, however well-intentioned. This is time-consuming work that ideally should entail patient consultations in the field with people directly affected, not simply in a distant capital city. And these consultations should start early, not only when a first draft has already been completed.

Broad participation in lawmaking not only improves the quality of the law, but it is also a significant factor in improving its implementation. It helps create a consensus in favour of the law. It may stimulate organized support of the law and active pressure for its enforcement, as opposed to indifference or passive resistance, which may impede implementation as effectively as active opposition does. At the least, participation publicizes legislation in the society at large, among those directly affected by it and those expected to enforce it.

Participation combined with drafting is not usually sufficient to ensure a workable law. Real experience with related problems and situations needs to be brought in as well. Examples offered should be local or national where suitable precedents exist, but no country should be afraid of comparative examples where other countries have already had relevant experiences. This is especially true where several countries, one after the other, have to implement the same treaty. The experiences of the first ones cannot rationally be ignored by the next.

The usefulness of technical assistance in developing legislation needs to be emphasized, as it was in Agenda 21 (para. 8.13). The way most governments are organized, lawyers frequently have little experience in formulating a particular type of agricultural or natural resources legislation, or even much experience with the subject matter. The great value of assistance in this situation is that it can bring in the missing expertise. Part of this will be in the form of the expert's exposure to the international consensus on particular issues, including the concerns that have informed the preparation of international agreements. Part of the added value will be the expert's personal experience in designing and drafting legislation of a particular kind. An even more important part will be the information that he or she has absorbed about the ways similar problems have been dealt with elsewhere, as well as about the successes and failures in implementing different legal provisions. Cross-cutting issues can be highlighted and comparative experiences shared.

REFERENCES

Boyle, A. & Freestone, D. (eds.). 1999. *International Law and Sustainable Development - Past Achievements and Future Challenges.* Oxford University Press, New York.

FAO. 2000. *Legal Framework Analysis for Rural and Agricultural Investment Projects: Concepts and Guidelines.* FAO Legal Paper Online No. 12 (www.fao.org/Legal).

Freestone, D. & Hey, E. 1996. *The Precautionary Principle and International Law: The Challenge of Implementation.* Kluwer Law International, The Hague.

Ginther, K., Denters, E. & De Waart, P.J.I.M. (eds.). 1995. *Sustainable Development and Good Governance.* Martinus Nijhoff, Dordrecht.

Gray, C.W. 1993. *Evolving Legal Frameworks for Private Sector Development in Central and Eastern Europe.* The World Bank, Washington, D.C.

Kiss, A. & Beurier, J.P. 2000. *Droit international de l'environnement (2ᵉ édition).* Pedone, Paris.

Kiss, A. & Shelton, D. 2000. *International Environmental Law (2ⁿᵈ edition).* Transnational Publishers, Ardsley, New York.

Lang, W., Neuhold, H. & Zemanek, K. 1991. *Environmental Protection and International Law.* Martinus Nijhoff, Dordrecht.

Sands, P. 1995. *Principles of International Environmental Law: Frameworks, Standards and Implementation.* Manchester University Press, Manchester.

World Commission on Environment and Development. 1987. *Our Common Future.* Oxford University Press, Oxford.

2

FOOD

Contents

I. INTRODUCTION

The 1992 Rio Declaration on Environment and Development proclaimed that human beings are entitled to a healthy and productive life in harmony with nature (principle 1), and Agenda 21 contains numerous references to food security, food safety and the rural poor. The right to food had been proclaimed, long before, in the 1948 Universal Declaration of Human Rights, and then reaffirmed in the 1996 International Covenant on Economic, Social and Cultural Rights.

Food security, however, remains a challenge in both developed and developing countries, although some progress has been made. In the period 1990–92, there were about 816 million undernourished people in the world – a figure that fell to 777 million by 1997–99. However, progress was unequal. The average rate of decline in the number of chronically undernourished has slowed in the last years, from 8 million a year in 1999 to 6 million a year in 2001. Consequently, the annual reduction required to reach the World Food Summit target of halving the number of under-nourished people by 2015 is now 22 million people per year. Continuing at the current rate, it will take more than 60 years to reach the target. (FAO, 2001a)

Since UNCED, problems of lack of economic and physical access to food have continued to be addressed at the international and national levels. Increasingly, attention has turned to the role of law in combating hunger and malnutrition. On the one hand, important developments have occurred in the application of the concept of the right to food as a human right. On the other hand, changes in the international trade regime have accompanied developments regarding food safety and related regulatory measures. The World Trade Organization Agreement on Sanitary and Phytosanitary Measures, which adopts the Codex Alimentarius as the source of all international standards on food, underlines the importance of food safety and food trade in today's world.

In many countries, recent food contamination problems have contributed to increasing lack of confidence in food safety among consumers. While some of these food contamination cases were accidental and unforeseen, others could have been predicted and avoided if proper monitoring and early warning mechanisms and controls had been in place. Hence the need for surveillance programmes which provide early warning about emerging food quality and safety problems and enable effective controls at both national and international levels. (FAO, 2001a)

The chapter will explore these two dimensions: first, developments regarding the clarification and implementation of the right to food as a human right; and, second, developments concerning food law, in particular in food safety and quality.

II.   RIGHT TO ADEQUATE FOOD

The right to food was first recognized in the Universal Declaration of Human Rights in 1948, and further codified by the 1966 International Covenant on Economic, Social and Cultural Rights (ICESCR), which entered into force in 1976. In the ICESCR the right is recognized as part of an adequate standard of living, which also includes housing and clothing (art. 11-1), and it enjoys separate recognition (art. 11-2). The right to food is also closely related to the right to life, which is protected under article 6 of the International Covenant on Civil and Political Rights. (ICCPR)

As will be discussed below, the right to food has acquired a more refined definition with the adoption of General Comment 12 to article 11 of the ICESCR. In that Comment, the right to adequate food is defined as being realized "when every man, woman and child, alone or in community with others, have physical and economic access at all times to adequate food or means for its procurement". This implies the "availability of food in a quantity and quality sufficient to satisfy the dietary needs of individuals, free from adverse substances, and acceptable within a given culture", and the "accessibility of such food in ways that are sustainable and that do not interfere with the enjoyment of other human rights". (CESCR, GC 12) The right to adequate food also encompasses food security, which is defined by FAO to exist "when all people, at all times, have physical and economic access to sufficient, safe and nutritious food to meet their dietary needs and food preferences for an active and healthy life". (World Food Summit Plan of Action, para. 1)

According to the Committee on Economic, Social and Cultural Rights (CESCR), which is the treaty body of independent experts that monitors state reports on compliance with the ICESCR, the right to food implies the right to means of production or procurement of food of sufficient quantity and quality, free from adverse substances and culturally acceptable. This right can be fulfilled by individuals' own efforts or in community with others, and must be enjoyed by all without any adverse distinction based on race, religion, sex, language, political opinion or other status.

2.1. International Framework: Key Developments

2.1.1. International Activities

(a) International Conference on Nutrition

The International Conference on Nutrition (ICN), held in Rome from 5 to 11 December 1992, was a major world event where food and environmental problems were addressed at the global level for the first time by the international community. Organized by FAO and the World Health Organization (WHO), the ICN was attended by delegates from 159 countries and the European Union (EU), and representatives from 144 non-governmental organizations (NGOs) and 27 intergovernmental organizations. The ICN adopted the World Declaration on Nutrition and the Plan of Action for Nutrition. The Declaration reflects a worldwide consensus that, globally, there is enough food for everyone, that inequitable access to food is the main problem and that each individual has a fundamental right to nutritionally adequate and safe food. In the Declaration, states commit themselves to act in solidarity to assure sustained nutritional well-being for all people in a peaceful, just and environmentally safe world.

The Plan of Action, which is linked to the Declaration, sets out four overall objectives: ensuring continued access by all people to sufficient supplies of safe food for a nutritionally adequate diet; achieving and maintaining the health and nutritional well-being of all people; achieving environmentally sound and socially sustainable development to contribute to improved nutrition and health; and eliminating famines and famine deaths. The Plan contains policy guidelines to help states attain these basic objectives, and outlines nine action-oriented themes that governments should consider in their efforts to improve nutrition. (FAO, 1992)

(b) World Food Summit

Between 13 and 17 November 1996, nearly 10 000 delegates and journalists converged on FAO headquarters in Rome for the World Food Summit (WFS). Heads of State and Government, Ministers of Agriculture and other delegates from 185 countries and the EU joined representatives of NGOs, United Nations agencies and other international bodies for the Summit proceedings. NGOs, parliamentarians, farmers' associations and the private sector held parallel meetings in Rome, as did some 500 young people gathered for a four-day International Youth Forum on food security.

The aim of the WFS was to raise awareness about issues surrounding world hunger, namely the fact that in 1996 more than 800 million human beings were not able to meet their most basic nutritional needs. The overriding goal of the WFS was to garner high-level political support for making concrete progress in achieving global food security, and two documents were adopted at the opening session: the Rome Declaration on World Food Security, and the World Food Summit Plan of Action (PoA), which details the Declaration's policy statements. Reaffirming the right of every person to be free from hunger, the Heads of State and Government pledged their political will and shared commitment to ensuring that "all people, at all times, have physical and economic access to sufficient, safe and nutritious food to meet their dietary needs and food preferences for an active and healthy life", with an "immediate view to reducing the number of undernourished people to half their present level no later than 2015". (FAO, 1997)

The commitments contained in the PoA are intended to underpin diverse paths to a common objective – food security and a significant decrease in chronic hunger – at the individual, household, national, regional and global levels. These commitments cover seven interrelated areas for governments to address: (i) general conditions for economic and social progress conducive to food security; (ii) policies aimed at poverty eradication and access to adequate food; (iii) sustainable increases in food production; (iv) consideration of the contribution of trade to food security; (v) prevention of, preparedness for and response to food emergencies; (vi) optimal investment in human resources, sustainable production capacity and rural development; and (vii) cooperation in implementing and monitoring the PoA. (FAO, 1997)

(c)   Steps Since the World Food Summit

The WFS gave a much-needed boost to a right that many have considered to be only aspirational, unrealistic or at the very least too vague to implement in a meaningful way. The WFS reaffirmed the right to adequate food and the fundamental right to be free from hunger. It set as Objective 7.4 of the PoA the clarification of the content of this right and the search for better ways of implementing it, calling upon the UN High Commissioner for Human Rights (UNHCHR) to take the lead in that work, in cooperation with other agencies, human rights bodies and civil society. (FAO, 1997) Much work has been done by the UN human rights bodies, along with FAO and NGOs as active partners, since the WFS.

Action by NGOs: In recent years, NGOs have played an essential role in clarifying the content and ways of implementation of the right to adequate food. They have participated in consultations of the UNHCHR and the CESCR and lobbied actively for more progress in the field. They have consistently raised the question of the right to food in FAO fora, including the preparations and follow-up to the WFS.

NGOs produced a draft Code of Conduct on the Right to Adequate Food in 1997, as called for by the NGO Forum of the WFS. (FIAN, et al., 1997) More than 800 NGOs have declared their support for the Code and its implementation at the national level. In autumn 2001, NGOs called on FAO, in cooperation with the UNHCHR, to start intergovernmental negotiations on such a code, or "voluntary guidelines for food security", which were explicitly mentioned in Objective 7.4. NGOs have also identified the right to food and other related rights, in particular access to resources such as land, water and genetic resources, as one of the key strategic elements for their advocacy in the context of the World Food Summit: five years later.

Action by UN Bodies: The Commission on Human Rights has annually since 1997 reaffirmed that hunger constitutes an outrage and a violation of human dignity, and mandated the UNHCHR to work on Objective 7.4. The UNHCHR has convened three expert consultations to date, the first on the content of the right to food, the second on the role of international organizations and the third on implementation at the national level. The Commission has called for a fourth expert consultation, which should focus on the realization of the right to food as part of strategies and policies for the eradication of poverty. Finally, in 2000, the Commission established the mandate of a Special Rapporteur on the Right to Food, who reports to the Commission and to the General Assembly on ways to implement the right to food and on violations of that right. (Robinson, 2002)

Steps taken by FAO to implement the PoA after the World Food Summit include the adoption, in 1999, of a Strategic Framework for the years 2000–2015 to focus work on WFS goals and PoA priorities; a new annual publication series on the State of World Food Insecurity, also launched in 1999; and further development of indicators on food insecurity. In 1998 FAO published a book called "The Right to Food in Theory and Practice"

(FAO, 1998), and in 1999 it issued "Extracts from International and Regional Instruments and other Authoritative Texts Relating to the Right to Food" (FAO, 1999).

The governing body of FAO, the FAO Conference, adopted a resolution on the right to food in 1997 (FAO, 1997), building on the explicit statement in the FAO Constitution of the Organization's goal of "ensuring humanity's freedom from hunger". As lead agency of the UN Task Force on long-term food security in the Horn of Africa, established by the Advisory Committee on Coordination in 2000, FAO has stressed the right to food of everyone, and the importance of peace, democracy and other human rights in attaining that goal. (FAO, 2000) Nevertheless, progress in achieving the main goal of the WFS, reducing the number of hungry people, has been too slow. Therefore FAO convened a new meeting, the World Food Summit: five years later (WFS:fyl), to foster the political will and mobilize resources for a renewed commitment to the WFS goals.

(d)   World Food Summit: five years later

The WFS:fyl took place in Rome, from 10 to 13 June 2002. Like the initial WFS in 1996, this summit was attended by Heads of State and Government, Ministers and other delegates from 182 countries and the EU as well as representatives of NGOs, UN agencies and other international bodies. NGOs, farmers' associations, the private sector and other civil society organizations held parallel meetings and events in Rome.

The WFS:fyl's main outcome was the Declaration unanimously approved on the opening day entitled "International Alliance Against Hunger". Reaffirming "the right of everyone to have access to safe and nutritious food", the Declaration renewed the commitment made in 1996 to "halve the number of hungry in the world no later than 2025". It stressed the importance of strengthening the respect of all human rights, the rule of law and good governance to solve socio-economic problems and to achieve food security. It also called for the adoption of poverty reduction and food security strategies that increase agricultural productivity and food production and distribution, particularly through the promotion of equal access by men and women to land, water and food.

2.1.2. Legal Developments

(a) General Comment 12 on the Right to Adequate Food

Benefiting from the work of earlier expert consultations, the CESCR adopted in 1999 a General Comment 12 on the Right to Adequate Food, which constitutes an authoritative statement on the content of the right in article 11 of the ICESCR (see Box 1), as well as on violations of the right and on the national and international obligations of states. The General Comment states that "The right to adequate food is realized when every man, woman and child, alone or in community with others, have physical and economic access at all times to adequate food or means for its procurement". The core content of this definition is the availability of food in a quantity and quality sufficient to satisfy the dietary needs of individuals, free from adverse substances and acceptable within a given culture; and the accessibility of such food in ways that are sustainable and that do not interfere with the enjoyment of other human rights.

Box 1 - International Covenant on Economic, Social and Cultural Rights, Article 11

1. The States Parties to the present Covenant recognize the right of everyone to an adequate standard of living for himself and his family, including adequate food, clothing and housing, and to continuous improvement of living conditions. The States Parties will take appropriate steps to ensure the realization of this right, recognizing to this effect the essential importance of international co-operation based on free consent.

2. The States Parties to the present Covenant, recognizing the fundamental right of everyone to be free from hunger, shall take, individually and through international co-operation, the measures, including specific programmes, which are needed:
    (a) To improve methods of production, conservation and distribution of food by making full use of technical and scientific knowledge, by disseminating knowledge of the principles of nutrition and by developing or reforming agrarian systems in such a way as to achieve the most efficient development and utilization of natural resources;
    (b) Taking into account the problems of both food-importing and food-exporting countries, to ensure an equitable distribution of world food supplies in relation to need.

International law prescribes that the state is responsible for the enjoyment of human rights within its territory. However, the state may assign responsibilities to different levels of government, and should, through its national strategy or legislation, assign as precise a responsibility for action as possible, especially in addressing multidimensional and multisectoral problems such as food insecurity. Under the ICESCR, state parties are obliged to take all appropriate steps, to the maximum of available resources, to progressively achieve the right to food for all.

While it is important to create an enabling environment where each person can enjoy the right to food acquired through his or her own efforts, under the ICESCR it remains incumbent on the state to ensure that those who are unable to provide for themselves are adequately provided for, so that, as a minimum, no one suffers from hunger. The General Comment provides that the principal obligation of states is to take steps to progressively achieve the full realization of the right to adequate food. This obligation consists of the duty to respect, protect and fulfil the right.

The obligation to *respect* existing access to adequate food requires states not to take any measures preventing such access. The obligation to *protect* requires that states take steps to ensure that others do not deprive individuals of their access to adequate food. According to the General Comment, the obligation to *fulfil* incorporates the obligation to *facilitate* as well as to *provide*. To *facilitate* means that states must pro-actively engage in activities intended to strengthen people's access to resources and improve their livelihoods and food security; to *provide* means that whenever an individual or group is unable, for reasons beyond its control, to enjoy the right to adequate food, states must fulfil the right directly by providing adequate food. (CESCR, 1999)

(b) Towards Voluntary Guidelines on the Right to Adequate Food

As mentioned above, the development of a draft Code of Conduct on the Right to Adequate Food in the 1990s was led by NGOs. Three of them took the lead in the drafting: the International Jacques Maritain Institute, FoodFirst Information and Action Network and the World Alliance for Nutrition and Human Rights. The work was undertaken on the basis of the final words of Objective 7.4, which requested the UNHCHR to bear in mind "the possibility of adopting voluntary guidelines for food security", as well as on the basis of an explicit mandate by the NGO Forum of the WFS. The draft Code has the support of hundreds of NGOs as well as some governments.

The draft Code provides a definition of the right to food, lists obligations of states at the national and international level and addresses the roles of intergovernmental, non-governmental and corporate actors. (FIAN et al.,

1997) It has proven to be a useful tool for the clarification of the obligations contained in article 11 of the ICESCR, and it had an influence on the drafting of General Comment 12. (Borghi and Postiglione Blommestein, 2002)

Beyond the Code of Conduct's already proven influence and utility, NGOs wish to take the Code further, into the intergovernmental arena. It was one of the items on the NGO agenda for the WFS:fyl, and a number of NGOs have called upon FAO to initiate formal negotiations at the intergovernmental level for such a Code, in cooperation with the UNHCHR. The Declaration adopted at the WFS:fyl eventually invited the FAO Council (FAO's intersessional governing body) to establish at its forthcoming session (November 2002) an Intergovernmental Working Group, with the participation of stakeholders, "to elaborate, in a period of two years, a set of voluntary guidelines to support Member States' efforts to achieve the progressive realisation of the right to adequate food in the context of national food security". Once created, the Working Group will have to produce such guidelines within two years. FAO was asked, in close collaboration with relevant treaty bodies, agencies and programmes of the UN system, to assist the Working Group, which shall report on its task to the Committee on World Food Security.

2.2. Recognition and Application of the Right to Food at the National Level

Human rights are mainly codified internationally, although effective enjoyment of them depends largely on their application at the national level. Many countries have incorporated human rights into their constitutions and taken other legislative measures for their implementation. Rights can also be enforced through jurisprudence created by courts, and through national human rights institutions, such as Ombudsmen and Human Rights Commissions.

2.2.1. Constitutional Provisions

Over twenty countries recognize the right to food explicitly in their Constitutions. A few examples of these are given in Box 2. Many more countries have constitutional provisions that guarantee individual entitlements to food and other basic requirements for an adequate standard of living, notably in social security legislation and in land and labour law. Other provisions govern process rights, for example by combating *de facto* discrimination on the basis of race, sex, language, religion or other social status or by protecting freedom of association and assembly. All of these may be implicated in the protection of the right to adequate food. (FAO, 1998)

In industrialized countries that have a well-developed social security system, a specific constitutional provision or legislation on the right to food may not be necessary for the actual enjoyment of the right. On the other hand, in less developed countries which have weak or less comprehensive social security systems, and weak protection of other rights, such provisions can prove crucial as a first step to implement the right to food at the national level.

Box 2 - Some Constitutional Provisions on the Right to Food

BANGLADESH - Article 15
"It shall be a fundamental responsibility of the state to attain ... a steady improvement of the material and cultural standard of living of the people, with a view to securing to its citizens ... the provision of the basic necessities of life, including food".

NICARAGUA - Article 63
"It is the right of Nicaraguans to be protected against hunger. The state shall promote programmes which assure adequate availability and equitable distribution of food".

SOUTH AFRICA - Section 27
"Everyone has the right to have access to ... sufficient food and water.... The state must take reasonable legislative and other measures, within its available resources, to achieve the progressive realization of each of these rights".

UKRAINE - Article 48
"Everyone has the right to a standard of living sufficient for himself or herself ... that includes adequate nutrition".

2.2.2. Framework Legislation

In countries where food insecurity prevalence is high, a framework law can be a useful tool for the progressive implementation of the right to food, ensuring that the maximum of available resources is allocated to food security and rural development, while at the same time holding appropriate government organs accountable for the process and for the results. The General Comment to article 11 of the ICESCR, discussed above, specifically requests states to consider the adoption of a framework law in the implementation of the national strategy concerning the right to food. The Comment explains that the law should include provisions on its purpose; the goals to be achieved and the relevant time-frame for their achievement; the means by which the objectives can be reached, in particular the intended collaboration with civil society, the private sector and international organizations; the institutional responsibilities for the process; and the national mechanisms for monitoring of the process, as well as possible recourse procedures. The law should assign responsibilities, set benchmarks and guide further legislative action. In developing the legislation, state parties are called upon to actively involve civil society organizations. (CESCR, 1999)

Most state parties to ICESCR are also parties to the International Covenant on Civil and Political Rights and other human rights instruments. Moreover, they participated in the 1993 World Conference on Human Rights, which declared that all human rights are universal, indivisible, interdependent and interrelated. This means that in implementing specific rights, such as the right to adequate food, other rights – civil, cultural, economic, social and political – must also be respected. The obligations of conduct are thereby reinforced along with the obligations of results. Legislation reflecting a rights-based approach to food security, therefore, should be concerned not only with the achievement of an adequate nutritional status of the population, but with achieving the result through the best possible process.

Because food security and the right to food are multidimensional and cross-sectoral, they may require legislative measures in many different areas. Therefore the lack of specific implementing legislation does not necessarily suggest a regulatory vacuum or non-compliance with article 2 of the ICESCR, which commits state parties to take legislative measures for the implementation of the rights recognized in the treaty.

While a number of countries have constitutional provisions on food and nutrition, none has yet adopted specific implementing legislation, although a few countries are now considering such legal action. The Third Expert Consultation of the UNHCHR, held in March 2001, considered legislative measures to implement the right to food and recommended, as a first step, the careful auditing of existing national legislation, policy and administrative measures and available recourse procedures, followed by the adoption of an administrative agenda for change and amendment. A legislative agenda should then be set which may include the adoption of framework legislation. (UNHCHR, 2001) It is believed that the adoption of such legislation would be conducive to food security, as it would clarify the content of the right in a particular country and ensure that the rule of law is brought to bear on food security issues. (FAO, 2001d) Some guidelines for the development of such legislation are set out below.

The process of establishing legislation should itself be participatory and tailored to the particular circumstances of specific countries as well as their legislative environment and traditions. Framework legislation should take into account the fact that different government agencies are responsible for different aspects and therefore overall responsibility may be diffused. Appropriate legislation could assign responsibility for action more clearly to the different actors in a transparent way, thus facilitating accountability and public participation.

Framework legislation could not dictate food security policy in much detail, but it could establish the principles to which such policy should conform, and could define acts that are forbidden, so as to ensure, at the very least, respect for the right to food. It would also set in motion the review of other sectoral legislation for the protection of the right to food, establishing targets and benchmarks for the progressive realization of the right to food, and allowing for its monitoring by the general population, NGOs and communities. (CESCR, 1999)

While human rights law makes it clear that every human being has the right to access to adequate food, it does not, as such, define exact entitlements, especially transfer entitlements. Such entitlements depend on national legislation and custom, including the question of who is responsible for providing the transfer. In countries with weak social security systems, and with little or no entitlements outside the family in case of illness, unemployment or other events outside a person's control, the lack of food entitlements is particularly serious. Framework legislation could define entitlements and duty holders, as well as establish appropriate measures to enable the duty bearers to fulfil their responsibilities. (FAO, 1998)

Because human rights should always be ensured through effective recourse in case of violations, framework legislation should define the modalities of oversight by appropriate bodies (ombudsmen, human rights commissions and the courts), and identify which aspects are actionable. Without specific legislation, that is, with reliance only on constitutional or international legal provisions, recourse is ill-defined and may not be effective. Framework legislation should make clear who can claim recourse for which action or omission by which government organ. (FAO, 2001d)

2.2.3. Case Law

Case law on the right to adequate food remains scarce. However, in recent years some cases have addressed questions of justiciability and enforcement. For example, Switzerland's Federal Court, in *V. v. Eninwohner-gemeinde X. und Regierungsrat des Kantons Bern* (BGE/ATF 121 I 367, 27 October 1995), recognized that it lacked the legal competence to set priorities for the allocation of necessary resources to realize the right to a minimum state of existence, which includes food. However, the court determined that it could set aside legislation if it failed to meet the minimum standards required by the constitutional right. Thus the exclusion of three persons from social welfare legislation was found to be a violation of the right to food, despite their being illegal immigrants. (Ziegler, 2002)

The Constitutional Court of South Africa, in the *Grootboom* case (CCT 11/00, 4 October 2000), which concerned housing rights, made determinations that are of general relevance for the judicial enforcement of socio-economic rights and have received much attention worldwide. The case is particularly relevant since the Constitution of South Africa proclaims that everyone has the right to access to adequate housing (sec. 26) and provides that the state must fulfil that right to the maximum of available resources, a wording that closely correlates with the content of food and housing rights in the ICESCR.

The case concerned hundreds of persons who had been evicted from privately owned land, where they had been squatting without permission. The judgement examined the measures taken by public authorities in light of the constitutional obligation to (1) take reasonable legislative and other measures to (2) progressively achieve the right (3) with available resources. The judgement reviewed the state's housing programmes and concluded that they fell short of the required obligations, in that no provision was made for relief for people in desperate need. In addition, the manner in which the evictions were carried out was found to be in breach of the state's obligations in regard to housing. The court issued a declaratory order that the state has an obligation to devise, fund, implement and supervise measures to provide relief to those in desperate need of access to housing.

The Indian Supreme Court has also intervened in cases concerning the right to food. A recent petition claimed that starvation deaths were occurring in certain regions, while amounts of grain in silos reserved for famine situations were in excess of legislative requirements. The petitioners requested that people at risk of starvation be provided food on the basis of their right to food, derived from their constitutional right to life. The court issued an interlocutory order requiring that food-for-work schemes be implemented in areas where starvation deaths had recently occurred. (Langford, 2001)

2.2.4. Non-judicial Implementation

Important as judicial enforcement may be, it is not the only way of implementing socio-economic rights or other human rights at the national level. In Colombia, the ombudsman (*Defensor del Pueblo*) serves a number of important functions, including awareness-raising, initiation of legislative and other state action, investigation of alleged violations and invalidation of acts which contradict recognized rights. As the right to food is one of the constitutionally recognized rights, the ombudsman could take various steps, including demanding the adoption of a policy to ensure access to food for all, initiating court action and establishing protective programmes for the enjoyment of the right to food.

In Mozambique, the government has made considerable progress in facilitating access to productive resources for those who lack them as well as providing direct aid for groups that are unable to provide for themselves. More important than financial resources have proven to be political will and organizational capacity. These, coupled with limited but well-utilized financial resources, have enabled the government to make considerable progress in reducing poverty and food insecurity.

In Norway, a parliamentarily endorsed policy established the goal of ensuring food security as defined by the WFS, and created a normative framework linked to the three kinds of state obligations laid out in General Comment 12, i.e., the duty to respect, protect and fulfil. This led to the development of a guiding matrix facilitating the identification of ongoing activities, strategies and programmes toward these ends.

The South African Human Rights Commission (SAHRC) is constitutionally mandated to promote, protect and monitor constitutionally protected human rights, which include the right to food and other socio-economic human rights. The SAHRC has the power to request information from any relevant government organ on its activities directed toward the realization of the rights in question, and to issue recommendations to Parliament. For the purpose of monitoring socio-economic rights, the SAHRC has developed questionnaires or "protocols" to obtain information. It also has the power to subpoena government officials in case the information is not forthcoming. (UNHCHR, 2001)

III. LAW ON FOOD CONTROL, FOOD SAFETY AND STANDARDS

In parallel to recent developments regarding the right to adequate food, the last decade has witnessed significant change in the regulatory frameworks governing food control, food safety and food standards. Some of the observed empirical and legislative trends at the international and national levels are set out below.

3.1. International Framework: Key Developments

3.1.1. World Trade Organization Agreements

The Uruguay Round of Multilateral Trade Negotiations in 1994 led to the establishment of the World Trade Organization (WTO) in January 1995. Agriculture was included in the trade talks in a significant way for the first time and it was agreed to reduce tariff barriers for many agricultural products in order to encourage free trade. Two agreements relevant to food were concluded within the framework of the WTO: the Agreement on the Application of Sanitary and Phytosanitary Measures (SPS Agreement) and the Agreement on Technical Barriers to Trade (TBT Agreement). These set important parameters governing the adoption and implementation of food quality and safety measures.

The SPS Agreement was drawn up to ensure that countries apply measures to protect human and animal health (sanitary measures) and plant health (phytosanitary measures) based on the assessment of risk, or in other words, based on science. The aim is the establishment of a multilateral framework of rules and disciplines that will guide the development, adoption and enforcement of harmonized sanitary and phytosanitary measures and minimize their negative effects on trade. The use of international standards is intended to allow countries to prioritize the use of their often limited resources and to concentrate on risk analysis and scientific investigations.

Under the SPS Agreement, Codex Alimentarius standards, guidelines and recommendations have been granted the status of a reference point for international harmonization. With regard to food safety measures, WTO members should base their national standards on international standards, guidelines and other recommendations adopted by Codex where they exist. As long as a country employs these standards, its measures are presumed to be consistent with the provisions of the SPS Agreement. They also serve as the basic texts to guide the resolution of trade disputes.

The TBT Agreement, which had been in existence as a multilateral agreement since the Tokyo Round (1973–1979), was revised and converted into a multilateral agreement through the Uruguay Round. It covers all technical requirements and standards (applied to all commodities), such as labelling, that are not covered under the SPS Agreement.

3.1.2. Codex Alimentarius

As noted, the Codex Alimentarius (Codex) is the main instrument for the harmonization of food standards. It constitutes a collection of internationally adopted food standards, maximum residue limits for pesticides and veterinary drugs and codes of practice. The objectives of Codex are to protect the health of consumers, to ensure fair practices in food trade and to promote the coordination of all food standards work undertaken by national governments. Each government must ensure that the legislation underlying its country's food control system is scientifically based and must work to establish equivalency and transparency among national food control systems.

The Codex Alimentarius Commission has prepared six important instruments in the years since Rio. Of these, so far only the Codex Guidelines for the Production, Processing, Labelling and Marketing of Organically Produced Foods (1999), which refer to genetically modified foods, have been adopted. These Guidelines were developed in light of the growing production of and international trade in organically produced foods, with a view to facilitating trade and preventing misleading claims. The Codex Alimentarius Commission is the primary forum in which the food safety aspects of genetically modified organisms are presently being addressed.

Instruments still being developed include the proposed draft Guidelines for the Labelling of Foods Obtained Through Certain Techniques of Genetic Modification/Genetic Engineering, proposed draft Principles for the Risk Analysis of Foods Derived from Modern Biotechnology, the proposed Revised Code of Ethics for International Trade in Food and proposed draft Guidelines for the Conduct of Food Safety Assessment of Foods Derived from Recombinant DNA Plants.

In the food labelling area, the Codex Committee on Food Labelling has been working to amend the Codex General Standard for Labelling Prepackaged Foods: Labelling of Foods Obtained Through Certain Techniques of Genetic Modification/Genetic Engineering. As part of the amendment process of the General Standard, the Committee is also working on proposed draft Guidelines for the Labelling of Foods Obtained through Certain Techniques of Genetic Modification/Genetic Engineering.

3.2. National Framework: Main Trends

3.2.1. Empirical Trends

In 2020, the world's population is expected to reach 7.6 billion, with most of the growth taking place in developing countries. Expanding populations pose great challenges to world food systems: agricultural yields and animal husbandry practices must improve; pre- and post-harvest losses must decrease; food processing and distribution systems must become more efficient; and new technologies and strategies must be adopted to meet the needs of growing populations. Some of these may compromise food safety and the nutritional value of food. Developing countries in particular must cope with poor post-harvest infrastructure, including the lack of safe water, electricity, storage facilities, roads and means of transport.

Between the years 1995 and 2020 the developing world's urban population is expected to double, to 3.4 billion. Urbanization creates great demand for food, and the increasing population density, expansion of slums, proliferation of street sellers and general degradation of civic amenities create health hazards. These developments, along with associated changes in the way food is produced and marketed, have increased the potential for new risks. Existing risks are rising because of a reduction in the supply of fresh potable water, climate change, migration, escalating poverty and increasing tourism and trade. The growing volume of international trade in agricultural products, in particular, makes the rapid transmission of food hazards more likely and reaction more problematic.

In both urban and rural areas, much has changed in the way food is produced, prepared and sold. New technologies allow food products to travel farther and stay fresh longer, while scientific advances have improved the identification of food hazards and the management of risk. At the same time, advanced technologies have created new food dangers.

Food-borne disease outbreaks in recent years have provoked a serious loss of confidence in the food supply both in the developed and the developing world. Particularly in the last decade, public concern over the safety of food has increased dramatically. Some well-known diseases have persisted while new ones have appeared, such as variant Creutzfeldt-Jakob disease. Even as some diseases come under control, others, such as antibiotic-resistant salmonella, emerge. For example, *E. coli* O157:H7 is an important new food-borne pathogen which has caused several major outbreaks.

In addition to microbes, food has been affected by chemicals and environmental contaminants. Misuse of pesticides during manufacture and storage can lead to high levels of residues, and heavy metals and other contaminants enter food through soil or water. Most recently, there has been contamination from dioxins entering the animal feed supply and from food additives. Antibiotic drug residues arising from improper animal feed or treatment is alleged to contribute to the growing antibiotic resistance of microorganisms, and animal feed affected with mycotoxins can result in the contamination of milk and meat.

The increasing use of GMOs in food production has been another important trend in the years since Rio. Modern biotechnology permits the artificial transfer of genetic material from one organism to another, including across species boundaries, which can broaden the range of alterations that can be made to food and can expand the spectrum of possible food sources. Several genetically modified foods, such as toma-toes, potatoes, raspberries, banana, soybean and melon, have become available, mainly in developed countries. A large proportion of the food consumed in some industrialized countries is derived from genetic modification.

Advances through genetic modification of food have the potential to improve the world's food supply and reduce the potential for losses due to pests, diseases, transport and storage. However, experts disagree on the safety, nutritional value and environmental effects of GMOs. On the one hand, advocates argue that the methods for transferring genes are more precise and predictable than in traditional plant breeding, and that the risks of harmful effects are very small. They also argue that any potential danger is mitigated because adverse changes in food due to gene transfer can be detected before the foods are marketed. In contrast, critics argue that the consequences of genetic modification of food are unpredictable, and that considerable scientific evidence will be needed to prove that such foods are safe. They also argue that it may be difficult or impossible to reverse course once genetic modifications have become widespread. The lack of adequate data causes many to argue that governments should apply the precautionary principle before clearing the use of genetic engineering in human food.

Increasing numbers of consumers are concerned about how their food is produced, processed, handled and marketed. Thus a new market for agricultural products has arisen to meet rising consumer demand for organically produced agricultural products and foodstuffs. Organic agriculture involves very tight restrictions on the use of fertilizers and pesticides, and the prohibition of the use of genetically modified organisms (GMOs) at all stages of food production, processing and handling. It also aims to produce food while respecting ecosystems, preserving soil fertility and preventing pest problems.

Media interest in genetically modified foods and in food-borne disease outbreaks has raised public awareness, and in many countries consumers are becoming more organized and more active. Citizens are demanding protection in the whole food supply chain, from primary producer to end consumer, i.e., from farm to fork. Improved access to scientific knowledge, including through the internet, has helped consumers to gain a better understanding of food safety issues. Consumers have become more discriminating and insist on better protection. They expect that both domestic and imported foods will meet basic quality and safety standards, and will conform to requirements relating to food hygiene, labelling, additives and residues. Concepts such as the Hazard Analysis Critical Control Point system have gained greater currency, and have raised awareness of food safety issues around the world. Countries are making choices about how to address food safety issues without unlimited resources.

Nonetheless, the economic effects of food-borne disease remain ill understood. Developing countries in particular have limited capacities to collect and analyse data on potential food-borne risks. In recent years more research has been carried out to capture the economic implications of food safety decisions, and reforms of national food control systems, including through legislation, may follow.

3.2.2. Legislative Trends

Some trends can be observed in recent years in changes made to national legal frameworks governing food.

(a) Reviewing and Consolidating Food Legislation

National legal frameworks governing food control and food safety vary widely in their complexity and their coverage. Some countries have no food legislation whatsoever, relying solely on, for example, standards of the Codex Alimentarius Commission. Other countries have had the same food legislation in place for decades. Laws and regulations may not have been updated or have constantly been amended, creating a maze of rules which are difficult to understand for regulators, industry and consumers.

Typically the legal framework governing food in a particular country has evolved over many years and is a blend of political, societal, economic and scientific forces. It is often influenced by the need to develop a regulatory framework for the domestic market or to promote exports. The whole system can therefore lack coherence and become quite complex. Although some sectoral regulation is inevitably necessary in any food control system, the general trend is to address food issues comprehensively in a basic food law, accompanied by implementing regulations and standards.

The most recent example of modernizing legislation into a coherent and transparent set of rules is provided by the recent EU Regulation (EC) No. 178/2002, adopted on 28 January 2002. EU food legislation had been developed with a focus on economic and trade needs, and an overall structure was lacking. The purpose of the Regulation is to provide a basis for a high level of protection of human health and to restore consumer confidence in food. The Regulation sets out the basic framework of guiding principles and definitions for future European food law, establishing the European Food Safety Authority and laying down procedures on matters of food and feed safety. An important element of the Regulation is the responsibility of food and feed businesses to ensure that only safe food and feed is placed on the market. Food is considered to be unsafe if it is potentially injurious to health, unfit for human consumption or contaminated in such a manner that it would not be reasonable to expect it to be used for human consumption.

Another jurisdiction that has adopted new basic food legislation is Indonesia: Act No. 7 on Food of 1996. Besides protecting consumer health, one of the purposes of the law is to provide the country with a modern law to promote the international competitiveness of the nation's products. More recently, the Russian Federation adopted a Federal Law FZ29 of 2000 containing general requirements for safeguarding food quality and food safety. Both New Zealand and Australia have made numerous amendments to their state and territorial legislation, based on a treaty signed between them in 1995, which established a system for the development of joint food standards. In Australia, the State of Tasmania adopted a new Food Act in 1998 and the State of New South Wales enacted a new Food Regulation and the Food Production (Safety) Act of 1998.

Developments are not limited to the larger countries. In Mauritius, the Food Act (and Regulations) of 1998 provides for a modernization and consolidation of food safety law, while other countries such as Belize, Cambodia, Cape Verde and Chile have made efforts to update their food legislation. At the time of writing, Haiti was in the process of adopting a basic food law, and Bhutan, Ghana and Swaziland had begun consideration of legislative changes to their food control and food safety systems.

In many of the former socialist states, such as Albania, Estonia, Hungary, Latvia and Lithuania, new basic food laws have been created where they previously did not exist. Nearly all these countries have aspirations to join the EU, so harmonization of laws and regulations is important. In Lithuania, for example, the Law on Food, adopted in 2000, specifically states that the administrative institutions shall implement the food safety requirements of the EU, FAO, WTO and the Codex Alimentarius Commission.

However, as noted above, national food legislation is not limited to basic food laws. The legal framework governing food control may consist of a variety of legal texts, often arising from governments responding to precise situations and needs. In such cases the legislation may be restricted to specific products or food-related issues. For example, after the Bovine Spongiform Encephalopathy (BSE) crisis, numerous countries adopted specific regulations in order to limit the import of meat products. Illustrative is the Order (No. 10/2001) adopted by Cape Verde in order to prohibit bovine importation from areas infected by BSE, or, similarly, the Meat Control (Importation of Meat and Meat Products) Regulations adopted by Kenya in 2001. More comprehensive legislation on beef products, including safety and quality control systems, was adopted by countries such as Norway (Act of 1997 Relative to Meat Production) and South Africa (Meat Safety Act of 2000).

(b)   Incorporating Prevention: The HACCP Approach

Food law has traditionally consisted of legal definitions of unsafe food, along with the prescription of enforcement tools for removing unsafe food from trade and punishing responsible parties after the fact. It has generally not provided food control agencies with the clear mandate and authority to prevent food safety problems. The result has been food safety programmes that are reactive and enforcement-oriented rather than preventive. To the extent possible, modern food laws should not only contain the necessary legal powers and prescriptions to ensure food safety, but also charge the competent food authority or authorities with building prevention into the system.

To adopt a preventive approach, countries might incorporate a quality assurance system in their basic food legislation. For example, the 1996 Indonesian Food Act states that any person who produces food to be traded must implement a quality assurance system. The Hazard Analysis Critical Control Point system (HACCP) is the most important quality assurance system that is applied at all stages in the production, processing and handling of food products. It monitors all the critical steps in the food chain and identifies where the problems might occur, although it is up to the food operator in question to take the appropriate precautions in order to prevent contamination.

The HACCP system is firmly established and required by the food legislation of many developed countries, in particular the United States and EU members. In New Zealand, as well, the Food Amendment Act of 1996 defines food safety programmes as ones that are based on HACCP, and in Hungary a 1999 decree adopted under the Food Act of 1995 determines the criteria of HACCP to be applied by the food producer. Similarly, in Lithuania the 2000 Law on Food states that HACCP must be applied at food handling establishments.

In some of the food sectors, such as milk, meat and fish processing, the implementation of HACCP may sometimes be well advanced. In other sectors, such as aquaculture, implementation may be slower. This may stem from the importance accorded to sectors that may have the potential for significant exports. Due to worldwide trade liberalization, a growing number of countries are becoming significant importers and exporters of food, and exporting countries are increasingly being forced to meet the requirements of their trading partners and to comply with all kinds of import rules and procedures. Many developed countries, such as the United States and EU countries, have now made implementation of the HACCP system a specific legal requirement for imported food products. As a result, many developing countries have been prompted to implement the strict HACCP regulations by means of adopting similar regulations in their own national legislation. (Boutrif and Bessy, 1999)

However, HACCP can be expensive to implement and the costs of meeting the standards have proven to be a major problem for many developing countries. Therefore, in some countries and for some products, implementation of the HACCP system is only required where it concerns export products. The need to gain access to the European and American markets is often more influential in stimulating new regulations than protecting consumers in the home market. Thus, the Sri Lanka Fish Products (Export) Regulations of 1998 require implementation of HACCP for fish processing establishments that are allowed to export fish products. Similarly, the Belize Agricultural Health Authority (Food Safety) Regulations of 2001 establish that all food exporting enterprises shall be required to comply with HACCP guidelines.

(c)   Exercising Control from Farm to Fork

Some twenty-five years ago, government agencies were used to inspecting the end product in order to determine whether food was safe and met the required specifications. However, during the 1980s developed countries increasingly arrived at the conclusion that it is impossible to provide adequate protection to the consumer by sampling and analysis of the final product. Many hazards enter the food chain at a variety of different points. Some can be controlled along the food chain through the application of good practices, such as good agricultural practices, good manufacturing practices and good hygienic practices, but classic inspection procedures are not sufficient to address all the relevant hazards in food production and to provide the necessary level of protection to consumers. Safety and quality must be built into the product right from its production through to consumption.

The introduction of preventive measures at all stages of the food production and distribution chain, rather than relying on inspection and rejection at the final stage, also makes better economic sense because unsuitable products can be stopped earlier along the chain. Thus there has been a shift over the years from retrospective control performed by government at the end of the line to control throughout the food chain. The overall trend in national food legislation is that all actors, from producer, processor, transporter and vendor to consumer – i.e., from farm to fork – are now being charged with responding to food safety and quality issues. The recent EU Regulation (EC) No. 178/2002 refers to the new integrated approach as follows:

> "In order to ensure the safety of food, it is necessary to consider all aspects of the food production chain as a continuum from and including primary production and the production of animal feed up to and including sale or supply of food to the consumer because each element may have a potential impact on food safety".

Equally, the Chilean *Reglamento sanitario de los alimentos* of 1996 states that the regulation applies to all stages of the food chain, from production to the sale of products, including transport and distribution. The Lithuanian Law on Food of 2000 also declares that all stages of preparation and sale of food to the consumer must be handled in accordance with the requirements of the law "from the field to the table". The Latvian Food Law applies to all activities carried out in relation to food before its ultimate consumption. Finally, the definition of "food safety system" in the Belize Agricultural Health Authority (Food Safety) Regulations of 2001 includes any system employed in the production of food "from the farm or sea or other source of the food to the table for human consumption".

Another key element of the integrated farm to fork approach is the concept of traceability, which means that it should be possible to trace and follow a food-producing animal, food, feed or any substance to be incorporated into a food or feed, through all stages of production, processing and distribution. Because unsafe food and feed will have to be withdrawn from the market, food businesses should have systems in place to identify their suppliers (one step below in the food chain) as well as those they have supplied (one step above). Thus, under the Estonian Food Act of 1999, food business operators have a recording obligation: they may only use raw material for food which is of identifiable origin, and they must maintain written records of obtained raw material for food and of the amount of food handled and distributed.

The application of the principle of traceability has been influenced by recent food scares that have demonstrated that identification is of vital importance. For example, the recent BSE crisis led to a traceability scheme for beef products under EU Regulation (EC) No. 1760/2000. For GMOs, the concept of traceability with regard to their deliberate release into the environment was introduced in EU Directive 2001/18, which will take effect from October 2002. However, the Directive does not provide for a complete approach towards implementation of the traceability principle. Therefore, proposals for new EU regulations concerning genetically modified (GM) food and feed and the traceability and labelling of food and feed products from GMOs are currently under preparation. The proposals streamline and unify existing provisions on GM food, including for the first time GM feed and, importantly, require the industry to have systems in place that identify to whom and from whom GM products are made available. It is expected that the proposals should enter into force in 2003 at the latest.

(d) Shifting Roles of Government and Industry

Inherent in the new integrated approach is the tendency to emphasize the primary responsibilities of the economic operators in the food and feed industry. Activities at all stages of the production and distribution process need to be carried out in such a manner that food products comply with the relevant provisions of food safety legislation. Recent food legislation shifts the focus of government activity from implementation and control, as it was previously, to auditing and oversight. This reflects current thinking that limited public resources and expertise are better applied to monitoring, and that industries themselves should guarantee the safety of products they place on the market.

For government regulators, therefore, the trend is clearly away from an enforcement-oriented approach and toward a more collaborative approach. This means that instead of simply seeking out and punishing violations, for example, legislation may charge food inspectors with the task of educating owners of food businesses with regard to proper procedures; assisting them in setting up their own controls; and auditing how food enterprises are exercising their own controls. Of course the end product sold by the retailer must meet the regulatory standards, and it must still be adequately and effectively controlled, and so government continues to have a back-up function, although it mainly monitors the controls exercised by the food industries themselves.

This approach is clearly illustrated in Estonia's 1999 Food Act, which outlines the supervisory responsibilities of government. The Act specifically states that the food business operators are required to verify the conformity of food, raw material for food and the handling thereof with established requirements, and to implement measures in order to ensure such verification. Similarly, the recent Lithuanian Law of 2000 on Food provides for growing industry responsibility and a system of auto-controls. Also in Australia, legislative changes reflect a shift from a prescriptive rules-driven approach to one that focuses on measures taken by the food industry itself.

(e)   Establishing an Independent Food Control Authority

In many countries, responsibility for food control is shared among government ministries such as Health, Agriculture, Fisheries, Environment, Trade and Tourism. The roles and responsibilities of these units are quite different, and this sometimes leads to problems such as duplication of regulatory activity, increased bureaucracy, fragmentation and a lack of coordination. For example, the regulation and surveillance of meat and seafood is often separate from the regulation of other kinds of foods and food products. Similarly, export inspection systems are often located within the Ministry of Commerce or Trade while other food control activities are carried out by the Ministry of Health or Agriculture.

In addition to the fragmentation of responsibilities by sector, the national constitution or legislation may allocate different powers to federal/ national, state/provincial and municipal/local authorities. There may be wide variations in the level of expertise and in the availability of resources among different agencies or regions, and the responsibility for protecting public health may conflict with other policy goals, such as the facilitation of trade or the development of the agro-industrial sector. Controls may be exercised effectively in the urban centres, but sporadically in the regions. Some sectors of the food chain may be intensely scrutinized, because of the multiplicity of inspectors, whereas others may receive little or no regulatory attention.

Duplication among regulatory authorities results in increased costs of inspection, placing a greater burden on the economy and on industry, especially on small-scale producers in developing countries. This situation also prevails in some developed countries, although in many cases potential problems have been reduced through memoranda of under-standing or other agreements between government units. These avoid duplication of efforts and confusion over roles and functions.

To combat the fragmentation of responsibilities, there is a growing ten-dency to restructure institutions by establishing a national food safety authority. Increasingly these authorities are becoming independent agencies not under the auspices of any ministry, enabling them to act independently and to serve in a coordinating role. Independent national food safety and control authorities have recently been established by principal or subsidiary legislation in countries such as Belize, Canada, Cape Verde, Ireland, Latvia and Spain. In 1995, Australia and New Zealand established one food authority for both countries.

National food authorities are generally responsible for policy development, risk assessment, standards development and coordination of food control activities. Day-to-day inspection responsibilities may remain with existing national, provincial or local agencies, or the authority may be charged with running the inspection programme. The legislation establishing the authority will prescribe the relationship of the authority to other inspection agencies, if any, and the jurisdiction of all relevant actors. The legislation also defines the authority's mandate, powers and responsibilities as well as its organizational structure.

The Irish Government initiated a review of its food safety systems in 1996, and the outcome was a recommendation to establish the Food Safety Authority of Ireland (FSAI) as a statutorily independent and scientific body, overseeing the regulation of the food industry. On 1 January 1999, the FSAI was formally established under the Food Safety Authority of Ireland Act. The FSAI operates the national food safety compliance programme and is also responsible for creating public awareness on food safety matters. This includes managing public relations and developing and implementing communications and educational policy for consumers, industry and enforcement officers. Similarly, the Canadian Food Inspection Agency was created in 1997 and is responsible for all federal food inspection, compliance and quarantine services. It develops and manages inspection, enforcement, compliance and control programmes and sets standards. It also collaborates with other levels of government and with NGOs, industry and trading partners, providing laboratory support, issuing emergency food recalls and conducting inspection, monitoring and compliance activities from farm to fork.

On a regional level, the establishment of the European Food Safety Authority (EFSA) under Regulation (EC) No. 178/2002 is considered to be a milestone. As a scientific risk assessment body that covers the whole food chain, the core function of EFSA will be to provide independent scientific advice which will form the basis for future policy and legislation, including on GMOs. In addition, EFSA is responsible for the operation of a rapid alert system for food and feed.

Belize has gone yet one more step, combining animal health and plant protection and some food safety responsibilities into one agency, the Belize Agricultural Health Authority. It carries out inspections, and after an initial period with external funding support, it is expected to act on a fee-for-service basis and to become self-sustaining. The Belizean model has triggered much interest in the Caribbean region, where discussions and feasibility studies are being carried out on the establishment of a central Caribbean Agricultural Health and Food Safety Agency.

(f)   Regulating Organic Production

With the organic industry constantly growing over the past decade, and with the increase in international trade in organic products, governments have begun to regulate organic agriculture mainly with a view to entering regulated markets and protecting consumers from fraudulent practices. International standards were developed first for the private sector by the International Federation of Organic Agriculture Movements: the International Basic Standards for Organic Production and Processing. Then, under Codex, the abovementioned Guidelines for Production, Processing, Labelling and Marketing of Organically Produced Foods were adopted to serve as minimum standards for the organic farming industry, for use by governments and private certification bodies. They are also useful in the development of national laws and regulations on organic agriculture.

The EU was the first organ to enact legislation on organic production through Regulation 2092/91, which was adopted in response to rising consumer interest in organic products. The regulation describes the minimum standards for organic farming and covers rules on production, labelling and inspection. It is intended to allow the organic industry to benefit from fair competition among producers and to gain credibility vis-à-vis consumers.

The technical details contained in the regulation may be amended, amplified or further described in order to take account of experience gained by the organic industry. Member states of the EU must complement Regulation 2092/91 with their national legislation, setting up their own inspection schemes and designating their own inspection authorities. States must meet the requirements of the regulation, although they may also enact more strict legislation concerning rules of production for organic agriculture. Denmark's Organic Foods Act of 1999, for instance, has stricter standards in some areas of the organic production process, including strict rules for the transportation and slaughtering of organically produced livestock.

As the EU is a large importer of organic products, it encourages many countries to enter the organic production market. In turn, several countries willing to access the EU market have used Regulation 2092/91 as a model for developing their domestic legislation. For example, in Central Europe, Hungary's regulations on organic agriculture (Decree No. 140 of 1999) were modelled after the EU legislation, including the establishment of an inspection system, in order to support the country's export opportunities. Estonia's Organic Agriculture Act (No. 823 of 1997) also follows the EU model and is intended to lay the foundations of a system that will assure the quality of ecologically or bio-dynamically (organically) grown and handled foodstuffs, and the development of environmentally sustainable agricultural production. Likewise, in North Africa, Tunisia's 1999 basic law on organic agriculture follows the EU model, as do the law's implementing regulations, enacted from 1999 through 2001. With this legislation, Tunisia's organic industry can access the foreign markets, including the EU market, while also supplying its domestic market.

(g) Regulating Street Foods

The images of the working father returning home for a hot lunch and of family dinners prepared by mother at home are outdated in most developed countries, and in the developing world growing urbanization is causing similar changes. Working families, greater distances between home and work and escalating time pressures mean greater numbers of people eating food outside the home. Street foods, i.e., food and drinks that are sold for immediate consumption at (often unapproved) points of sale, are an essential part of the food service landscape of most cities, especially in many developing countries, and they fill an important gap.

Street food vending employs millions, in many cases women, and street food vendors meet basic food needs of large groups of people far from their homes during the working day. However, food safety can be a major concern, as street foods are generally prepared and sold under unhygienic conditions, with limited access to safe water, sanitary services, refrigeration and garbage disposal facilities. Hence street foods pose a higher risk of food poisoning from microbial contamination and cross-contamination, as well as from improper use of food additives, adulteration and environmental contamination. Surveys of street foods in Africa, Asia, Latin America and the Caribbean confirm these concerns.

Protection of consumers against health hazards from street foods calls for comprehensive measures, in particular at the local level. Legislation should be accompanied by community outreach programmes including training for food vendors, education of consumers and infrastructure support. However, regulation in many countries has not kept pace with the changes in food preparation, sale and consumption of street foods. Legislation that was developed with another model in mind may contain no provisions specifically dealing with the issue of street foods, and may not even have existing general provisions that can be interpreted to apply to street foods.

The Codex Alimentarius Commission (Codex), which, as noted, sets food safety standards worldwide, has also been working on street foods. Through its Regional Coordinating Committees, Codex has created guidance documents that will serve as the basis for national and local regulations on street foods. The first regional document was produced for Latin America and the Caribbean in 1995. Guidelines produced for Africa followed in 1997, setting policies for licensing vendors, establishing street food advisory services and educating consumers about hygienic practices. These documents will serve as the basis for a regional code of practice, which may be adapted by each country and enforced by local authorities.

Regulation of street foods can take place through a specific mention in the main food law, through subsidiary legislation issued under the law, through local by-laws and administrative decrees or through codes of practice. If the main food law gives the Minister broad power to take action to prevent food-borne disease and to regulate the production and sale of food in the country, this should be a sufficient basis on which to elaborate regulations on street foods. On the other hand, the advantage of regulating street foods through municipal by-laws or decrees is that local solutions can be found for local problems, as local authorities are most familiar with the regulatory needs and staffing and resource constraints. Several countries, including Burkina Faso, Ghana, India, Nepal, Philippines, Senegal and South Africa, have recently taken steps toward regulating the quality and control of street foods. Development and implementation of codes of hygienic practices have also been successfully tried in some developing countries. This promises to be an area of continuing interest, research and concern in the coming years.

3.2.3. Guidelines for Food Legislation

The preceding section outlined some of the trends that have appeared in national legislation regulating food safety and food control in recent years. Some government officials seeking to update their food legislation have requested FAO to provide updated guidelines for the development of modern food legislation, in view of the fact that the 1979 FAO/WHO Model Food Law in circulation is woefully outdated and inadequate. Legal expertise in food legislation, regulation and standards is not widely available, and the Model Food Law, despite its weaknesses, has filled a gap.

As noted in Chapter 1, the process of developing and updating national legislation should be carried out with extensive stakeholder and agency participation and consultation, in order to take account of local economic, political, institutional and legal circumstances. Therefore the development and use of model laws should in general be discouraged. However, because the 1979 FAO/WHO Model Food Law is still in circulation and government officials continue to apply it, it has been decided to update it and FAO is currently drafting a new version. The New Model Food Law is not expected to be enacted wholesale, but instead should be considered as a blueprint for the development of legislation tailored to national needs.

A modern basic food law generally contains provisions falling into the following categories: definitions and principles to be applied in the law's interpretation; the objectives and scope of the law; the administrative structures that will operate under authority of the law, including inspection and licensing services; offences and penalties; legislation that the law repeals or amends; and the areas in which subsidiary regulations can be elaborated. Regulations usually cover such matters as: (i) contents, handling, packaging and labelling of food products; (ii) specific food products, such as novel foods, baby foods and special dietetic foods; (iii) organizational or coordinating matters concerning, for example, the functioning of the Food Board, the issuance of licences and the conduct of the inspection and analysis services; and (iv) schedules that may contain lists of inspection and analysis fees, models for application forms or certificates and other detailed matters.

The form of the law each country decides to enact will depend on the nation's legal system and legislative tradition. In general, however, a food law will generally be kept as basic as possible, with specific requirements regarding food additives, residues, contaminants, labelling and food standards dealt with in subsidiary legislation. Because all details are confined to the regulations and standards, changes can be more easily and quickly made. For example, regulations and standards may need to be changed in response to scientific advancements, and instead of having to approach Parliament to amend the law, the relevant Minister or Ministers will be given the power to issue any appropriate regulations or schedules and can therefore act to take account of the new developments.

IV. CONCLUSION

Since Rio, the international trade of food has grown enormously as countries rely on each other to secure an adequate and varied food supply through the import and export of food products. Opportunities for growth are encouraged through free trade on the basis of the WTO agreements. In the coming years, countries will have improved access to export markets, but this will be accompanied by greater competition and the need to ensure confidence in the safety of the food supply. This can be achieved through the application of the "farm to fork" principle, according to which all links in the food chain are now being checked to assure food safety and quality, and through the incorporation of a preventive approach to food safety.

On the other hand, new and more sophisticated technologies may raise new risks of food-borne disease, which do not respect national boundaries. Citizens concerned about biological, chemical and environmental hazards, including the potential risks from GMOs, will likely continue to call for greater attention and resources to be allocated to food safety issues. National, regional and international information-sharing can assist in combating consumers' fears, and research can improve the scientific understanding of food-related hazards.

Equally, continuing interest in combating food insecurity and hunger through a human rights approach, building on recent developments, gives rise to some optimism that the right to adequate food may become more widely recognized as a "real" human right, clearer and better implemented in the future. Until now, the right to food and other socio-economic rights have suffered from lack of attention and ideological battles, and are in many respects still underdeveloped and frequently misunderstood. Sustained attention and commitment to defining and enforcing the right to adequate food, whether through voluntary guidelines, an international code of conduct, increased legislative activities at the national level or heightened awareness in governments, courts and human rights bodies, can only help in meeting the goals of reducing the numbers of the world's hungry.

REFERENCES

Borghi, M. & Postiglione Blommestein, L. (eds.). 2002. *For an Effective Right to Adequate Food.* In *Proceedings of the International Seminar on The Right to Food: A Challenge for Peace and Development in the 21ˢᵗ Century, Rome, 17–19 September 2001.* Presses Universitaires de Fribourg, Fribourg.

Boutrif, E. & Bessy, C. 1999. *Basic Approaches to Consumer Protection - FAO/WHO Model Food Act: Control Procedures.* In *Conference on International Food Trade Beyond 2000: Science-Based Decisions, Harmonization, Equivalence and Mutual Recognition, Melbourne, Australia, 11–15 October 1999.* FAO, Rome.

CESCR. 1999. *General Comment No. 12, the right to adequate food (Article 11 of the Covenant).* E/C.12/1999/5, Committee on Economic, Social and Cultural Rights.

FAO. 1992. *Final Report of the International Conference on Nutrition,* Rome.

FAO. 1997. *Rome Declaration on World Food Security* and *World Food Summit Plan of Action.* Report of the World Food Summit, Part One, Rome.

FAO. 1998. *The Right to Food in Theory and Practice,* Rome.

FAO. 1999. *Extracts from International Instruments on the Right to Food.* Legislative Study No. 68, Rome.

FAO. 2000. *The Elimination of Food Insecurity in the Horn of Africa: A Strategy for Concerted Government and UN Agency Action.* Inter-Agency Task Force on the UN Response to Long-term Food Security, Agricultural Development and Related Aspects in the Horn of Africa, Rome.

FAO. 2001a. *The State of Food Insecurity in the World,* Rome.

FAO. 2001b. *New Challenges to the Achievement of the World Food Summit Goals,* CFS:2001/INF.7 and INF.7/Add.1/Rev., Rome.

FAO. 2001c. *Fostering the Political Will to Fight Hunger.* CFS: 2001/INF.6, Rome.

FAO. 2001d. *Contribution to the Third Expert Consultations of the High Commissioner for Human Rights, Bonn, Germany, 12–14 March 2001,* Rome.

FAO/WHO. 1976. *Guidelines for Developing an Effective National Food Control System,* Rome.

FAO/WHO. *Guidelines for Strengthening Food Control Systems* (forthcoming).

FIAN, WANHR & IJMI. 1997. *Draft International Code of Conduct on the Right to Adequate Food. Background paper submitted by FoodFirst Information and Action Network (FIAN), the World Alliance for Nutrition and Human Rights (WANHR) and the International Jacques Maritain Institute (IJMI) to the Expert Consultation of the High Commissioner for Human Rights on the Right to Food, Geneva, 1 and 2 December 1997.*

Langford, M. 2001. *Right to Food in International Law: Obligations of States and the FAO*, LLM Thesis, European University Institute, Department of Law, Florence.

Robinson, M. 2002. *The Right to Food: Achievements and Challenges.* Report to the *World Food Summit: Five Years Later*, Geneva.

UNHCHR. 2001. *Report of the High Commissioner of Human Rights on the Right to Food.* E/CN.4/2001/148, Geneva.

Ziegler, J. 2001. *Report on the Right to Food.* Special Rapporteur, E/CN.4/2001/53, Geneva.

Ziegler, J. 2002. *Report on the Right to Food.* Special Rapporteur, E/CN.4/2002/58, Geneva.

3

ANIMALS

Contents

I. INTRODUCTION

No assessment of the veterinary regulatory environment since the Rio Conference can ignore the dramatic influence of animal disease outbreaks within the last several years. The increase in intensive livestock farming in industrialized countries during this century might have suggested that infectious animal diseases would be confined to the developing world. However, during the last ten years, animal disease emergencies, both infectious and vector-borne, have been occurring with increasing frequency even in the developed world.

The recent outbreaks of bovine spongiform encephelopathy (BSE) and foot and mouth disease (FMD) first appeared in the 1990s in the United Kingdom and then spread to other parts of Europe. Although the extent of the effects of these two diseases is not yet known, together they have already taken an extraordinary toll in human and animal life and have caused severe financial impacts both nationally and internationally. They have also had the effect of raising worldwide awareness of animal diseases, those affecting animals alone and those affecting both animals and humans.

Animal disease control is one of four distinct subject areas addressed by what is commonly called veterinary legislation. The regulation of the veterinary profession is the second; the control of veterinary drugs is the third; and the control of animal feeds is the fourth. Each of these elements will be addressed in this chapter, although the bulk of the discussion will centre on the first, as legislation in this subject area has evidenced more noticeable trends since Rio.

II. INTERNATIONAL FRAMEWORK

In the last decade there have been a number of economic, biological and other trends which have affected the incidence and the control of animal diseases worldwide. By extension, they have also informed regulatory efforts during this period. Some of these are observable empirical trends; others fall under the heading of developments in the international framework of agreements and organizations related to animal health.

2.1. Empirical Trends

2.1.1. Animal Movement and Trade

Within the past few decades, increases in the movement of animals have aided the spread of animal diseases. Trade liberalization is one explanation, as countries have been seeking to benefit from lowered barriers to regional and international trade in animals and animal products. Infrastructure improvements in response to expanding industrial needs have also contributed to the rapid spread of animal diseases. Road construction as well as modernized sea and air freight systems have greatly facilitated the transport of animals around the world. Modern animal transport systems unfortunately assist in the transmission of animal disease, since the animals being transported generally originate from different herds or flocks and they are often confined together for long periods in environments that foster disease spread.

Paradoxically, the greater potential for economic gain through easier access to international trade has been accompanied by greater risks of even more debilitating animal diseases with wider-ranging economic effects. The outbreaks of FMD in dairy herds in Saudi Arabia and in sheep in Kuwait in 2000 probably resulted from the importation of cattle or sheep from Eastern Africa. Another instance of the long-distance spread of FMD occurred in 1999 in North Africa. Regulation of transport means, transport procedures and imports and exports; introduction of livestock tracking systems; and implementation of other mechanisms to facilitate trade while safeguarding animals and humans can lower those risks to some degree, but the reality is that in the current circumstances some diseases have easier pathways to cause greater harm.

2.1.2. Economic and Structural Factors

The economic effects of the increased movement of animals have been coupled with other economic factors affecting the appearance and results of animal diseases. In order to properly control animal diseases, government authorities must have the financial wherewithal to carry out agreed-upon measures, such as purchasing and distributing vaccines, setting up surveillance systems and providing other resources to implement disease control strategies. Most of the countries which have been most directly affected by animal disease outbreaks in recent years do not have the resources required to carry out all of these necessary activities, and thus some gaps necessarily occur. And as a more general matter, veterinary services may get less attention than other "sexier" issues and thus they may get a smaller piece of the economic pie when budgets are devised.

The structural adjustment programmes adopted in many developing countries mainly in the 1980s have also had significant effects in the last ten years. Structural adjustment required widespread privatization of government-owned enterprises and the devolution of government services to private actors, on the assumption that the private sector would act more efficiently and cost-effectively than the public sector. Downsizing official animal health services was also intended to take some of the burden off of developing country budgets.

Some of the weaknesses of this approach have only become apparent in recent years. In the field of animal disease control, privatization meant that the sale of veterinary medicines, the administration of vaccines and the provision of clinical services gained primary importance, whereas surveillance, early warning, laboratory diagnostic services and disease control programmes fell to a secondary role. Less attention was paid to "public good" issues like the control of animal diseases and the obligations to manage and report on disease outbreaks. Coupled with the weakened financial state of many veterinary departments, the result was an increase in animal disease outbreaks and the resurgence of many diseases heretofore thought eliminated. Some examples of this are the appearance of BSE (United Kingdom 1986), the Nipah virus (Malaysia 1999) and the bird flu influenza virus (Hong Kong 1997). Zoonotic diseases that had lain dormant have also been breaking out in recent years, such as leptospirosis (Thailand 1995 and 2000, Ecuador 1998, Peru 1998, USA 1998), monkeypox (DR Congo 1996 and 1997), Rift Valley Fever (Senegal 1986, Egypt 1993), visceral leishmaniasis (Brazil 1993, Kenya 2000) and arbovirus (USA 1999).

The privatization activities connected with structural adjustment were often accompanied by moves to decentralize government services, as part of the same effort to reduce the government's role in animal disease control. The decentralization of many government veterinary departments has meant that veterinary officers are often placed under the control of regional and local authorities, which also means a weakened chain of veterinary command which should otherwise facilitate notification of disease outbreaks and a coordinated response to disease emergencies.

2.1.3. Political and Social Instability

Political upheaval can have dramatic effects on animal disease outbreaks and disease control programmes. Of the 40 poorest countries in the world, 24 are either in the midst of armed conflict or have recently emerged from it. Civil strife can cause refugee movements, with refugees often fleeing with livestock and introducing animal diseases into previously unaffected areas. The Gulf War, the genocide in Rwanda and the civil war in Burundi were all followed by sudden movements of people and livestock, which caused widespread outbreaks of animal disease: rinderpest in the case of Kurdish refugees fleeing into Turkey, and foot and mouth disease in the case of Rwanda, Tanzania, Uganda and the Democratic Republic of the Congo. In Somalia and Southern Sudan, conflicts have been hindering progress in the control of rinderpest, and in Zimbabwe the recent conflicts over land reform issues are preventing the implementation of normal animal health practices.

2.1.4. Climate Variability and Change

Climate variability and climate change have implications for the incidence, spread and control of animal diseases. Periods of drought due to changes in weather patterns can cause the extensive migration of herds in search of water and grazing, which can favour the spread of disease due to increased contact among livestock, and between livestock and wildlife. The introduction of contagious bovine pleuropneumonia in the early 1990s into Botswana and Tanzania was due to the movement of only a few infected animals from endemic areas.

Climate change characterized by global warming is expected to cause more frequent storms and flooding, which may already be observed in the floods in Mozambique in 2000 and 2001. Scientists measuring ice at the two poles have concluded that the Earth's temperature has been rising in recent years and will continue to do so. Rising sea levels can be expected to displace some human populations, perhaps resulting in migration into wilderness areas where infectious agents can be transmitted. Higher temperatures, increased humidity and more extensive surface water may result in increased insect populations and a higher incidence of vector-borne diseases. It appears increasingly likely that climate changes and altered weather patterns will affect the range, intensity and seasonality of many vector-borne and other animal diseases.

2.2. International Developments

In addition to the empirical changes outlined above, the last decade has seen several new international agreements, programmes and organizations which directly or indirectly address veterinary issues.

2.2.1. World Trade Organization Agreements

The three relevant agreements under the World Trade Organization (WTO) are the most significant regulatory development in the international arena in terms of impact on the animal sector. The Uruguay Round of Multilateral Trade Negotiations which established the WTO included negotiations on reducing non-tariff barriers to international trade in agricultural products. The agreements relevant to the animal sector are the Agreement on Agriculture, the Agreement on the Application of Sanitary and Phyto-sanitary Measures (SPS Agreement) and the Agreement on Technical Barriers to Trade. These Agreements entered into force with the establishment of the WTO on 1 January 1995.

Animal health, as it relates to trade, is covered by the SPS Agreement which concerns the application of food safety and animal and plant health regulations. The Agreement encourages governments to "harmonize" their sanitary measures, by basing those national measures on international standards, guidelines and recommendations. Significantly, the SPS Agreement permits governments to set more stringent requirements than the international standards, i.e., to their own "appropriate" level of sanitary and phytosanitary protection. However, the Agreement also provides that all national sanitary measures must be based on an analysis of scientific evidence and the risks involved, and transparent. They must not unjustifiably discriminate between countries, and one measure should not be preferred over another if the end result is the same.

These principles have wide implications for governments seeking, for example, to regulate trade in live animals or animal products. Whereas earlier, countries could enact restrictive animal quarantine or import rules which were in fact disguised trade restrictions, under the WTO scheme all such sanitary measures, where they depart from international standards, must be scientifically justified.

2.2.2. *Office international des épizooties*

The *Office international des épizooties* (OIE), or World Organization for Animal Health, is an intergovernmental organization created in 1924, based in Paris, with 158 member states. Member countries of the OIE commit to collecting information on animal diseases present in their territories, which the OIE analyses and disseminates in order to facilitate prevention and control by other potentially affected states. The OIE also more generally collects and distributes scientific information on animal diseases and the methods used to control them, and assists member countries in disease control activities. Finally, the OIE develops rules and standards which member countries can use as models in developing their own national measures to prevent the outbreak and spread of animal diseases. This last standard-setting role of the OIE is extremely significant in light of the SPS Agreement, which identifies the OIE as the source for international standards for animal health.

In the world economy, the unimpeded flow of international trade in animals and animal products requires rules that permit governments to prevent the spread of transmissible diseases to animals and to human beings without creating unjustified trade barriers. The sources for international norms which have been prepared by the OIE are the International Animal Health Code (2001), the Manual of Standards for Diagnostic Tests and Vaccines (2000), the International Aquatic Animal Health Code (2001) and the Diagnostic Manual for Aquatic Animal Diseases (2000). These promote the harmonization of regulations applicable to trade in animals and animal products. The two Health Codes provide standards for international trade, whereas the Diagnostic Manuals establish standardized diagnostic techniques and vaccine control methods for use in international trade.

International Animal Health Code: The 10th edition of this Code was published in 2001. The Code is divided into four parts, with the first containing general provisions for animal health, the second, recommendations applicable to specific diseases, the third, appendices and the last, model international veterinary certificates. Among the general provisions in the Code are guidelines and principles for conducting transparent, objective and defensible risk analyses for international trade. The components of risk analysis described in the Code are hazard identification, risk assessment, risk management and risk communication. Because of the variations in animal health situations in different countries, the Code offers options to importing countries, incorporating the view that only by considering the animal health situation in the exporting country can the importing country precisely articulate the requirements which are to be met for imports.

Manual of Standards for Diagnostic Tests and Vaccines: This Manual, from 2000, is the companion volume to the Code and provides a wealth of essential internationally agreed scientific and technical information to complement the International Animal Health Code's trade provisions. The aims of the Manual are to facilitate international trade in animals and animal products and to contribute to the improvement of animal health services worldwide. By describing internationally agreed laboratory methods for disease diagnosis, as well as requirements for the production and control of biological products (mainly vaccines), its objective is to harmonize these important elements of animal disease prevention, surveillance and control.

International Aquatic Animal Health Code: This Code was last revised in 2001, with the aim of facilitating trade in aquatic animals and aquatic animal products. It gives detailed definitions of the minimum health guarantees required of trading partners in order to avoid the risk of spreading aquatic animal diseases, and includes sections on import risk analysis and import/export procedures. The Code also sets out detailed rules for "Diseases Notifiable to the OIE". Less detailed chapters cover additional diseases classified as "Other Significant Diseases" (of lesser economic importance, limited geographical distribution or too recent definition to justify inclusion in the primary list). The Code also contains sections on health control and hygiene, and includes model international health certificates for trade in live and dead aquatic animals.

Control of Veterinary Drugs: A seminar on quality control of veterinary drugs was held in Niamey, the Niger in 1997, organized by OIE and the Niger. Biologists, pharmacists and veterinarians responsible for the registration and control of veterinary drugs in Benin, Burkina Faso, Cameroon, Central African Republic, Chad, Côte d'Ivoire, Madagascar, Mali, the Niger, Senegal and Togo gathered to discuss quality control, marketing authorization, good manufacturing practices and export licensing for vaccines and drugs.

At the end of the seminar, fifteen recommendations were adopted with the aim of alleviating any deficiencies still existing in francophone African countries in terms of veterinary drug control, registration and quality. Among the most important recommendations were:

- the creation or strengthening of national laboratories for the control of veterinary drugs and the designation of regional reference laboratories, which would receive technical support from the OIE Collaborating Centre in Fougères;

- the development, or strengthening, of national legislation on veterinary drugs with a team of state inspectors to ensure compliance;

- the improvement of quality control of veterinary drugs, and especially of vaccines, with technical support of the Pan-African Veterinary Vaccine Centre;

- the continuation of information and training activities already undertaken by the OIE in the field of veterinary drug control.

All these recommendations should help to strengthen regional cooperation in francophone Africa, with the aim of stemming the proliferation of unauthorized veterinary drugs.

2.2.3. Codex Alimentarius Commission

The Codex Alimentarius Commission (Codex) is a subsidiary organ of FAO and the World Health Organization (WHO). The SPS Agreement designates Codex as the authority for all matters related to international food safety evaluation and harmonization. The main task of Codex is to develop scientific methodologies, concepts and standards to be used worldwide for food additives, microbiological contaminants and veterinary drug and pesticide residues. Among the most important subjects addressed by Codex in the years since Rio is whether the "precautionary principle", which applies in many other international contexts, should also explicitly apply under Codex. This issue was most recently addressed in the Codex Committee on General Principles in 2001.

The Codex standards for Veterinary Drugs Residues in Food include: (a) Guidelines for the Establishment of a Regulatory Programme for Control of Veterinary Drug Residues in Foods (1993), in order to assure citizens of a safe and wholesome food supply; (b) a Recommended International Code of Practice for Control of the Use of Veterinary Drugs (1993), which sets out guidelines for the prescription, application, distribution and control of drugs used for treating animals, maintaining animal health or improving animal production; (c) a Glossary of Terms and Definitions (1993), developed with a view towards providing information and guidance to the Codex Committee on Residues of Veterinary Drugs in Food; and (d) a list of Codex Maximum Residue Limits for Veterinary Drugs (1999). Draft Guidelines for Residues at Injection Sites were considered at Codex's December 2001 session.

The Ad Hoc Intergovernmental Task Force on Animal Feeding is now discussing the text of a proposed draft Code of Practice on Good Animal Feeding which will apply to feed manufacturing and to the use of all feeds other than those consumed while animals are grazing free range. The main objective of this Code is to encourage adherence to good practice during the procurement, handling, storage, processing and distribution of feed for food-producing animals, and a further objective is to encourage good feeding practices on the farm.

2.2.4. Emergency Prevention System for Transboundary Animal and Plant Pests and Diseases

In 1994, FAO established the Emergency Prevention System for Transboundary Animal and Plant Pests and Diseases (EMPRES). The migration of agricultural pests and diseases across borders has caused major losses and emergencies, at times leading to famine and triggering trade restrictions. EMPRES is designed to bolster existing crisis management to permit early and rapid action, raising efficiency and lowering costs. The initial focus was on two transboundary pest and disease components: animal diseases and the desert locust. For the locust component, see Chapter 4.

The programme's focus is on major transboundary livestock diseases, including rinderpest and other epidemic animal diseases (contagious bovine and caprine pleuropneumonias, FMD, *peste de petit ruminants*, Rift Valley Fever and lumpy skin disease). These diseases are among the most contagious and are a serious burden on the economies of the countries in which they occur.

2.2.5. Programme Against African Trypanosomiasis

The Programme Against African Trypanosomiasis (PAAT) was created in 1997 by an international alliance of FAO, WHO, the International Atomic Energy Agency and the Interafrican Bureau for Animal Resources of the Organization for African Unity, to promote integrated trypanosomiasis control through coordinated international action. PAAT treats the tsetse/trypanosomiasis problem as an integral part of development and poverty alleviation in tryps-affected areas, as part of its ultimate goal of improving food security and sustainable agricultural and rural development.

2.3. Regional Organizations

Several regional organizations are in the process of harmonizing their legislation in order to improve international trade and expand their export markets. Some of the legislation addresses animal health or animal-related issues.

2.3.1. Andean Community

The Andean Agricultural Health System, established in 1992 through Decision 328 of the Andean Community (which consists of Bolivia, Colombia, Ecuador, Peru and Venezuela), has made it possible to coordinate and carry out sanitary activities; assist in harmonizing trade-oriented plant and animal health legislation; monitor the onset of epidemics or diseases; carry out joint action programmes; and help settle trade-motivated disputes between member countries. The Decision establishes objectives, elements, structures and regulations that should be applied within the system. The Andean Community countries are currently working together on a project to update and improve the contents of Decision 328.

In 2000 the Community adopted Decision 483 establishing requirements and harmonized procedures for the registration, control, sale and use of veterinary products in member countries, in order to facilitate trade, ensure their proper use and improve their quality while minimizing risks to animal and human health and the environment.

2.3.2. Caribbean Community

The Caribbean Community (CARICOM) has drafted a model Act entitled the "Animals (National & International Movement & Disease Prevention) Draft Act". This Act has as its objectives the control of the movement of animals and the prevention of the introduction and spread of animal diseases within the member countries of CARICOM (Antigua and Barbuda, Bahamas, Barbados, Belize, Dominica, Grenada, Guyana, Haiti, Jamaica, Montserrat, Saint Kitts and Nevis, Saint Lucia, Saint Vincent and the Grenadines, Suriname and Trinidad and Tobago). It addresses the importation of animals and animal-related products, establishes conditions for quarantine, gives powers to inspectors and sets out a list of prescribed diseases.

2.3.3. Economic Community of Cattle and Meat

In March 1992 in Nouakchott, Mauritania, at a conference jointly sponsored by the Economic Community of Cattle and Meat (*Communauté économique du bétail et de la viande,* CEBV) and the Permanent Interstate Committee for Drought Control in the Sahel (*Comité Permanent Inter-Etats de Lutte contre la*

Sécheressse dans le Sahel, CILSS), representatives of twelve nations in the Sahel and coastal West Africa adopted a modified version of an action plan to improve the efficiency of livestock trade in the central corridor of the Sahel, by lowering administrative and procedural barriers to regional commerce. The representatives also recommended that Burkina Faso, Côte d'Ivoire and Mali implement a pilot effort to promote regional economic integration. The Nouakchott Plan is an integrated approach to reform that is intended to harmonize the interests of governments, which would like to see their economies grow, and private sector actors, which are the direct beneficiaries of reform. These include livestock producers and traders, professional organizations, private transporters and the consumers of livestock products. National coordinating committees were established, made up of government officials from a variety of organizations and private actors representing stakeholder groups. While the committees were at first largely informal, in less than a year they obtained legal recognition.

In 2000, the member countries of the CEBV – Benin, Burkina Faso, Côte d'Ivoire, the Niger and Togo – announced their intention to extend the market to cover all West African countries. Such a market would be in line with the integration goal of the Economic Community of West African States.

Discussions have also been under way for the CEBV to be folded into the *Union économique et monétaire ouest-africaine* (UEMOA). The Council of Ministers and the Commission of UEMOA have approved the concept and at the end of 2000, the Council of Ministers invited the Commission to finalize efforts in this regard.

2.3.4. Economic Community of West African States

As part of its trade promotion programme adopted in 1992, the Economic Community of West African States (ECOWAS) carried out market surveys of veterinary medicines in 1995. Furthermore, in an attempt to better coordinate national policies, an annual meeting of heads of national veterinary services and directors of animal vaccine laboratories of the member states has been institutionalized, with the first meeting held in October 2000. The member countries of ECOWAS are Benin, Burkina Faso, Cape Verde, Côte d'Ivoire, the Gambia, Ghana, Guinea, Guinea-Bissau, Liberia, Mali, Mauritania, the Niger, Nigeria, Senegal, Sierra Leone and Togo.

2.3.5. European Union

The European Union (EU) has adopted numerous Directives, Regulations and Decisions during the last ten years related to animal health. There are Directives establishing conditions for intra-community trade of bovine, swine, ovine and caprine animals; conditions for imports from third countries of poultry and eggs, fresh poultry meat, semen, ova and embryos; and conditions governing the sale of aquaculture animals and products, among others. The legislation applies within the territories of the EU member countries (Austria, Belgium, Denmark, Finland, France, Germany, Greece, Ireland, Italy, Luxembourg, Netherlands, Portugal, Spain, Sweden and the United Kingdom).

With regard to animal disease control, the EU has had to focus a great deal of attention on foot and mouth disease (FMD). The EU's FMD control policy in the early 1990s was designed to achieve high livestock health status prior to the advent of the Single Market on 1 January 1993. This required free trade in livestock within the member states. The EU decided to adopt a policy of non-vaccination based on two reports, one identifying FMD vaccine/research laboratories and the use of poorly inactivated vaccine as the likely source of more than a third of the primary outbreaks between 1977 and 1987, and the other showing that it would be cheaper to compensate for outbreaks than to continue mass prophylactic vaccination Union-wide. Another perceived advantage of the non-vaccination policy was the potential for international trade.

The initial outlook appeared to be that non-vaccination was appropriate, and that the financial benefits of FMD-free status far outweighed the costs incurred in stamping out new introductions of the disease (Italy in 1993; Greece in 1994 and 1996); in each of those instances the disease was eradicated without recourse to vaccination. However, it remains to be seen whether the costs of the latest outbreaks in the late 1990s and early 2000s may alter these calculations. In 2002 the EU was considering implementing a vaccination policy, likely not prophylactically, but for emergency situations.

With regard to Bovine Spongiform Encephelopathy (BSE), in 2000 the EU banned meat and bone meal in all animal feeds and also excluded all cattle over 30 months old from the food chain unless tested for BSE. These rules were intended to harmonize the measures applicable in Europe, as previously a number of EU member countries had imposed their own rules to contain the spread of BSE.

The EU has also been active in the last ten years in the regulation of veterinary drugs control. Directive 96/22/EC of 1996 prohibits the use of certain substances in stockfarming; Directive 96/23/EC, also of 1996, establishes measures to monitor certain substances and residues in live animals and animal products. Decision 97/747/EC of 1997 fixes the levels and frequencies of sampling to be carried out under Directive 96/23/EC; Decision 98/179/EC of 1998 sets out detailed rules for official sampling for the monitoring of certain substances and residues; and Decision 98/140/EC of 1998 lays down rules for checks by Commission veterinary personnel.

2.3.6. Southern African Development Community

In 1992, the Southern African Development Community (SADC) became a formal treaty organization with the signature of the SADC Treaty and Declaration at Windhoek, Namibia. Its founding member states were Angola, Botswana, Democratic Republic of the Congo, Lesotho, Malawi, Mauritius, Mozambique, Namibia, Seychelles, South Africa, Swaziland, Tanzania, Zambia and Zimbabwe. One of the Community's core mandates is food, agriculture and natural resources, which encompasses sanitary and animal husbandry policies. Its Food, Agriculture and Natural Resources Directorate must develop, promote and harmonize member states' husbandry policies.

2.3.7. Southern Common Market

The Southern Common Market (*Mercado Común del Sur*, MERCOSUR) has as members Argentina, Brazil, Paraguay and Uruguay. MERCOSUR was quite active in veterinary regulation in the last decade. For example, Resolution No. 6/96 establishes sanitary regulations for the transit of specific kinds of animals within MERCOSUR. In 1997 various regulations were issued dealing with animal health matters. Regulation No. 2 includes technical information concerning pharmaceutical products for veterinary use; Regulation No. 3 deals with registration of antimicrobial products; and Regulation No. 4 addresses the production and control of vaccines, antigens and solvents for poultry farming. Finally, Resolution No. 45/98 of 1998 establishes a glossary of terms and definitions for residues in veterinary medicines.

III. NATIONAL LEGISLATION

In addition to the developments in the international arena outlined above, the decade since Rio has seen a number of changes and trends in countries' national legal frameworks relating to animal issues. One of the main trends is that an increasing number of FAO member countries have requested assistance in revising their existing veterinary legislation or drafting new laws covering animal diseases and animal movements, as well as the control of veterinary drugs and drug residues. Many countries still have colonial-era legislation for the control of animal movement and animal disease, the regulation of the veterinary profession, the control of veterinary drugs and even the structure of veterinary services delivery. While the age of existing legislation does not *per se* argue for its amendment or replacement, there have been important international developments which have caused many countries to take a new look at their veterinary legislative frameworks.

As noted earlier, the WTO SPS Agreement identifies the OIE as the main source of internationally agreed standards in animal health, and many countries are seeking to harmonize their legislation with the Agreement and with the standards established by the OIE. Countries that have joined the WTO, or that intend to trade with or within the EU, are looking closely at their laws, regulations and standards in order to ensure that these meet agreed international standards and do not run afoul of international obligations. Each country must assess its legal framework in order to determine whether its legislation meets the country's particular needs in light of its economy, trade, policies, government structures and, perhaps most importantly, its international commitments. In particular, countries must ensure that their sanitary measures do not depart from international norms.

Although specific guidance to countries seeking to amend their veterinary legislation is difficult without a close examination of the country's general and specific legal framework, there are some broad principles regarding legislation on veterinary issues which can prove useful and have wider application. Elements of national veterinary laws are examined in more detail below, and at the same time any observed trends since Rio are noted.

3.1. Animal Health

The following list of elements has been used in recent years by FAO as a guide for updating existing animal health legislation or preparing new laws. An examination of the presence or absence of these elements can help determine whether there are gaps in the existing legal framework for animal health and how they might be filled. However, not all of the matters outlined here are essential in all countries, as the contents of a particular country's laws and regulations depend on the policy priorities and exigencies of that country at that particular time.

Scope and definitions: The scope provisions describe the ambit of the animal diseases law and provide the tools for its interpretation. A provision in the law stating its purpose, objectives or scope generally precedes all others. For example, article 1 of the German Act on Animal Diseases dating from 2001 states that the Act deals with the fight against animal diseases. Such a provision serves to explain why the law was enacted, what purpose it is intended to serve and what areas are covered by the law. The 1992 Veterinary Law of Kyrgyzstan was enacted for purposes of the protection of animal health and the prevention of diseases common to animals and people.

Countries often include a list of definitions of the main terms employed in the animal diseases law. There has been a clear trend in the last several years for countries to closely consult internationally agreed sources such as the OIE and Codex, along with other national legislation on related issues, in drafting definitions.

Enabling provisions, administration and powers of delegation: An animal diseases law must define the nature and the limits of the powers to be exercised under it and should designate those who will exercise authority under the law. The Sri Lanka Animal Diseases Act of 1992 provides for the appointment of a Director of Animal Production and Health and subordinate or substituting officers. Most animal diseases laws vest power in the Minister responsible for agriculture, who can then in turn delegate necessary powers to the Chief Veterinary Officer (CVO). For example, the Animal Health Act of Australia, of 1995, provides in article 10 that the Minister may delegate to the Secretary, Chief Veterinary Officer or Deputy Chief Veterinary Officer any of his or her functions under the Act, other than the power of delegation.

As will be discussed below, there has been a trend in recent years of countries acknowledging the weaknesses of systems that rely solely on professionally trained veterinarians for animal health activities. Particularly in light of many governmental efforts to decentralize activities to the regions (where there may be fewer trained veterinarians), legislation needs amending to ensure that community veterinary health workers are permitted to carry out certain extension activities and treatments. This may include, for example, the power to prescribe and dispense certain veterinary drugs. Also, in the context of an emergency when there may not be sufficient staff strength for all the required tasks, the CVO must also be able to press other Ministry staff as well as private veterinarians into service. Under Kyrgyzstan's 1992 Veterinary Law, for example, veterinary activity is to be performed by the state veterinary service of the Ministry of Agriculture as well as by other ministries, institutions, organizations, enterprises and veterinarians in private practice.

Another trend is to combine animal health, plant health and food safety into one agency. This is discussed in Chapter 2.

Reporting requirements: Animal disease laws must impose a duty on both government officials (veterinary officers, extension agents, border guards) and private citizens (farmers, private veterinarians) to report the appearance of certain diseases, even before the existence of the disease can be diagnostically confirmed, as is the case for example in article 3 of the 1997 Animal Disease Act of Morocco.

Inspection: Most animal diseases laws contain a set of provisions establishing administrative structures to carry out the activities necessary to enforce the law. For example, the law will in some fashion set up an inspection service within the veterinary department, or at the least, veterinary officers should carry out an inspection function (including taking samples) in addition to their other tasks. The Sri Lankan Act of 1992, for instance, outlines the powers of the Director of Animal Production and Health and appointed officers to take measures to prevent or contain animal diseases.

The law does not usually delve into great detail on the functioning of the various structures it establishes, but instead describes mandates, defines roles and outlines some other basic rules. Subsidiary regulations may contain the operational details. For example, Regulations No. 184 of 2001 charge the Belize Agricultural Health Authority with veterinary inspection functions, outlining specific procedures for control of the manufacture, placing on the market and importation of veterinary products and animal feeds.

Power to impose and lift quarantine: An animal diseases law must provide the Minister with the power to declare certain areas under quarantine, with concomitant restrictions. These may concern, among other things, the movement of animals or animal products. For example, Part 3 of the Australian Act outlines the conditions for declaring a quarantine area. As noted above, under the SPS Agreement all of these quarantine restrictions must have a scientific foundation and be based on risk assessment. The law should also contain a procedure for review of areas under quarantine and the lifting of quarantine where the danger has abated.

Assistance from forces of public order: The Minister must be able to request the assistance and presence of the forces of public order in carrying out control measures such as those associated with the imposition of quarantine, inspection, slaughter, road blocks and the like.

List of quarantinable diseases: All animal diseases acts must have a list of diseases that may lead to a potential declaration of quarantine by the Minister. For example, article 38 of the Animal Diseases Act of Sri Lanka (1992) defines as "disease" any infectious or contagious disease among animals or birds listed in the first schedule. Containing the list of diseases in an annex or schedule is desirable because the list may change over time. The necessity to add diseases also means that the competent authority is given the mandate to declare other diseases to be "diseases" under the act (e.g., article 2 of Botswana's Diseases of Animals Act of 1979). Equally, a particular disease may have to be deleted from the list when the country determines that that particular disease is no longer a danger in its territory.

Power to declare emergency: The Minister or his/her delegate must have the power to declare an animal disease emergency. Ideally, such a declaration should trigger the release of funds to combat it, and there must be sufficient funds set aside and immediately available upon the declaration of an animal disease emergency anywhere in the country.

Import controls: Animal diseases laws regulate the import, and often also the export, of live animals and all kinds of animal products. For example, article 6 of the Diseases of Animals Act of Botswana provides that no person shall, without the consent of the Director of Veterinary Services, import or export any animal or any other product of animal origin.

In a country where there is an outbreak of a particular animal disease, the law should permit post-import quarantine of animals and animal products, or possibly the temporary ban on imports altogether. It should however be borne in mind that the principles of the WTO SPS Agreement would prohibit discrimination against imported animals and animal products. Moreover, as noted, all measures intended to protect animal health must be scientifically justified.

Slaughter: Certain animal diseases have no cure or are best stamped out through a slaughter programme. The animal diseases act must give the Minister or CVO the power to order the destruction of dead and dying animals, with all details contained in standing orders or in decrees or orders to be issued rapidly as needed. Article 6 of the Moroccan law states that on the proposition of the CVO, the Minister of Agriculture can order, first, the destruction of all animals infected or suspected of being affected; second, the destruction of all animals of a specific farm where there are some animals infected; and third, animals belonging to surrounding farms.

Compensation: Rapidly compensating farmers whose animals have died or whose animals are slaughtered may be absolutely essential to arresting the spread of certain diseases. The law should indicate whether and under what conditions compensation is permitted and how it shall be authorized and carried out. Regulations or standing orders can contain details such as how compensation will be calculated and whether compensation will be in kind or in cash. There are arguments in favour of each, and policymakers will have to weigh them before the emergency arises. The basic questions with regard to compensation should be regulated by the act itself. In the German Animal Diseases Act, for example, there is a specific chapter outlining in detail in which cases how much compensation will be paid.

Collection of data: Under the animal diseases act or its accompanying regulations, some person or department should be charged with collecting and analysing epidemiological data so that the disease status of the country – and its various regions – can be monitored. This information should be shared on a regional and international basis.

Animal and farm registration: It is advisable that the law establish a system of control to identify farms and track animals in the country, and there has been growing interest in such systems in recent years. Article 17(h) of the German Animal Diseases Act, for example, provides that the Minister may introduce an obligation to register animals or animal products. Such measures offer benefits even in the absence of animal disease outbreaks, as through extension activities farmers can be sensitized to proper zoosanitary procedures. Several countries in Eastern and Southern Africa, including Malawi and Rwanda, have launched efforts to regulate livestock identification and movement.

Offences and penalties: Offences against the animal diseases law must be defined, and their associated penalties listed. The level at which the penalties are set depends on the particular country and situation, and they should be linked to the nature of the offence. Many countries complain that the level of the penalties in their animal diseases laws is too low, because the laws are outdated and the currency has lost its value over time. A recent trend in some laws is to apply the concept of "penalty units" rather than fixed amounts, so that inflation will not erode the punitive and deterrent value of penalties as the legislation ages.

Another trend in the last ten years is the inclusion of forfeiture provisions in some laws: provisions like article 77 of the German Animal Diseases Act allow the government to seize vehicles and other property used in the commission of an offence.

Repeal and savings: Where a new animal diseases law makes significant changes to an existing system, laws or regulations already in force may have to be amended or repealed. In such cases the new law will have to list which provisions in which other laws are to be repealed or altered. However, in order not to dismantle the existing system entirely, many laws contain a provision stating that any regulations made under any provision repealed under the new law remain effective, just as if they had been issued under the new law itself.

Regulations: The general form of the basic animal diseases law depends on the legislative traditions of the particular country, but in most cases the best policy is to limit the contents of the basic law to the enabling provisions together with a few very general principles. The advantage of this approach, in all legal systems, is that because the law is basic and all details are confined to the regulations and standards, changes can be more easily and quickly made.

In most cases, the animal diseases law will contain a provision or provisions listing the many subject matters that the Minister may address through regulations in order to carry out the purposes of the law. The list of regulations may be extremely detailed or it may simply give broad outlines to the kinds of topics that the Minister may address. There may be a trend toward the latter, to avoid later accusations that the government acted *ultra vires* in elaborating regulations on particular issues. In any case, the Minister's powers are rarely limited, as in almost all cases the law will contain a general statement that the Minister may "make all regulations he or she deems necessary to achieve the purposes of this law". A good example of this is the Animal Diseases Act of Sri Lanka which states in article 37 that the Minister may make regulations in respect of all matters that are required in the Act.

In preparing regulations and standards, countries that have amended their veterinary legislation or prepared new veterinary regulations in the past ten years have been taking full advantage of OIE and Codex standards and lessons learned in other countries. National standards developed in this fashion complement international ones while respecting local needs and conditions.

3.2. Veterinary Profession

The veterinary profession has seen remarkable developments in the last ten years. Advances in DNA technology have improved vaccines, risk analysis has been borrowed from the field of nuclear energy and quality assurance has been introduced widely, including Good Clinical Practice, Good Laboratory Practice and Good Management Practice in Veterinary Medicine. Finally, there has been a dramatic increase in the use of Geographical Information Systems to map the presence of disease worldwide.

Many of the elements of national laws addressed above under animal diseases laws also apply to laws governing the veterinary profession, often called "veterinary surgeons laws". Accordingly, the specific elements outlined above are not repeated here, nor in the following sections on the regulation of veterinary drugs and animal feeds. Only those new elements specific to these subject matters will be explored.

The scope and purpose of most veterinary surgeons laws is to regulate the practice of veterinary medicine and to protect consumers from unlawful acts by animal health care providers. Laws regulating the veterinary profession usually create a statutory body, such as a Veterinary Council, to carry out a variety of registration and certification functions. For example, the Council will have responsibility for examining and certifying new veterinary graduates and immigrant veterinarians; registering veterinarians and other animal health care providers; and generally policing the activities of registered veterinarians and other providers. Disciplinary measures have to be provided for, ranging from suspension of the licence to practise, to fines, compulsory retraining, expulsion from registration or imprisonment. The veterinary board or council should be independent of the national veterinary service.

Another important purpose of veterinary surgeons laws is to determine those remedies and vaccines that can be sold and dispensed by each class of animal health care practitioner. One notable change in recent years is the increasing involvement of non-veterinarians in the provision of veterinary services. This is partly as a result of the decentralization of ministries of agriculture and also a result of some of the economic factors outlined in Part II of this chapter. Often formal and informal groups of livestock owners employ animal health assistants or, more often, lower-level para-veterinary agents (such as community veterinary health workers), particularly in the rural areas. These non-veterinarians are called upon to provide primary services such as administering remedies against easily diagnosable diseases, prescription drugs and vaccines.

These empirical trends are at times in tension with existing veterinary surgeons laws, which establish strict rules for who may prescribe certain medications and carry out certain procedures. In many cases, these changes have meant that legislation governing the veterinary profession has had to be amended. Ghana and Rwanda have recently begun efforts to revise their veterinary legislation to take account of these developments.

As suggested, another observed trend is the privatization of veterinary services, with many activities previously carried out by government officers now being carried out by private veterinarians. In some cases major disease outbreaks in the last ten years have meant that governments have had to rely on private veterinarians to carry out vaccination campaigns or otherwise to assist in the control and eradication of disease. Legislative amendments to permit this delegation of duties to private actors in such cases are required.

3.3. Veterinary Drugs

Veterinary drugs, including growth promoters, are increasingly used in attempts to improve food animal production. Legislation for the control of veterinary drugs generally sets up a national authority to register all veterinary medicines for use in the country. The distribution, sale or administration of unregistered drugs is prohibited under the law. The law also identifies who may prescribe veterinary drugs, how they must be stored and disposed of, what information must be contained on the label and what records must be kept. To harmonize with the changes to veterinary surgeons laws as discussed in the previous section, existing veterinary drugs legislation may also need to be amended as countries may wish to relax the requirement that certain drugs be prescribed only by veterinarians. Portugal adopted in 1999 a Decree-Law regulating the production, trade, storage, transport and use of veterinary drugs. Cameroon's 2000 Act on Veterinary Pharmacy similarly provides a legal framework for the trade, distribution and import of veterinary drugs.

The law may also detail who may prepare veterinary medicines, using what techniques and under what conditions. Withdrawal periods before slaughter and/or permissible maximum residue levels (MRLs) for meat and milk may also be established in the regulations, although frequently such rules are found in regulations issued under a country's food safety laws rather than in its veterinary legislation.

Producer compliance with veterinary drug regulations should be monitored by national testing laboratories according to nationally or internationally accepted sampling protocols and assay methods. Many developing countries lack the capacity to operate quality assured testing programmes for detection of regulated residues in food animals and their products. Since 1990, within the EU a group of laboratories have been accorded responsibility for the effectiveness of analytical residue control programmes, including methods and materials. These laboratories assess programmes in EU member countries as well as countries trading with the EU.

Draft legislation currently under consideration in Mozambique is based on a comparative study of the regimes in seven neighbouring countries, with which Mozambique has substantial trade. The major innovation inspired by the comparative study is bringing control of veterinary and human medicines under the oversight of a single agency and subjecting them to the Medicines Law. Veterinary treatments that fall under the Pesticides Law (e.g., insecticides) will be regulated under that Law. New procedures under the Medicines Law are proposed for registration of veterinary drugs on the advice of a Veterinary Medicines Commission. Distribution of veterinary drugs through veterinarians is permitted although some will be obtainable only through pharmacies.

3.4. Animal Feeds

Animal feeds laws regulate the import, manufacture, registration, sale, advertising and use of animal feeds and the raw materials used in their manufacture. Generally the law appoints a Registrar of Animal Feeds who has responsibility for registering animal feeds and raw materials used in animal feeds, and listing them in the Register also established in the law. Other administrative provisions may establish an Animal Feeds Committee which is responsible for providing technical advice to the relevant Minister (usually the Minister responsible for agriculture) on all issues relating to animal feeds in the country, in particular the detailed standards that will apply under the law. The internal workings of the Committee are generally set out in subsidiary regulations or in the Committee's own by-laws. Most important, the Committee advises on the contents of the schedules to the law, such as which raw materials and animal feeds are permitted; which ingredients are prohibited; and other matters. The Committee will also advise on any regulations to be proposed under the law.

Generally the law will provide that any person intending to import or manufacture raw materials or animal feeds will have to apply for a licence, and it is an offence under the law to do these activities without such a licence. For example, Egypt adopted a Ministerial Resolution in 1999 regulating feed, feed production, circulation and control. This resolution states that the approval of the Technical Apparatus of the General Union of Poultry Producers is necessary to obtain the licences for production or import of feed.

Licences can be suspended or revoked for any of the reasons enumerated in the law, although the law should also establish procedures for allowing any licence holder to appeal any such decision.

Inspection should also be authorized to control locales where raw materials or animal feeds are imported, manufactured, sold, advertised or used. Inspections are intended to assess the manufacturing processes and the quality control procedures at that establishment. Naturally, any inspectors authorized or appointed under the law may take samples and request documents. Regulations under the law may set out procedures for the taking and marking of samples.

Some animal feeds laws provide that the Registrar may grant provisional registration for the import or manufacture of certain raw materials or animal feeds. This gives flexibility to the Registrar to exempt certain raw materials and animal feeds from the strict registration requirements, for example where a manufacturer has only produced a small amount and cannot pay the full fee. Similar flexibility is also granted in regard to imports: the law may provide that the Minister, acting on the advice of the Committee, may waive normal requirements and permit the import of any raw material or animal feed for research purposes. The Committee can also impose conditions on any importation permitted in this fashion.

Recording responsibilities under the law include those falling on the Registrar as referred to above; in addition, the law may provide that any person who imports or manufactures raw materials or animal feeds must keep records of the quantities dealt with.

Animal feeds laws also enumerate requirements for the sale or use of particular animal feeds and the use of certain additives, providing that they may only be used in relation to the particular species associated with that raw material. A schedule will contain prohibited substances which may not be used for any animal species.

Some animal feeds laws prohibit the advertisement of any unregistered raw material or animal feed, of any raw material or animal feed for a purpose for which it is not intended or in a false or misleading manner or that is contrary to any of the conditions under which it was registered.

IV. CONCLUSION

Recent disease outbreaks even in the most developed countries have raised a great deal of public interest in the causes, prevention and economic effects of animal diseases. The World Food Summit in 1996 recognized the importance of epidemic diseases of livestock to both international trade and world food security. On that occasion, governments and civil society committed to strive for effective prevention and progressive control of such diseases.

Effective control requires efficient disease detection systems, competent diagnostic laboratories and close cooperation among official veterinary services, private veterinarians, farmers, industry, consumers and other organizations. Existing legislation and the concomitant institutional set-up may not foster cooperative effort or joint management and may hinder the effective delivery of veterinary services. Legislative frameworks may also fail to regulate important areas such as veterinary drugs and animal feeds. Comprehensive solutions are needed.

Inadequacies at national level due to outdated or weak legislative frameworks have been compounded by developments at the international level, which are not yet reflected in many countries' legislative systems. The adoption of the WTO SPS Agreement, which underlined the importance of harmonized international standards and of scientific justification, gave prominence to the *Office international des épizooties* and its important standard-making work. This has spurred many countries to take a closer look at their veterinary legislation to determine whether it meets present needs. Efforts are under way, at national and regional level, to review and revise the legislative frameworks in many countries. It is hoped that some of the analysis and recommendations in this chapter may aid in that endeavour.

REFERENCES

Bruckner, G., Donaldson, A.I., James, A., McDermott, J., Leyland, T., Morris, R.S., Permin, A., Rweyemamu, M., Ward, D. & Webb, R. 2001. *Fostering the Policy Dialogue in Support of Improved Animal Health and Veterinary Public Health as an Entry Point for Poverty Reduction and Sustainable Livelihoods for Livestock Farmers.* FAO, Rome.

Centres for Disease Control and Prevention. *Health Topics A to Z* (www.cdc.gov/health/diseases.htm).

FAO. 1991. *Guidelines for Strengthening Animal Health Services in Developing Countries,* Rome.

FAO. 1997. *Principles for Rational Delivery of Public and Private Veterinary Services, with Reference to Africa,* Rome.

FAO/IAEA Training & Reference Centre. *Veterinary Drug Residues* (www.iaea.or.at/trc/vet-intro.htm).

Fingleton, J. 2001. *Mozambique. Veterinary Pharmacology Legislation.* FAO, Rome.

Future Trends in Veterinary Public Health, Weekly Epidemiological Record, No. 19, 14 May 1999.

Improved Control of Veterinary Drugs, World Veterinary Association Bulletin, Vol. 15, No. 2, June 1998.

Smith, L.D. 2001. *Reform and Decentralization of Agricultural Services: A Policy Framework.* FAO, Rome.

Vapnek, J. 1999. *Legal and Institutional Measures to Combat African Swine Fever.* FAO Legal Paper Online No. 3 (www.fao.org/Legal).

WTO. 1998. *Understanding the World Trade Organization SPS Agreement* (www.wto.org/english/tratop_e/sps_e/spsund_e.htm).

4

PLANTS

Contents

I.   INTRODUCTION

Modern methods of travel, trade and communications have led to enormous increases in the movement of people, commodities and conveyances. Natural and national borders that once were effective barriers to the introduction and spread of unwanted organisms or material have shifted or have become more porous, as a result of political or other developments. Continental countries with land borders have always had difficulty monitoring and controlling the movement of pests across the borders, but expansion in the international movement of people and goods is causing increasing difficulties even in island nations, as the volumes of modern air and shipping traffic breach their natural defences against pest introduction.

To address these changing circumstances, and to keep pace with other international developments with regard to plants and plant products, countries and groups of countries have taken action to amend existing laws, regulations and international agreements, especially in the following three areas: (a) plant protection, including pest control and plant quarantine; (b) pesticide control; and (c) seeds and plant variety protection. This chapter will explore developments in these areas, all of which fall under the main heading of Plants.

II.   INTERNATIONAL FRAMEWORK: KEY DEVELOPMENTS

2.1. Plant Protection

Although the devastating effects of plant pests, including diseases and weeds, have been known throughout history, it is only recently that legal standards have been promulgated to prevent the spread of plant pests and to protect plant resources. It may be that in the past plant pests were viewed as divinely imposed and therefore beyond human control – like the recurring plagues of locusts in the Bible – but in more recent times the global community has worked to develop cooperative mechanisms to protect people, animals, plants and the environment from them. The growing importance of international trade has also been an impetus for regulatory change.

2.1.1. WTO Agreement on Sanitary and Phytosanitary Measures

The adoption of the World Trade Organization (WTO) Agreement on Sanitary and Phytosanitary Measures (SPS Agreement) is undoubtedly the most significant international development relating to plants in the last ten years. The SPS Agreement establishes rules regarding sanitary and phytosanitary measures, guiding countries that are seeking to protect human, animal or plant life and health without impinging on international trade. The Agreement articulates a number of principles that are reflected in other later agreements and that are being incorporated into national legislation. The most important effect of the SPS Agreement is that it is binding and enforceable through the WTO dispute settlement procedure.

As a general matter, international agreements designed to address a specific global problem may adopt differing approaches to regulation. Some agreements outline desired goals and offer guidelines on courses of action; others establish precise standards to be met by parties to the agreement. Still others do not themselves establish standards, but instead recognize existing organizations as the source of present and future international standards in a particular subject area. Chapter 2 discussed the role of Codex Alimentarius (Codex) in establishing food safety standards, and Chapter 3 introduced the *Office international des épizooties* (OIE) as the international standard-setting organization for animal health and animal disease control. Along with Codex and the OIE, the SPS Agreement identifies the International Plant Protection Convention (IPPC) as the third source for international standard-setting, and as such the IPPC serves as the basis for the harmonization of plant protection legislation.

2.1.2. Revision of the International Plant Protection Convention

The IPPC is an international treaty relating to plant health. It was initially adopted by the FAO Conference in 1951 and came into force in 1952, superseding previous international plant protection agreements. It was revised in 1979 and its amendments came into force in 1991, and finally was further amended in 1997 to reflect the mandate articulated in the SPS Agreement that the IPPC would be the standard-setting organization for phytosanitary matters. The new wording of the Convention is currently awaiting acceptance, and will come into force 30 days after acceptance by two-thirds of the contracting parties.

In addition to its significant implications for international trade, the 1997 text of the IPPC embodies a number of other themes. For example, the 1997 text emphasizes cooperation and the exchange of information on plant protection. It also promotes the harmonization of phytosanitary measures and toward that end creates a procedure to develop International Standards for Phytosanitary Measures, and promotes their use. The text formalizes the IPPC Secretariat and the procedures for standard-setting, and outlines modern phytosanitary concepts, such as pest risk analysis to support phytosanitary measures, the designation of pest free areas and the phytosanitary security of export consignments after certification. Finally, the text makes provision for contracting parties to provide technical assistance to other contracting parties, especially developing countries, with the objective of facilitating implementation of the IPPC.

The 1997 text of the IPPC provides for the establishment of a Commission on Phytosanitary Measures that will serve as the IPPC's new governing body. The members of the Commission are the parties to the Convention and its functions are to review the state of plant protection in the world, provide direction to the work programme of the IPPC Secretariat and approve standards. The Commission is scheduled to meet annually, although special sessions may also be called. An Interim Commission on Phytosanitary Measures (ICPM) has been established until the new text comes into force.

The 1997 text reflects several conceptual shifts. One is changing the focus from national defensive responses to an international joint plan of action on plant protection. Another is that application of the text is not limited only to the protection of plants in agriculture and agricultural trade, but rather extends also to the protection of natural flora and the environment. In addition, the text applies both to direct and indirect damage by pests such as weeds. The IPPC has always been an important agreement for promoting trade in agricultural, horticultural and forestry products, but as governments become more concerned about the adverse impact of weeds and other invasive organisms on biodiversity and natural habitats as well as on commercial crops, the Convention is also acquiring an increasingly important role as a framework to be applied to matters of environmental protection.

2.1.3. Phytosanitary Standards Under the IPPC

The IPPC is a formal international convention, but the standards developed and adopted under its aegis are not in themselves binding. They do however become binding on WTO members, in that member states are required to base their phytosanitary measures on the international standards developed within the framework of the IPPC. Countries are not restricted to IPPC standards, however: they may establish their own standards so long as they justify any deviation from existing international standards through risk analysis. Risk analysis must also be used where countries develop their own requirements in the absence of any international standard. This practice is widespread, as there are only a limited number of standards established under the IPPC, as compared to standards established by the OIE and Codex.

The IPPC Secretariat became functional at FAO headquarters and established its standard-setting programme in 1992, the same year as the Rio Conference. The Secretariat has the responsibility for coordination of the work programme and for the global harmonization of phytosanitary measures under the IPPC. 1994 saw the first meeting of the Committee of Experts on Phytosanitary Measures, which was replaced by the Interim Standards Committee in 2000 and the Standards Committee in 2000. This is a group of phytosanitary experts from around the world that meets bi-annually to review draft standards, taking into consideration comments submitted by governments, and to comment on the suitability of documents prepared by the Secretariat.

The first international standards for phytosanitary measures (ISPMs) were approved by the FAO Conference in 1995, and since 1998 they have been approved by the ICPM. A number of ISPMs have been prepared and adopted, as shown in the following box. Many of these standards are already being used as the basis for the resolution of trade disputes between WTO members.

International Standards for Phytosanitary Measures

ISPM 1- Principles of Plant Quarantine as Related to International Trade (1995): intended to reduce or eliminate the use of unjustifiable phytosanitary measures as barriers to trade;

ISPM 2 - Guidelines for Pest Risk Analysis (1996): describes the process of pest risk analysis to assist National Plant Protection Organizations in the preparation of phytosanitary regulations;

ISPM 3 - Code of Conduct for the Import and Release of Exotic Biological Control Agents (1996): lists the responsibilities of government authorities and of exporters and importers of biological control agents;

ISPM 4 - Requirements for the Establishment of Pest Free Areas (1996): outlines the requirements for the establishment and use of pest free areas in connection with phytosanitary certification of plants and plant products for export;

ISPM 5 - Glossary of Phytosanitary Terms (1999): lists terms and definitions relevant to phytosanitary systems worldwide and provides a harmonized internationally agreed vocabulary;

ISPM 6 - Guidelines for Surveillance (1997): describes the components of surveillance and monitoring systems for pest detection or for the provision of information for use in pest risk analysis, the establishment of pest free areas or the preparation of pest lists;

ISPM 7 - Export Certification System (1997): describes the components of a national system for the issuance of phytosanitary certificates for export;

ISPM 8 - Determination of Pest Status in an Area (1998): describes the content of a pest record, and outlines the use of pest records and other information in the determination of pest status in an area;

ISPM 9 - Guidelines for Pest Eradication Programmes (1998): describes the components of a pest eradication programme which can lead to the establishment or re-establishment of pest absence in an area;

ISPM 10 - Requirements for the Establishment of Pest Free Places of Production and Pest Free Production Sites (1999): describes these requirements, similar to pest free areas;

ISPM 11 - Pest Risk Analysis for Quarantine Pests (2001): provides details for the conduct of pest risk analysis to determine whether pests are quarantine pests;

ISPM 12 - Guidelines for Phytosanitary Certificates (2001): describes principles and guidelines for the preparation and issue of phytosanitary certificates;

ISPM 13 - Guidelines for the Notification of Non-compliance and Emergency Action (2001): describes the actions to be taken by countries regarding the notification of instances of failure of an imported consignment to comply with specified requirements;

ISPM 14 - The Use of Integrated Measures in a Systems Approach for Pest Risk Management (2002): provides for the development and evaluation of integrated measures in a systems approach as an option for pest risk management for import;

ISPM 15 - Guidelines for Regulating Wood Packaging in International Trade (2002): describes phytosanitary measures to reduce the risk of introduction and/or spread of quarantine pests associated with wood packaging material;

ISPM 16 - Regulated Non-quarantine Pests: Concept and Application (2002): describes the concept of regulated non-quarantine pests and identifies their characteristics;

ISPM 17 - Pest Reporting (2002): describes the responsibilities of and requirements for contracting parties in reporting the occurrence, outbreak and spread of pests in areas for which they are responsible.

2.1.4. Emergency Prevention System for Transboundary Animal and Plant Pests and Diseases

Agricultural pests often migrate or spread across borders and can cause major losses. Damage can be catastrophic, leading to famines and sometimes triggering trade problems. Developing countries are frequently not able to react sufficiently quickly to such events, and extensive emergency operations as well as international assistance may become necessary.

Although there may be effective control methods for the particular pests and diseases, crisis management inevitably involves delays, a low efficiency/cost ratio and an inability to contain the problem before it has had a chance to spread. For all these reasons, as noted in Chapter 3, in 1994 FAO established the Emergency Prevention System for Trans-boundary Animal and Plant Pests and Diseases (EMPRES) in order to minimize the risk of such emergencies. Initial priority was given to two transboundary pest and disease problems: the desert locust and animal diseases.

The locust programme initially focused on the nine countries bordering the Red Sea and Gulf of Aden which have historically been a source of many outbreaks and plagues: Djibouti, Egypt, Eritrea, Ethiopia, Oman, Saudi Arabia, Somalia, Sudan and Yemen. The programme is now being extended to West Africa.

2.1.5. Regional Plant Protection Organizations

Regional Plant Protection Organizations (RPPOs) provide coordination on a regional level for the activities and objectives of the IPPC. The role of regional organizations has been expanded in the 1997 text of the IPPC to specify their cooperation with the Secretariat and the Commission. In addition to promoting the objectives of the IPPC, RPPOs disseminate information relating to the IPPC and cooperate with the ICPM and the IPPC Secretariat in developing international standards. They also develop regional standards in harmony with international ones.

There are in existence nine RPPOs, one of which has been established since Rio: the Pacific Plant Protection Organization was created in 1995 upon a resolution of the South Pacific Conference, by the member countries of the Secretariat of the Pacific Commission. An agreement was signed in 1993 to establish the Near East Plant Protection Organization, although it has not yet begun to function.

2.1.6. Commission for Controlling the Desert Locust in the Western Region

In November 1997, the FAO Conference recommended that "locust-affected countries re-evaluate existing regional locust control structures in order to achieve an appropriate and efficient geographic coverage taking into account the effectiveness of these structures, and to establish a realistic financial provision that would assist affected member Nations to take common action". As a result of these recommendations, FAO invited countries affected by the desert locust (Algeria, Chad, Libyan Arab Jamahiriya, Mali, Mauritania, Morocco, the Niger, Senegal and Tunisia) as well as the secretariats of the two existing regional organizations, the FAO Commission for Controlling the Desert Locust in North West Africa and the *Organisation commune de lutte antiacridienne et antiaviaire*, to meet to develop a common strategy. Two meetings were held in Rome in the first half of 1999 and participants unanimously agreed that a new common regional cooperation body should be established within the FAO framework.

A ministerial meeting on the restructuring took place in Rome in November 1999, and confirmed that a new organization should be established. The meeting requested the Director-General of FAO to convene a Legal and Technical Consultation on a draft Agreement for the Establishment of a Desert Locust Control Commission for the Western Region. The Agreement was approved by the FAO Council in November 2000, and, thus far, five member nations have deposited their instruments of acceptance: Algeria, Chad, Mali, the Niger and Senegal.

2.2. Pesticides

2.2.1. FAO Pesticides Management Guidelines

Pesticides are chemicals used to kill pests, such as insects, fungi, weeds, nematodes, rats, mice, mites, ticks and snails. Pesticides may also kill other organisms, and most are poisonous to humans. FAO has prepared a number of guidelines for pesticides management, which are frequently used as the basis for the development of policies and practices in countries looking to initiate or improve their pesticide management schemes. The FAO pesticides management guidelines encourage responsible trading practices by assisting countries in establishing controls to regulate the quality and suitability of pesticide products as well as the safe handling and use of such products. The guidelines address such topics as registration and control of pesticides; legislation; personal protection for those working with pesticides; good labelling practices; pesticide storage and stock control; and tender procedures for the procurement of pesticides. A number of such guidelines have been issued or reissued by FAO within the last ten years.

Guidelines on Good Labelling Practice (revised) (1995): FAO first published "Guidelines on Good Labelling Practice for Pesticides" in 1985. They are intended for use by those involved in the pesticide industry as well by national regulatory personnel. The document provides guidance on the preparation of pesticide labels including specific recommendations for content and layout. Since 1985 there have been considerable changes in regulations and requirements, and accordingly these guidelines have been revised and updated. The new document, adopted in 1995, contains four main sections and appendices. The first section identifies the main objectives and considerations in preparing a label; the second identifies the information that must appear on a label; the third addresses writing a label with maximum clarity while taking into consideration the level of knowledge of users; and the last discusses the establishment of toxicity and hazard classifications for a product. The appendices contain examples of labels, hazard statements, agricultural practice statements and other summaries of specific and generic labels.

FAO Manual on the Submission and Evaluation of Pesticide Residues Data for the Estimation of Maximum Residue Levels in Food and Feed (1997): The FAO manual on pesticide residues data compiles information and principles which are currently used to estimate maximum residue levels (MRLs) and supervised trials of median residue levels. The aims of the FAO Manual are to:

- clarify, update and consolidate the procedures used to evaluate experimental data and related information;
- improve transparency in the work of the FAO panel which develops these guidelines;
- define and provide guidance on the type, amount, quality and format of data submissions required for the estimation of MRLs on which the Codex MRLs are based;
- facilitate the acceptance of Codex MRLs by governments and foster their use under the SPS Agreement;
- serve as a source of information and instruction for all those directly involved in the activities of the FAO panel; and

- assist member countries in evaluating residue data for the registration of pesticides and in developing their national evaluation systems.

Pesticide Storage and Stock Control Manual (1995) and *Guidelines on the Prevention of Accumulation of Obsolete Pesticide Stocks* (1995): Because pesticides are usually stored before use, FAO has developed a "Pesticide Storage and Stock Control Manual" to convey the importance of pesticide storage practice and stock control. Most developing countries have outdated and deteriorated stocks of pesticides that can no longer be used as prescribed on the label, and such stocks are often stored in poor conditions that pose a threat to human health and the environment. With the exception of a few newly industrialized countries, developing countries do not have adequate facilities to dispose of such stocks in a safe and environmentally sound manner. In view of the danger as well as the high costs of safe and environmentally sound disposal, the long-term solution to obsolete stocks lies in preventive measures: improved stock management and reduction of stocks.

The objective of the "Guidelines on the Prevention of Accumulation of Obsolete Pesticide Stocks" is to raise awareness about the mechanisms by which obsolete pesticide stocks accumulate and to enhance the formulation of policies and procedures aimed at prevention of such accumulation. The guidelines are useful for aid agencies, the pesticide industry and governments of developing countries, in particular ministries of agriculture and ministries of health.

Provisional Guidelines on Tender Procedures for the Procurement of Pesticides (1994): The guidelines on tender procedures are intended to instruct both suppliers and procurers of pesticides on the steps to be taken to ensure that pesticides obtained are of the required quality and are suitably packaged and labelled, taking into account local transport and warehousing conditions. The recommendations are relevant to all procurement agencies – government agencies, donors and private dealers – regardless of the ultimate user of the pesticides. The guidelines are designed to minimize problems commonly encountered in developing countries, such as supply of sub-standard and inappropriate formulations, contained in unsuitable packaging of poor quality with inadequate labelling. This can lead to leakage, degradation of contents and misuse.

Manual on the Development and Use of FAO Specifications for Plant Protection Products, 5th edition (1999): The establishment of voluntary standards to reduce risks associated with the use of pesticides is one of FAO's primary objectives in plant protection. The development of FAO specifications was a vital tool in this regard, designed to ensure that pesticides complying with the specifications are satisfactory for the purpose for which they are intended and that they do not present unexpected hazards. FAO specifications may be used (i) as part of a contract of sale so that a buyer may purchase a pesticide with some guarantee of the quality expected; and (ii) for the competent authority to check that the quality of the formulation on the market is the same as that registered. The specifications are intended to enhance confidence in the purchase and use of pesticides and, at the same time, to contribute to better pest control measures and agricultural production. The 5th edition of the Manual describes in detail a new procedure for the development of FAO specifications, under which the data requirements have been expanded dramatically. Now, specifications will apply only to products for which the technical materials have been evaluated by FAO, instead of to any notionally similar product, as under the previous procedure.

2.2.2. Convention on the Prior Informed Consent Procedure for Certain Hazardous Chemicals and Pesticides in International Trade

The Convention on the Prior Informed Consent Procedure (PIC) for Certain Hazardous Chemicals and Pesticides in International Trade, adopted in 1998 but not yet in force, represents an important step towards protecting the world's peoples and environment from the dangers of highly dangerous pesticides and chemicals. It will establish a first line of defence against future harm by preventing unwanted imports of dangerous chemicals, particularly in developing countries. Previously, the PIC system was grounded primarily on two non-binding instruments: the 1985 FAO Code of Conduct on the Distribution and Use of Pesticides, and the 1987 UNEP London Guidelines for the Exchange of Information on Chemicals in International Trade. In 1989, both the FAO Code and the UNEP Guidelines were amended to include specific provisions on PIC.

The PIC procedure helps participating countries learn more about the characteristics of potentially hazardous chemicals that may be shipped to them, initiates a decision-making process on the future importation of these chemicals and facilitates the communication of the importing country's decision to other countries. The Convention gives importing countries the power both to decide which chemicals they want to receive and the choice of excluding those they cannot manage safely. If trade does take place, the Convention imposes requirements for labelling and the provision of information on potential health and environmental effects.

Pesticides and chemicals are subject to PIC if their use has been entirely prohibited or severely restricted, refused approval for first-time use or withdrawn from the market because of environmental or health reasons, as a result of a final government regulatory action. The PIC procedure normally applies to any such pesticide or chemical upon notification to and listing by FAO or UNEP. It is implemented through a joint FAO/UNEP Secretariat, FAO being the lead agency for pesticides and UNEP the lead agency for other chemicals.

2.2.3. Convention on Persistent Organic Pollutants

Persistent Organic Pollutants (POPs) are chemical substances that persist in the environment, bioaccumulate through the food web and pose a risk of adverse effects to human health and the environment. POPs are highly toxic, causing an array of adverse effects among humans and animals, notably morbidity, disease and birth defects. In addition, POPs concentrate in living organisms through bioaccumulation. Though not soluble in water, POPs are readily absorbed in fatty tissue, where concentrations can become enormously magnified. Fish, predatory birds, mammals and humans are high up the food chain and so absorb the greatest concentrations. When they travel, POPs travel with them, and thus POPs can be found in people and animals thousands of kilometres from any major POPs source. With the appearance of these substances in regions where they have never been used or produced and the consequent threats they pose to the global environment, the international community called for urgent global action to reduce and eliminate releases of such chemicals.

The POPs Convention was adopted in Stockholm in 2001. It covers a dozen POPs including pesticides, industrial chemicals and hazardous by-products of combustion: aldrin, chlordane, DDT, dieldrin, dioxins, endrin, furans, heptachlor, hexachlorobenzene, mirex, toxaphene and polychlorinated biphenyls (PCBs). Most of the 12 chemicals are subject to an immediate ban, except for a health-related exemption which has been granted for DDT, as it is still needed in many countries to control mosquitoes. The exception will permit governments to protect their citizens from malaria – a major killer in many tropical regions – until they are able to replace DDT with cost-effective and environmentally friendly alternatives.

In the case of PCBs, although they are no longer produced, hundreds of thousands of tonnes are still in use in electrical transformers and other equipment. Under the Convention, governments may maintain existing equipment in a way that prevents leaks until 2025, to give them time to arrange for PCB-free replacements. In addition, a number of country-specific and time-limited exemptions have been agreed for other chemicals: for example, governments agree to reduce releases of furans and dioxins, which are accidental by-products and thus more difficult to control, "with the goal of their continuing minimization and, where feasible, ultimate elimination".

The Convention sets out control measures covering the production, import, export, disposal and use of POPs, according to which governments are to promote the best available technologies and practices for replacing existing POPs while preventing the development of new POPs. To carry out their commitments, countries will draw up national legislation and develop action plans. Although the control measures will apply to the initial list of 12 chemicals cited above, a POPs Review Committee will consider additional candidate chemicals for the POPs list on a regular basis, thus ensuring that the treaty remains dynamic and responsive to new scientific findings.

2.3. Seeds and Plant Variety Protection

In 1996 FAO developed a Special Action Programme on Seeds to ensure that emerging trends in seed development are more appropriately and effectively addressed. The programme aims, among other things, to develop national seed policies, plans and programmes, to define seed security strategies and to train and organize farmers.

A great deal of attention has been paid to plant variety protection in recent years. The justification for protecting new plant varieties is to encourage plant breeders to invest the time and resources necessary to improve existing varieties. The argument is that without exclusive rights, breeders will not have sufficient incentives to develop new varieties. In addition, the grant of exclusive rights to plant breeders is intended to benefit society, as it should encourage research and development into new breeding techniques and new varieties, thereby reducing the need for government funding in these areas. An international system of protection for plant varieties expands these benefits by facilitating access to new varieties created in other states. The assumption is that once breeders are assured that their rights will be protected in other states, they will be more willing to make their new varieties available.

Two international agreements relating to plant variety protection have come into force since Rio, the World Trade Organization Agreement on Trade-Related Aspects of Intellectual Property Rights, which became effective in 1995, and the 1991 UPOV Act (*Union internationale pour la protection des obtentions végétales*), which came into force in 1998. These two treaties contain comprehensive rules for their member states regarding the protection of plant varieties.

2.3.1. 1991 UPOV Act

The 1991 UPOV Act requires states to protect at least fifteen plant genera or species upon becoming members of the Act, and to extend protection to all plant varieties within ten years. A variety is eligible for protection if it is novel, distinct, uniform and stable. Once protection is granted, prior authorization must be obtained from the breeder by any person seeking to use reproductive or vegetative propagating material of the variety for: (1) production or reproduction; (2) conditioning for the purpose of propagation; (3) offering for sale; (4) selling or marketing; (5) exporting; (6) importing; or (7) stocking for any of these purposes. (Art. 14)

The 1991 UPOV Act requires national treatment, meaning that whatever rights member states grant to their nationals in their own plant variety protection laws, they must also grant to nationals of other 1991 Act member states. For example, if a 1991 Act member chooses to grant more expansive exclusive rights to breeders than the exclusive rights required by the 1991 Act, it must grant those rights to breeders from all other 1991 Act member states. The Act also contains a compulsory licence provision, meaning that a member may restrict a breeder's exclusive rights only in the public interest. However, equitable remuneration must be paid to the breeder whose rights are limited.

2.3.2. WTO Agreement on Trade-Related Aspects of Intellectual Property Rights

The WTO Agreement on Trade-Related Aspects of Intellectual Property Rights (TRIPS Agreement) requires its member states to protect new plant varieties using patent rights, a *sui generis* system of protection (that is, a system of its own kind) or some combination thereof. The TRIPS Agreement is unusual in that it seeks to establish universal, minimum standards of protection across the major fields of intellectual property, including patents, copyrights, trademarks, industrial designs, integrated circuits and trade secrets. Although the TRIPS Agreement devotes only minimal attention to plant varieties, its article 27(b)(3) has done more to encourage the legal protection of plant varieties than any other international agreement.

TRIPS is part of a set of trade-related treaties on a variety of subjects going far beyond intellectual property rights. Other treaties adopted during the Uruguay Round of Multilateral Trade Negotiations covered agriculture, sanitary and phytosanitary measures, technical standards, textiles and trade in goods and services. TRIPS was only one part of a global "package deal", under which developing countries agreed to provide minimum standards of effective intellectual property protection, and in exchange developed countries agreed to open their domestic markets to goods and other products manufactured by producers in the developing world. (Helfer, 2002) The TRIPS Agreement is binding on all WTO members except for the least developed countries, which have until 2006 to implement the treaty's obligations.

III. TRENDS IN REGIONAL AND NATIONAL LEGISLATION

3.1. Regional Developments

In the development of regional trading blocs, policymakers are increasingly drawing attention to the need to harmonize standards so as to facilitate trade. One of the first stated tasks of the newly created African Union, for example, is to assess the web of food safety, phytosanitary and animal health standards on the continent, and to make recommendations for harmonization in order to remove barriers to trade. Interest in the harmonization of standards for trade purposes has triggered the development of standards at the regional level, where regional standard-setting organizations exist. These regional standards must be consistent with the SPS Agreement and other applicable international obligations, although they may address areas not yet covered by international standards. For example, a regional organization may develop a standard for surveillance of a particular pest in the region, although that standard will be based on science and on the existing IPPC surveillance standard.

The relationship between a regional economic grouping and its relevant standard-setting organization varies. At one end of the spectrum might be the North American Free Trade Agreement and the North American Plant

Protection Organization, where the standards established by the latter have direct legal effect. At the other end of the spectrum, standards established by the European Plant Protection Organization are not binding on European Union members, although they are persuasive and are most often taken on board. As noted, however, regional standards, whatever their effect, must be based on science and on what has already been agreed at the international level.

3.1.1. Plant Protection

Andean Community: The Andean Community has recognized the importance of public knowledge on the phytosanitary situation of its member countries and has approved Resolution 419 of 1996, which contains a sub-regional pest and plant diseases inventory that is intended to be updated. This Resolution arose from Decision 328 of 1992, which proclaimed the necessity of surveillance against exotic pests and diseases of plants.

Caribbean Community (CARICOM): In 2001 FAO prepared a model plant quarantine law for the Caribbean region, following country consultations and a discussion of the draft law at a meeting of the Caribbean Plant Protection Commission. The Commission recommended that a more detailed discussion be carried out, and a meeting of Caribbean countries was held in August 2002 to finalize the draft. Individual countries wishing to follow the regionally agreed guidelines will have to enact a nationally tailored version of the model law to ensure that the legislation captures local circumstances and needs.

The existence of harmonized plant quarantine laws is intended to facilitate trade in agricultural products among CARICOM countries and with other trading partners. It should also facilitate compliance with the WTO, as the model law applies the concepts and terminology of the SPS Agreement and the 1997 text of the IPPC. Harmonized legislation should also provide a good foundation for incipient regional efforts to create a Caribbean Agricultural Health and Food Safety Agency, as noted in Chapter 2.

Comité de sanidad vegetal del Cono Sur (COSAVE) and the *Mercado Común del Sur (MERCOSUR)*: COSAVE is an RPPO established in 1989 within the framework of the IPPC through an agreement among its member countries (Argentina, Brazil, Chile, Paraguay and Uruguay). Its main objective is regional plant protection. After the formation of the WTO and

MERCOSUR, it started to develop regional standards to harmonize phytosanitary regulations and procedures in order to facilitate regional and international trade in agriculture products. Phytosanitary standards issued by COSAVE make possible the harmonization of plant protection methods among the member countries, while preventing phytosanitary measures being used as barriers to the regional and international trade. To accomplish this objective, NPPOs may use COSAVE's standards to establish their own phytosanitary regulations, and as technical references to solve any bilateral controversy on the application of such regulations.

The interaction between COSAVE and MERCOSUR assists in creating effective regional phytosanitary measures. COSAVE standards are horizontal, and support the vertical standards of MERCOSUR. MERCOSUR's vertical standards apply the concepts designed by COSAVE to develop normative and practical procedures related to regional and international trade. COSAVE standards are not compulsory, but the developed guidelines are incorporated into MERCOSUR's community legislation as provided in Resolutions GMC 12/93 and 59/94. COSAVE also carries out the initial phases of pest risk analysis, identifying which pests are of quarantine concern. It then develops the later phases, establishing the phytosanitary requirements for each specific product from specified origins.

COSAVE has adopted the following standards since Rio:

- Guidelines for the Development and Adoption of Regional Standards in Plant Protection (1995), which describe the process of elaboration and adoption of COSAVE regional standards;
- Principles of Plant Quarantine in Relation to International Trade (1995), which are intended to reduce or eliminate the use of unjustified phytosanitary measures as barriers to trade;
- Glossary of Terms Related to the Registration of Phytosanitary Products (1996), which describes the officially accepted terms concerning regulations of phytosanitary products;
- Guidelines for the Establishment of a System of Phytosanitary Certification for Export (1998), which describe the elements of a national system of phytosanitary certification;
- Guidelines to Authorize Official Inspectors to Issue Phytosanitary Certificates (2000), which outline the responsibilities of NPPOs and the basic levels of training, knowledge and authority that their officers need to have to issue phytosanitary certificates in conformity with the IPPC;

- Procedures for the Approval of Quarantine Treatments (2000), which describe procedures used by COSAVE in order to recognize quarantine treatments used by the respective NPPOs of the member states;
- Labelling of Phytosanitary Products (2000), which prescribes the contents and form of compulsory labels for phytosanitary products.

European Union (EU): With Directive 77/93/EEC, the EU established a Community Plant Health Regime, specifying the phytosanitary conditions, procedures and formalities to which plants and plant products are subjected when introduced into or moved within the EU. In particular, this directive prohibits the introduction into member states of certain harmful organisms which were listed in an inventory. For the sake of clarity and internal consistency, the directive has been amended on a number of occasions, often substantively. Directive 95/44/EC of 1995, for example, establishes the conditions under which certain harmful organisms, plants, plant products and other objects listed in the annexes to Directive 77/93/EC could be introduced into or moved within the EU, for experimental or scientific purposes and for work on varietal selections. It was finally consolidated in Directive 2000/29/EC of 8 May 2000.

Gulf Cooperation Council (GCC): FAO assisted the Gulf Cooperation Council in the revision of a draft Plant Quarantine Law for the Gulf Region in 2001. At a meeting with legal and quarantine experts from the six Gulf countries (Bahrain, Kuwait, Oman, Qatar, Saudi Arabia and United Arab Emirates), the contents and format of the law were agreed upon. The law is intended to harmonize quarantine activities in the region and facilitate compliance with the SPS Agreement, and has since come into force.

Pacific Plant Protection Organization (PPPO): The Pacific Plant Protection Organization in 2001 agreed to guidelines for drafting biosecurity laws in the region, which have been used to draft legislation for Kiribati and Niue.

North American Plant Protection Organization (NAPPO): NAPPO has been very active in preparing and reviewing regional standards in the last ten years. Some of the most important include:

- Guidelines for the Use of Irradiation as a Phytosanitary Treatment (1997), which offer guidance for the evaluation, adoption and use of irradiation as a phytosanitary treatment;

- Accreditation of Laboratories for Phytosanitary Testing (1998), which outlines criteria for the accreditation of diagnostic laboratories to perform specific functions in support of phytosanitary certification;
- NAPPO Glossary of Phytosanitary Terms (1999), which is intended for use within NAPPO and by the NPPOs in the NAPPO region, and which includes only those terms that are defined in NAPPO standards or other current NAPPO policy documents that do not occur in the FAO Glossary of Phytosanitary Terms;
- Guidelines for Preclearance Programs (2000), which contain a framework for establishing preclearance programs between NAPPO member countries;
- Accreditation of Individuals to Sign Federal Phytosanitary Certificates (2001), which describes the responsibilities of NPPOs and the base level of knowledge, skills, ability and authority appropriate for NPPO officials to sign phytosanitary certificates under the IPPC;

and a number of other standards on pest free areas, on the pest status of particular pests in the region and on the import of particular products into the NAPPO area.

3.1.2. Pesticides

Andean Community: The Andean Community issued in 1998 Decision 436 concerning the registration and control of chemical pesticides for agricultural use. It establishes requirements and harmonized procedures for the registration and control of chemical pesticides for agricultural use, to regulate their use and correct handling in order to prevent and minimize damage to health and the environment as well as to facilitate trade in the sub-region. Manufacturers, importers, exporters and wholesalers of pesticides for agricultural use are required to be registered by the competent national authority. Special permits are also required for research and scientific experiments.

COSAVE and *MERCOSUR*: For pesticides, a 1997 COSAVE standard establishes procedures and criteria for the harmonization and adoption of procedures and analytical methods for phytosanitary products and their residues in accredited laboratories in the region. In 2002, two standards were elaborated on pesticides: one outlines the requirements for proper labelling of phytosanitary products, including the contents and form of labels that are required for particular formulations, and the other describes and codifies the internationally accepted formulations for use in the region. An earlier standard (1995) set out the requirements that must be considered for the accreditation of bodies that will assess the efficacy of phytosanitary products.

In the area of biological control, COSAVE has adopted several standards regarding biological control agents (BCAs), the first on their import, quarantine and release (1996). Another standard elaborated basic procedures and requirements for the registration of BCAs and other biological control products (1997), and a recent standard addressed the establishment and functioning of quarantine laboratories for BCAs in the region (2000). The member states of MERCOSUR decided with Resolution 48/96 of 1996 to establish a common list of products that can freely be circulated in the common market. They also agreed on a process aimed at harmonizing national pesticides registries.

EU: Directive 99/45/EC relates to the classification, packaging and labelling of dangerous preparations. Classification is to be carried out based on the degree of hazard of the particular product, and member states are also required to follow certain packaging requirements before placing such products on the market. Directive 94/43/EC establishes uniform principles for the evaluation and authorization of plant protection products.

Directive 98/8/EC concerns the authorization and placing on the market of biocidal products; the mutual recognition of authorizations within the EU; and the establishment at EU level of a list of active substances which may be used. Member states are required to prescribe that a biocidal product may not be placed on the market and used within their territory unless it has been authorized in accordance with the directive. Products must be classified, packaged and labelled in accordance with the directive as well.

Directive 2000/80/EC of 4 December 2000 amended Annex I of Directive 91/414/EEC concerning the placing of plant protection products on the market, so as to consolidate that Annex and include a further active substance. The directive provides that after inclusion of an active substance in Annex I, member states must, within a prescribed period, grant, vary or withdraw, as appropriate, the authorizations of the plant protection products containing the active substance. In particular, plant protection products should not be authorized unless account is taken of the conditions associated with the inclusion of the active substance in Annex I and the uniform principles laid down in the directive.

European Plant Protection Organization (EPPO): EPPO issued Guidelines on Good Plant Protection Practice in 1998. The main purpose of the EPPO recommendations is to provide guidance on whether to use plant protection products and how to use them safely and effectively. EPPO also approved a standard for the efficacy evaluation of plant protection products in 1999, which describes how the risk of resistance to plant protection products can be assessed and, if appropriate, systems for risk management can be proposed.

Permanent Interstate Committee for Drought Control in the Sahel (Comité Permanent Inter-Etats de Lutte contre la Sécheresse dans le Sahel, CILSS): In 1999 CILSS revised its Common Regulation for the Registration of Pesticides. The main objective of the regulation is to combine the expertise on pesticide evaluation and management in all CILSS member states for purposes of pesticides registration. The revision was adopted as Resolution 8/34/CM/99 by the 34th session of the CILSS Council of Ministers, held in N'Djamena, Republic of Chad.

3.1.3. Seeds and Plant Variety Protection

Andean Community: Decision 345 of 1993 of the Andean Community established a common regime for the protection of plant breeders' rights.

CARICOM: In 1995 FAO prepared a model Seed Law for the Caribbean, which incorporates updated definitions and concepts relating to seed certification and control, and draws on the national seed policies and plans which most countries have already considered and adopted. A number of countries have carried out discussions at the national level intended to lead to enactment of national legislation based on the model law.

EU: Directive 98/44/EC of 1998 on the Legal Protection of Biotechnological Inventions provides that "biological material which is isolated from its natural environment or produced by means of a technical process" may be patentable. Member states must adjust their national patent laws to take account of the provisions of this directive. For the purposes of the directive, inventions which are new, which involve an inventive step and which are susceptible of industrial application shall be patentable even if they concern a product consisting of or containing biological material or a process by means of which biological material is produced, processed or used. Plant varieties and essentially biological processes for the production of plants shall not be patentable.

Regulation EC/2100/94 on plant variety rights establishes an EU system as the sole and exclusive form of EU intellectual property rights for plant varieties. Generally the system tracks the 1991 UPOV Act, with minor differences. EU plant variety rights cover varieties of all botanical genera and species, including hybrids between genera or species. A Community Plant Variety Office is established for the implementation of this regulation.

MERCOSUR: In the seed area, MERCOSUR adopted in 2000 Resolution 1/00 which sets up criteria for the elaboration of standards for the production of certified propagating material with the aim of facilitating trade of seeds within member states. For plant varieties, the member countries of MERCOSUR signed an Agreement of Cooperation related to the Protection of Plant Breeding in 1998 (No. 2/98). The objective of the agreement is to adapt countries' plant protection legislation to the provisions of the 1978 UPOV Act. The agreement defines rules on plant variety protection regarding equal treatment (art. 1); denomination of varieties (art. 2); harmonization of technical examinations (art. 3); exchange of information (art. 4); harmonization of administrative procedures (art. 5); and cooperation (art. 6).

Organization of African Unity (OAU): The foreign ministers of the member states of the OAU issued a statement in 1999 calling for a hold on intellectual property protection for plant varieties until an Africa-wide system has been developed that grants greater recognition to the cultivation practices of indigenous communities. However, at a subsequent meeting of the *Organisation Africaine de la propriété intellectuelle*, patent officials from sixteen francophone African nations recommended that their countries adopt the 1991 UPOV Act.

3.2. National Trends

3.2.1. Plant Protection

As noted earlier, the most important influence on national legislation relating to plant protection in the last ten years has been the adoption of the SPS Agreement and the new revised text of the IPPC (1997). Many countries are amending their existing plant protection laws, or enacting new ones, to ensure that their legislation uses the new definitions from the IPPC and the Glossary of Phytosanitary Terms, and that their laws reflect the concepts and rules of the SPS Agreement.

Another recent development is the trend toward the establishment of a central national food safety authority, discussed in Chapter 2. Such central authorities often draw together food safety, animal health and phytosanitary matters under one roof, and coordinate national inspection activities in two or more of these fields. El Salvador's *Ley de sanidad vegetal y animal* of 1995 abrogates earlier legislation and combines the protection of plant and animal health. Under the law, Consultative Councils of Plant Health and Animal Health will draw on government representatives, producers, professional associations, academic institutions and other organizations. Peru's *Servicio nacional de sanidad agraria* is a decentralized government body charged under the *Ley marco de sanidad agraria* of 2000 with addressing all risks to the agricultural health of the country, whether zoosanitary or phytosanitary. Central food and sanitary authorities may also be established as agencies not under the auspices of any ministry, so as to ensure their independence.

National plant protection laws can follow many forms, but there are certain elements that FAO has been advising countries to include when updating phytosanitary legislation or preparing new phytosanitary laws. The following discussion centres on these elements, although it should be borne in mind that not all matters outlined here are essential in every country. The decision of what to include and what to exclude will depend on the international obligations, policy priorities, existing structures, budgetary constraints and human resources of a country at the time of enactment.

Title and preliminaries: The title and preamble outline the ambit of the plant protection law, stating its purpose and scope. The preamble has no real legal effect, but instead outlines why the law was enacted, what purpose it is intended to serve and what areas are covered by it. For example, the draft Plant Quarantine Act for Ghana is termed "an Act to provide for the efficient conduct of plant quarantine in Ghana and to assist in the prevention of the importation or spread of plant pests". Similarly, a bilateral agreement between Croatia and Bulgaria on plant protection signed in 1996 aims to protect plants and plant products through the prevention of the introduction and spread of plant pests and diseases on the territory of the contracting parties.

One notable development in the years since Rio is that whereas existing plant protection legislation in many countries provides that the Minister can take action only to prevent the introduction of a plant pest, newer laws adopt the concepts of the 1997 text of the IPPC, which recognizes that even pests already established in a country may be regulated at borders if they are under official control within the country.

Definitions: All phytosanitary laws include a list of definitions of the main terms employed. Because the SPS Agreement requires countries to rely on international standards developed by the IPPC for phytosanitary matters, the definitions in recently drafted plant protection laws use the language and concepts established under the 1997 text, including the Glossary of Phytosanitary Terms. In fact, the existence of these global reference points for phytosanitary terminology has been one impetus for many countries to seek to harmonize their legislation using these terms. Countries can also introduce their own terms to meet national needs: for example, the draft plant protection legislation for Sudan introduces the term "pests of national concern". This innovative concept is designed to ensure that the Act will apply to all pest control programmes, pest management activities and pests, even those of purely domestic interest.

It must be emphasized that in all legislation, no matter the subject matter, the list of definitions is not a glossary of terms in general. The definitions that are included must be only those that appear in the body of the law, and the definitions should not be overly detailed but should be designed solely for the purpose of application and interpretation of the law.

Administration: The Administration part of a modern phytosanitary law contains the enabling provisions, which are those that define the nature and the limits of the powers to be exercised under the law and also identify the persons or institutions in whom those powers are to be vested. Normally a phytosanitary law vests power in the Minister responsible for agriculture, although naturally he or she may delegate necessary powers to the National Plant Protection Organization (NPPO). The duties assigned to the NPPO in the law are usually those listed in the 1997 text of the IPPC. For example, the draft legislation for Sudan sets out in detail the mandate and responsibilities of the NPPO, and those details are based on the IPPC.

In many countries, the initial screening of plant products in the possession of ship and airline passengers is done by officers of the Customs Department rather than the Ministry responsible for agriculture. Accordingly, recent phytosanitary laws may state that although the Ministry responsible for agriculture has the ultimate authority for all plant protection inspection activities (because it is the Ministry with the relevant expertise in plant health matters), the Minister may nonetheless call upon officers of other ministries to assist with implementation of the Act. Where the delegation clause is restricted only to government officials, however, this may conflict with a recent trend in many countries for NPPOs to out-source some of their inspection and other activities to contracted parties. A restrictive delegation clause would have to be amended if an NPPO intended to privatize certain government functions.

Because plant protection intersects with other government departments, quasi-governmental agencies and the private sector, it is important that the law make provision for coordination. Most modern phytosanitary laws establish a mechanism for consultation and joint decisionmaking such as a Plant Protection Board, which has as its essential mandate the provision of advice to the Minister responsible for agriculture on all matters related to plant protection in the country. The specific membership will vary from country to country but, in general, all the relevant governmental bodies and stakeholders should be represented, to ensure that all parties interested in and affected by plant protection issues in the country will be able to give their inputs. This also fosters transparency in decisionmaking. Due to the technical complexity of many matters the Board will be called on to address, for example in carrying out pest risk analysis, it must have representation from scientific experts or must be able to constitute technical committees to draw upon their expertise.

Finally, an important administrative provision that may be included in newer phytosanitary laws, which does not often appear in older laws, establishes a Phytosanitary Emergency Fund which can be used when the Minister declares a phytosanitary emergency. The Board generally has the task of developing the applicable criteria for when an emergency should be declared, which triggers activation of the Fund. Alternatively, the law may not specifically create a Fund, but may simply provide that the Minister has a right to go to Cabinet for funds to be appropriated from consolidated revenue in the case of a phytosanitary emergency.

Imports: There are two main regulatory approaches to imports of plants, plant products and other regulated articles (such as biological control agents). Some countries will evaluate all imports in order to assess the risk of allowing the item into the country; others will establish *a priori* a list of commodities and relevant conditions imposed, based on already demonstrated risk. An example of the first category is a Croatian ordinance of 1998 which establishes phytosanitary measures for the import of seed potatoes, requiring the importer to provide a certificate of import and other information before permission to import will be granted. An example of the second category is the 1995 Malian Decree on plant protection, which contains a list of prohibited articles, and imposes restrictions and conditions on the import of other plants and plant products.

An important provision generally empowers the Minister to prohibit the entry of any plant, plant product or other regulated article in order to protect plant resources or the environment. This permits the Minister, for example, to prohibit the entry of alien plant species which might cause harm to local flora, and also living modified organisms (LMOs) for the same reason. As will be discussed below, all such prohibitions must be scientifically based or they risk violating the concepts of the SPS Agreement and the IPPC.

It should also be borne in mind in relation to LMOs that here they are being regulated only for the purposes of protecting the plant resources or the environment of the country. Governments that have other concerns in relation to LMOs, such as public health and the economy, may wish to address LMOs comprehensively in other legislation. Norway, for example, enacted a Decree Relative to Impact Assessment Pursuant to the Genetic Engineering Act in 1993, which makes provision for the assessment of risk to the environment and public health upon the release of genetically modified organisms.

Scientific justification: Perhaps the most important change in phytosanitary regulation in the years since Rio is that requirements for the import of plants, plant products and other regulated articles should have a scientific basis. All decisions on imports that are not based on international standards must be based on pest risk analysis. In practice, an importer will apply for an import permit, stating the type of commodity, its source and its end use. The authority then evaluates the application based on an assessment of the risk (using pest risk analysis), and if the risk is acceptable, or can be properly managed, the import permit will be issued. Original phytosanitary certificates from the country of origin may be required. For example, under the *Ley de protección fitosanitaria* (1997) of Costa Rica, the State Phytosanitary Service is responsible for issuing phytosanitary certificates "in conformity with operative norms" as well as norms established by the Ministry of Agriculture. (Art. 59)

The most effective way to comply with the principle of transparency expressed in the SPS Agreement is to collect all scientifically justified requirements that the Minister develops in regard to the importation of certain plants, plant products and other regulated articles into a document entitled "Commodities and their Import Requirements". This could be issued as a schedule to the primary law (so that it can be amended easily), or it could be kept more informally as an official document retained by the NPPO and made available on demand to potential trading partners.

Costs of treatment: Different treatments or levels of control will be imposed based on the assessed risk. Treatment costs or costs of removal and destruction almost always fall on the importer, even in older phytosanitary laws. However, many modern laws also address the issue of how to calculate those costs. While it is relatively easy to bill the importer for the treatment imposed where it is a private company that has carried it out, where it is the Ministry itself that does the work, costing is more difficult. Newer phytosanitary laws may develop a formula to calculate costs, thus avoiding the necessity in each case of having to calculate fuel prices, hours of overtime for inspection and so forth, in order to bill the importer. Draft plant protection legislation in the Bahamas, for example, establishes such a costing formula.

Ports of entry: The import permit, if granted, will state that a particular article may be imported for a particular purpose at a particular port of entry. Because there may be a number of sea ports and airports where citizens and visitors may try to bring in plants and plant products but where the NPPO does not have a presence, phytosanitary laws generally provide that plants, plant products and regulated articles may only be imported at official ports listed in a schedule to the law. The law will also provide that it is an offence to bring plants and plant products into the country except at these prescribed ports.

Containment and eradication of pests: In order for the Ministry responsible for agriculture to be able to take action in regard to pests in the country, it must know when pests have appeared. Phytosanitary laws generally impose a duty on land owners to inform the NPPO where the existence of a regulated pest is suspected. Similarly, postal workers and customs officers have a duty to inform the NPPO upon the arrival of plants, plant products or other regulated articles.

The powers accorded to the Minister responsible for agriculture to declare an area infested, to restrict or prohibit the movement of plants, plant products and people into and out of the area, to regulate when planting and replanting may take place, to modify or remove the restrictions and to declare the area no longer infested (i.e., lift the quarantine), have not changed much in recent years. Even the oldest colonial-era legislation usually has such provisions. However, newer laws make clear that where a land owner does not carry out the ordered treatment, the Ministry may do so, but it is the land owner who pays. Albania's 1993 Law on Plant Protection Service, for example, provides that where there is a risk from the spread of a pest, the producer must take control measures; if he or she does not, the necessary action is taken by the Plant Protection Service but with the cost borne by the producer.

In some cases, the Minister retains discretion to waive the requirement of payment for reasons of poverty, or for expediency. This ensures that treatment and/or destruction will not be delayed in cases where the owner does not have the financial wherewithal to carry it out, or cannot be found, or where there are larger national issues at stake. Albania's law establishes an exception to the requirement that the costs be borne by the farmer, for those pests "specially indicated" by the Ministry of Food and Agriculture.

Compensation: Whether to permit compensation for the destruction of plants or plant products is a policy decision, to be decided by each government before enactment of a phytosanitary law. There are strong arguments in favour of a compensation policy. For one thing, farmers will be more likely to draw the attention of the NPPO to the presence of a pest if they know that the government will assist in any associated losses, and this could limit the spread of the pest. Similarly, where there is compensation, farmers may be more likely to agree to the destruction of healthy plants, and to the creation of a buffer zone, both of which can assist in hindering the spread of a disease. Hungary's new Plant Protection Act of 2000 specifically provides for indemnification in the case of damage caused by quarantine measures.

Nonetheless, the law should make clear that compensation may be payable only in limited circumstances, and should define them. Canada is unusual in having enacted a law specifically addressing compensation for farmers whose agricultural products are found to be contaminated with pesticide residues where the farmer properly used the product. However, the law states that compensation is only payable where the loss suffered is not due to any fault of the farmer. Furthermore, compensation is only payable when the farmer takes prescribed steps with regard to minimizing the loss, and to pursuing legal action against other parties. (Pesticide Residue Compensation Act)

Pest free areas: Under the 1997 text of the IPPC, where the NPPO takes certain steps to eradicate a pest from an area, imposes certain phytosanitary measures to keep the area free of the pest and institutes a monitoring system to verify that the area remains free of the pest, it can declare the area pest free. Newer phytosanitary laws, such as the draft plant protection law for the Bahamas, include a provision permitting the Minister to make such a declaration.

Once the NPPO implements the proper surveillance and monitoring activities in relation to a particular pest in a particular area and achieves the required results, the Minister may add the area to a schedule which lists pest-free areas in the country. Of course it is then up to the importing countries to make their own assessment of the actual implementation of the phytosanitary measures and monitoring system by the exporting country, and to decide accordingly whether to accept that the area is in fact pest free.

Exports: Plant protection laws generally make clear that exporters are responsible for applying for the appropriate documentation from the Ministry responsible for agriculture in order to meet the importing countries' requirements. Cuba's Plant Health Regulations (Decree-Law of 1994), for example, establish that certificates and permits may be required by the Ministry of Agriculture for the import and export of agricultural or forestry products. Whereas older laws were based on quality assurance, current export regulations are generally based on importing countries' requirements.

Enforcement: All phytosanitary laws outline some of the enforcement powers of inspectors, for example that they may enter premises and stop and search persons and vehicles where they suspect that a violation of the law is taking place. Also, at any time that an inspector feels that a home owner, a traveller or an importer is not being cooperative, he or she may call upon a representative of the forces of public order, such as a police officer, to assist in enforcing the law. In order to prevent the introduction or spread of pests, inspectors must have the power to take immediate action, including treating and destroying infected goods. For instance, the Lithuanian Phytosanitary Law of 1999 grants to officers of the State Plant Protection Service the power to take specific decisions during the control of plants, plant products and other objects at import.

To protect property owners, importers and travellers, inspectors are required to follow certain procedures where they treat or destroy objects seized under the law. In addition, where the actions are taken with respect to imported goods, the Minister should inform the exporting country's NPPO. This stems from the duty imposed on NPPOs under the 1997 text of the IPPC to notify trading partners not only of the requirements for import, but also of any incidents of non-compliance. Too often the exporting country's NPPO does not know what problems may have befallen its goods when they arrive overseas.

Appeals: Although the law generally does not provide for any liability of the government or its officers for official actions taken, importers and land owners generally have the right to appeal against decisions by inspectors to destroy, dispose of or treat plants, plant products or other regulated articles. The details of the appeals procedure are set out in regulations.

Offences and penalties: The Act should list all the acts and omissions that constitute an offence under the law, including selling items knowingly imported into the country contrary to the law, preventing an inspector from carrying out his or her duties under the law and falsely filling out documents required under the law. Responsibility for enforcement of the law may be assigned to the courts, to the Minister, to the head of the plant protection service or to the inspectors themselves. For example, under the Lithuanian Phytosanitary Law, action may be taken by "officers of the State Plant Protection Service in accordance with the procedure established by the laws of the Republic of Lithuania". (Art. 14) In addition, a trend in modern phytosanitary legislation is to state explicitly that inspectors who abuse their power or improperly share information acquired in the course of their duties have violated the law.

One new provision often appears, stating that it is not simply the plants, plant products and packaging that may be seized where an offence has been committed, but also anything used in the commission of an offence. Draft plant protection legislation in the Bahamas, Ghana and Namibia includes such a provision. This would permit, for example, the government to seize vehicles used to transport illegally imported plants, plant products and regulated articles. The inclusion of this provision (to be applied at the discretion of the court in appropriate cases) is intended to make the penalties under the law a greater deterrent.

The penalties should be set at a level that is sufficiently high to deter and to punish. It is expected that a judge imposing the fine will link the punishment to the nature of the offence, and to its magnitude. Usually such a judge may impose a prison sentence, or both a fine and imprisonment.

New legislation often adopts creative ways of avoiding the effects of inflation which in some countries makes penalties derisory only a few years after enactment. The new draft standards bill in Ghana, for example, provides that any person who commits an offence under the law is liable, upon summary conviction, to a fine expressed in "penalty units". One penalty unit is equivalent to one-third of the prevailing national daily minimum wage multiplied by 30. The penalty unit concept thus provides for automatic increases in the levels of fines in line with inflation. Some countries have considered other alternate strategies to calculate fines, including by multiplying by a certain factor the monthly salary of a civil servant at a certain grade; basing the fine on a percentage value of an offending shipment; or enacting a separate law multiplying all existing fines in all existing legislation by a certain figure (such as 1 000).

Fixed penalties: Another development in recent phytosanitary laws is the institution of a system of on-the-spot fines ("fixed penalties") which can be paid in lieu of a regular court appearance, much in the same way that traffic fines are paid in many countries. The draft CARICOM legislation includes this procedure. Spot fines are intended to be used in the case of arriving airline passengers or pleasure yacht owners who do not declare that they have plants, plant products or other regulated articles in their possession. The advantage of a fixed penalty scheme is that offenders are subject to enforceable and immediate punishment without having to enter into the court system, which would otherwise be onerous and might have negative effects on tourism. On the other hand, in some countries a spot fine system can open up possibilities for corruption, and thus each country has to ensure that the fixed penalty scheme is an appropriate feature in its own context.

Regulations: All laws grant power to the Minister to issue regulations to carry out the purposes of the law. The provision usually states that this power is unrestricted, but recent laws tend to list in detail the areas in which the Minister may act, so as to avoid any future challenge to regulations issued. For example, the draft plant protection law for Namibia lists no less than 15 subject matters that the Minister may address through regulations, in addition to granting broad power to take all necessary action to further the objectives of the law.

Naturally the power to issue regulations includes the power to establish the format for application forms, permits, certificates and other documents that will be issued under the law. An annex to Portugal's Decree-Law No. 14 of 1999 contains model forms that are to be used in the implementation of the law, which concerns the production, circulation, import and export of plants or plant products; and Decree-Law No. 91/98 contains model import permit application forms. In many countries such documentation is now available and may even be submitted electronically, a trend that can be expected to increase in the future.

3.2.2. Pesticides

Although as described above there have been significant international developments in the pesticides arena, these have not had a great deal of effect on the structure of national legislation regarding pesticides. Accordingly, the following broad outlines of the contents of modern pesticides laws can be described as follows.

Title and preliminaries: Whereas common law countries generally separate their legislation on plant quarantine from legislation regulating pesticides, civil law countries tend to combine them. For example, Namibia is considering adoption of a law on plant quarantine, as well as a separate law on pesticides to replace the 1947 South African legislation which regulated pesticides, farm feeds, fertilizers and stock remedies in one Act. By contrast, Chad adopted a Plant Protection Law No. 14/PR/95 which addresses the registration of pesticides and more generally the protection of plants and plant products, and the Niger did the same in its Plant Protection Ordinance of 1996. Hungary also adopted a law in 2000 which addresses the practice and management of plant protection as well as the marketing and use of pesticides. (Act XXXV on Plant Protection)

Definitions: The definitions in modern pesticides laws are generally drawn from the Convention on the Prior Informed Consent (PIC) Procedure for Certain Hazardous Chemicals and Pesticides in International Trade. Malta's Pesticides Control Act of 2001, for example, contains updated definitions including "active ingredient" and "residue".

Administration: The most important administrative elements of a pesticides law are the appointment of a Registrar of Pesticides (who keeps a Register of Pesticides containing enumerated information), and the establishment of a Pesticides Board. The Austrian Federal Act on Plant Protection Products (1997), for example, establishes a Plant Protection

Register at the Federal Office for Agricultural Research, which at the beginning of each year issues the list of registered pesticides.

An observed trend in recent years is that pesticides boards have become more cross-sectoral, with representation not only from the Ministry of Agriculture but also the Ministry of Health and the Ministry of Trade, among others. The Plant Protection Ordinance of the Niger creates a broad-based "National Committee on Phytopharmaceutical Products", to advise the Minister of Agriculture on the registration and use of pesticides. Burkina Faso's Law No. 006/98/AN also establishes a National Pesticides Control Commission. The Namibian draft pesticides legislation establishes a Pesticides Board consisting of representatives of a variety of ministries, to evaluate applications for registration of pesticides, license premises which manufacture pesticides and persons who apply pesticides for profit, manage the Development Fund established under the Act, propose and prepare regulations to be made under the Act and generally to advise the Minister on all issues relating to pesticides in Namibia. Industry is generally not represented on pesticides boards, as the regulated should not act in the role of regulators.

Pesticides laws generally provide that the Minister can appoint or designate inspectors to enforce the law. Inspectors should be given the power to inspect locales where pesticides are manufactured, imported, packed, repacked, labelled, stored, sold, distributed or advertised, and also to search land, premises, aircraft, vessels or vehicles without a warrant if they suspect that the law is being violated. Great Britain's Pesticides Act 1998 (Cap. 26) amends the Food and Environment Protection Act, among other things to provide for the enforcement of controls on pesticides by local authorities. Like inspectors under most modern plant quarantine laws, they may request the assistance of customs officers or police officers in these tasks.

Registration of Pesticides: The basic rule behind modern pesticides laws is that in order to be lawfully imported, manufactured, packed, repacked, labelled, stored, sold, distributed, applied, possessed or used in a country, a pesticide must be registered under the law. Canada's Pest Control Products Act of 2000 makes it a violation to sell or import into Canada any product that has not been registered, that does not conform to prescribed standards or that is not packaged or labelled as required. Pesticides laws often list the permissible pesticides in a regulation or schedule to the main act, or to the contrary, list banned pesticides. Singapore recently adopted a law on the registration of pesticides

(Control of Plants Rules No. S606 of 2001), which sets out the pesticide products that may be used in the cultivation of plants in Singapore. Pesticide products are listed in a table that includes information such as the pesticide registration number, ingredients and intended use. Portugal, by contrast, issued Decree No. 238 in 2001 to include 13 more active substances within the Annex of its Decree-Law on Pesticide Trade which lists banned substances.

Depending on the policy decisions of the government, exemptions from the registration requirements may be made for certain kinds of pesticides, such as those used in paint, those manufactured solely for export and others. The Netherlands amended its Pesticides Act 1962 in 2001 so as to permit the entry of certain pesticides considered "indispensable". The amending Act sets forth the criteria to be applied in determining whether the pesticide may be admitted, including whether it is urgently needed; whether no valid alternative is available, taking into account public health and the environment; and whether certain requirements of novelty, resistance and cost-effectiveness are met. (Act No. 68 of 2001)

Requirements for registration may also be waived for pesticides imported for purposes of scientific research and evaluation, so long as the importer seeks a permit under the law. And finally, registration may not be required where the authority specifically exempts certain pesticides, which it might do, for example, as to a pesticide whose registration has been cancelled but where stocks of that pesticide already in the country need to be used up.

Applications for registration must be made according to the details in the law and its regulations. One recent trend is for the law to specify that the Board must treat information supplied in connection with an application as proprietary information of the applicant, for a period of time specified in the law (for example ten or 15 years, or some other time period). The draft pesticides law for Namibia, for example, establishes such a requirement. Registrations are valid for the period of time specified. The Moroccan Law on the Use of Pesticides in Agriculture of 1997 is typical, providing that registrations are valid for ten years.

Where the Board refuses an application (for reasons enumerated in the law), it must notify the applicant of the reasons for that refusal. This permits the applicant to make an appeal as outlined in the section of the law dealing with appeals. Usually the law permits applicants whose applications were refused for incompleteness of information to supplement them within a specific time.

Registration may be granted unconditionally, or in some jurisdictions, for limited purposes; or it may be denied. The Pesticides Control and Management Act of Ghana (1996), for example, grants or denies registration depending on the classification of the pesticide as: (i) for general use; (ii) for restricted use; (iii) suspended; or (iv) banned.

It is important to note that a comprehensive law will make clear that any time the applicant intends to change the formulation, trade name, pesticide active ingredient or concentration of the pesticide, or where someone other than the original applicant intends to manufacture, import, pack, repack or label that pesticide, a new application must be submitted. Normally, the less significant changes must simply be notified in writing to the Pesticides Board. The Board may cancel a registration for enumerated reasons, but must give the applicant notice and the opportunity to submit a written justification as to why the cancellation should not go forward.

Licences: Under most pesticides laws, only those persons who are in possession of a valid licence are permitted to manufacture, pack, repack, label, sell, store or distribute a pesticide. The Plant Protection Ordinance of the Niger provides that a licence, issued by the Minister, is necessary for the import, production, preparation and conditioning of phytopharmaceutical products. Similarly, Nicaragua's *Ley básica para la regulación y control de plaguicidas, sustancias tóxicas, peligrosas y otras similares* of 1998 applies to all activities carried out in relation to pesticides, including import, export, distribution, storage and trade. Some laws also provide that anyone intending to apply pesticides for profit must apply for a Pest Control Operator's Licence. The "for profit" ensures that farmers applying pesticides on their own land do not fall within this rule.

Applications for licences must be submitted in the form specified in the law, and will be approved or denied by the Board for listed reasons. Portugal's Decree No. 341 of 1998, for example, establishes principles to be applied in evaluating and authorizing the use of pesticides, with particular attention to environmental effects. Normally, just as with Registration, applicants submitting incomplete applications are permitted to supplement them with the missing information, and licences are valid for a certain period of time from the date of issue. The Pesticides Board usually has the power to revoke a licence, giving the applicant an opportunity, as with cancellation of registration, to submit written arguments against that revocation. Aggrieved applicants may generally file appeals in accordance with procedures established in subsidiary regulations.

Use of pesticides: Requirements regarding the use of pesticides might provide that employers whose employees work with pesticides must follow certain procedures. Additionally, the law generally provides that pesticides must be disposed of in a manner which does not harm human or animal health or the environment. Albania's 1993 Law on Plant Protection Service, for instance, provides that expired or ineffective pesticides and their packaging must be disposed of in appropriate places, according to procedures set by the Ministries of health and agriculture.

Presentation of pesticides: Pesticides laws generally provide that containers for pesticides must meet specified standards, and must have an approved label attached. The labelling requirements will normally apply to the external container (where a container has an inner bag), and must apply to the smallest unit that can be sold separately. Larger containers of pesticides containing several smaller containers must also display a label, where consumers are likely to see that larger container. Interestingly, one observed trend in recent years is to require the use of pictograms, acknowledging the illiteracy of some users. It is intended that regulations prepared under the draft pesticides legislation in Fiji will include such a provision.

Normally, the law will make it an offence to advertise an unregistered pesticide or to advertise any pesticide in a false or misleading manner. Austria's new federal Act No. 105 of 2000 includes provisions regarding the appropriate advertising of pesticides.

Analysis: Generally, the law will give the Minister the power to appoint persons to be analysts under the law. Analysts are required to follow certain procedures for taking and marking samples, and may be required to issue a certificate of analysis.

Offences and penalties: One important provision in most modern pesticides laws specifies that it is an offence to reveal information to another person, where that information was acquired while carrying out duties under the law. Draft pesticides legislation in Fiji and Namibia contains such a prohibition. This is in acknowledgement of the fact that pesticides manufacturers may have confidential information regarding the method of manufacture, and an inspector who gains access to such information during an inspection must not share it. Other offences might include giving false information on applications or altering any document issued under the law, interfering with an inspector or manufacturing or doing other prohibited activities without a proper licence. Ghana's Pesticides Control and Management Act of 1996 contains such a comprehensive list of offences.

The penalties should be commensurate with the crime; often outdated penalties are one impetus for countries wishing to update their pesticides legislation, since the fines may be derisory if the laws have been on the books for a long time. The suggestions for innovative penalty provisions in plant protection laws, discussed above in section 3.2.1., apply equally to pesticides laws.

3.2.3. Seeds and Plant Variety Protection

Little legislation purely on seeds has been enacted in the last ten years, as many countries have instead been focused on the development of national seed policies and plans. In the Caribbean, in particular, many countries have conducted national workshops and public meetings to develop and agree upon their national seed policies, which will guide the development of national legislation tailored to national needs. Another reason for the lack of legislative activity in relation to seeds is that countries have been focused on plant variety protection, as will be discussed below. Although a number of countries have enacted combined legislation on seeds and plant varieties, the two are discussed separately here. The trends in plant variety protection will be discussed in section (b), whereas the next section outlines the main provisions generally found in seed laws.

(a)   Seed Legislation

Preliminary provisions: Seed laws generally contain preliminary provisions consisting of the short title, the scope of the law and the definitions of terms. Cameroon's Law on Seed Activity of 2001, for example, aims to protect the seed sector against unfair competition and to protect plant breeders' rights.

The law may come into force on the date the Minister selects, and different parts of the law can become effective on different dates. This can assist a Minister in gradually introducing agencies and structures, rather than activating them all at once.

The definitions will include such matters as what is certified seed (i.e., of which progeny), and how it has to have been handled in order to qualify as certified seed. Some countries have certified I and certified II seed, which refers to the particular generations and genetic purity of the seed. In some countries certified II seed applies not only to the progeny of certified I seed but also to the progeny of certified II seed, but this will depend on the dilution of genetic purity. Cameroon has three varieties: basic seed, certified seed, and standard seed, with only the first two subject to certification by the Seed Administration. Tunisia's Law No. 99-42 on seeds, plants and plant varieties uses the same three categories.

Administration: Like plant protection laws and pesticides laws, seed laws normally establish a National Seed Committee to serve as an advisory body to the Minister of Agriculture on all matters relating to seeds, seed certification and variety release. Peru's General Seed Law of 2000, for instance, establishes a National Seed Commission as a consultative organ of the Ministry of Agriculture; similarly, Nicaragua's National Seed Council is charged with the study, analysis and development of government seed policy (*Ley de producción y comercio de semillas* of 1998).

The membership of the Committee depends on the circumstances in the country: where there is a particularly strong industry such as rice or cocoa, the Committee may require more input and therefore a wider variety of actors on the Committee. The Philippines' National Seed Industry Council includes representatives from government, the agricultural university, research institutes, farmers' organizations and the seed industry (Act No. 7308 of 1992).

The seed law should next establish a seed quality control and certification agency, a seed multiplication unit and a cadre of seed inspectors. Nigeria's National Agricultural Seeds Decree of 1992, for example, establishes a "National Seed Service Unit" which is responsible for the certification and quality control of seeds. Current seed laws ensure that the seed multiplication unit is independent from the certification agency, to avoid any conflict of interest that would arise if the same organ that is multiplying the seed were also certifying it.

The need for a seed multiplication unit may be felt only in countries with emerging seed programmes; in others, seed multiplication activities may have already been assumed by the private sector either because of a lack of financing from the government or because the programme is so advanced that activities are more efficiently carried out by the private sector as a business. Nonetheless, even in those countries with an established seed programme, the government should set up a seed multiplication unit to multiply seeds and planting materials for crops the private sector does not consider viable.

The seed law will have to outline the duties of seed inspectors, including taking seed samples and sending them to a designated laboratory. Where inspectors suspect an offence in violation of the law is being or has been committed, they may enter premises, by invitation or by force, and seize seed, documents or other items believed to have been used in violation of the law. The model Seed Law for the CARICOM region includes such powers for inspectors.

Certified seed: The seed law will have to establish criteria for certifying seed. In determining whether seed should be certified, the law may impose certain requirements, for example directing the certification agency to consider whether the seed is of known derivation, has been produced on designated land and has been sown, cultivated, produced, inspected and tested in the appropriate manner. Nigeria's National Agricultural Seeds Decree of 1992, for example, outlines the genetic identity of certified seed (sec. 14).

Certified seed producers: Under a seed law, individuals or companies may apply for registration as certified seed producers if they wish to produce certified seed. Trade in other seed is generally not regulated. The 2000 Seed Law of China, for instance, establishes that any unit or individual must apply for a licence to produce commodity seed. In deciding on applications for registration, the certification agency must use specified criteria, and may impose conditions on the registration and cancel the registration if there are unacceptable changes in the applicant's situation. The agency usually keeps a register of certified seed producers, listing particulars of the application, any conditions and other required information. Argentina's Resolution No. 42/00 of 2000, updating rules for the registration and certification of seeds, provides that all persons interested in producing certified seed must be registered in the National Register for Trade and Certification. Similarly, Bolivia's Resolution No. 41 of 2001 provides that every person intending to produce seeds needs to be registered in the National Register of Seed Producers.

Imported seed: Normally, any person wishing to import seed into the country must apply to be a licensed seed importer, and he or she will be listed in the register of licensed seed importers to be kept by the certification agency. In China, the Seed Law sets out in Chapter VIII that companies involved in the seed import-export business shall obtain an international trade licence according to the Law of Foreign Trade. Under the Seed Law of Paraguay (2000), all natural and legal persons, whether public or private, interested in importing seeds shall be registered in the National Register of Seed Traders. No one may import certified seed into the country unless he or she is registered as a licensed seed importer, the seed conforms to the certification standards and the details of the origin and variety of the seed, among other information, accompanies the seed upon its importation.

Given the developments in the international trading system, it is advisable for the law to give the Minister the power to recognize seed certified in foreign countries as certified seed under the law. This will facilitate import, so that country A can stipulate that any seed certified in country B will be designated "certified seed", without the need for the testing and other requirements of the relevant provisions of the law.

Seed inspectors: One unique provision in modern seed laws permits a person whose stock of seed has been found defective not only to remove the defect, if possible, but also to choose instead to use the seed for food or feed (except where the seed has been treated with hazardous chemicals) if he or she does not wish to remove the defect. This gives more choice to the farmer rather than giving blanket authority to the certification agency to order the farmer to destroy the seed.

Offences: The law will of course have to define specific violations, such as selling certified seed or seed marked with "certified" or a related word unless such seed is in fact certified; obstructing a seed inspector's exercise of his or her powers under the law; tampering with samples taken by a seed inspector; altering certificates, registers or other documents with intent to deceive; improperly using information obtained in the course of employment or appointment under the law; and allowing one's employees to violate the provisions of the law. The 2000 Seeds Act of Canada, for example, provides that "every person who, or whose em-ployee or agent, contravenes any provision of this Act or any regulation made thereunder is guilty of an offence punishable on summary conviction" (sec. 9).

(b) Plant Variety Protection Legislation

Recently, in various parts of the world, many countries have enacted legislation on plant variety protection. Austria (1993), Chile (1994),

Hungary (1996), India (2001), Lithuania (1996), Paraguay (1994), Tunisia (1999), Ukraine (1993), the United States (1994) and Uruguay (1997) are only some of the countries that have chosen to regulate plant varieties since the Rio Conference. This flurry of activity may be due to the fact that many countries are facing mandatory obligations under the WTO TRIPS Agreement (see section 2.3.2.): as noted, article 27.3(b) of TRIPS requires state parties to provide protection for plant varieties "either by patents or by an effective *sui generis* system or by any combination thereof". Most of the TRIPS obligations became binding on developed nations in 1996, whereas for developing countries and countries in transition to market economies the TRIPS requirements became obligatory in 2000. Least developed nations are not required to implement the treaty's substantive obligations until 2006.

Unlike earlier intellectual property rights agreements, TRIPS not only specifies the minimum substantive requirements for various forms of intellectual property, but also requires its members to adopt "effective" provisions within their national laws to permit those whose intellectual property rights are being infringed to enforce them. (Art. 41.1) A country's choice of how to protect plant varieties, however, will depend on the universe of its international obligations, specifically, how much discretion it has depending on whether it is a member only of one of the UPOV Acts, a member of TRIPS and one of the UPOV Acts, a member of TRIPS alone or not a member of any of these agreements.

Members of the 1991 or 1978 UPOV Act only: Only two states are not members of the WTO but are members of one of the UPOV Acts – the Russian Federation and Ukraine. These countries must comply with the numerous requirements of the UPOV Act to which they are a party. Ukraine, which is a member of the 1978 Act, does not have to protect all plant varieties, although the Russian Federation, as a member of the 1991 Act, does. On the other hand, as a member of the 1978 Act, Ukraine may impose certain reciprocity requirements on those varieties that it does protect. For both countries, their national treatment obligations are limited to those states that are members of the same UPOV Act.

Members of TRIPS and the 1978 UPOV Act: Twenty-nine countries are members of TRIPS and the 1978 UPOV Act. Countries in this category must comply with all of the 1978 Act requirements. They must also meet the four main TRIPS requirements when they legislate on plant varieties: first, the law must apply to all plant varieties (i.e., all species and all botanical genera); second, it must grant to plant breeders the exclusive right to control particular acts with respect to the protected varieties, or at least the right to compensation when third parties engage in certain acts; third, the law must provide national treatment and most favoured nation treatment to breeders from other WTO member states; and finally, it must implement procedures that enable breeders to enforce the rights granted to them under the law.

Members of TRIPS and the 1991 UPOV Act: Because the 1991 UPOV Act grants more protection for plant breeders' rights than does the 1978 Act, countries that are members of TRIPS and the 1991 Act have less discretion than members of TRIPS and the 1978 Act in choosing how to protect plant varieties. Twenty-one nations fall in this category. These states must comply with TRIPS, and, naturally, with all of the other provisions of the 1991 Act. In particular, these states must adopt all of the exclusive rights contained in article 14 of the 1991 Act regarding breeders' rights, i.e., the breeder's prior authorization must be obtained for the use of reproductive or vegetative propagating material of the protected variety for the purpose of: (1) production or reproduction, (2) conditioning for the purpose of propagation, (3) offering for sale, (4) selling or marketing, (5) exporting, (6) importing and (7) stocking for any of these purposes.

Japan is one of the countries that has enacted a law and regulations relating to plant varieties modelled on the 1991 Act. The Seeds and Seedlings Law, enacted in 1998, aims to promote the breeding of plant varieties and the distribution of seeds in Japan by providing a system for the registration and protection of plant varieties. The Law contains provisions related to the labelling of designated seeds and seedlings. The Seeds and Seedlings Law Enforcement Regulations of 1998 outline the application procedure for variety registration and list the particulars to be contained in an application, including the seed or strain of the variety.

TRIPS members only: States that are parties to the TRIPS Agreement but not members of either UPOV Act enjoy a great deal of discretion. At present this category contains approximately 94 of the 144 member states of the WTO. As members of TRIPS, these countries are required to comply with the four core obligations of article 27.3(b), but how they choose to comply is a matter of choice. States are free to model their national laws protecting plant varieties on the 1978 UPOV Act, the 1991 UPOV Act, the patent provisions of TRIPS or some combination of the above. Each of these approaches achieves, in different ways, the principal policy goal of an intellectual property rights system: creating adequate incentives for plant breeders to develop and market new varieties. The approach chosen will depend on the needs of that nation's agricultural industry and farming sectors, its desire to encourage foreign investment relating to plant breeding and biotechnology and its international trade objectives.

Although "TRIPS only" states have wide discretion in how to implement the Agreement's core obligations, most countries that have adopted plant variety protection laws have followed one of the two UPOV Acts. Examples of countries that have followed the UPOV model are Dominica, which enacted a Protection of New Varieties of Plants Act in 1999, and Belize, whose Protection of New Plant Varieties Act of 2000 is nearly identical to it. The Act provides for the grant and protection of breeders' rights, establishing a Register of Plant Breeders' Rights which will be maintained by the Registrar of Companies and Intellectual Property. The Act establishes criteria for the grant of a right (novelty, distinctness, homogeneity and stability); outlines the scope of the right; states the requirements of eligibility to apply; and includes provisions on the termination, invalidation and forfeiture of rights.

India's Protection of Plant Varieties and Farmers' Rights Act of 2001 is a notable counter-example to the trend of following the UPOV model. The Act protects breeders' rights while also recognizing farmers' rights by allowing farmers to register the varieties they cultivate. It also contains benefit-sharing provisions that allow individuals and communities to claim compensation for their contributions to plant genetic diversity. Finally, the Act requires inventors to disclose the source and geographical origin of biological material used in their inventions. Other proposed laws that deviate from the UPOV model include bills in Bangladesh, Nicaragua, Thailand and Zambia.

The most notable trend, however, is the large number of TRIPS members that have not enacted any plant variety protection laws despite the 2000 deadline for developing nations to enact such laws. According to a May 2000 study, 80 percent of African countries, 80 percent of countries in the Asia-Pacific region and 56 percent of Latin American and Caribbean states which should have implemented TRIPS article 27.3(b) by 2000 had not done so. This reluctance can be attributed to the controversial nature of article 27.3(b) (Helfer, 2002), and to the fact that the article was scheduled to be reviewed in 1999 but was not. The pace of implementation is unlikely to increase until WTO members resolve issues regarding the scope of plant variety protection during the Doha Round of trade negotiations that commenced in November 2001.

Not members of TRIPS or either UPOV Act: Countries that are not members of either TRIPS or a UPOV Act have no obligation to protect plant varieties or plant breeders' rights. However, they may find that intellectual property issues arise if, for example, they must implement obligations under other treaties to which they may be parties, such as regional or bilateral agreements. In addition, the actions of other countries are likely to have effects even on countries that are not members of TRIPS or UPOV. The globalization of trade makes it increasingly more difficult for countries to chart an independent course, and thus countries that are not yet members of TRIPS may wish to consider which choices they intend to make.

IV. CONCLUSION

Since Rio, there have been some major international advances regarding plants. First, there are new international instruments concerning matters that previously were not covered by universal international law. For example, the 2001 Convention on Persistent Organic Pollutants can be seen as a response to the calls made in Agenda 21 to regulate harmful pollutants. Second, there was further development of existing instruments, such as the voluntary PIC procedure under the FAO Code of Conduct on the Distribution and Use of Pesticides and the UNEP Guidelines for the Exchange of Information on Chemicals in International Trade, which became the PIC Convention in 1998.

The WTO SPS Agreement identified the International Plant Protection Convention as the source of internationally agreed standards on phytosanitary measures, and the new revised text of the IPPC adopted a number of new and innovative concepts and structures. The influence of the SPS Agreement will continue to be far-reaching, as numerous countries seek to update their legislation to incorporate the concepts and language of that Agreement and the 1997 text of the IPPC.

At the regional level, economic blocs and standard-setting organizations developed a variety of standards based on international norms and adapted to regional needs. A number of meetings were held and draft model legislation prepared to assist in meeting the harmonization goals of the SPS Agreement. In the coming years, countries will be tailoring their national legislation to regional models to take account of their priorities, resources, legal systems and policy goals.

In the area of plant variety protection, a number of countries have begun to take steps to conform with the WTO TRIPS Agreement, which requires states to implement some form of protection for plant varieties. Interest in plant variety protection, plant breeders' rights and intellectual property rights in general can be expected to increase in the coming years, as countries take note of their international obligations not only under the WTO, but also under the Convention on Biological Diversity and the new International Treaty on Plant Genetic Resources for Food and Agriculture. Guidance from FAO and other international organizations will continue to be useful in providing information and comparative assessments of potential national choices.

REFERENCES

Comité Permanent Inter-Etats de Lutte Contre la Sécheresse dans le Sahel. *Convention for the Registration of Pesticides* (www.cilss.org).

Comunidad Andina. *Normativa Andina* (www.comunidadandina.org).

Comité de Sanidad Vegetal del Cono Sur (www.cosave.org.py).

European Plant Protection Organization (www.eppo.org).

Genetic Resources Action International (GRAIN). 2000. *For a Full Review of TRIPs 27.3(b), An Update on Where Developing Countries Stand with the Push to Patent Life at WTO* (www.grain.org/publications/tripsfeb00-en-p.htm).

Helfer, L. 2002. *Intellectual Property Rights in Plant Varieties: An Overview with Options for National Governments,* FAO Legal Paper Online No. 31 (www.fao.org/Legal).

IPPC Secretariat (www.ippc.int/cds_ippc/IPP/En/default.htm).

Leskien, D. & Flinter, M. 1997. *Intellectual Property Rights and Plant Genetic Resources: Options for a sui generis System,* Issues in Genetic Resources, No. 6, IPGRI, Rome.

Mercosur. *Secretaria Andina del Mercosur* (www.mercosur.org).

North American Plant Protection Organization (www.nappo.org).

UNEP. 2001. *Persistent Organic Pollutants* (www.chem.unep.ch/pops).

UNEP/FAO. 1998. *Rotterdam Convention on the Prior Informed Consent (PIC) Procedure for Certain Hazardous Chemicals and Pesticides in International Trade* (www.pic.int).

Vapnek, J. 1995. *Model Seed Legislation for the Caribbean Region.* FAO, Rome.

Vapnek, J. 2001. *Strengthening Phytosanitary Capabilities (CARICOM).* FAO, Rome.

5

AGROBIODIVERSITY

Contents

I. INTRODUCTION

On 3 November 2001, the International Treaty on Plant Genetic Resources for Food and Agriculture (Treaty) was adopted by the FAO Conference at its 31st session in Rome, by Resolution 3/2001, with 116 favourable votes, no dissenting votes and two abstentions (Japan and the United States).

The Treaty is a new, legally binding instrument which seeks to ensure the conservation and sustainable management of plant genetic resources for food and agriculture, as well as the fair and equitable sharing of the benefits arising from their use (art. 1.1). At the crossroads of agriculture, commerce and the environment, the Treaty also aims to promote synergy in these areas (preamble). As one commentator put it, this newly born treaty is "the latest innovation to address the intersection of international environmental, agricultural and trade law". (Earth Negotiations Bulletin, 2001)

Once in force, the Treaty will succeed the International Undertaking on Plant Genetic Resources (Undertaking), a soft law instrument adopted by FAO in 1983, and the first international agreement to deal with sustainable management of plant genetic resources at the global level. The Undertaking was adopted by Resolution 8/83 of the FAO Conference to "ensure that plant genetic resources of economic and/or social interest, particularly for agriculture, will be explored, preserved, evaluated and made available for plant breeding and scientific purposes". (Art. 1) Three other resolutions containing agreed interpretations were subsequently adopted and annexed to the Undertaking. As of June 2002, 113 countries had adhered to it.

Secretariat functions for the Undertaking have been performed by the FAO Commission on Genetic Resources for Food and Agriculture (Commission), an intergovernmental forum that was also created in 1983 to facilitate policy dialogue and technical discussions on genetic resources of relevance to food and agriculture. Its mandate, initially limited to plant genetic resources, was broadened in 1995 to cover all components of agrobiodiversity. As of June 2002, 161 countries and the European Union were members of the Commission.

As the Treaty is one of the most significant developments in agriculture and natural resource management since Rio, this chapter briefly describes is gestation, highlights its main provisions, discusses implementing measures and outlines the arrangements to be made in preparation for its entry into force.

II. DEVELOPMENT OF THE INTERNATIONAL TREATY ON PLANT GENETIC RESOURCES

Unlike some recent biodiversity or environment-related conventions, such as the 2001 Convention on Persistent Organic Pollutants (POPs) or the 2000 Cartagena Protocol on Biosafety, for which the negotiations were swiftly completed in a matter of two or three years, the present Treaty's gestation was not an easy one. It is the result of a hard-fought seven-year negotiating process, which began in November 1994 at the 1st extraordinary session of the Commission, and continued through June 2001 following three regular and five extraordinary sessions. The nego-tiations also included an informal expert meeting and six intersessional meetings of the Chairman's Contact Group.[1] The process was eventually concluded within an open-ended working group which met in Rome during the 121st session of the FAO Council, from 30 October to 1 November 2001, only two days before the Treaty's formal adoption.

The adoption of the Treaty fulfils the request in Resolution 7/93 of the FAO Conference that the Director-General of FAO provide a negotiation forum for "the adaptation of the International Undertaking on Plant Genetic Resources, in harmony with the Convention on Biological Diversity", and for "consideration of the issue of access on mutually agreed terms to plant genetic resources, including *ex situ* collections not addressed by the Convention".

This move was partly in response to biodiversity-related developments which had occurred about the same time. In particular, when the agreed text of the Convention on Biological Diversity (CBD) was adopted in Nairobi in May 1992, Resolution 3 of the Final Act stated that access to *ex situ* collections not acquired in accordance with the CBD, as well as farmers' rights, were outstanding matters for which solutions should be sought within the FAO Global System on Plant Genetic Resources – that is, primarily through the Undertaking. Similarly, a month later at the UN Conference on Environment and Development (UNCED), Chapter 14 of Agenda 21 ("Promoting Sustainable Agriculture and Rural Development") had called for the strengthening of the FAO system on plant genetic

---

[1] The Contact Group comprised 40 countries and the European Union.

resources, including through steps to realize farmers' rights, as well as the "adjustment" of that system in line with the CBD.

Earlier, between 1989 and 1991, the original text of the Undertaking had already been the subject of a series of "agreed interpretations", which aimed to find an equitable balance between the interests of developing and developed countries, and between the rights of farmers (informal innovators of farmers' varieties) and of breeders (formal innovators of commercial varieties and breeders' lines). This process helped attract a broader acceptance of the Undertaking over the years, through the following decisions of the FAO Conference:

- Resolution 4/89 (1989), which simultaneously (a) recognized farmers' rights and (b) stated that plant breeders' rights (i.e., rights based on the UPOV Acts (Acts of the Union for the Protection of New Varieties of Plants) were compatible with the Undertaking;

- Resolution 5/89 (1989), which conceptualized the notion of farmers' rights as the "rights arising from the past, present and future contributions of farmers in conserving, improving, and making available plant genetic resources, particularly those in the centres of origin/diversity. These rights are vested in the International Community, as trustee for present and future generations of farmers, for the purpose of ensuring full benefits to farmers, and supporting the continuation of their contributions"; and

- Resolution 3/91 (1991), which (a) recognized the sovereign rights of nations over their plant genetic resources and (b) established that farmers' rights should be implemented through an international fund for plant genetic resources.

The three resolutions were then incorporated into the text of the Undertaking as Annexes 1, 2 and 3. This gradual evolution resulted in key shifts in the Undertaking's conceptual grounds, particularly as regards the recognition of: (i) its compatibility with plant breeders' rights as provided for by UPOV; (ii) the need to realize farmers' rights; and (iii) state sovereignty over plant genetic resources.

These moves helped address some of the concerns that had been voiced by a number of countries, both developed and developing. The Undertaking was originally founded on "the universally accepted principle that plant genetic resources are a *heritage of mankind* and consequently should be available without restriction". (Art. 1, emphasis added) Some developed countries, concerned that such a heritage-based approach could undermine the rights of plant breeders, had adhered to the Undertaking with reservations; hence, the explicit recognition of plant breeders' rights in Resolution 4/89. This, however, was counterbalanced by the simultaneous recognition of farmers' rights, stemming from "the enormous contribution that farmers of all regions have made to the conservation and development of plant genetic resources, which constitute the basis of plant production throughout the world", a position that was largely advocated by developing countries.

At the same time, those decisions contributed to paving the way for the revision of the Undertaking in a manner consistent with related legal instruments. In this connection, Resolution 3/91 explicitly stated, on the one hand, that "breeders' lines and farmers' breeding material should only be available at the discretion of their developers during the period of development", echoing to some extent the 1991 amendment to the UPOV Act; and, on the other hand, that "nations have sovereign rights over their plant genetic resources", and that "the concept of mankind's heritage, as applied in the International Undertaking on Plant Genetic Resources, is subject to the sovereignty of the states over their plant genetic resources". Such language reflected an obvious move from a heritage-based approach towards a sovereignty-based approach, a position that had already prevailed at the time in the draft text of the CBD, and which was later repeatedly confirmed in various UNCED and post-UNCED legal documents. Resolution 3/91 therefore clearly contributed to closing the gaps between the Undertaking and related conventions, in particular with the draft CBD.

III. CORE OF THE TREATY

3.1. Underlying Principles

As finally approved, the Treaty – while articulating the specific nature and needs of the agriculture sector – reflects some of the major principles of contemporary international environmental and biodiversity law, as enunciated, for example, in the Rio Declaration or in the CBD.

The *sovereign rights of states* over their plant genetic resources is one of those principles. It is clearly affirmed in the very first paragraph of the preamble to Resolution 3/2001 by which the Treaty was adopted, as well as in the second-to-last paragraph of the preamble and in article 10 of the Treaty itself, particularly in relation to access rights. Conversely, no reference is made in the Treaty to the "heritage of mankind", a concept that was central to the Undertaking. Instead, the notion that plant genetic resources are a "common concern of all countries" is used in the Treaty's preamble, in line with similar wording in the preamble to the CBD ("Affirming that the conservation of biological diversity is a common concern of humankind"). The Treaty and the CBD are therefore in full harmony in this regard.

The principle that plant genetic resources should be *conserved and used in a sustainable way* is also unequivocally stated in the Treaty – where the term "sustainable" appears no less than 24 times, and "sustainably" twice. Article 6, more specifically, spells out the type of measures that should be taken to promote sustainability in this context, including the following: (i) encouraging farming systems that enhance the sustainable use of agrobiodiversity and other natural resources; (ii) maximizing intra- and inter-specific variation for the benefit of farmers, especially those who apply ecological principles in maintaining soil fertility and combating diseases, weeds and pests; (iii) broadening the genetic base of crops and increasing the range of genetic diversity available to farmers; and (iv) promoting increased world food production compatible with sustainable development.

Access to information related to plant genetic resources is another principle that is addressed by various provisions of the Treaty. According to article 13.2-a, for instance, non-confidential information regarding catalogues, inventories, technologies, results of research, etc. on plant genetic resources is to be made available to contracting parties through the global information system provided for in article 17. This system is to be developed by Treaty members, in collaboration with the CBD's Clearing-House Mechanism, in order to facilitate information exchange "on scientific, technical and environmental matters related to plant genetic resources for food and agriculture", with a view to contributing to the sharing of benefits therefrom.

Furthermore, there is ample provision in the Treaty for *participation in decisionmaking* by interested stakeholders on various aspects of plant genetic resource conservation and use, first in the preamble (para. 8), then in articles 6.2-c and 9.2-c.

3.2.   Groundbreaking Provisions

It is in light of the above principles that the substantive provisions of the Treaty should be read. Some of these are groundbreaking. First and foremost, farmers' rights have now been formally endorsed by a legally binding instrument at the global level. The relevant provisions of the Treaty are article 9 (see Box 1) and paragraphs 7 and 8 of the preamble, which largely borrowed from, and built upon, the aforementioned FAO Conference Resolutions 4/89, 5/89 and 3/91, which conceptualized the notion of farmers' rights under the Undertaking.

Box 1 - Article 9: Farmers' Rights

9.1. The Contracting Parties recognize the enormous contribution that the local and indigenous communities and farmers of all regions of the world, particularly those in the centres of origin and crop diversity, have made and will continue to make for the conservation and development of plant genetic resources which constitute the basis of food and agriculture production throughout the world.

9.2. The Contracting Parties agree that the responsibility for realizing Farmers' Rights, as they relate to plant genetic resources for food and agriculture, rests with national governments. In accordance with their needs and priorities, each Contracting Party should, as appropriate, and subject to its national legislation, take measures to protect and promote Farmers' Rights, including:

  (a)   protection of traditional knowledge relevant to plant genetic resources for food and agriculture;
  (b)   the right to equitably participate in sharing benefits arising from the utilization of plant genetic resources for food and agriculture; and
  (c)   the right to participate in making decisions, at the national level, on matters related to the conservation and sustainable use of plant genetic resources for food and agriculture.

9.3. Nothing in this Article shall be interpreted to limit any rights that farmers have to save, use, exchange and sell farm-saved seed/propagating material, subject to national law and as appropriate.

This important landmark in contemporary treaty law represents a major step toward wider acknowledgement and genuine implementation of the rights conferred on informal innovators ("traditional farmers"), to rest on an equal footing with the rights already granted to formal innovators ("modern breeders") by existing conventions, and reaffirmed by this Treaty in paragraph 6 of the preamble and articles 6.2(c)) and 7.2(b), in particular.

The scope of the Treaty covers all plant genetic resources for food and agriculture (art. 3). Within this broader framework, another key element of the Treaty is the provision for a *Multilateral System of Facilitated Access and Benefit-Sharing* for plant genetic resources, to which the whole of Part IV – articles 10 through 14 – is devoted. The system aims to provide facilitated access to an agreed list of over 60 plant genera, including 35 crops and 29 forages, established on the basis of interdependence and their importance for food security (art. 11). The current agreed list, which includes most crops that are considered essential to world food security, is appended to the main body of the Treaty as Annex I.

Contracting parties agree to provide to each other facilitated access in accordance with the conditions specified in article 12.3, in particular that recipients "shall not claim any intellectual property or other rights that limit the facilitated access to plant genetic resources for food and agriculture, or their genetic parts or components, in the form received from the Multilateral System". The subject of heated discussions during the negotiations of the Treaty, this clause was opposed by some countries which were concerned that it could impinge on their intellectual property laws and policies, while other countries viewed it as consistent with theirs. With a view to its interpretation and implementation, this provision will surely need to be further debated within the Treaty's Governing Body.

By pooling these resources in such a way, and dealing with them through multilateral arrangements, countries forgo the possibility of bilateral arrangements. This being the case, the benefits resulting from the use of genetic resources – including commercial use – do not return to the country of origin, but are to be shared in a fair and equitable manner through multilateral mechanisms. In addition, they should flow primarily to farmers in all countries, especially in developing countries and countries with economies in transition, who conserve and sustainably utilize plant genetic resources for food and agriculture (art. 13).

The Treaty makes provision for benefits accruing from the use - including the commercial use – of the material accessed under the Multilateral System to be shared fairly and equitably, through a variety of actions (art. 13). These include partnerships and collaboration with the private and public sectors of countries in development and in transition. There will be increased opportunities for developing joint strategies for the conservation and sustainable use of plant genetic resources; for the facilitation of research partnerships and the pooling of resources to exploit plant genetic resources; for access to relevant research and technologies; and for access by germplasm providers to information and training.

It should be noted in this connection that, in 1993, the FAO Conference adopted the International Code of Conduct for Plant Germplasm Collecting and Transfer to promote the rational collection and sustainable use of genetic resources, to prevent genetic erosion and to protect the interests of both donors and collectors of germplasm. The Code is based on the principle of national sovereignty over plant genetic resources and sets out standards and principles to be observed by the countries and institutions that adhere to it. It proposes procedures for collection; provides guidelines for collectors; and extends responsibilities and obligations to the sponsors of missions, the curators of genebanks and the users of genetic material. It calls for the participation of farmers and local institutions in collecting missions and proposes that users of germplasm share the benefits derived from the use of plant genetic resources with the host country and its farmers. A primary function of the Code is to serve as a point of reference until such time as individual countries establish their own codes or regulations for germplasm exploration and collection, conservation, exchange and utilization.

But it is the provisions of the Treaty regarding the sharing of the monetary benefits arising from commercial use that represent the real conceptual breakthrough in this connection. For the first time, someone who obtains a commercial profit from the use of genetic resources administered multilaterally will be obliged, by a Standard Material Transfer Agreement, to share such profits fairly and equitably, and to make an equitable payment to the multilateral mechanism. Such payments are to be used by the Governing Body of the Treaty as part of its funding strategy for benefit-sharing (art. 13.2(d)).

The Treaty distinguishes between mandatory and voluntary payment. Payment is mandatory on the commercialization of a product that is a plant genetic resource and that incorporates material accessed from the Multilateral System, when this product is not available without restriction to others for further research and breeding. Payment is voluntary when such product is available.

The Governing Body shall, at its first meeting, determine the level, form and manner of the payments, in line with commercial practice. It may also decide to establish different levels of payment for various categories of recipients trading in such products, and from time to time review the levels of payment. Furthermore, the Governing Body may assess, within five years of the entry into force of the Treaty, whether mandatory payment shall also apply in cases where commercial products are available without restriction for further research and breeding (art. 13.2(d)(ii)). The contracting parties shall also consider modalities of a strategy of voluntary benefit-sharing contributions by food processing industries that benefit from plant genetic resources (art. 13.6).

Such monetary benefit-sharing is part of a larger whole. In article 18, the Treaty establishes a funding strategy, which will mobilize funding for priority activities, plans and programmes, in particular in developing countries and countries with economies in transition. Moreover, the contracting parties are to take the necessary and appropriate measures within relevant international mechanisms, funds and bodies to ensure that due priority and attention are given to the effective allocation of predictable and agreed resources, taking into account the priorities established in the Global Plan of Action for the Conservation and Sustainable Use of Plant Genetic Resources for Food and Agriculture adopted in 1996 by 150 countries at the Leipzig International Technical Conference on Plant Genetic Resources for Food and Agriculture. The Plan is intended as a framework, guide and catalyst for action at community, national, regional and international levels. It seeks to create an efficient system for the conservation and sustainable use of plant genetic resources, through better cooperation, coordination and planning and through the strengthening of national capacity.

Last, but not least, the Treaty for the first time provides an agreed international framework for the *ex situ* collections of plant genetic resources held in trust by the International Agricultural Research Centres (IARCs) of the Consultative Group on International Agricultural Research (CGIAR) and by other relevant international organizations. An international network of *ex situ* collections was created in 1989 under the auspices of FAO in collaboration with CGIAR. In 1994, 12 CGIAR centres signed agreements with FAO whereby they placed most of their collections (some 500 000) in that network and agreed to hold the designated germplasm in trust for the benefit of the international community, and not to claim ownership or seek intellectual property rights over the germplasm and related information. The signature of agreements between IARCs and other such organizations and the Treaty's

Governing Body is foreseen for the purpose of making the collections' material available within the context of the Multilateral System, and under the terms and conditions set out in article 15.

Other important provisions of the Treaty include those dealing with: (i) the promotion of international networks for cooperation on plant genetic resources (art. 16); (ii) the institutional arrangements to be put in place for the operation of the Treaty (arts. 19 and 20); and (iii) compliance, dispute settlement, amendments, reservations and termination (arts. 21–35). A number of these provisions relate to the future functioning of the Treaty, whose Governing Body is made up of all contracting parties. The parties shall in turn elect the Chair and Vice-chairs of the Governing Body, who will form the Bureau (art. 19), with a Secretary appointed by the Director-General of FAO (art. 20).

IV. IMPLEMENTING THE TREATY

4.1. Paving the Way: Interim Arrangements

During the year following its adoption, the Treaty will remain open for signature at FAO Headquarters (art. 25), with the Director-General of FAO performing depository functions (art. 34). As of June 2002, in addition to the European Union, 56 countries had signed the Treaty, including 35 developing countries and 20 developed countries. Moreover, seven countries had already deposited their instrument of ratification (Canada, Eritrea, India, Jordan, Sudan), of acceptance (Cambodia) or of approval (Guinea). The Treaty will enter into force three months after its ratification by 40 contracting parties (art. 28).

In the interim, various institutional and financial arrangements, described in Resolution 3/2001, should be adopted to prepare for the Treaty's future implementation. They mainly consist of the following:

- the Interim Committee for the Treaty will be the FAO Commission on Genetic Resources for Food and Agriculture;

- states that are members of FAO, the International Atomic Energy Agency, the UN and its specialized agencies are invited to participate in the Interim Committee's work;

- at its first meeting, which should take place in 2002, the Interim Committee will adopt its rules of procedure. It will further prepare, for consideration by the Treaty's Governing Body: (i) draft rules of procedure, draft financial rules and a budget proposal for the Treaty; (ii) a draft standard agreement for facilitated access, with proposed terms for commercial benefit sharing; (iii) draft agreements on *ex situ* collections; and (iv) proposed procedures to promote compliance;

- an Expert Group of technical and legal experts on plant genetic resources exchange will be established to formulate recommendations on the terms of the standard agreement for facilitated access; and

- the Interim Committee will initiate the establishment of cooperation with relevant treaty bodies and international organizations, including the CBD's Conference of Parties.

These tasks and others will keep negotiators and experts busy for quite some time. Progress in these matters will be indispensable if the Treaty is to attract, before long, the required number of ratifications to become effective. To this end, mobilizing appropriate resources will be essential, as well as strengthening cooperation among all those active in the area of agrobiodiversity. Contracting parties will also have to prepare for compliance with the Treaty, particularly in terms of building the capacities and acquiring the tools necessary to exercise their rights and fulfil their obligations.

4.2. Promoting Compliance: National Legislation

Among the chief measures to be taken in this respect are the design or adjustment of domestic policies and laws relating to agrobiodiversity to meet the Treaty's requirements, as explicitly stated in articles 4 and 6 of the Treaty. Mechanisms to promote compliance will also include legal assistance to countries in development and in transition on matters covered by the Treaty (art. 21). Moreover, the terms of the Standard Material Transfer Agreement, by which commercial benefits will be fairly and equitably shared, will be a major conceptual task, for which new national implementing legislation will also be required.

New legislation will be especially needed in such novel areas as farmers' rights (art. 9.2), as they are crucial in providing an incentive for the conservation and development of plant genetic resources which constitute the basis of food and agriculture production throughout the world (Esquínas-Alcázar, 2000 and 1987). The process of conceptualizing and writing laws in this area has started only very recently. India is the first country to have passed a law in this area: the Protection of Plant Varieties and Farmers' Rights Act 53 of 31 August 2001 (Sahai, 2000), already mentioned in Chapter 4. The 2000 OAU "African Model Legislation for the Protection of the Rights of Local Communities, Farmers and Breeders, and for the Regulation of Access to Biological Resources", in Part V on farmers' rights, is another illustration of emerging efforts towards the formal sanction of farmers' rights.[2] Some of the relevant provisions of both texts, abstracted in Box 2, are clearly inspired by, if not modelled after, the concept of farmers' rights as developed under the Undertaking and reaffirmed by the Treaty.

In the broader area of genetic resources, some 50 countries have already introduced, or are developing, laws and other policy measures to regulate access modalities and provide for benefit sharing. The majority of countries contemplating such laws are developing countries. Regional groups, national governments or state governments already regulating access to genetic resources to ensure prior informed consent and benefit-sharing include: the Andean Pact (Bolivia, Colombia, Ecuador, Peru, Venezuela); Australia (the states of Western Australia and Queensland); Brazil (at the federal level and the states of Acre and Amapa); Cameroon; Costa Rica; the Republic of Korea; Malaysia (the state of Sarawak); Mexico; the United States (within Yellowstone and other national parks) and the Philippines. (GRAIN, 2002)

In general, existing access legislation recognizes sovereign rights over biological resources, sets forth the administrative process for access and establishes conditions for access. Much of the existing national access legislation applies to all genetic resources and, like the CBD, does not distinguish between different sectors of biodiversity, or between resources maintained *in situ* or *ex situ*. In the Syrian Arab Republic, however, specific legislation is being developed in line with the Treaty. In view of its novelty, this legislation is described hereafter in some detail.

---

[2] General references to farmers' rights may be found in a few other texts, such as Costa Rica's 1998 *Ley de biodiversidad*, which provides: (i) "*El Estado reconoce la existencia y validez de las formas de conocimiento e innovación y la necesidad de protegerlas, mediante el uso de los mecanismos legales apropiados para cada caso específico*" (art. 77); and (ii) "*El Estado otorgará la protección indicada en el artículo anterior, entre otras formas, mediante [...] derechos de los agricultores*" (art. 78). Another example is Bangladesh's draft Plant Varieties Act of 1998, which recognizes farmers' rights in article 22.

Box 2 - Farmers' Rights in Two Recent Texts

African Model Legislation (2000)	Indian Act (2001)
Recognition of Farmers' Rights 24(1) Farmers' Rights are recognized as stemming from the enormous contributions that local farming communities … have made in the conservation, development and sustainable use of plant and animal genetic resources that constitute the basis of breeding for food and agriculture production; and (2) For farmers to continue making these achievements, therefore, Farmers' Rights have to be recognized and protected. **Application of the Law on Farmers' Varieties** 25(1) Farmers' varieties and breeds are recognized and shall be protected under the rules of practice as found in, and recognized by, the customary practices and laws of the concerned local farming communities, whether such laws are written or not. (2) A variety with specific attributes identified by a community shall be granted intellectual protection through a variety certificate which does not have to meet the criteria of distinction, uniformity and stability. This variety certificate entitles the community to have the exclusive rights to multiply, cultivate, use or sell the variety, or to license its use without prejudice to the Farmers' Rights set out in this law. **Farmers' Rights** 26(1) Farmers' Rights shall … include the right to: a) the protection of their traditional knowledge relevant to plant and animal genetic resources;` b) obtain an equitable share of benefits arising from the use of plant and animal genetic resources; c) participate in making decisions, including at the national level, on matters related to the conservation and sustainable use of plant and animal genetic resources; d) save, use, exchange and sell farm-saved seed/propagating material of farmers' varieties; e) use a new breeders' variety protected under this law to develop farmers' varieties, including material obtained from genebanks or plant genetic resource centres; and f) collectively save, use, multiply and process farm-saved seed of protected varieties.	**Definitions** 2(k) "farmer" means any person who- (i) cultivates crops either by cultivating the land himself; or (ii) cultivates crops by directly supervising the cultivation of land through any other person; or (iii) conserves and preserves, severally or jointly, with any person any wild species or traditional varieties or adds value to such wild species or traditional varieties through selection and identification of their useful properties. (l) "farmers' variety" means a variety which- (i) has been traditionally cultivated and evolved by the farmers in their fields; or (ii) is a wild relative or land race of a variety about which the farmers possess the common knowledge. **Chapter VI - Farmers Rights** 39(1) Notwithstanding anything contained in this Act, a farmer- (i) Who has bred or developed a new variety shall be entitled for registration and other protection in like manner as a breeder of a variety under this Act,… (iii) Who is engaged in the conservation of genetic resources of land races and wild relatives of economic plants and their improvement through selection and preservation shall be entitled in the prescribed manner for recognition and reward from the National Gene Fund; Provided that material so selected and preserved has been used as donors of genes in varieties registrable under this Act, (iv) shall be deemed to be entitled to save, use, sow, resow, exchange, share or sell his farm produce including seed of a variety protected under this Act in the same manner as he was entitled before the coming into force of this Act; Provided that the farmer shall not be entitled to sell branded seed of a variety protected under this Act.

4.3. A Pioneering Effort: The Syrian Arab Republic's Draft Law

With assistance from FAO, the Government of the Syrian Arab Republic is formulating legislation on exchange of plant genetic resources. The draft legislation mandates bilateral arrangements between specified Syrian authorities and any party seeking access to Syria's plant genetic resources. The legislation has a broad scope. In addition to facilitated access to plant genetic resources, it provides for the fair and equitable sharing of benefits derived from their use, and recognizes the rights of farmers and local communities. (Cantarella and Cooper, 2002)

What makes the Syrian legislation noteworthy is that it is the first national legislation to be drafted in conformity with the Treaty; in fact, Syria signed the Treaty at the World Food Summit: five years later in Rome in June 2002. The draft legislation not only embodies the principles of the Treaty, but also provides for the mechanisms to facilitate access under the multilateral system (MLS) established in the Treaty. The legislation is also consistent with the CBD.

The Syrian legislation sets forth three basic access and benefit-sharing arrangements: one under the MLS, and the other two for access not pursuant to the MLS – one for applicants requesting access for non-commercial purposes and one for commercial purposes. The legislation is designed to avoid unnecessarily cumbersome access procedures, both for the applicants and for the Syrian authorities. As such, the legislation provides for simple procedures and standard terms and conditions in the case of access requests made under the Treaty and applications for non-commercial purposes. The access regime allows applicants to define their intentions with respect to access and avoids the need to infer the nature of the access from the description of the project in the application. Nonetheless, the ultimate determination as to what type of access is appropriate rests with the Syrian authority.

4.3.1. Access Under the Treaty

The terms of access for plant genetic resources for food and agriculture under the MLS are in complete accordance with the Treaty. Access shall be provided solely for the purposes of utilization and conservation for research, breeding and training for food and agriculture, and is contingent on the applicant's acceptance of the Standard Material Transfer Agreement provided for in the Treaty. (The Syrian legislation provides for an interim MLS Material Transfer Agreement to be used pending the adoption of the Standard Material Transfer Agreement by the Governing Body of the Treaty.) The legislation incorporates the list of crops covered under the MLS. Additionally, it establishes that plant genetic resources on this list held in national *ex situ* collections (including those held by Syrian universities and research institutes), as well as those held *in situ* on government lands, are included under the MLS. The list of crops may be amended in accordance with any amendments to the Treaty's list, or if the Syrian authorities independently determine that additional plant genetic resources should be made available.

4.3.2. Access Other Than Under the Treaty

As noted, the terms of access other than under the Treaty are determined according to the purpose for which access is sought.

(a) Non-commercial Purpose

Applicants who desire access to plant genetic resources solely for academic, educational, scientific or public use purposes must execute a non-commercial Material Transfer Agreement. No rights to commercialization are granted to the applicant, nor may the applicant claim any rights, including intellectual property rights, over the plant genetic resources or any derivatives or associated traditional knowledge. Additionally, the legislation allows the Syrian authority discretion to enter into umbrella agreements with Syrian universities and research institutes and international institutes based in Syria, to facilitate academic, research and not-for-profit activities.

(b) Commercial Purpose

Applicants who desire access for any commercial purpose must execute a Commercial Material Transfer Agreement. Commercial purposes include use or exploitation of plant genetic resources for financial gain, including but not limited to sale, product development, market research, pre-market approval and pursuit of intellectual property (or any other) rights. The applicant and the Syrian authority negotiate these agreements in consultation with relevant stakeholders on a case-by-case basis, and in reference to the conditions of access and benefit sharing provided in the subsidiary regulations to the draft legislation. These draw upon the "Bonn Guidelines on Access to Genetic Resources and Fair and Equitable Sharing of the Benefits Arising out of their Use", adopted at CBD's 6th Conference of Parties in April 2002. (CBD, 2002) The terms of the

Commercial Material Transfer Agreement must be reviewed by a Policy Advisory Body, which, before granting access, will advise on both the adequacy of the terms proposed and of the consultation process with stakeholders.

For access for commercial purposes, while rights over the plant genetic resources themselves cannot be acquired under any circumstances, the issue of rights over derivatives, other than proximate derivatives, is also to be addressed on a case-by-case basis. Thus, a Commercial Material Transfer Agreement could potentially permit a recipient of plant genetic resources to acquire intellectual property rights in a technology, process or end product derived from such plant genetic resources, but not the plant genetic resources themselves or their proximate derivatives.

4.3.3. Sustainable Use and Benefit Sharing

Recognizing that the goals of conservation, sustainable use and benefit sharing can only be achieved if plant genetic resources are accessed, the Syrian legislation balances access to, and protection of, plant genetic resources. It provides a clearly defined regulatory scheme that facilitates access by informing applicants of the Syrian requirements before they submit their applications. Moreover, the legislation provides streamlined procedures for applicants making requests under the Treaty or seeking access for non-commercial purposes, and eliminates restrictive administrative requirements that would create disincentives for undergoing the access process. Consequently, the regime facilitates access for precisely those applicants whom the Treaty aims to assist.

In order to protect the plant genetic resources and to promote benefit sharing, the procedures for applications made for commercial purposes or for those that might involve transfer of any rights over the plant genetic resources require full prior informed consent procedures and negotiation of mutually agreed terms on a case-by-case basis. The legislation also sets out the range of conservation and sustainable use activities that should be promoted by the authority through policies and programmes that are largely derived from the Treaty.

4.3.4. Farmers' Rights

Consistent with the Treaty's goals, the access regime of the draft Syrian legislation also protects the rights of local communities and farmers' rights. The legislation provides for the protection of traditional knowledge, the right of farmers and local communities to participate in decisionmaking at the national level on matters related to the conservation and sustainable use of plant genetic resources and the sharing of benefits arising from the use of plant genetic resources. The legislation also requires consultation with farmers and local communities prior to granting consent for collecting *in situ* plant genetic resources. The legislation provides for public disclosure of information provided in applications, which increases transparency and can contribute to involving stakeholders in the access process. Finally, the legislation does not apply to or affect customary exchange of plant genetic resources between farmers.

V. CONCLUSION

The International Treaty on Plant Genetic Resources for Food and Agriculture is the first legally binding instrument that deals specifically with agrobiodiversity at the global level, providing for the conservation and sustainable use of plant genetic resources for food and agriculture. It is grounded on contemporary principles of natural resource and biological diversity law, such as sovereignty of states over their plant genetic resources coupled with the duty to protect and use them sustainably, along with the principles of access to information and of participation in decisionmaking by interested stakeholders. Thus, notwithstanding its distinctiveness in terms of agrobiodiversity, the Treaty may be viewed as belonging to the wider family of modern biodiversity-inspired international legal instruments.

The Treaty addresses conservation measures – both *in situ* and *ex situ* – as well as the rights of traditional farmers and of modern breeders. Its centrepiece is the multilateral system of facilitated access to plant genera that are essential to food security, and of equitable sharing of the benefits arising from their use, under conditions to be set out in the Standard Material Transfer Agreement after the Treaty's entry into force.

In view of this, contracting parties will need to develop new legislation or to adjust existing laws in the area of agrobiodiversity. In particular, making benefit sharing and farmers' rights a reality, at the national level as well as between nations, will represent a challenge in the coming years – and one of the manifold tasks to be steadily addressed in implementing the Treaty.

REFERENCES

Cantarella, C. & Cooper, H.D. 2002. *Formulation of Draft Legislation on Plant Genetic Resources for Syria.* FAO, Rome.

Convention on Biological Diversity (CBD). 2002. *Report of the Ad Hoc Open-ended Working Group on Access and Benefit-sharing.* UNEP/CBD/COP/6/6, 31 October 2002.

Earth Negotiations Bulletin. 2001. *Negotiations on the International Treaty on Plant Genetic Resources for Food and Agriculture: 30 October - 3 November 2001.* Vol. 9, No. 213 (www.iisd.ca/biodiv/iu-wg).

Esquínas-Alcázar, J. 1987. *Plant Genetic Resources: A Base for Food Security.* CERES, No. 118, Vol. 20/4, 1987.

Esquínas-Alcázar, J. 2000. *Agricultural Biological Diversity and Farmers' Rights.* World Conference on Bioethics, Gijón, Spain.

Erosion, Technology and Concentration Group (ETC). 2001. *The Law of the Seed!* Erosion, Technology and Concentration Group. Vol. 3, No. 1 (www.etcgroup.org/documents/trans_treaty_dec2001.pdf).

FAO. 1999. *Progress Report on the International Network of* ex situ *Collections Under the Auspices of FAO,* CGRFA-8/99/7, Rome.

FAO. 2002. *A Treaty on Plant Genetic Resources* (www.fao.org/ag/magazine/0112sp3.htm).

Genetic Resources Action International (GRAIN). 2002. *Biodiversity Rights Legislation* (www.grain.org/brl/index.cfm).

Mekouar, M.A. 2001. *A Global Instrument on Agrobiodiversity: The International Treaty on Plant Genetic Resources for Food and Agriculture.* Environmental Policy and Law [also published in 2002 as FAO Legal Paper Online No. 24 (www.fao.org/Legal)].

Sahai, S. 2000. *India's Plant Varieties Protection and Farmers' Rights Act* (www.ciroap.org/food/PVP_SUNS.PDF).

Swaminathan Research Foundation. 1996. *Agrobiodiversity and Farmers' Rights. Proceedings of a Technical Consultation on an Implementation Framework for Farmers' Rights,* Madras.

6

WATER

Contents

I. INTRODUCTION

Despite illustrious precedents (the Mar del Plata Water Action Plan, 1977, and the Dublin Statement on Water and Sustainable Development, 1992), water resources were not a prominent issue at the Rio Conference on Environment and Development. However, since then water resources have been gaining an ever higher profile through the work of the United Nations Commission on Sustainable Development at its 1994 and 1998 sessions and the 1997 Special Session of the General Assembly convened to debate and adopt the draft United Nations Convention on the Law of the Non-navigational Uses of International Watercourses. All called for a concerted effort to develop more integrated approaches to the management of water resources and for a stronger focus on the needs of poor people and poor nations. In a similar vein, the United Nations Millennium Declaration issued in 2000 at the specially convened UN Millennium Assembly called upon United Nations member states "to stop the unsustainable exploitation of water resources by developing water management strategies at the regional, national and local levels which promote both equitable access and adequate supplies".

These concerns have gained further prominence and momentum due to other recent and significant developments, notably, the preparation of the World Water Vision launched at the World Water Forum held in The Hague in March 2000, which is in the nature of a policy statement; the Ministerial Declaration on Water Security in the 21st Century adopted by the parallel Ministerial Conference held in The Hague; and, most recently, the Ministerial Declaration adopted by water ministers at the Ministerial Session of the International Conference on Freshwater in Bonn in December 2001 (the "Bonn Conference"), and the Abuja Declaration on Water adopted by the water Ministers of African countries at their meeting in Abuja, Nigeria, in April 2002.

These policy pronouncements reveal that water security is the main goal inspiring the international community's emerging agenda for the 21st century. Indeed, water security has inspired the Preliminary Assessment of Policy Progress since Rio, a document prepared by the United Nations World Water Assessment Programme (WWAP) for the Bonn Conference, and the first World Water Development Report due to be presented by WWAP at Rio plus 10. In particular, in both the Bonn Ministerial Declaration and the WWAP Preliminary Assessment, water governance issues, including a supportive legal and institutional framework, are seen to play a central role in achieving water security.

II.   INTERNATIONAL DEVELOPMENTS

The drafting and adoption of domestic water resources legislation is largely inspired and informed by domestic policy, but can also be guided by regional or global standards reflected in multilateral conventions, treaties and agreements, and by the rights and obligations created by them.

The only global convention on water resources is the UN Convention on the Law of the Non-navigational Uses of International Watercourses (UN Convention), which was adopted by an overwhelming majority of votes at a specially convened session of the United Nations General Assembly in May 1997, but which is not yet legally binding. Similarly, the widely respected Helsinki Rules on the Uses of International Watercourses (1966) developed by the International Law Association (ILA), and the subsequent complementary rules, are non-binding. Both the UN Convention and the Helsinki Rules carry only the moral weight that accrues to the UN Convention from the fact of its emanating from an overwhelming majority vote of states gathered at a special session of the UN General Assembly; and to the Helsinki Rules from the respect commanded by the ILA members who took part in the drafting of the Rules.

Both the UN Convention and the Helsinki Rules spell out the rights and obligations of countries in respect of the water resources of rivers, lakes and underground aquifers which form, or are crossed by, international boundary lines. That is, the scope of application of the provisions of the UN Convention and of the Helsinki Rules is limited to that fraction of the total water resources of any country which belong to rivers, lakes and underground aquifers which form, or are crossed by, international boundary lines (also commonly referred to as "transboundary water resources" or "transboundary rivers, lakes and aquifers"). Although conceivably these provisions would require domestic legislation to implement them, they are in a way too general to provide much guidance for countries wishing to review their water legislation.

By contrast, two water resources conventions in force, both of which operate on a large-scale regional level, the 1992 UN Economic Commission for Europe Convention on the Protection and Use of Transboundary Watercourses and International Lakes (ECE Convention), and the 1995 Protocol on Shared Watercourses in the Southern African Development Community Region (SADC Protocol), revised in 2001, carry rather more specific obligations. Although these concern only the "transboundary" water resources of state parties, they are precise enough that useful guidance can be drawn from them in the drafting of the domestic legislation concerning the totality of states' water resources. For example, under the revised SADC Protocol member states are to have domestic legislation in place providing for the licensing of water resources abstraction and for the permitting of wastewater disposal. And, under the ECE Convention, member states have undertaken to have domestic legislation in place regulating point-source wastewater disposal, and to adopt water quality objectives and water quality criteria consistent with the parameters provided in an annex to the Convention.

The European Union's Framework Water Policy Directive of 2001 is another regional instrument which is the source of binding rights and obligations for the EU member states. In contrast to the UN Convention, the Helsinki Rules and the two regional conventions mentioned earlier, the EU Directive covers all water resources in all of the EU member states, regardless of whether the resources are "transboundary" or fully domestic. EU member states are under an obligation to adapt their domestic water resources legislation to the precise regulatory, economic and institutional requirements laid down in the directive in regard to, in particular, licensing of the abstraction of water resources for use, wastewater discharge permitting, implementation of the polluter-pays and user-pays principles, the marketing of water rights and patterning of the government water administrations along river basin lines.

In addition to these global but non-binding, and regional and binding, instruments, many more multilateral and bilateral water resources treaties, agreements and conventions exist, generally covering a designated "transboundary" river, lake, basin or, more infrequently, a designated aquifer. Depending on the level of specificity of the rights and obligations which stem from them, these instruments tend to be the source of inspiration for the domestic water legislation of the states which are party to them. Significant examples of multilateral water resources treaties laying down precise enough obligations to require and inspire legislative action by member countries are the lower Mekong River Basin Treaty of 1995, the Danube Convention of 1994 and the Rhine Convention of 2000.

III. TRENDS IN NATIONAL LEGISLATION

In response largely to concern about the growing scarcity of water resources relative to projected needs in the years since Rio, and aware of the desirability of fostering greater efficiency of use while being mindful of equity and ecological considerations, the governments of growing numbers of countries have felt compelled to review their existing water laws and to prepare the blueprint of new laws. These draft bills, in a large number of cases, have since been enacted into law. A comparative analysis of these new and proposed water laws discloses a number of discrete trends, which will be presented below.

3.1. Growing Incorporation of Water Resources into the Public Domain

The last remaining vestiges of "private" groundwaters and of exclusive riparian rights in surface watercourses have been steadily eroded by the ever-expanding sphere of "public" waters. Public waters may include those waters held in the public domain (ownership) of the state, as in the water resources legislation adopted in Italy in 1994, in Morocco in 1995 and in Zimbabwe in 1998, all of which bring all groundwater resources within the public domain. Alternatively, where ownership of water is a notion repugnant to the legal system, water resources have been vested in the state in trust for the public, such as in South Africa's 1998 National Water Act, which adapts the "public trust" doctrine developed by courts in the United States. Finally, the state may be vested with superior user rights, which is the approach reflected in Uganda's 1995 Water Resources Act and in the Australian state of New South Wales' Water Management Act of 2000. Whatever the legal underpinning, the result has been to bring all or most of the nation's water resources under the scope of the government's allocative authority.

3.2. Checking Government Authority to Allocate and Re-allocate Water Resources for Use

As a result of water becoming public property – or acquiring by statute some comparable status as earlier outlined – the ownership rights of individuals have been eroded, and generally they can only claim user rights. Such rights accrue from the pronouncements of courts in adjudication-type proceedings (as in some Western states of the United States) or, as a more general trend, from a grant made by the government and recorded in a permit, licence, concession or like instrument. The relevant discretionary authority the government enjoys in making grants and allocating water has traditionally been checked by the courts of law or through the hierarchical review (appeal) opportunities available internally through the granting process.

These traditional review mechanisms are available *after* an allocation decision has been made and a permit granted. By contrast, a new generation of checks and balances tends to operate *before* such decisions and the relevant grants are made. These are basically aimed at improving the quality of decisionmaking, obviating the need for most *post facto* review. These new checks and balances which operate before allocation decisions stem from Environmental Impact Assessment (EIA) requirements for proposed water abstractions; water resources planning determinations; minimum flow requirements of surface watercourses; and the formal reservation of quantities of water for specific purposes.

3.2.1. Environmental Impact Assessment Requirements

EIA requirements for proposed new water abstractions have been introduced by France's 1992 Water Act, by Spain's 1999 extensive amendments to the 1985 Water Act and by Cameroon's 2001 industrial and commercial water abstraction licensing regulations. In addition, the adoption of EIA requirements for designated surface water development projects, for designated groundwater extractions and for artificial recharge projects has become mandatory, as of March 1999, for all member states of the European Union by virtue of Council Directive 97/11/EC of 3 March 1997, amending Directive 85/337/EEC on the assessment of the effects of certain public and private projects on the environment. In the Argentine province of Mendoza, regulations have been introduced in 1999 mandating the preparation of a "Water Impact Statement" by the provincial government water administration, for all water development and other projects.

3.2.2. Water Planning Mechanisms, Processes and Instruments

Water planning mechanisms, processes and instruments feature in recent water legislation as a preferred mechanism for informed, forward-looking and participatory decisionmaking with regard to the management and development of water resources, in particular for water use allocation and for pollution prevention and control. For example, the preparation and periodic review of River Basin Management Plans is a mandatory requirement for member states of the European Union in the recent EU Framework Water Directive. Prior to this directive, France introduced and regulated through the 1992 Water Act a complex water resources planning system based on General Water Plans (*Schémas directeurs d'aménagement et de gestion des eaux*) covering one or more basins, and on Detailed Water Plans (*Schémas d'aménagement et de gestion des eaux*) covering one or more sub-basins or an aquifer. Determinations under approved plans become binding on governmental decisionmaking, and at least one groundwater allocation decision reportedly has been challenged in court and quashed on the basis of its being at variance with the relevant approved basin plan.

South Australia's catchment-level "water allocation planning", which was introduced by the 1997 Water Resources Act, fixes volumes of water that can be taken from a catchment area for use. The Act will become the source of rules for governmental allocation decisions and relevant grants of water rights. Zimbabwe's catchment-level "outline planning", provided for in the 1998 Water Act, sets forth priorities for the allocation of water, and under the Act governmental allocation decisions cannot depart from approved outline plans. Also in the U.S. state of Texas, legislation passed in 1997 institutes a complex water planning system at regional and at state level, and gives the planning determinations a binding effect which they did not have under previous legislation.

On a less ambitious scale, New South Wales' Water Management Act of 2000 calls for the formation of statutory water resources management plans in respect of designated "water management areas". The plans, which will be in effect for ten years at a time, are to be formed by local committees and will cover water resources allocation and sharing, environmental protection, drainage and floodplain management. In Victoria, another Australian state, recent (2001) amendments to the 1989 Water Act provide for "streamflow management plans", which will limit total abstractions, to be prepared in respect of surface water resources under stress.

In all these cases, and others still (Morocco, South Africa and Uganda), planning determinations are not simply strategic but are fully binding on governmental water abstraction licensing decisions.

3.2.3. Minimum Flow Requirements

Minimum flow requirements seek to protect the ecology and fish life of watercourses and act as a limit on the government's abstraction licensing authority by barring any abstractions from watercourses above established limits. Minimum flow requirements may be designed specifically to protect riverine fish life, to protect the scenic and recreational values of streams and to attain ambient water quality objectives or to meet some other policy objective. Extensive amendments made in 1999 to Spain's 1985 Water Act provide for the establishment of minimum flow requirements in rivers, aimed at protecting the riverine environment. The subsequent Act approving the National Water Master Plan, adopted in mid-2001, explicitly grants such minimum flow requirements priority call on available river flows.

3.2.4. Reserving Volumes or Flows

Reserving volumes or flows for given purposes also puts limits on the government's abstraction licensing authority in that the water reserve cannot be allocated except for the stated purposes. Such a reserve features in South Africa's 1998 National Water Act, according to which the government is under a statutory duty to reserve water resources for ecological purposes or for the purposes of supplying water to satisfy basic human needs. Under Spain's 2001 Act approving the National Water Master Plan, the government has authority to set aside entire rivers, sections of rivers, aquifers or other water bodies for conservation in their pristine state (so-called "environmental reserve"). The reservation may entail a ban on the granting of water abstraction rights from the identified water bodies.

In the Australian state of Victoria, the recent amendments to the 1989 Water Act allow fixing a permissible annual volume of water which can be extracted from designated aquifers under stress, thus effectively limiting total groundwater extractions from such aquifers and having the same effect as a declared reserve. In Jamaica, the 1995 Water Act vests in the government authority to reserve a "source of supply" for a public purpose, and applicants for the abstraction and use of reserved water for a reserved purpose take precedence over competing applications, and override existing abstractions. Under Mexico's water legislation, the federal government has authority to set aside water resources for domestic and public water supply purposes, for the generation of hydro-power, to meet the minimum flow requirements of watercourses and to protect aquatic ecosystems in general. The federal government is under a general obligation to see to it that the reserved water resources are kept in a quantitative and qualitative state which is consistent with the objectives of the reservation.

3.3. Fostering Controlled Trading in Water Rights

Increasingly, lawmakers have been turning to trading in water rights in the pursuit of efficiency of water allocation and use. Because trading of water rights empowers users to make allocative decisions instead of government, part of the expanding allocative authority vested in the government, which was observed earlier, is returned to the users.

Unregulated water trading is known to operate perhaps only in Chile. There, water is regarded as a commodity which can be freely traded through the sale of the relevant government grants. Yet, in the years since Rio, a fierce debate has been raging due to government proposals to penalize the hoarding (non-use) of water, on the logic that incentives are needed to ensure that water is put to actual use. In other countries, regulations on water trading seek to minimize the possibilities of unwelcome "third-party" effects, such as effects on the environment, on the interests of the area from where water is taken for use in another area, on cultural values, on resource availability to meet priority requirements and, generally, on marginal groups.

The trend towards a regulated approach to trading of water rights is borne out in the statutory and case law of the Western United States, and in the water legislation of such diverse jurisdictions as Mexico (1992), the Canadian province of Alberta (1996), the Australian states of South Australia (1997) and New South Wales (2000), South Africa (1998) and Spain (1999).

It bears emphasizing, however, that in countries where water has traditionally been regarded as an appurtenance of the irrigated land where it is used, the trading of water rights separately from land rights is forbidden, as for example under Morocco's recent water legislation (1995). Also, under Cameroon's industrial and commercial water abstraction licensing regulations adopted in 2001, trading is not permitted as such licences are not transferable. In the Argentine province of Mendoza, where water rights cannot be traded either, under regulations issued in 1999 the available surpluses can be allocated by the provincial water administration acting as a clearinghouse between willing suppliers and willing takers of surplus water. No monetary transaction takes place between the parties, but the supplier pays half of the water abstraction charge he or she would otherwise be liable for, and the taker pays the water abstraction charge for the duration of the abstraction.

3.4. Charging for Water Abstraction

Charging for water abstraction in general, and for the extraction of groundwater in particular, seeks to influence the demand for water and constitutes the chief non-regulatory mechanism available to control water abstraction and use. It is generally practised in combination with the regulatory mechanisms described earlier, such as in all the examples reviewed below.

In Mexico, for instance, charges on industrial and municipal abstractions were levied annually even before enactment of the 1992 National Waters Law. Relevant rates are set each year by the Federal Law on Levies, and are calculated so as to reflect the relative scarcity of water resources and the different kinds of use – except for irrigation, as to which no water abstraction charges are levied. Also, in Germany, charge rates vary according to use, and tend to be higher for groundwater extraction. In France, water abstraction charging has been practised since 1964. Charges vary according to volume, kind of use, location and source – with groundwater extraction being charged at 2 to 3.5 times higher than surface water abstractions, although legislation was tabled in Parliament in mid-2001 to end the current practice of different sectors being charged different rates. As a result, industry, agriculture and households in any given area would pay the same amount per cubic metre of water abstracted. This same approach is under consideration in Portugal.

Water abstraction charging has a long history in England and Wales also, where charges are set at a level that enables the Environment Agency to cover its costs in performing its function of water custodian. The levels and rates of charges are set accordingly, and ostensibly do not seek to influence the behaviour of water abstractors. Charges are based on the annual quantity of water authorized for abstraction, not on actual volumes abstracted. No charges are levied on groundwater extractions of 20 cubic metres a day or less for agricultural purposes, whereas all other groundwater extractions are charged.

In the Netherlands, a groundwater extraction charging mechanism has been in effect since 1995, with the revenue used in part to fund research into developing groundwater policy plans and the remainder paid to the Finance Ministry as part of general taxation. In the U.S. state of Arizona, a tax is levied on all users of groundwater according to the volume consumed. The proceeds from this tax are directed to purchasing existing water rights and retiring them from use, to conducting water augmentation programmes and to sponsoring research on water conservation.

3.5. Curbing Water Pollution

Well-tested regulatory and economic instruments for the prevention and abatement of water pollution from point sources (notably, industrial outfalls and municipal sewers) feature in many recent water pollution control laws. Such instruments range from discharge permits linked to effluent quality standards and quality objectives/standards for the receiving water source, to charging for discharging waste in water bodies (the well-known "polluter-pays" principle).

The more recent statutes bear evidence of a growing concern for pollution of surface and, more urgently, underground water resources from diffuse sources, such as the runoff and drainage of cropland in rural areas. The complex and insidious threat posed by diffuse pollution sources has been addressed by the more recent generation of water laws through a shift in the focus of regulation from the discharge itself – which it would be difficult if not impossible to track down to a specific outfall – to the land use giving rise to a diffuse discharge.

Thus, cultivation practices have been increasingly attracting regulatory restrictions aimed at preventing, abating or minimizing pollution from substances such as the nitrates employed in agriculture. Just before the Rio Conference, in December 1991 the European Union adopted Directive 91/676/EEC concerning the protection of waters against pollution caused by nitrates from agricultural sources, directing member states to designate nitrate-sensitive (or nitrate-vulnerable) areas and to draw up a code or codes of good agricultural practice. Within the designated areas, the provisions of such code or codes become mandatory for farmers. Furthermore, the polluter-pays principle mentioned earlier is making inroads in the agricultural sector, which has traditionally been impermeable to charging policies. In France, for instance, in 2001 legislation was tabled in Parliament *inter alia* introducing a tax on nitrogen-based pollution of water resources, whether surface or underground, from agriculture.

The diffuse impact of point sources like waste dumps and landfills is also attracting increasing attention. For instance, under a statute – technically, an amendment to the 1959 Water Rights Act – adopted in 1997 by Austria, most landfills will require a permit. The operator must provide adequate security, in particular with regard to future precautionary measures. If the precautions taken prove insufficient, the government may impose additional or alternative requirements. In extreme cases, the disposal of waste can be suspended temporarily or the landfill can even be closed. Furthermore, the government may appoint a monitoring body at the expense of the licence holder. The licence holder must submit annual reports indicating the type, quantity and origin of wastes deposited in the preceding year and the results of the monitoring programme.

Other legislation focuses not on the land use but on the area where the diffuse pollution is occurring and on specific activities that can cause or worsen pollution. In Spain, for example, under the 1999 amendments to the 1985 Water Act, the government has the authority to declare an area experiencing groundwater pollution or the risk of it as a "protected aquifer area". In such areas, groundwater withdrawals may be limited or frozen pending the adoption of a recovery plan for the aquifer. In addition, the government's prior consent will be required for the siting of facilities, the extraction of inert materials or any other activity potentially impairing the quality of the underground water. A similar approach is reflected in the Water Management Act of 2000 of the Australian state of New South Wales, which mandates the formation by the local community of legally binding "aquifer management plans".

3.6. User Participation in the Management of Water Resources

The formation of groupings of water users for the development and management of sources of irrigation water is widely known and provided for in the legislation of most of Latin America, Spain and Italy in Europe and many South Asian countries. Customary law regarding user participation also plays a dominant role in some jurisdictions, such as the island of Bali (Indonesia), and in many oases in the Saharan and Sahelian regions of Africa. Apart from these well-known and established trends, water users are increasingly being called upon by legislation to participate (a) in the micromanagement of water resources under stress and (b) in the internal structure of the government water administration. Both can be seen as different but complementary manifestations of a budding public-private sector partnership aimed at building consensus and support for difficult water allocation and management decisions, and at sharing government responsibilities with concerned users.

The direct involvement of users in the micromanagement of water resources under stress is a regular feature in much recent water legislation. Often, such schemes arise in connection with groundwater resources in areas experiencing accelerated groundwater depletion and/or severe ground-water pollution. In the U.S. state of Texas, Groundwater Conservation Districts were traditionally formed on petition and vote by affected property owners, but tend now, on the basis of a 1997 statute, to be formed also at government's instigation of a property owners' vote. This will generally occur where government, based on its own studies, creates a district in so-called "critical areas", i.e., areas experiencing overdraft, insufficient supply or contamination.

Although these districts have varied powers including issuing permits, spacing wells and setting the amount of withdrawals, most have not imposed such regulatory mechanisms, instead opting for voluntary self-restraint and educational programmes. As such, they leave untouched land owners' rights to pump groundwater. Under New South Wales' Water Management Act of 2000, water users must be represented in the groundwater management committees established for the management of aquifers under stress.

In Spain, the 1999 water legislation provides for the compulsory formation of water users' groups from among the users of an aquifer, when the aquifer is being, or is at risk of becoming, overexploited. These groups are to share groundwater management responsibilities with the government, in particular in the management and policing of groundwater extraction rights. In Mexico, since 1995 a number of "Groundwater Technical Committees" (*Comités Técnicos de Aguas Subterráneas* – COTAS) have been established under the auspices of the *Comisión Nacional de Aguas* (CNA), to allow the participation of users, together with federal, state and local agencies, in the formulation and implementation of programmes and regulations for aquifer preservation and recovery. The establishment of these committees is not contemplated in the 1992 National Waters Act and, as a result, their legal status is unclear. The COTAS are consultative organizations, the decisions of which may – or may not – be taken into account by the CNA. Against this backdrop, in the state of Guanajuato, where groundwater overdraft is particularly severe, despite being in legal limbo the COTAS have been promoted with enthusiasm, and are considered as full-fledged users' organizations, covering all groundwater users and stakeholders within the aquifer.

Water User Groups (WUGs) for the management of water supply points, and Water User Associations grouping any number of WUGs, are regulated by Uganda's 1995 Water Statute. South Africa's 1998 National Water Act also provides for the formation of water user associations from among water users wishing to undertake water-related activities for their mutual benefit.

The thinking behind the establishment of river basin authorities and agencies responds, in part, to the same concern of having stakeholders take part in water-related decisionmaking. To this end, users and their interests are represented in the governmental organs which make up the structure of such authorities and agencies. Thus, for instance, under the 1999 amendments to the Water Act, Spain's River Basin Authorities (*Confederaciones hidrográficas*) include users' representatives in their decision-making and advisory organs. Similarly, users' representatives make up at least two-thirds of the total membership of the board of directors of France's Water Agencies (*Agences de l'eau*). They are also represented on the Agencies' advisory Basin Committees and Local Water Committees, which were created by the French 1992 Water Act as part of the water resources planning process at the level of sub-basins or groundwater aquifers.

Irrigators hold a minority of seats on the board of directors of Morocco's new Basin Authorities, which are being formed pursuant to the 1995 Water Act. In South Africa, water users and environmental interest groups will be represented in the decisionmaking structure of the new Catchment Management Agencies established under the new Water Act. A similar approach is reflected in Zimbabwe's 1998 Water Act, which provides for the establishment of Catchment and Sub-catchment Councils and for the representation of water users on them. In Mexico, amendments made in 1997 to the water legislation then in force have enabled the election of water users to the Lerma-Chapala Basin Council, which is a forum for coordination of the various interests at stake but does not have decisionmaking authority. Similar councils are being formed in other river basins of the country.

Under Brazil's 1997 federal Water Act, water users will be represented in the basin committees, alongside the representatives of civil society and of the federal, state and municipal governments concerned. The functions of such committees are akin to those of their Mexican counterparts. By contrast, the representation of water users in the basin committees provided for by the Australian state of South Australia's 1997 Water Act is not mandatory. However, users who possess the required professional qualifications and/or have a special knowledge of the area can be appointed to such committees, although in a personal capacity and not as representatives of any constituency.

3.7. Growing Attention to the Interface Between Statutory and Customary Water Rights

Customary law in many countries still plays an important role in water management, particularly at the community level. Customary water laws are rarely a single and unified body of norms, and vary widely from region to region, sometimes even between villages in the same region. Customary rules governing access to water have been documented in many countries, the best-known example being perhaps the allocation system of irrigation water and relevant water rights practised since time immemorial on the island of Bali, Indonesia. Another example of customary law is riparianism, which is or has been practised in a variety of forms in many common law countries.

Most recently, however, riparian rights have been increasingly replaced by statutory rights. For example, the post-Rio legislation of jurisdictions like Jamaica (1995), Uganda (1995), South Africa (1998), Zimbabwe (1998) and New South Wales (2000) adopts statutory water rights regarding the abstraction and use of water resources and eliminates ownership or possession of riparian land as a prerequisite to the claim and exercise of water abstraction rights.

Other countries fall along a wider spectrum. At one end, the Water Act (1974) and subsequent irrigation regulations (1982) of Indonesia openly acknowledge the traditional system of irrigation water allocation and rights practised in the island of Bali, and grant it equal dignity to the statutory allocation and rights system inaugurated by the legislation. In a similar vein, the 1998 Irrigation Law of Bolivia recognizes as *de facto* organizations water users' groups formed on the basis of customary norms. Draft legislation under consideration in Namibia, to replace the 1964 Water Act in force, does not privilege one over the other, but instead requires the government to take due account of existing customary practices and rights in granting statutory water use permits. The existence of such rights and practices not only enters the decisionmaking process leading to the grant or denial of a statutory right; it also attracts special terms and conditions to be entered in a grant of said statutory rights, for the specific purpose of protecting existing customary rights and practices. The legislation being mooted seeks to map out the scope of the interaction between statutory water rights and customary rights in general, and to minimize opportunities for conflict.

IV. CONCLUSION

What lies ahead on the agenda of water laws for the new century is the further refinement of water allocation mechanisms, which must strike a dynamic balance between equity and efficiency in allocation and use. Water allocation structures and policies must reflect the uncertainties of water availability under regulated and unregulated flow conditions, while at the same time they must take into account the security and dependability of water rights sought by users and investors. Another challenge is reconciling the development of water resources with conservation and with protection of the water quality of water bodies, not just for further use but also for the survival of water-dependent habitats.

Both these challenges call for the creative use of economic mechanisms, in addition and as a complement to robust regulation. Experience suggests that success is more likely where the laws promote the sharing of responsibility for difficult management decisions with those who stand to be affected the most by regulatory and non-regulatory water resources management mechanisms.

REFERENCES

Bogdanovic, S. 2001. *International Law of Water Resources - Contribution of the International Law Association (1954-2000).* Kluwer Law International, The Hague.

Burchi, S. 1994. *Preparing National Regulations for Water Resources Management - Principles and Practice,* Legislative Study No. 52, FAO, Rome.

Burchi, S. 2000. *Current Developments in Water Legislation,* 11 Water Law 3.

Burchi, S. 2001. *2001 Year-end Review of Comparative International Water Law Developments,* 12 Water Law 6.

Caponera, D. 1992. *Principles of Water Law and Administration - National and International.* A.A. Balkema, Rotterdam.

FAO. 1999. *Issues in Water Law Reform,* Legislative Study No. 67, Rome.

Garduño Velasco, H. 2001. *Water Rights Administration - Experience, Issues and Guidelines,* Legislative Study No. 70, FAO, Rome.

7

FISHERIES

Contents

I.   INTRODUCTION

Since Rio, the ecosystems dimensions of fisheries management have drawn increasing attention from national governments, the UN system and the fishing industry. In particular, UNCED recalled in Chapter 17 of Agenda 21 that the world's marine environment, including the oceans, seas and the adjacent coastal areas, "forms part of an integral whole that is an essential component of the global life-support system and a positive asset that presents opportunities for sustainable development".

FAO, in the State of World Fisheries and Aquaculture 2000, confirms this view, stating that:

> "fish are an integrated part of an aquatic ecosystem, a system in which modifications in one area have the potential to affect other areas. Thus, it is increasingly regarded as necessary, first to monitor the state of the aquatic ecosystem, and then to manage human interventions within that ecosystem. Only within such a framework will it be possible for capture fisheries to continue to be a source of food and income for future generations". (FAO, 2000)

The implication is that fisheries governance does not stop at regulating fishers and their gear or fish farmers and aquaculture facilities. Because capture fisheries or aquaculture activities often occur in water bodies such as lakes or in coastal marine areas which are influenced by other natural factors and are subject to other competing uses, fisheries and aquaculture need to be managed with these considerations in mind.

It is beyond the scope of this chapter to discuss competing uses of aquatic areas, zonal management including coastal zone management and related legislation. Only trends in legislation directly governing fisheries and aquaculture are addressed. This is preceded by a brief discussion of the international legal framework relating to fisheries management and aquaculture, due to the huge influence that this has on national legal frameworks. In this context, a brief explanation of the terms "fishery", "fisheries management" and "aquaculture" is required.

A fishery is characterized by the categories of people involved, species or type of fish, area of water or seabed, method of fishing, class of boats, purpose of the activities or a combination of the foregoing features. Fisheries management is "[t]he integrated process of information gathering, analysis, planning, consultation, decision-making, allocation of resources and formulation and implementation, with enforcement as necessary, of regulation or rules which govern fisheries activities in order to ensure the continued productivity of the resources and accomplishment of other fisheries objectives". (FAO, 1997) Aquaculture can be defined as the farming of aquatic organisms, and encompasses a wide range of aquatic farming processes differing by species, environment and systems used. Aquaculture farms can be land- or water-based and can be found in freshwater, brackish or marine (mariculture) environments. The sector involves a wide variety of issues such as land tenure, water use and water quality, but also health management, food safety, disease control and genetic engineering.

Fishery management approaches may differ according to the fisheries activities they seek to govern and may entail activity-specific laws or regulations. For example, an inland fishery is clearly distinguishable from a marine fishery, and capture fisheries is distinguishable from aquaculture. Legislation must respond to these individual characteristics, and the related legal issues vary dramatically.

II. INTERNATIONAL LEGAL FRAMEWORK

This section addresses trends in the international arena regarding fisheries governance and management. For reasons of space, it does not address regulation of fisheries by regional fisheries bodies, although they also can play an important role in initiating major trends in national legislation or in establishing specific conservation and management measures that will need implementation through national legislation.

2.1. Capture Fisheries

UNCED and its outcomes are said to be a new beginning for international lawmaking, marking the transition from international environment law and international economic law to an international law of sustainable development. (Boyle and Freestone, 1999) In respect of fisheries law, particularly marine capture fisheries, Chapter 17 of Agenda 21 calls on states "to pursue the protection and sustainable development of the marine and coastal environment and its resources" in accordance with the 1982 UN Convention of the Law of the Sea (1982 UN Convention).

After UNCED, the international community adopted a two-tiered approach to deal with the problems of over-fishing. The first was the negotiation of international agreements on specific marine fish stocks and high seas fishing, while the second, which had commenced prior to UNCED, was the development of soft law instruments for the conservation and management of fisheries. Soft law instruments include Chapter 17 of Agenda 21 itself and, most significant, a Code of Conduct for Responsible Fisheries (Code of Conduct), discussed below.

Chapter 17 called for an intergovernmental conference under the auspices of the United Nations to promote effective implementation of the 1982 UN Convention and to take effective action to deter re-flagging of fishing boats. Pursuant to this commitment, the UN Conference on Straddling Fish Stocks and Highly Migratory Fish Stocks in 1995 adopted the Agreement for the Implementation of the Provisions of the United Nations Convention of the Law of the Sea of 10 December 1982 Relating to the Conservation and Management of Straddling Fish Stocks and Highly Migratory Fish Stocks (UN Fish Stocks Agreement). At the same time, FAO was working on an agreement to reduce fishing on the high seas contrary to internationally agreed conservation and management measures. In November 1993, the FAO Conference adopted the Agreement to Promote Compliance with International Conservation and Management Measures by Fishing Vessels on the High Seas (Compliance Agreement).

In the meantime, a work plan had been developed in 1992 for the elaboration of a Code of Conduct for Responsible Fisheries. In the run-up to UNCED, a Conference on Responsible Fishing, held in Cancún, Mexico in May 1992, adopted the Cancún Declaration on Responsible Fishing, which called upon FAO to begin development of such a Code. The final text of the Code was adopted in November 1995. The Compliance Agreement was intended to be an integral part of the Code.

The Code of Conduct is intended to cover much more than marine fisheries and high seas fishing. (Edeson, 1996) FAO has produced non-legal technical guidelines to provide general advice in support of the implementation of the Code. These include guidelines on fishing operations; vessel monitoring systems; the precautionary approach to capture fisheries and species introduction; the integration of fisheries into coastal area management; fisheries management; conservation and management of sharks; aquaculture development; good aquaculture feed manufacturing practice; inland fisheries; responsible fish utilization; and indicators for sustainable development of marine capture fisheries.

The Code of Conduct was followed by four international plans of action developed under the auspices of FAO: the International Plan of Action for Reducing Incidental Catch of Seabirds in Longline Fisheries, the International Plan of Action for the Conservation and Management of Sharks, the International Plan of Action for the Management of Fishing Capacity and the International Plan of Action to Prevent, Deter and Eliminate Illegal, Unreported and Unregulated Fishing. Other important international fisheries instruments are the Rome Consensus on World Fisheries, the Rome Declaration on the Implementation of the Code of Conduct for Responsible Fisheries and the Kyoto Declaration and Plan of Action.

The influence of these international law developments and instruments on national legislation cannot be underestimated. Not only have they given impetus at the national level for practical implementation of environmental concepts such as sustainable development and the precautionary principle or precautionary approach in the field of fisheries, but states have also acted to give effect to specific provisions of international fisheries instruments, particularly the Compliance Agreement and the UN Fish Stocks Agreement. Both Agreements seek to enhance responsible fishing or conservation and sustainable use of living marine resources although they emphasize different means to that end.

The Compliance Agreement focuses on ensuring compliance with international conservation and management measures through effective use of flag state responsibility (i.e., ensuring that vessels do not fish on the high seas without authorization). The UN Fish Stocks Agreement reinforces flag state responsibility but emphasizes that conservation and management of straddling and highly migratory fish stocks shall be undertaken through cooperation facilitated largely by regional fisheries bodies (RFBs). This latter requirement, along with the further restriction that non-members of a fisheries management body shall not have access to the fishery resources to which the measures of that fishery management body apply, has had an extraordinary impact in fisheries conservation and management in restricting freedom of fishing on the high seas. (Freestone and Makuch, 1998)

The hard law and soft law instruments adopted in recent years influence and reinforce one another. The preambles of the two Agreements refer to Agenda 21 and to the issues identified in the Cancún Declaration. They also use the term "responsible fishing", which is clearly drawn from the Code of Conduct. Equally, soft law instruments such as the Code of

Conduct call on states to become parties to fisheries agreements and to implement them. These connections give a basis for using soft law instruments as aids to interpretation.

2.2. Aquaculture

Aquaculture is one of the fastest-growing food production systems in the world, and developing countries are the largest producers. Aquaculture offers a number of opportunities to contribute to poverty alleviation, employment, community development, reduction of over-exploitation of natural aquatic living resources and food security in tropical and sub-tropical regions. National legislative action on aquaculture, like capture fisheries, has been similarly influenced by international instruments and developments.

Soft law instruments important to aquaculture include the Kyoto Declaration on Aquaculture, the Bangkok Declaration and Strategy ("Aquaculture Development beyond 2000", adopted at the Bangkok Conference on Aquaculture in the Third Millennium), Chapters 15 and 17 of Agenda 21 and the Code of Conduct.

The first major international Conference on Aquaculture was held in Kyoto, Japan, in 1976. The resulting Kyoto Declaration on Aquaculture was the most important precursor to UNCED in aquaculture, focusing on technology and science, networking, training and institutional development. The Conference was a landmark event that raised awareness of the opportunities offered by, and constraints to, the development of aquaculture.

The Bangkok Conference on Aquaculture in the Third Millennium aimed to reassess the direction of aquaculture development and to propose strategies for sustainable development, with emphasis on regional and global cooperation. "Aquaculture Development Beyond 2000: the Bangkok Declaration and Strategy" is the major output of the Conference. The Declaration states that aquaculture should continue to develop towards its full potential and that policies and regulations should promote practical and economically viable farming and management practices that are environmentally responsible and socially acceptable. National aquaculture processes should be transparent and should take place within relevant national policies, regional and international agreements, treaties and conventions.

Another important soft law instrument is Agenda 21. Chapter 15 draws attention to the special importance of aquatic biological and genetic resources for food and agriculture. Chapter 17 points to aquaculture development as one of the ways forward for coastal states to "obtain the full social and economic benefits from sustainable utilization of marine living resources" in areas under national jurisdiction.

The Code of Conduct sets out principles and international standards with a view to ensuring the effective conservation, management and development of living aquatic resources, with due respect for ecosystems and biodiversity. Article 9.1.1 provides that "States should establish, maintain and develop an appropriate legal and administrative framework which facilitates the development of responsible aquaculture". Though mainly addressed to states, the Code calls upon all those involved in aquaculture to apply it. Governments and the private sector, including interest groups, aquaculture producers and farmers associations, should ensure an enabling environment for sustainable development of aquaculture.

In addition to the principles and guidelines contained in the afore-mentioned instruments, there are regional and technical guidelines that are being developed with a view to ensuring sustainable aquaculture. These include regional guidelines for aquaculture development prepared by the Southeast Asian Fisheries Development Centre; the "Asia Regional Technical Guidelines on Health Management for Responsible Movement of Live Aquatic Animals", developed under the Asia Pacific Regional Aquatic Animal Health Programme and the Beijing Consensus and Implementation Strategy; a supporting manual of procedures; and the "Asia Diagnostic Guide". In 1998, FAO organized the Bangkok Technical Consultation on Policies for Sustainable Shrimp Culture which was followed in 2002 by the FAO/Government of Australia Expert Consultation on Good Management Practices and Institutional and Legal Arrangements for Sustainable Shrimp Culture. The latter produced a set of legal and institutional arrangements for sustainable shrimp aquaculture, which were recommended for adoption by the FAO member states. These arrangements point to the need for a regulatory framework to support the development of sound aquaculture practices.

It is in the area of genetically modified organisms (GMOs) that one finds legally binding instruments of relevance to aquaculture. Globally, more than a dozen transgenic fish are being developed for aquaculture in developed countries. It seems likely that aquatic GMOs will soon be available for sale to consumers. The most significant international action regarding GMOs is the adoption of the Cartagena Protocol on Biosafety under the Convention on Biological Diversity. Its objective is to protect biological diversity from the potential risks posed by the transfer, handling and use of living modified organisms (LMOs) resulting from modern biotechnology. It contains reference to the precautionary approach and establishes an advance informed agreement procedure for ensuring that countries are provided with the information necessary to make informed decisions before agreeing to the import of such organisms into their territory.

Finally, as discussed in Chapter 3, the Agreement on Sanitary and Phytosanitary Measures (SPS Agreement) of the WTO recognizes the *Office international des épizooties* (OIE) as the relevant international organization responsible for the development and promotion of international animal health standards, guidelines and recommendations affecting trade in live animals and animal products. At present the OIE International Aquatic Animal Health Code is the only source of international standards recognized under the SPS Agreement for health certification requirements for international trade in fish and shellfish. Although OIE standards are not binding in themselves, countries that become members of the WTO are bound to follow international standards where they exist.

III. TRENDS IN NATIONAL LEGISLATION

3.1. Legislative Trends in Capture Fisheries

3.1.1. From Open Access to Limited Access

Over-fishing has led to the collapse of many of the worlds fisheries, in many instances because of the existence of open access regimes where the fisher chooses where and when to fish and how much fish to take. Such regimes were justified largely on the erroneous belief that the oceans and other water bodies hold infinite fish resources. In addition, the oceans, in particular the high seas, were *res communis* so that everyone had a right to fish and no one had ownership over the resource or the right to limit access. While many large areas of oceans are now subject to the jurisdiction of coastal states, and high seas fishing is subject to rights and obligations under the 1982 UN Convention, one may be surprised to find that many states have only recently begun to regulate domestic fishing or to consider stringent control over fishing.

In many Southeast Asian states located to the West of the South China Sea, for example, an individual has an unquestionable right to take to the sea to fish, provided that he or she complies with whatever requirements or regulation is in place. In Thailand, an act such as registration of a fishing vessel which is a prerequisite for entering the coastal marine fishery is a mere formality. In this situation, the fisheries management authority in general considers its role to be one in the service or support of fishers or for the promotion and development of fishing. In Tonga, fishing, particularly small-scale fishing, is considered a livelihood, and no licences have been issued for medium- to large-scale commercial fishing until recently. In many cases government regulation is seen as an unnecessary hindrance to the right to fish. However, the trend today is that governments are realizing that in order to ensure the long-term sustainability of fishery resources, the once open access regime for fishing can no longer continue. To this end, Thailand and Tonga, among others, are considering legislation which could make the right to fish subject to significant controls.

Given that it could still be a matter of opinion whether anyone has a right to fish in certain jurisdictions, governments like Iceland enacted fisheries legislation that attempts to clarify the issue as follows:

> "Marine resources that are found in Iceland waters and are utilized are the common property of the Icelandic nation. The purpose of this legislation is to ensure the preservation of and sensible utilization of these resources thereby guaranteeing full employment and stable settlement of the country. The issuing of fishing permits, in accordance with this legislation, does not constitute any claims to ownership or irrevocable claims by individual parties over fishing rights". (Law Concerning the Management of Fisheries of 1990)

Senegal makes a similar statement in its 1998 fisheries legislation.

Even countries that have never before regulated fisheries, such as Ethiopia, are considering new policies and legislation to properly manage the significant increase in fishery activities and to prevent over-exploitation. As a land-locked country, Ethiopia's fishery activities occur entirely in inland water bodies such as rivers, lakes and reservoirs. The proposed fisheries laws for Ethiopia set out the basic framework for fisheries management and contain many of the principles referred to above, including the precautionary approach.

Other jurisdictions have focused more on asserting the right of the government to manage fisheries resources. Thus Namibia recently stated in legislation that the management, protection and utilization of marine resources in Namibia and Namibian waters shall be subject to its Marine Resources Act of 2001. Cameroon and the Marshall Islands set out the right of the government to manage and control the fisheries resources in stronger terms. A similar approach, in the context of inland fisheries, can be found in Malawi's legislation.

3.1.2. Towards the Use of Property Rights

Related to the trend away from open access to limited access regimes is the move towards creating property rights in fisheries resources and the allocation of such rights. The move from an open access to a limited access regime is in essence a move from one form of administration of property rights to another.

A property rights regime can be a state property regime, private property regime or common (collective) property regime. The most universal is the state property regime, although most states do not commonly depend on "property" or know and administer it as such, but rather on the distribution of fishing rights on the basis of jurisdiction or sovereignty. In such a regime, the state is the custodian of the fishery resource and can decide to leave the resource to free use (open access), can choose to exploit the resource directly through its own agencies or can allot rights to citizens to exploit the resource. The most widely used and practical system of administering the last variant is that the state grants licences to individuals or groups to fish, and in this way controls access to the resources. At the other end of the scale is the common property regime whereby a local community instead of an individual holds exclusive rights to harvest fish in a certain geographical area. (Leria and Van Houtte, 2000)

The developments in Eastern Europe and the former Soviet Union illustrate the effects of the different property regimes. Before the shifts to market economies, fisheries were maintained at an almost constant level by centralized economic plans. However, during the transition period, the fisheries operated under an open access system which stimulated competition but at the same time increased the risk of over-exploitation of the stocks. Therefore, new fishing regulations have been established that set out fish licensing and catch quota regimes, to minimize the risk of collapse. For example, Lithuania enacted a Law on Fisheries in 2000.

Under the private property regime, normally the authorized user who has received a licence has a personal right to fish or harvest and such right is renewed regularly. More recently, licensing schemes have begun to permit the authorized user to sell or lease the right to fish. Such a property regime requires the setting of the total allowable catch (TAC) for a specific fishery, and establishes systems for allocation of the TAC, the transferability and leasability of the rights and the manner in which such rights can be enforced. Iceland has institutionalized the individual quota system in legislation, as has New Zealand. In Africa, Angola and Mozambique have legislative provisions that will enable the use of a property rights system in the future.

3.1.3. From Development to Sustainable Utilization

Fisheries management prior to Rio generally emphasized optimum utilization of fishery resources. In respect of marine capture fisheries, this perspective is reflected in the 1982 UN Convention, which calls on states to optimally utilize fisheries resources. Many fisheries management authorities at that time focused on building capacity or encouraging entry into the fisheries industry to increase fish production for individual profit, revenue generation or domestic consumption. Fisheries management was also an exclusive mandate, often devoid of considerations of the impact of fishing or fisheries activities on associated matters such as the environment. Conversely, other industries did not consider the impact of their activities on fisheries.

There has been a gradual shift in focus to a more "rounded" approach to fisheries management – one that not only ensures exploitation of the resource for economic gain, but also ensures that the resource is maintained at biologically, environmentally and economically sustainable levels. The shift in focus which has been forged in international fora is slowly becoming entrenched in domestic policy and eventually has found its way into legislation. A few examples demonstrate this. Whereas in the past the statement of purpose in fisheries legislation might refer to allocation of a quota levy, the development of fishery or the management of fishery, in recent times one sees an inclusion of a statement of principles and policy relating to sustainable utilization of fishery resources, as in Namibia, Nauru, New Zealand, Papua New Guinea and South Africa. For example, the Marine Resources Act of Namibia (2000) has as its purpose to "provide for the conservation of the marine ecosystem and the responsible utilization, conservation, protection and promotion of marine resources on a sustainable basis; for that purpose to provide for the exercise of control over marine resources; and to provide for matters connected therewith". The South Africa Marine Living Resources Act of 1998 has a similar provision.

While preambular provisions of a fisheries act are usually not enforceable, these statements of purpose are given effect in the law's operational provisions, i.e., in the mechanisms it establishes. More significantly, the strong reference in such laws to conservation of the ecosystem and to long-term sustainable utilization is important for it stamps them as very much of the new era of fisheries management. (Edeson, 1999b)

Similarly, management action was, in the past, based primarily on scientific (biological) information directly affecting the species or fish stock in question. Little or no consideration was given to the effect of fishing on species associated with or dependent on the target species or on the aquatic environment. National legislation now calls for the effects of fishing on non-target or associated species or the aquatic environment to be considered in determining the types of management measures that should apply in a fishery, and to what extent. Legislation that demonstrates this trend can be found in New Zealand and South Africa. Laws of other jurisdictions may not necessarily refer to environmental protection, as in New Zealand, or allow for environmental impact assessments, as in South Africa. Nevertheless, other management actions required under fisheries laws may have the effect of protecting the environment. Sustainable use of the fish stocks and the protection of the environment are now key elements in the recently developed legislation and institutions of Albania, Hungary, Lithuania and Romania.

A related and interesting feature is an increase in references to the precautionary approach or principle. Such references are viewed as an effort by states to give effect to international fisheries instruments or agreements, particularly principle 15 of the Rio Declaration, the UN Fish Stocks Agreement and the Code of Conduct. Even if the precautionary approach is only mentioned in a preambular provision or a broad policy statement and may at best be used only as an aid to interpretation, its significance should not be underestimated, for it "represents a major change in the traditional approach of fisheries management, which until recently has tended to react to management problems only after they reached crisis levels". (Freestone and Hey, 1996)

3.1.4. Improved Enforcement

As countries seek to ensure that only sustainable levels of fishing activity are allowed in zones under national jurisdiction, several innovative mechanisms and legislative approaches to fisheries monitoring, control and surveillance have emerged, in particular to curb illegal, unreported and unregulated (IUU) fishing.

(a)   Vessel Monitoring Systems

The use of satellite-based vessel monitoring systems (VMS) is a recent development in fisheries monitoring control and surveillance (MCS). VMS ensures that fishing vessels provide reports in real time. VMS can be seen as a direct response to IUU fishing, in particular fishing that is unreported due to problems with radio reporting systems and other conventional means of reporting vessel positions.

At this time, VMS is focused on position reporting, although other VMS information, namely, sighting reports, catch reports, notifications (entry/exit into the exclusive economic zone, port entry, etc.) and analyses, can also be generated by VMS. VMS is currently considered a complementary tool to conventional MCS tools such as sea and air reconnaissance. VMS is in use or in various stages of trial and implementation in many countries and by regional fishery bodies. In the case of one regional fishery body, the Forum Fishing Agency (FFA), the member countries that are mostly developing countries sought to overcome their individual limited resources for MCS by establishing a regional VMS.

The issues in the implementation of VMS which are dealt with in legislation are: requiring the installation of VMS components, namely automatic location communicators or vessel tracking units; protecting VMS components; ensuring confidentiality of VMS information; and using VMS information in fisheries enforcement in courts, particularly the admissibility of VMS information such as vessel positions. (Cacaud, 1998) Recent legislation on VMS in Europe, North America, Southern Africa and the South Pacific has sought to address these issues.

(b)   "Long-arm" Approach to Enforcement

Another mechanism that has emerged in fisheries law enforcement is a provision in national fisheries legislation commonly referred to as the

"Lacey Clause", from the Lacey Act of the United States. The provision extends the arm of the law, basically by making it unlawful to import fish that has been taken contrary to the laws of another country. (Kuemlangan, 2000) A common example of violation of the laws of another state is the taking of fish without a licence where such licence is required by that states' fisheries legislation.

A typical Lacey Act provision states that anyone who lands, imports, exports, transports, sells, receives, acquires or purchases any fish taken, transported or sold contrary to the law of another state is guilty of an offence and liable to a fine. Such a clause was first adopted in the FFA region by Papua New Guinea in 1994, followed by Nauru in 1997 and Solomon Islands in 1998. New Zealand has introduced in a recent amendment to its principal fisheries legislation a Lacey Act-type clause, which prohibits its nationals from fishing in another jurisdiction in contravention of that jurisdiction's laws. An interesting aspect of the New Zealand legislation is that the prerequisite element of bringing fish into the country is not necessary, although such extra-territoriality applies only to New Zealand nationals and vessels.

(c)   Alternatives to Criminal Proceedings

Despite innovative efforts such as enactment of Lacey Act clauses, enforcement of fisheries provisions through criminal laws and procedures has a number of drawbacks. There is a high standard of proof, and there may be difficulties in using evidence generated by VMS due to the hearsay rule. In many jurisdictions, extended delays plague the criminal law system. One solution, now applied in the United States, the FFA region and many civil law countries, is the adoption of civil and administrative processes and penalties for dealing with fisheries offences. (Kuemlangan, 2000) This approach presents the advantages of expedited proceedings, lower standards of proof, possibilities for negotiated settlements and hearings which do not necessarily follow strict rules of evidence. Civil penalty schemes for fisheries violations treat certain violations of fisheries laws as civil wrongs penalized by civil penalties, while the right of the offender to decide that he or she be tried under the normal judicial process is preserved.

While only a few countries have adopted administrative proceedings to deal with fisheries offences, many states in the Caribbean, Indian Ocean and South Pacific regions have adopted a system of compounding of offences in order to deal swiftly with fisheries violations. The main element of such a scheme is that instead of resort to traditional court proceedings, the person in whom powers to compound offences is vested (usually the Minister responsible for fisheries or the chief executive officer in the fisheries administration) decides to accept sums of money – usually not more than the maximum of fines allowed – from the offender if it is believed that an offence has been committed. Other requirements in more recent legislation are that offences may be compounded only with the consent of the alleged offender and that the Minister or chief executive officer may be empowered to release any article seized in relation to the offence. The offender retains the right to have the matter against him or her heard in normal judicial fora.

3.1.5. Requiring Fisheries Management Planning

Fisheries management planning involves the development of a plan which describes a particular fishery and its particular problems, the actors involved in the fishery and the objectives for the development of the fishery, and which outlines the measures for control of fishing to ensure the sustainable utilization of the fishery resource. The management plan may be linked to mechanisms that limit entry or restrict fishing. For example, some of the provisions might provide that a licence may be refused on the grounds that to issue it would undermine the objectives of a fishery plan. The fisheries management plan should be developed with input of technical experts, and provisions should be included to monitor its implementation.

For many countries, the development of a fishery plan used to be an administrative process and the prerogative of the fisheries management authority. In such countries, fishery management planning was a good management technique but not a mandatory requirement. In recent years, however, more countries have embraced the management planning concept and have eventually required the development of fishery plans in legislation. The Australian state of Queensland prescribed the development and implementation of management plans for the state's major fisheries in legislation in 1994. Papua New Guinea first introduced the use of fishery plans in the same year. Nauru introduced its version of fishery plans, the "fisheries strategy", in 1997. Solomon Islands legislatively introduced fishery management and development plans for the first time in 1998. Malawi and Senegal also legislatively introduced fisheries management plans in legislation in 1997 and 1998, respectively. These are but a few of the many countries that have adopted the use of fishery plans in fisheries management in the last decade.

3.1.6. Increased Participation and Devolution of Functions

National fisheries management, like many natural resource management regimes, heavily concentrated management authority in the central (national) government or its agencies. In recent years, however, the effectiveness of these top-down management approaches has been questioned. The main criticisms include: (a) the lack of consultation with stakeholders or with the regulated, which results in the lack of a legitimate basis for regulations or management measures and, consequently, non-compliance; (b) implementation and enforcement in such systems relies heavily on adequate technical capacity and other resources, of which there are never enough, thus adding to the high rate of non-compliance; and (c) resource users do not appreciate that the sustainable use of the fisheries resources is vital to their livelihood or the nation's economy because they do not feel part of or "owners of" the management process and measures.

Recent legislation has expanded the scope of involvement of stakeholders so that there is broader participation both at the decisionmaking and implementation levels. The expansion of involvement of stakeholders has been in three main areas: (i) consultation, whereby the management authorities solicit the views of persons who are interested in or could be affected by the management decision, so that their views can confirm or cause an amendment to the proposed management decision or regulation as appropriate; (ii) formal representation of stakeholders on consultative, advisory or decisionmaking institutions within the fisheries management framework; and (iii) devolution of management or implementation powers, or both, to lower-level governments and stakeholder communities or groups. Examples of the expansion of participation in the consultation process can be found in the fisheries legislation of Barbados, New Zealand and the Philippines. In the context of fisheries management plans, it is argued that the participation of stakeholders in the preparation of such plans increases the opportunity for their effective implementation.

Broad participation through formally established institutions is a more common practice than participation through direct consultation or devolution of powers. Barbados and Mauritius facilitate such participation through Advisory Committees, whereas Malawi has an Advisory Board and South Africa has Consultative Advisory Forums. In formerly communist regimes, Albania established Central and Local Consultative Commissions whereas Lithuania has a Fisheries Board.

Participation of stakeholders by means of the third approach (i.e., devolution of powers) is a more progressive form of participation in fisheries management compared to the other two. It is also the most difficult to institutionalize because it involves laws relating to political governance which may implicate the constitution or other fundamental laws on governance or decentralization. Nevertheless, recognition of the important role to be played by communities whose livelihoods depend on fishing, and transfer of fishery management functions to such communities or to lower-level governments, has been slowly gaining popularity (as well as controversy) over the last decade. Canada, New Zealand and the United States, which have been negotiating with native or aboriginal communities for years, have developed schemes to recognize or give deference to native rights to fish or manage fisheries. In Japan, fisheries cooperatives have enjoyed some form of exclusivity in fishing and management over coastal resources falling within their domain.

The Philippines has been a leader in the developing world in the devolution of fisheries management powers. The government formalized the decentralization of fisheries management powers to municipalities in 1991 through legislation and consolidated it in subsequent legislation in 1998. In the Marshall Islands, Local Government Councils are responsible for the management, development and sustainable use of the reef and in-shore fisheries, extending up to five miles seaward from the baseline from which the territorial sea is measured.

A variant of devolution regimes is co-management, as seen in Malawi. There, since 1993, participatory fisheries management programmes have been introduced whereby local-level institutions and the Department of Fisheries jointly make decisions. This scheme has replaced the former centralized management system.

3.1.7. Food Safety Regulation for Fish and Fish Products

In many developing countries, seafood exports are an important source of revenue and there is growing interest in government policies and practice relating to fish and fish product exports. Although food safety is generally the purview of ministries or agencies concerned with food and human health (see Chapter 2), in some countries government may decide that seafood safety is best regulated by the authorities responsible for the fisheries sector, and this may require legislative action.

Food safety issues affect fisheries particularly in the post-harvest sector. The main trend is the introduction of the Hazard Analysis and Critical Control Point (HACCP) system into the European Union (EU) and the United States, and its recognition as a food safety assurance mechanism by Codex Alimentarius. The EU and the United States have both made fish and fishery products the first category of foods in the food industry subject to mandatory application of HACCP systems. The EU issued the first regulation for fish products "laying down the health conditions for the production and the placing on the market of fishery products" in 1991 (Directive 91/493). In May 1994, the EU adopted an additional regulation which made it mandatory to impose more precise rules for the application of health checks. The United States adopted a seafood HACCP regulation, Procedures for the Safe and Sanitary Processing and Importing of Fish and Fishery Products, in December 1997.

These developments have caused the major seafood-exporting countries to adopt or meet the standards established by the importing countries. For example, Namibia and South Africa, which have significant exports to the EU, require that seafood processors and exporters meet Directive 91/493. The directive concerns both domestic (EU) and third country (non-EU) production. It defines EU standards for handling, processing, storing and transporting fish. It must be noted that processed bivalve molluscs (as well as tunicates, marine gastropods and echinoderms) are subject to both Directive 91/492 and Directive 91/493. Directive 91/493 lays down rules on conditions applicable to factory vessels, on-shore plants, packaging, storage and transport. Provisions that may require more details are set concerning auto-controls, parasites (all visible parasites must be removed), organoleptic, chemical and microbiological checks. National authorities responsible for standards, food safety and fisheries management are also charged with encouraging exporters to meet HACCP and ISO 9000 standards and guidelines, with the ultimate objective of formally adopting these systems through regulation.

In Tonga, seafood exporters to the United States have taken it upon themselves to implement HACCP and other applicable requirements of the seafood safety regulations administered by the U.S. Food and Drug Administration. It is a matter of Tonga government policy that regulations for the processing of seafood and a certification system for seafood exports are to be introduced soon. To this end, draft seafood safety regulations are currently under consideration for promulgation under the principal fisheries legislation. The United Republic of Tanzania is one of the few countries to adopt regulations (the Fish Quality Control and Standards Regulations of 2000) to specifically implement HACCP.

3.1.8. Legislative Implementation of International Fisheries Instruments

The 1993 FAO Compliance Agreement and the 1995 UN Fish Stocks Agreement address the nature of state obligations at the international level; both agreements seek to define with a degree of specificity which is unusual in global fisheries agreements the precise ways in which state parties should meet those obligations. Implementing legislation will be necessary in most countries to meet these requirements as a precondition to state ratification or acceptance. This will usually call for new legislation, although, depending on the legislation already in place, some countries may be able to implement the Agreements through changes to current legislation or through subsidiary legislation.

(a) Compliance Agreement

The Compliance Agreement reinforces the effectiveness of international fisheries conservation and management measures by redefining and reinforcing the concept of flag state responsibility for the activities of fishing vessels flying the flag of a state party. It also seeks to provide means to ensure the free flow of information on all high seas fishing operations. (Moore, 1995) The agreement requires the following issues to be implemented in the national legislation of its parties:

- designation of the national authority responsible for carrying out the duties of the flag state under the agreement;
- provisions that make it unlawful for flag vessels to undermine the effectiveness of international conservation and management measures, and that provide a mechanism for authorities to ensure that the law is respected;
- mandatory fishing authorizations for flag vessels fishing on the high seas;
- mandatory conditions for flag vessels receiving a fishing authorization;
- proper marking of fishing vessels;
- information on fishing operations;
- enforcement measures and sanctions;
- establishment and maintenance of records of flag vessels fishing on the high seas;

- duties of the flag state to provide FAO with information.

The Compliance Agreement has not yet entered into force but the parties to the agreement have started to give effect to it through legislation. At the time of writing, the following countries had enacted legislation or made amendments to existing legislation to implement the provisions of the agreement: Australia, Canada, Namibia, New Zealand, Norway, Seychelles, South Africa, Saint Vincent and the Grenadines and the United States. The style with which these countries have legislated on the essential components of the Compliance Agreement, and the scope of their legislative action, varies as the countries attempt to reflect their national situations and respond to their particular needs. Time does not permit an examination of the details of these national efforts, although it can be said that these countries have clearly charted the general approach on how to incorporate the requirements of the agreement into national legislation. (Edeson, Freestone and Gudmunsdottir, 2001)

(b)   UN Fish Stocks Agreement

The UN Fish Stocks Agreement entered into force in December 2001. The main elements that need legislative implementation are:

- Coastal states and distant water fishing states are required to ensure that the conservation and management measures which are created within the exclusive economic zone (EEZ) and on the high seas are compatible.
- Parties to the agreement are to apply general principles for the conservation and management of straddling fish stocks and highly migratory fish stocks, including the precautionary approach, on the high seas as well as within their EEZ.
- Flag states must meet certain obligations with respect to their vessels fishing on the high seas for straddling fish stocks and highly migratory fish stocks.
- State parties are obliged to join regional fisheries management organizations or arrangements, or to agree to comply with the conservation and management measures those bodies create. Otherwise they will not be allowed to fish in the areas where such measures apply.
- Non-flag states are subject to innovative enforcement provisions, and a new concept of port-state jurisdiction in respect of fishing vessels applies.

- States will have to apply detailed provisions on peaceful dispute settlement.

The agreement is complex and therefore difficult for states to legislate on. Nevertheless, a number of countries have enacted legislation to implement it, namely: Australia, Canada, Iceland, Namibia, New Zealand, Norway, Seychelles, South Africa, Saint Vincent and the Grenadines and the United States. In most cases, both the Compliance Agreement and the UN Fish Stocks Agreement are implemented through the same legislation, as in New Zealand. (Edeson, Freestone and Gudmunsdottir, 2001)

3.2. Legislative Trends in Aquaculture

Aquaculture is affected by a variety of issues and hence regulated under a wide range of legislation. Studying the legal regime of a particular country involves paying attention to laws and regulations dealing with various topics such as the use of freshwater, environmental issues, food safety, fish health and land tenure. Many of the issues and concerns involved are not unique to aquaculture and may be regulated in a more general legislative regime. In addition, many of the laws and regulations in place today were not even developed with aquaculture in mind and thus are often applied to the sector in an inconsistent manner. Conflicts may arise within the range of legislation applicable to aquaculture or among the agencies and institutes involved.

The rapid and largely unregulated expansion of the aquaculture industry has caused and is causing significant environmental damage, and governments are increasingly recognizing that uncertain and inappropriate legislative arrangements are seriously hindering the sustainable development of the sector. Despite the limitations outlined above, aquaculture laws and regulations across the globe have developed some commonality in terms of approach and the required minimum elements for their sound management. The following discussion highlights the most significant trends and initiatives in national aquaculture legislation in recent years.

3.2.1. New Legal Frameworks for the Control of Aquaculture

Over the last decade, aquaculture has become increasingly subject to legislative control in a variety of countries. The way in which national legislation deals with aquaculture, however, still varies significantly. For example, much of the independent Pacific Islands still lack any specific rules on aquaculture in their legislation, but many nowadays include a statement about aquaculture in national policy and development plans. Other countries have simply included a reference to aquaculture in a traditional "enabling clause" in their basic fisheries legislation, without detailed criteria for setting up or operating an aquaculture establishment. Some basic fisheries laws provide for the adoption of a separate aquaculture regulation, which in many cases has not yet been developed.

A recent example of a basic law simply authorizing future regulation on aquaculture is the fisheries legislation of Sierra Leone, which states that the Director of Fisheries may issue licences for aquaculture operations "in such form and in accordance with such requirements as may be prescribed". (Fisheries (Management and Development) Decree of 1994) The Republic of Congo's fisheries legislation of 2000 has similar provisions.

Due to the pressure of the expanding industry, however, there is a noticeable tendency to regulate and control the aquaculture sector more thoroughly. In fact, many of the recently adopted fisheries laws deal with certain aspects of aquaculture. In some cases the fisheries and aquaculture sectors are even mentioned side by side, indicating that the legislature attaches a similar importance to both sectors. Examples include Madagascar (Fisheries and Aquaculture Ordinance of 1993), Albania (Law on Fishery and Aquaculture of 1995), Burkina Faso (Forestry Code of 1997), Malawi (Fisheries Act of 1997) and Costa Rica and Guatemala, which are currently in the process of drafting new fisheries laws that include specific provisions on aquaculture.

Eritrea's Fisheries Proclamation of 1998 is a typical example with more detailed provisions regulating aquaculture, providing that no person shall culture fish or other aquatic organisms except by authorization; no applicants shall be granted authorization unless they meet certain criteria; authorization is granted subject to specified terms and conditions; and activities may be suspended or terminated where such conditions are violated. The rights of the operator of the aquaculture facility are to be protected. Similar legislation is under consideration for enactment in Tonga, to ensure that aquaculture is better controlled.

Many countries have not enacted complete aquaculture legislative texts but have simply enacted specific provisions to deal with specific issues. Such countries are often responding to a precise and urgent need, and methodical preparation and enactment of comprehensive legislation may not be feasible at the time. For example, aquaculture-exporting countries have increasingly been forced to adopt food security laws to comply with the quality standards required by importing countries. Other countries may enact specific provisions to protect their mangroves, which are often intensively cut to facilitate aquaculture operations. Thus, in 1995 Ecuador elaborated regulations on the conservation, management, use and development of mangroves. (*Reglamento para la ordenación, conservación, manejo y aprovechamiento del manglar*) Likewise, Guatemala (*Reglamento para el aprovechamiento del manglar*, 1998), Mozambique (under the Forestry and Wildlife Act of 1999) and Costa Rica (*Permisos de uso en áreas de manglar*, 2001) responded to this specific need.

Although some of the regulations referred to above may provide useful building blocks for modern aquaculture legislation, they are only part of the legislation necessary for the sustainable development of the sector. Increasingly it is being recognized that issues such as registration and access, planning and management and the many environmental impacts of aquaculture should be dealt with in a more consistent manner in order to protect the industry, the environment, other resource users and consumers. There is a growing interest in developing and setting up comprehensive regulatory frameworks related to aquaculture, the importance of which was emphasized in article 9.1.1 of the Code of Conduct: "States should establish, maintain and develop an appropriate legal and administrative framework, which facilitates the development of responsible aquaculture".

The need for such legal framework has been recognized by countries that have become farmed-shrimp producers, such as the Philippines. Its Fisheries Code of 1998 provides for the development, management and conservation of fisheries and aquatic resources and includes a range of issues such as the use of public lands, leasing of fishponds, the establishment of an aquaculture Code of Practice, incentives and disincentives for sustainable aquaculture practices and the establishment of an Aquaculture Investment Fund. Similar efforts have been made in Sri Lanka (Fisheries and Aquatic Resources Act of 1996 and Aquaculture Management Regulations of 1996). Mozambique adopted an extensive Aquaculture Regulation in 2001 that regulates access to aquaculture and the protection of the environment, among other matters. Other countries that are currently in the process of drafting and discussing a specific set of rules for aquaculture include Cyprus and Suriname.

In Chile the *Ley general de pesca y acuicultura* of 1989 (amended in 1991) has provided the necessary building blocks for a modern aquaculture law. Over the last decade this law has been implemented by a number of government decrees and resolutions relating to aquaculture issues. Similar efforts have also been made in Mexico (*Ley de pesca*, 1992) and Peru (*Ley general de pesca*, 1992 and *Ley de promoción y desarrollo de la acuicultura*, 2001). The basic objective of the Peruvian legislation is to optimize the economic benefits of aquaculture in harmony with the preservation and conservation of biodiversity. A comprehensive approach is also pursued in the 1995 Aquaculture (Regulation) Act of the Indian state of Tamil Nadu.

Drafting comprehensive legal frameworks for aquaculture is not limited to developing countries. Certain Australian states have promulgated comprehensive legal frameworks, such as Tasmania (Marine Farming Planning Act of 1995; Living Marine Resources Management Act of 1995) and New South Wales (Fisheries Management Act of 1994; Fisheries Management (Aquaculture) Regulation of 1995). Other countries that are currently discussing revision of their aquaculture legislation include the United States, where a bill was introduced in 1995 to amend the National Aquaculture Act of 1980, and Canada, where a Legislative and Regulatory Review of Aquaculture was published in 2001. The Government of New Zealand published a discussion document in 2000 that recognizes that the law governing aquaculture (the Marine Farming Act of 1971) is out of date and that a new legal framework is needed to provide more certainty to everyone involved in the industry.

3.2.2. Aquaculture and Sustainable Development

Particular emphasis is nowadays placed on developing an aquaculture industry that is environmentally and economically sustainable. For example, in India the Guidelines for Sustainable Development and Management of Brackish Water Aquaculture of 1995 recognize the need for measures for sustainable aquaculture development and the need to reduce or eliminate the environmental impacts of the industry. The guidelines refer to experiences in other countries where intensive shrimp farming has led to environmental degradation and subsequent threats to the long-term sustainability of the industry. Similarly, under the Philippines' Fisheries Code of 1998, a Code of Practice for aquaculture will outline principles and guidelines to promote the sustainable development of the industry. Similar statements as to the concept of sustainable development can be found in other recent laws such as the

2001 Peruvian aquaculture law, and in recent government policies and programmes, such as Mexico's *Programa de Pesca y Acuacultura* of 1995–2000 and Viet Nam's Aquaculture Development Programme for 1999–2010.

In 2000 the Federation of European Aquaculture Producers (FEAP), which is currently composed of twenty-six national aquaculture producer associations from twenty-two European countries, adopted a Code of Conduct for European Aquaculture. The Code is intended to assist with the development of policies to achieve environmental, economic and social sustainability of the aquaculture production sector. It states that individuals, cooperatives and companies that engage in aquaculture shall consult and collaborate with European, regional and national authorities for the development and implementation of policies, practices and regulations.

3.2.3. Coastal Aquaculture as Part of Integrated Coastal Management

Aquaculture is dependent upon the use of limited natural resources such as land and water. Due to economic development and population growth, these resources are becoming increasingly scarce and aquaculture currently faces serious competition from other resource users.

Conflicts over the allocation and sharing of natural resources have already taken place and are likely to become more frequent in future. For example, in India several large corporations entered the aquaculture sector in the late 1980s. In 1991 the Indian Government issued the Coastal Regulation Zone Notification SO 114(E), which prohibits setting up new industries or expanding existing ones within the coastal zones. Local fishers protested, but in 1996 the Indian Supreme Court issued a final judgment affirming the Notification, thereby banning all non-traditional aquaculture within 500 m of the high water mark. To deal with the new situation the government constituted an Aquaculture Authority to ensure the closure, demolition and removal of non-traditional aquaculture activities by 1997. In practice, however, demolition has been limited and the situation remains uncertain.

In order to balance the diversity of interests involved in aquaculture there is a tendency to base future developments on integrated coastal management plans. Governments recognize that choices need to be made in advance among the different resource uses taking into account their individual and combined impacts on the environment. Long-term planning also provides the predictability that is required for investment and reduces the possibility of conflicts among actual and potential users. However, integrated coastal area management is not specific to aquaculture and is therefore often regulated in basic environmental laws, such as the 1994 National Environment Management Act of the Gambia and the 1994 Environment Protection Act of Seychelles. More specific legislation addressing coastal area management can be found in countries like Estonia (Law on the Protection of Marine and Freshwater Coasts, Shores and Banks of 1995) and Barbados (Coastal Zone Management Act of 1998).

The idea of integrating the aquaculture sector into coastal area management is gradually gaining ground and has now been implemented in legislation in some cases. For example, the Coastal Zone Management Act of 1998 of Belize specifically includes aquaculture proposals that should be dealt with in Coastal Zone Management Plans. Besides that, an Advisory Council is to be established whose members may include persons with competence and experience in aquaculture. Chapter 1 of the Philippines' Fisheries Code of 1998 declares that it will be state policy to "manage fishery and aquatic resources, in a manner consistent with the concept of an integrated coastal area management in specific natural fishery management areas, appropriately supported by research, technical services and guidance provided by the State".

There are a number of tools to integrate aquaculture into coastal areas, such as the use of EIAs, the creation of protected areas, restrictions on private ownership or the recognition of indigenous rights. One of the most important tools is zoning, whereby land and water areas are set aside for certain types of aquaculture. The Chilean *Ley general de pesca y acuicultura* of 1989 defines particular zones in the coastal area for the exercise of aquaculture. Outside these areas aquaculture activities are forbidden. Another example of zoning can be found in the Tasmanian Marine Farming Planning Act of 1995, which provides for the designation of so-called Marine Farming Development Plans of areas where marine farming may occur. The Plans are developed following a process of public consultation that takes account of the physical suitability of potential aquaculture sites, the current legal situation and the desire to minimize impacts on other users of the coastal zone.

3.2.4. Towards Coordinated Authorization Processes

A major feature of aquaculture legislation is the use of government authorizations to exercise control over aquaculture establishments. Authorizations can take the form of a licence, permit, concession or lease and are commonly subject to certain conditions. They constitute a good basis for governments to regulate the limited natural resources available and allow governments to integrate the siting of aquaculture farms within their integrated coastal management plans. Authorizations are also useful for controlling the environmental effects of aquaculture operations, often through the requirement of an EIA.

Authorization procedures may be required during different stages of the aquaculture process. A licence is commonly obligatory before setting up an aquaculture establishment, but in many cases additional licensing requirements may be imposed to regulate the actual operation of an aquaculture farm. Malaysia, for example, requires the aquaculturist to apply for a licence to operate the system following its construction (Fisheries Act of 1995 and the Fisheries (Marine Culture System) Regulations of 1991).

The authorization process can be a complicated affair for the aquaculturist, since the approval and operation of an aquaculture project involve a variety of laws and agencies. This is particularly the case when access to public land and water is involved. Not only are fishery or aquaculture authorities implicated, but also land use planning institutions, water institutes, health agencies and environmental protection authorities. Usually a number of documents are needed before an applicant may establish or operate an aquaculture farm, such as land concessions, water licences, effluent discharge permits and other types of environmental licences. The challenge in aquaculture law now is to remove existing legal and bureaucratic obstacles and to increase the cost-effectiveness of aquaculture operations. The trend is toward the unification of licensing requirements and the streamlining of approval procedures through the creation of a single or lead aquaculture agency which controls the application process.

The initiatives that have been taken over the years to streamline application procedures are promising. For example, in Chile one single application for aquaculture activities is required under the *Reglamento de concesiones y autorizaciones de acuicultura* of 1993, and in Albania a single aquaculture licence is issued by a board constituted by representatives of the Committee of Environmental Protection and other ministries concerned (Law on Fishery and Aquaculture of 1995 and its Regulation of 1997). In Mexico, a special office for aquaculture development handles all the required permits, concessions and authorizations for establishing an aquaculture farm (Fisheries Law of 1992 and its Regulation, modified in 1999).

In the U.S. state of Florida, an Aquaculture Permitting Section has been created within the Department of Environmental Protection that is working to consolidate permits, licences and other regulatory requirements, which will allow the aquaculturist to submit a single application and pay a single fee for any marine aquaculture activity (1996 Florida Laws (Ch. 96.247)). Finland has introduced a new permit system in the Environmental Protection Act of 2000, according to which all fish farm impacts (including water, waste and health) will be evaluated as a whole. In Malta the issuance of an aquaculture permit follows joint consultation by the Director of Fisheries, the Chairman of the Malta Maritime Authority and the Chairman of the Planning Authority (Fisheries Conservation and Management Act of 2001).

3.2.5. Increasing Environmental Restrictions

There is growing concern about the environmental impacts of aquaculture activities, given the degree of ecological hazard that can be involved. Environmental concerns increasingly form a part of licensing procedures, from the potential environmental impacts of establishing an aquaculture activity to the impacts that arise through the actual operation of an aquaculture farm. Environmental legislation related to aquaculture has become more stringent over the years.

(a) Environmental Impact Assessments

In order to prevent environmentally unsustainable developments, Environmental Impact Assessments (EIAs) are increasingly required before aquaculture farms may be established or operated. Submission to an EIA is usually a precondition for the issuance of a general aquaculture licence, and the EIA addresses various factors such as the proposed size of the aquaculture farm and the sensitivity of the area involved. In developed countries it is now routine to make use of EIAs, and the procedures are generally laid down in exhaustive detail. For example, intensive fish farming is one of the categories subject to an assessment of possible environmental impacts under EU Directive 85/337/EEC on

Water Quality, updated by Directive 92/43/EEC. A further amending Directive 97/11/EC has extended application to intensive farming of all marine finfish, in effect from March 1999.

Developing countries also increasingly subject aquaculture activities to an EIA, usually in basic environmental laws. The 1994 National Environment Act of the Gambia and the 1994 Environment Protection Act of the Seychelles contain detailed regulations on carrying out an EIA before initiating aquaculture projects in sensitive areas. Likewise, the 1997 Environment Protection Act of Mozambique requires an environmental licence and mandatory EIA for marine and fresh water aquaculture projects.

In some cases reference to the requirement of EIA is made in a specific fisheries or aquaculture text. For example, the 1996 Aquaculture Management Regulations of Sri Lanka require the performance of an EIA (based on the National Environment Act), while some other countries have developed special guidelines relating to EIA for aquaculture operations, such as the United Republic of Tanzania and – with particular attention to shrimp farms – Viet Nam. The 1998 Fisheries and Marine Resources Act of Mauritius also has such a specific requirement.

(b) Chemicals

The overuse and misuse of chemicals in the aquaculture industry, causing pollution and contamination of the aquatic environment, is an area of growing concern. A particular problem is that the expanding aquaculture industry has adopted chemicals originally developed for use in other sectors, most notably the agricultural sector. In addition, aquaculture farms are extremely vulnerable to poor water quality, and the improper use of chemicals can negatively affect the quality of the aquaculture product and subsequently harm human health. While the overriding consideration should be minimizing the use of chemicals in aquaculture, it is recognized that some chemicals are needed.

Chemical contamination is basically controlled legislatively in two ways. The first concerns direct prohibitions or restrictions on the use of specific chemicals that are harmful to the environment. The use, import, distribution or sale of particular hazardous chemicals can be made a criminal offence, while such activities in relation to less dangerous chemicals can be made subject to authorization schemes and licensing requirements. Generally, this type of control legislation is not formulated exclusively in relation to aquaculture farming, but is found in basic environmental laws or more specific acts related to the use of chemicals. In some cases lists of chemicals that can be used in aquaculture have been set up, including rules on how these chemicals have to be used, for example in China, Malaysia, Sri Lanka, Thailand and Viet Nam.

The second tool to regulate chemicals in the environment consists of a system of wastewater discharge licensing. Again, such licences are in most instances likely to be regulated under the same general environmental or water legislation. However, the Australian Great Barrier Reef Marine Park (Aquaculture) Regulations of 2000 specifically regulate the discharge of waste from aquaculture operations which may affect animals and plants in the Great Barrier Reef Marine Park.

(c)   Introduction and Movement of Species

One of the potentially serious effects of aquaculture on the environment is the introduction of exotic species into environments where they may compete with, or replace, native species. Such introductions are generally unintended, though some can also be the result of deliberate actions such as sea ranching (see section 3.2.8.). As a result, countries have increasingly introduced legislation that prohibits the introduction of non-indigenous species or limits the movement of fish and other aquatic organisms. For example, in Peru the 2001 *Ley de promoción y desarrollo de la acuicultura* contains a provision on the introduction of new species in order to protect the ecosystem. Some of these restrictions are also justified by the desire to prevent the spread of diseases. (See section 3.2.6.)

Special attention is being given to GMOs. Primarily, restrictions incorporate a precautionary approach towards the introduction and release of GMOs for the purpose of prevention of environmental harms. Illustrative is the Federation of European Aquaculture Producers (FEAP) statement in its Code of Conduct for European Aquaculture that it does not endorse the use of GM fish in aquaculture since it is concerned about the maintenance of natural characteristics and biodiversity. However, because genetic research may play an important role in future global food production, this position may be reviewed "if such developments are acceptable to the consumer and do not pose any safety or environmental problems". (FEAP Code, art. B.2.a)

In many developed countries stringent legislation on the introduction and use of GMOs has now been adopted. In the European Union, for example,

Directive 90/219/EEC addresses the contained use of GM micro-organisms, whereas Directive 90/220/EEC governs the deliberate release of GMOs into the environment. In addition, Regulation 258/97 on Novel Foods and Novel Food Ingredients establishes that labelling is mandatory for food products containing GMOs, where authorization was granted after 1997 under Directive 90/220/EEC. Other examples include Norway's Gene Technology Act of 1993, Chile's biosecurity regulations of 1999 and Australia's Gene Technology Bill of 2000.

Although there is widespread concern in developing countries about the need to regulate GMOs, only a few specific regulations have been adopted so far in this area. In some countries the issue is considered to be sufficiently addressed by existing legislation on the introduction and movement of fish and other aquatic products. In others, strict regulations related to the use of GMOs in aquaculture do exist. In the Philippines, for example, a National Committee of Biosafety identifies and evaluates potential hazards before introduction, and the 2001 Aquaculture Regulation of Mozambique contains a special provision on genetic manipulation.

3.2.6. Preventing Fish Diseases

Increasingly, disease outbreaks are being recognized as a major problem for the aquaculture industry, affecting trade, production and economic and social development. These can be prevented through restrictions on the introduction and movement of fish and other aquatic products.

In the European Union, Directive 91/67/EEC (as amended) on the marketing of aquaculture animals and products seeks to secure the free movement of fish for aquaculture purposes, but also imposes restrictions for the purpose of preventing the spread of disease. In Norway, the 1997 Act to Prescribe Measures in respect of Fish and Other Aquatic Animal Disease has as its objectives to prevent, reduce and eliminate infectious diseases in fish and other aquatic animals. The Act is implemented by numerous decrees, including one on control and supervision measures, and others on the disinfection and cleaning of aquaculture facilities and the disinfection of water flowing into and out of aquaculture-related operations. Recent legislation in Japan is also aimed at preventing the spread of fish disease via imports of marine animals for use in aquaculture or propagation of stocks (Law to Partially Amend the Law on the Protection of Fishery Resources, 1996).

Increasing attention to the control of disease can be seen in the fisheries legislation of developing countries as well. In the Eritrea Fisheries Proclamation of 1998, the prevention of the spread of disease and the protection of the quality of aquatic organisms is one of the main reasons to suspend the operation of or close aquaculture facilities. Honduras adopted new fish disease regulations (*Reglamento de salud pesquera y acuícola, 2000*), and in Peru the 2001 *Ley de promoción y desarrollo de la acuicultura* contains a provision on disease control. Mauritius also has provisions on control of fish diseases in the Fisheries and Marine Resources Act of 1998.

Another noteworthy initiative is the Australian National Strategic Plan for Aquatic Animal Health 1998-2003 (Aquaplan), which is intended to assist in the development of a national approach to emergency preparedness and response, and to the overall management of aquatic animal health. This comprehensive strategy is to be jointly developed by government and industry consistent with existing health management arrangements. Key programmes of the Aquaplan consist of quarantine, surveillance, monitoring, reporting, research and development, as well as law and policy.

3.2.7. Food Safety and Health Issues

Similar to the case of capture fisheries, HACCP has increasingly been incorporated in the aquaculture legislation of many importing countries of aquaculture products. As noted, the United States and many countries of the EU are at the forefront of such legislative developments. In addition, in 1999 the Russian Federation adopted new veterinary and sanitary requirements regarding the import of fish and aquaculture products. Specific legislation on the safety of fish and aquaculture products can also be found in Pakistan (Fish Inspection and Quality Control Act of 1997).

While the implementation of safety assurance systems in exporting countries may be well advanced in the fish-processing sector, the application and enforcement of such systems at aquaculture farm level is relatively new. The 1998 Fishery Products (Export) Regulations of Sri Lanka implement Directive 91/493/EEC for aquaculture products, at processing and farm levels. Jamaica adopted the Aquaculture, Inland and Marine Products and By-products Act of 1999, which provides for the inspection and certification of various categories of aquaculture, inland and marine products intended for export and for the licensing of persons and facilities engaged in the production, harvesting, processing, handling, storage and transport for export of such products. The Act includes the development of a HACCP plan.

Another important development is that, from January 2002, labelling for origin and species has become mandatory in the EU for fishery and aquaculture products offered for retail sale to final consumers (Regulations Nos. 104/2000 and 2065/2001). So-called eco-labelling can create a market-based incentive for environment-friendly production, although it can be controversial. In this regard, the Code of Conduct provides that "States should ensure that international and domestic trade in fish and fishery products (including aquaculture products) accords with sound conservation and management practices through improving the identification of the origin of fish and fishery product treated".

3.2.8. Regulating Sea Ranching

Given the growing pressure on the world's fisheries, the aquaculture industry provides useful alternatives to meet the future needs of the ever-increasing human population. However, it is expected that established techniques of aquaculture – basically the rearing of (shell) fish in ponds, cages and other kinds of enclosures – may soon be insufficient to meet those future needs. Limited resources and potentially harmful environmental effects call for alternatives to conventional aquaculture. The enhancement of natural stocks of fish, or sea ranching, is now being considered as a viable long-term alternative.

Stock enhancement or sea ranching is basically a combination of aquaculture and traditional fishing. After being reared in aquaculture farms to a desired stage of development, the cultivated fish are released into the wild in order to grow to a harvestable size in the sea. Natural stocks are supported and increased and even new stocks may be created. Enhancement practices can take the form of introduction of new species, fertilization, altering species composition including elimination of undesirable species and genetic modification of introduced species. Currently, in order to facilitate recapture, sea ranching is commonly conducted with migratory stocks that return to their natal streams to spawn, like salmon, or with certain types of shellfish or molluscs. The concept of sea ranching has evolved rapidly in recent years in countries like Chile, Japan, Norway and parts of North America.

Until recently the concept of sea ranching had been given little attention in fisheries and aquaculture legislation. The Philippines' Fisheries Code of 1998 defines sea ranching as the release of young fishery species reared in hatcheries and nurseries into natural bodies of water for subsequent harvest at maturity, or the manipulation of fishery habitat, to encourage the growth of wild stocks. The Code provides for demarcated areas, i.e., areas with boundaries defined by markers and assigned exclusively to specific individuals or organizations for sea ranching, among other purposes. In 1990 Norway launched a seven year Programme for the Development and Encouragement of Sea Ranching (PUSH), which included char, cod, lobster and salmon. A special committee was appointed under the programme and given the task of considering legal aspects of sea ranching. Although not built directly on the recommendations of the committee (Hallenstvedt, 1999), a new Law on Sea Ranching was adopted in 2000.

Legislation may be required not only to permit sea ranching, but also to protect it. An example of limiting capture fisheries in order to promote sea ranching is provided by the Chilean *Ley general de pesca y acuicultura* of 1989, amended in 1991. The law prohibits the capture of species that swim up the river from the sea to spawn (or vice versa), with the species to be defined by decree. Similar efforts to protect rights in areas close to the production sites have occurred in the Canadian provinces of Nova Scotia and Newfoundland. Nevertheless, the uncertainty for the investor in sea ranching remains. It is expected that the main legal issue in the future will be whether ranched fish can be subject to some sort of continuing property right or right of preferential harvesting. (Howarth and Leria, 1999)

3.2.9. Enforcement and Self-Regulation

Until the 1990s, aquaculture was rarely mentioned in any enforcement provision, and where aquaculture was dealt with under a basic fisheries law, the law enforcement sections had often been drafted with only capture fisheries in mind. Progress has certainly been made in the more recently adopted fisheries and aquaculture laws. In many countries, practising aquaculture without authorization, discharging wastewater from aquaculture facilities without a permit or importing fish or aquatic organisms without authorization all result in some sort of defined penalty. In general, the enforcement systems that have been adopted mirror traditional sanctions schemes, including administrative measures (such as the revocation or suspension of licences) and fines. In addition, one often finds provisions outlining the rights, duties and responsibilities of enforcement officers, such as the right to enter, inspect and search aquaculture facilities.

However, due to the overlap of laws and institutions involved in aquaculture, the implementation of enforcement mechanisms remains difficult. A major problem, particularly in developing countries, is limited budgets and insufficient staff, which means that aquaculture rules often cannot be properly enforced. Other options than the classic "command and control" mechanisms are therefore being explored in order to encourage farmers to make more efficient use of resources and to take full responsibility for mitigating or minimizing environmental changes caused by their aquaculture operations.

In particular, there appears to be a growing interest in the use of economic instruments, such as subsidies and tradeable permits. The Philippines' Fisheries Code of 1998 is illustrative of developments in this field, charging the responsible authority with formulating incentives and disincentives, including effluent charges, user fees and negotiable permits, to "encourage compliance with the environmental standards and to promote sustainable management practices" (sec. 48).

Even before legislation is introduced, voluntary options such as guidelines or codes of conduct are also considered to have great value in promoting the sustainability of aquaculture over the long term. Adherents to codes of conduct may for example agree to implement self-monitoring and control systems. Non-binding guidelines may also set up eco-labelling schemes, on the assumption that some consumers will pay a premium for environmentally friendly goods. Although guidelines and codes are voluntary, their effectiveness can be enhanced through the creation of additional incentives to encourage compliance. For example, the authorization to engage in aquaculture activities or the membership of an aquaculture organization can be made dependent on compliance with the applicable code or guideline.

Voluntary codes and guidelines can be developed at the international level, such as the Code of Conduct, which contains special provisions on aquaculture development. Codes and guidelines can also be developed regionally: as noted above, FEAP's Code of Conduct for European Aquaculture is an important document that establishes and recommends guiding principles for the aquaculture industry.

At the national level, some farmed-shrimp producing countries have prepared voluntary guidelines. In Malaysia a voluntary Code of Responsible Aquaculture Practices for cage culture and shrimp farming has been developed. Similar initiatives have taken place in the Philippines (Code of Practice for Aquaculture), Sri Lanka (Code of Good Management Practices for Shrimp Aquaculture) and Thailand (Code of Conduct for Shrimp Aquaculture). As noted above, in India the Guidelines for Sustainable Development of Brackish Water Aquaculture have been important for the sustainable development of the industry. In Japan, the development of aquaculture management has even led to a completely self-imposed and self-monitored system via Fisheries Cooperative Associations (FCAs), whose members engage in aquaculture according to FCA-management plans.

Another strategy for self-regulation consists of agreements between government and industry to protect the aquacultural environment, such as "eco-contracts" in Denmark or "covenants" in the Netherlands. The basic idea of these agreements is that pollution control cannot be achieved without close and active cooperation of industry. Therefore, binding objectives and targets for the reduction of pollution are laid down on a sector-by-sector basis. Then industry members party to such agreements work out plans and mechanisms and set time frames for the shared reduction of pollution. The scheme reduces the need for licences and permits for pollution and helps to limit bureaucracy and government control. However, these mechanisms can only be applied in legal systems with a tradition of consensus-seeking and joint problem-solving, and where the sectors of industry are well organized.

IV. CONCLUSION

Many fisheries resources that are targeted in capture fisheries know no maps, and building physical boundaries over large stretches of oceans to keep these resources in or out is obviously impossible. In addition, fishing activities on vast marine areas are hard to monitor and control, not only from an enforcement standpoint but also for lack of scientific information needed to drive fisheries management action. In this context, the search for innovative management approaches, frameworks and measures continues, and legislation will have to accommodate these innovations.

The high mobility of the resources and the vast areas they occupy or travel means that for many capture fisheries, there are many stakeholders and accordingly a wide range of interests to be considered in the development of management frameworks. Broad-based participation by stakeholders in areas under national jurisdiction and, beyond those areas, international cooperation amongst states, is vital to conservation and sustainable utilization of the resources. International arrangements are already driving national legislative action and can be expected to continue to do so.

With many of the world's capture fisheries being over-fished, aquaculture is often viewed as the industry that could meet the increasing shortfall in the supply of fish. Under pressure of growth in the industry, many countries have started to review their existing legislation or even to adopt new comprehensive regulatory frameworks. Enforcement, however, often remains the weak link, although there are effective and powerful alternatives including economic incentives and disincentives and voluntary instruments such as codes and guidelines.

Increased public concern over ecological matters has generated a variety of new concepts and approaches towards improved regulation. However, the economies of the large majority of countries, both developed and developing, are increasingly dependent upon the flow of trade. Environmental protection and trade goals have to be mutually supportive.

These diverse developments underline the need for fisheries and aquaculture legislation that is not based solely on biology as was the case in the past but that also takes into account socio-economic and environmental issues. As knowledge of the resource improves, as more sophisticated techniques are employed and as global solutions are sought, future legislation will have to keep pace.

REFERENCES

Boyle, A. & Freestone, D. (eds.). 1999. *International Law and Sustainable Development, Past Achievements and Future Challenges.* Oxford University Press, New York.

Cacaud, P. 1999. *Legal Issues Relating to Vessel Monitoring Systems.* In *Report of a Regional Workshop on Fisheries Monitoring, Control and Surveillance, Kuala Lumpur and Kuala Terenganu, Malaysia, 29 June-3 July 1998.*

Edeson, W. 1996. *The Code of Conduct for Responsible Fisheries: An Introduction,* 11 International Journal of Marine and Coastal Law.

Edeson, W. 1999a. *Closing the Gap: the Role of Soft International Instruments to Control Fishing*, 20 Australian Yearbook of International Law.

Edeson, W. 1999b. *Towards Long Term Sustainable Use: Some Recent Developments in the Legal Regime of Fisheries*. In A. Boyle & D. Freestone (eds.), *International Law and Sustainable Development, Past Achievements and Future Challenges*, Oxford University Press, New York.

Edeson, W., Freestone, D. & Gudmunsdottir, E. 2001. *Legislating for Sustainable Fisheries: A Guide to Implementing the 1993 FAO Compliance Agreement and the 1995 UN Fish Stocks Agreement*. The World Bank Law, Justice and Development Series, Washington, D.C.

FAO. 1997. *Fisheries Management*. FAO Technical Guidelines for Responsible Fisheries, Nos. 4 and 5, Rome.

FAO. 1997. *Hazard Analysis and Critical Control Point (HACCP) System and Guidelines for its Application* (www.fao.org/codex/standard/fh_basic.pdf).

FAO. 2000. *State of World Fisheries and Aquaculture 2000*, Rome.

Freestone, D. & Hey, E. 1996. *Implementing the Precautionary Principle: Challenges and Opportunities*. In D. Freestone & E. Hey (eds.), *The Precautionary Principle and International Law: The Challenge of Implementation*, Kluwer Law International, The Hague.

Freestone, D. & Makuch, Z. 1998. *The New International Environmental Law of Fisheries: The 1995 United Nations Straddling Stocks Agreement*, Yearbook of International Environmental Law 7.

Howarth, W. 1999. *Legislation for Sustainable Aquaculture: A Legal Perspective on the Improvement of the Holmenkollen Guidelines*. In N. Svennevig, H. Reinartsen & M. New, *Sustainable Aquaculture: Food for the Future*, A.A. Balkema, Rotterdam.

Howarth, W., Hernandez, R.E. & Van Houtte, A. 2001. *Legislation Governing Shrimp Aquaculture: Legal Issues, National Experiences and Options*, FAO Legal Paper Online No. 18 (www.fao.org/Legal).

Howarth, W. & Leria, C. 1999. *Legal Issues Relating to Stock Enhancement and Marine Ranching*. In A. Howell, E. Moksness & T. Svasand (eds.), *Stock Enhancement and Marine Ranching*, Blackwell, Oxford.

Kuemlangan, B. 2000. *National Legislative Options to Combat IUU Fishing*. In *Report and Papers Presented at the Expert Consultation on Illegal, Unreported and Unregulated Fishing, Sydney, 15-19 May 2000*, FAO Fisheries Report No. 666.

Leria, C. & Van Houtte, A. 2000. *Rights-Based Fisheries: A Legal Overview*. In M.H. Nordquist & J.N. Moore, *Current Fisheries Issues and the Food and Agriculture Organization of the United Nations*, Center for Oceans Law and Policy, Kluwer Law International, The Hague.

Moore, G. 1995. *The Food and Agriculture Organization Compliance Agreement*, 10 International Journal of Marine and Coastal Law.

Read, P. (ed.). 2000. *The Monitoring and Regulation of Marine Aquaculture in Europe*: Proceedings of the 1st Workshop Held at the University of Algarve, Faro, Portugal, 6–8 September, 1999, Journal of Applied Ichthyology, Special Issue No. 16.

Subasinghe, R. 1999. *Towards Sustainable Shrimp Culture Development: Implementing the FAO Code of Conduct for Responsible Fisheries. Paper presented at the Fifth Central American Symposium on Aquaculture, Aquaculture and the Environment: Together Towards the New Millennium, San Pedro Sula, Honduras, 18–20 August 1999.*

Van Houtte, A. 1996. *Preliminary Review of the Legal Framework Governing the Use of Chemicals in Aquaculture in Asia. In Proceedings of the Meeting on the Use of Chemicals in Aquaculture in Asia, Manila, 20–22 May 1996.*

Van Houtte, A. 1996. *Legal Aspects Concerning Aquaculture: Some Food for Thought*, Aquaculture Newsletter 14.

Van Houtte, A. 2001. *Establishing Legal, Institutional and Regulatory Frameworks for Aquaculture Development and Management. In Technical Proceedings of the Conference on Aquaculture in the Third Millennium, Bangkok, 20-25 February 2000.*

Van Houtte, A., Bonucci, N. & Edeson, W. 1989. *A Preliminary Review of Selected Legislation Governing Aquaculture.* FAO, Rome.

8

LAND

Contents

I.   INTRODUCTION

In most societies, land has played a central role throughout history. It has been the locus of productive activities and a source of political power. It has held special cultural and emotional significance, for families, communities and nations. Its sound management has contributed to environmental stability and economic well-being, while its abuse has helped undermine ecosystems and livelihoods. It has figured prominently in a wide variety of human conflicts, from inheritance disputes to wars.

The decade since Rio has been a period of intense activity in the reform of land laws around the world. Not surprisingly, developments in this area have not been uniform, in part because the contexts for reform have been so diverse. Perhaps more than any other subject in this volume, land law has deep roots in the unique history of each country, reflecting widely varying tenure systems, political regimes, colonial experiences, social institutions and religious practices. As a result, while broad traditions of land law are discernible, local variations within those traditions are often great.

Equally diverse are the issues and problems with which land law must contend. Around the world, there are vast differences in the ways people use and possess land and the ecological, economic and social settings in which they do so. There are huge variations in soil fertility; in the potential of land for different agricultural practices; in the relative importance of agriculture; in population densities and land availability; and in the extent to which landholdings are highly concentrated or more equitably distributed, to name just a few areas.

Despite this diversity, it is possible to identify some common impulses that have driven land law reform over the last decade, resulting in some broadly comparable legal developments in a number of countries around the world:

- *Market liberalization.* In many countries, the decade was characterized by efforts to install or enhance market economies, and reduce the role of the state in economic affairs. A central premise of this agenda asserts the importance of a functioning land market to the health of the overall economy. Thus, reform designed in various degrees to strengthen private, marketable rights in land was featured in all regions of the world, especially in countries in transition to market economies, but in other countries as well.

- *Poverty alleviation and food security.* In agricultural societies, access to land is central to livelihood strategies for the rural poor. Even in rapidly changing societies characterized by a shift away from agriculture, evidence shows that access to a small amount of land can play a vital role in supplementing income, meeting subsistence needs and shielding households from economic and natural shocks. Secure rights over land may encourage greater investment and productivity, and allow small farmers better to capitalize on the value of what is often their most important asset.

- *Democracy and decentralization.* Many countries have adopted policies aimed at moving important governance functions away from the centre and vesting greater responsibility and powers in local governments and communities. In some countries, this has been accompanied by a greater willingness to accommodate local people's choices regarding the nature of land rights and the institutions that govern them. Attempts to implement this perspective have taken a number of different forms, including efforts to accommodate customary and indigenous tenure arrangements within state land law frameworks and to locate basic land administration services within local governments.

- *Sustainable management of land and land-based resources.* According to the vision of sustainable development expressed at Rio and elsewhere, secure, long-term property rights are a prerequisite for the sound use of land. The absence of such rights weakens incentives to use land sustainably and to preserve its value into the future. This logic applies not only to individually held parcels of agricultural land, but also to land used in common, such as pasture or forests, where degradation can in part be linked to the failure to vest management rights and responsibilities in local stakeholders. In addition, in some parts of the world, severe inequalities in landholding often compel an over-reliance on marginal, environmentally fragile areas by the rural poor, as do government actions or inactions that facilitate the displacement of those with weak rights and limited political clout.

The attention given to land law reform over the last decade does not mean that such reform has been comprehensively achieved in most countries, or even that there is consensus about what the elements of reform should be. Indeed, there is considerable disagreement over whether the various agendas mentioned above complement one another or push in different directions. Some commentators argue, for example, that measures designed to improve the marketability of land may in fact undermine the ability of the poor to acquire and retain land. Others argue that there is an inevitable tension between a market-oriented approach and the recognition of customary rights or community interests in land. Nevertheless, while the experience of the last decade has been inconclusive and at times contradictory, it provides evidence of some noteworthy trends that are likely to dominate the law reform agenda for some time to come.

In the next Part, this chapter provides a brief overview of the treatment of land issues in international documents and fora over the last decade. This is followed in Part III with a discussion of how recent national legislative reforms have dealt with three important themes: strengthening private land rights; recognizing customary and indigenous rights; and improving access to land.[1]

II.   LAND RIGHTS IN INTERNATIONAL INSTRUMENTS

Land tenure, access and administration issues are generally not subjects of international law and hence have not been given detailed treatment in international treaties. The Rio documents and others, however, place considerable emphasis on the importance of these subjects, and alert governments to the need to address them, including through legislative action.

Thus, Chapter 14 of Agenda 21 states that "the main tools of Sustainable Agriculture and Rural Development are policy and agrarian reform, income diversification, land conservation and improved management of inputs". Governments are exhorted to "review and re-focus existing measures to achieve wider access to land" and to "assign clear titles, rights and responsibilities for land and for individuals or communities". They are further urged "to ensure equitable access of rural people, particularly women, small farmers, landless and indigenous people, to land, water and forest resources" and to "implement policies to influence land tenure

---

[1] This chapter primarily covers land law developments affecting access to and tenure over land. Issues concerning land management and planning more broadly are not dealt with in detail, given the treatment of these issues in other chapters of this book on forestry, mountains, fisheries (aquaculture) and wildlife. It should also be noted that this chapter focuses mainly on emerging land law trends in developing countries and countries in transition, rather than in developed economies, and on rural land rather than urban land.

and property rights positively with due recognition of the minimum size of landholding required to maintain production and check further fragmentation".

Chapter 10 of Agenda 21, on the Integrated Approach to the Planning and Management of Land Resources, acknowledges the centrality of "private property rights, the rights of indigenous people and their communities and other local communities" to achieving sustainable management, and highlights conflicts and competition over land as a prime cause of suboptimal land use. Similar broad indications of the importance of land rights may be found in Chapter 12 on combating desertification (urging particular attention to "the property rights of women and pastoral and nomadic groups living in rural areas"); in Chapter 3 on combating poverty; in Chapter 7 on human settlements; and in several of the chapters devoted to strengthening the role of major groups.

These themes were echoed and reinforced at various points in the decade following Rio. In 1996, the Rome Declaration of the World Food Summit highlighted the interrelationship between access to land, environmental sustainability and conquering hunger. The Summit's Plan of Action called upon countries to "[e]stablish legal and other mechanisms, as appropriate, that advance land reform, recognize and protect property, water, and user rights, and enhance access for the poor and women to resources. Such mechanisms should also promote conservation and sustainable use of natural resources (such as land, water and forests), lower risks, and encourage investment". The Eighth Session of the Commission on Sustainable Development in New York (April–May 2000) also gave detailed attention to land access and tenure issues, stressing the importance of well-defined and enforceable land rights and equal access to land, in particular for women and indigenous and local communities, and highlighting the need for adequate land administration systems.

The discrimination faced by women with respect to access to land received a significant amount of attention in international fora over the last decade, as several of the examples above indicate. Land was a major focus of the Fourth World Conference on Women in Beijing in 1996. The Plan of Action from that Conference included exhortations to states to "[u]ndertake legislative and administrative reforms to give women full and equal access to economic resources, including the right to inheritance and to ownership of land and other property, credit, natural resources and appropriate technologies". (Strategic Objective A.2)

Land rights of indigenous peoples have also been the focus of attention in international instruments, and in the jurisprudence of various international tribunals. Article 10(c) of the Convention on Biological Diversity (CBD), for example, protects the "customary use of biological resources in accordance with traditional cultural practices". According to a later interpretation of this article, a necessary condition of such protection is "security of tenure over traditional terrestrial and marine estates; control over and use of traditional natural resources". (CBD, 1997)

The most extensive international treatment of indigenous peoples' rights, both generally and concerning land, is found in International Labour Convention No. 169, which was adopted in 1989. This treaty has been influential during the last decade in promoting the cause of indigenous rights, particularly in Latin America, as eleven of the fifteen states that have ratified the Convention so far are from that region, and a further four have submitted it to their legislatures. Article 14 of the Convention states that the collective "rights of ownership and possession [of indigenous peoples] over the lands which they traditionally occupy shall be recognized". Governments are required to "take steps as necessary to identify" these lands and to "guarantee effective protection" of the recognized rights. Land is defined in article 13(2) as including "the concept of territories, which covers the total environment of the areas which the peoples concerned occupy or otherwise use".

There are other important international instruments, existing or proposed, which deal with indigenous rights over land and resources. Recent jurisprudence under the International Covenant on Civil and Political Rights interprets the Covenant's article 27 – relating to the right of indigenous peoples to enjoy their culture – to include rights to land, resources, subsistence and participation. Relevant regional agreements include the American Convention on Human Rights, under which a recent decision of the Inter-American Court on Human Rights has confirmed that indigenous peoples' territorial rights arise by virtue of traditional occupation and use and indigenous forms of tenure, rather than from grants, recognition or registration by the state. (Colchester, 2001) Finally, a United Nations draft Declaration on the Rights of Indigenous Peoples is currently under development, containing extensive provisions concerning the protection of indigenous rights over lands and requiring governments to title and demarcate such lands.

III. THEMES IN NATIONAL LEGISLATION

This section will examine three recurring themes that played a dominant role in efforts to reform land laws during the last ten years:

- the strengthening of individual private rights in land and the partial liberalization of land markets;
- the recognition of claims to land and resources by indigenous people and local communities, and attempts to accommodate plural tenure regimes within national legal systems; and
- efforts to facilitate access to land for the poor or for those often excluded from holding land rights, such as women.

The following discussion is not intended to be a comprehensive survey of national developments with respect to these themes; instead, it draws upon selected examples to illustrate important aspects and variations. Moreover, the above list should not be understood as describing universal trends. Some countries have moved significantly along one or more of these trajectories, while others have taken little action. Often reform efforts have been diluted by contradictory tendencies elsewhere within the same legal framework, sometimes even within the same piece of legislation. Finally, there tend to be broad regional variations in the extent to which any of these themes have been prominent. For example, Africa's preoccupation with the treatment of customary rights is not one that is shared in Eastern Europe.

3.1 Strengthening Private Individual Rights

3.1.1. Rebalancing the Role of Private Actors and the State

Law reform aimed at strengthening individual private rights in land has been a widespread phenomenon over the last decade. It was most conspicuous in the countries of the former Soviet Union and Central and Eastern Europe. But countries in most other parts of the world, from China to Latin America to Africa, also made significant moves in this direction.

Broadly speaking, these reforms share two complementary features. First, they involve an expansion of the types of rights that private persons can possess with respect to land – or in some countries, the recognition in the first instance that private land rights can exist at all. To varying degrees, the focus has been on defining an expanded "bundle of rights", in terms of the ability of private people to occupy and use land without unwarranted interference for a defined period or indefinitely, and to deal with their land, through sale, mortgage, inheritance or otherwise.

The necessary corollary to the widening of private rights is a corresponding reduction of the state's powers over privately held land. This includes diminishing the role of the state in decisionmaking about the use and transfer of land, areas in which state discretion has traditionally been dominant in many countries (at least formally). It means imposing greater restraints on the ability of the state to override private rights, and to acquire land compulsorily.

Once again, there are wide divergences between countries in terms of the pace and extent of change, in part reflecting the significantly different starting points from which countries have approached reform. In Central and Eastern Europe and the former Soviet Union, for instance, the dismantling of communism has required the crafting of almost entirely new legal frameworks governing land. As a consequence, the last decade has been a period of unparalleled activity in the drafting of land legislation. Virtually every country in the region, from Albania to Kyrgyzstan to the Russian Federation, has adopted laws that:

- redefine the nature of the rights and responsibilities that private persons may hold with respect to land;
- establish a process for the privatization of state-held land and collective farms, and the allocation of individualized rights; and
- create an institutional and procedural framework for the administration of private land rights and for the operation of markets in land rights.

As will be discussed below, the results of these activities have been extremely variable. Reforms in some countries have fallen far short of early expectations, due to a continuing or resurgent reluctance on the part of their governments to substantially reduce the state role in monitoring, approving and controlling land relations. Legal constraints on the efficient operation of land markets and the acquisition of secure private rights persist, to a greater or lesser degree, in almost all countries in the region. Nevertheless, when viewed in the aggregate, the changes accomplished in a relatively short period of time are impressive.

Though no other part of the world devoted such concentrated attention to these issues, legislative movements toward stronger private land rights were not confined to Central and Eastern Europe and the former Soviet

Union. The decade also witnessed important land law reforms in a number of Asian socialist or post-socialist countries, including China, Lao People's Democratic Republic, Mongolia, Viet Nam and, most recently, Cambodia. Laws from the early 1990s in Honduras, Mexico, Nicaragua and Peru exemplify efforts in a number of Latin American countries to reduce "paternalistic controls which have regulated property use and restricted property rights" and to introduce greater freedoms and efficiencies into land markets. (Hendrix, 1993) Important new land laws in a number of African countries, such as Burkina Faso, Côte d'Ivoire, Mozambique, the Niger, South Africa, the United Republic of Tanzania and Uganda, as well as constitutional provisions in Ghana and South Africa, have helped to clarify the nature of private rights over land and have reduced the discretion of government to interfere with those rights.

The next two sections will examine briefly how new laws have dealt with the closely related questions of: (a) where the ultimate "ownership" of land resides – with the state or with private landholders; and (b) the variety of ways in which private rights have both expanded and continue to be constrained. It should be noted that the focus here is on the substantive *content* of land rights. Equally if not more important are the legal and institutional mechanisms by which such rights can be exercised and protected in practice, issues which are dealt with below in section 3.1.4. on land administration.

3.1.2. State vs. Private Ownership

Countries in many parts of the world entered the 1990s with the ultimate ownership of all or most land vested in the state. This was particularly true, of course, in the case of socialist or post-socialist countries of Central and Eastern Europe and Asia. It was also true in most African countries, many of which asserted state ownership over land in their first post-colonial constitutions. In a number of other countries, from Guyana to Sri Lanka, the state has been by far the largest owner of agricultural land, and private rights over state land have been limited to leaseholds or use rights rather than full ownership.

For many countries engaged in land law reform, therefore, an initial consideration has been whether to change or leave intact the basic template of state-as-ultimate-titleholder. The outcome of this debate has been mixed, even within regions.

Over the course of the decade, an increasing number of former Soviet Republics have adopted provisions recognizing the possibility of private, individual ownership of agricultural land. For example, Kyrgyzstan, whose constitution originally prohibited private ownership, adopted a constitutional amendment allowing such ownership after a national referendum in 1998. The Constitution of the Russian Federation has recognized the possibility of private ownership since 1993, but it was only with the coming into effect of the new Land Code in 2001 that a mechanism for securing such ownership over agricultural land became available. (Rolfes, 2002) Armenia, Georgia, Ukraine and the Baltic Republics, among others, now allow private ownership of agricultural land. (In many of the countries of Central and Eastern Europe, private ownership was legally recognized even during the communist period, though difficult to exercise in practice.)

By contrast, in a number of former Soviet Republics, land remains legally in the hands of the state, and reforms so far have focused on leaseholds, use rights and the reorganization of collective farms. Belarus, for example, allows ownership of land only for purposes such as housing or gardening. Kazakhstan's 2001 Land Law provides only for leasing of agricultural land.

Law reforms in various parts of Asia also reveal different approaches. Cambodia's Land Law of 2001 allows private ownership of agricultural land, in place of the regime of user rights that was enshrined in earlier legislation. The Government of Sri Lanka has announced its intention to convert much of the state agricultural land – currently held by farmers under state grant and permitting schemes regulated by the Land Development Ordinance and other laws – to freehold title. In the case of China, Lao People's Democratic Republic and Viet Nam, by contrast, the principle of state ownership of land has been reaffirmed. However, within the framework of state ownership, there were significant moves towards stronger and more secure individual or household rights in land.

In Africa, as well, considerable debate has taken place in a number of countries about the desirability of the state retaining "radical title" over land, once again with mixed outcomes. Eritrea's Land Proclamation of 1994 unequivocally asserts state ownership of all land, with private rights over agricultural land limited to life usufructs. Mozambique's Land Law of 1997, which, as will be seen, significantly strengthens the land rights both of private investors and local communities, nevertheless keeps in place the basic principle that all land ultimately belongs to the state.

The United Republic of Tanzania's 1999 Land Act continues to vest land in the President as trustee for the people of Tanzania. Uganda's Land Act of 1998 goes further towards removing from the state a residual ownership interest in land, recognizing both private individuals and communities as potential owners.

The relative merits of vesting ultimate ownership or radical title in the state or in private persons are difficult to evaluate in the abstract. The mere fact of state ownership in itself provides little information about the nature and strength of the rights that private persons may acquire in land. Depending on whether state ownership is nominal or symbolic on the one hand, or active and interventionist on the other, private landholders may acquire rights that for all intents and purposes are equivalent in practice to full ownership. As the example of Hong Kong (amongst others) demonstrates, the fact that all land is held under long-term leases does not preclude the emergence of a vigorous real estate market.

Nevertheless, the issue often provokes strong passions in different ideological camps. Many socialist or post-socialist governments, for example, have been reluctant to abandon long-standing convictions that land properly belongs to the state, even while they have come to recognize the need for greater security, flexibility and marketability of private rights. Some observers, including some Western donors, tend towards the view that true reform requires the elimination of a state ownership interest from privately held land. And in countries where government intervention in land relations has traditionally been pronounced, some critics see the retention of the concept of underlying state ownership as a pretext for governments continuing "business as usual", however much new laws may constrain state action in theory.

3.1.3. Variations in the "Bundle" of Private Rights

Whether private rights are categorized as ownership, leasehold, user rights, permits or otherwise, the critical question is what the holders of those rights can do with them, and to what extent they are vulnerable to being taken away.

Here again law reforms during the last decade fall across a wide spectrum of approaches, with some countries recognizing expansive rights to use, sell, mortgage and modify landholdings, and others opting for more restricted rights packages.

Lithuania's Land Law of 1994 falls at the liberal end of this spectrum. It specifies that land owners shall have the right:

- to sell, devise, donate, mortgage, exchange or lease the land and to grant others temporary rights to occupy and use the land;
- to occupy and use the land for any business not prohibited by law and compatible with its defined purpose or use, and to construct any buildings allowed by planning and other legislation;
- to establish servitudes for others on the land;
- to make application to change the designated use of the land and to seek changes in any restrictions placed on the land by law, planning or the documents transferring the land initially;
- to apply to the courts for protection or compensation against violations of their ownership rights;
- in the course of farming, to make use of water and natural resources found on or under the land (but not to sell them commercially), in accordance with environmental and other laws governing mineral use; and
- to dispose of any produce grown on the land and to use the income without restriction.

Even in countries where the underlying ownership by the state is retained, there have been some notable expansions in private rights. In China, the 1998 Land Administration Law leaves in place the basic rule that agricultural land is to be held in collective ownership. At the same time, however, the law lays the groundwork for greater recognition of the rights of the individual cultivators who make up a collective. It provides for peasant contracts of 30 years, thus giving the individual cultivator formal rights over a specific parcel which can only be altered by the collective management through a specified procedure. "The new law", observes one recent commentary, "rests on the principle that by strengthening the security of tenure and the stature of the individual vis-à-vis the collective, the peasant will become a more careful protector of the quality of the land and a more efficient land user". (Valletta and Venable, 1999)

Viet Nam's Land Law of 1993 also did not change the principle of state ownership, but provided for the de-collectivization of agriculture by allowing farmers to obtain Land Use Certificates. These land use rights can be inherited, mortgaged, transferred, exchanged or leased. By 1999, about ten million households had been issued Land Use Certificates.

While private land rights have expanded in numerous ways over the decade, this expansion has frequently been diluted simultaneously by quite significant legislative constraints. Such constraints can take the form of prohibitions or controls on certain activities, or of underdeveloped legal frameworks that leave the rules concerning certain transactions unclear. (Giovarelli and Bledsoe, 2001) Thus, in many laws from Central and Eastern Europe and the former Soviet Republics, it was not uncommon during the past decade to find:

- full prohibitions or moratoria on the sale of agricultural land;
- artificially high "floors" imposed on the sale price of land;
- restrictions on the capacity of business entities or foreign nationals to acquire agricultural land;
- stipulations as to the qualifications of persons who can acquire farm land;
- unclear or non-existent rules concerning mortgaging and leasing of private land;
- affirmative obligations to use land in a certain way, with the possibility that land may be forfeited to the state if not used productively or if environmental or land use laws are violated; and
- the retention of broad powers on the part of the state to rescind land allocations.

These constraints may reflect a number of motivations working in tandem. The selling of agricultural land, for example, may provoke fears that inexperienced smallholders will be victimized by speculators, that food security will be undermined by agricultural land falling into the hands of non-cultivators, that the fabric of rural society will be destroyed and that migration to the cities will accelerate. Lingering attitudes from central planning days may account for the reluctance of governments to give up the power to insist that land be used for a specific purpose and to make tenure rights contingent upon the performance of land use obligations.

Laws in Kyrgyzstan and Ukraine, both of which allow ownership of land, provide interesting examples of the persistence of state intrusion that resemble (in spirit if not in detail) a number of countries in the region and elsewhere in the world. The Kyrgyzstan Land Code imposes significant restrictions on how land can be used. More importantly, it gives the state power to withdraw private land rights if land is used in contradiction to its use classification, or if there is failure to use agricultural land within three years of allocation. In practice these provisions are rarely used, but they contribute to a weakening of tenure security.

Similar uncertainty characterizes recent reforms in Ukraine, where state and municipal officials retain significant powers "to withdraw, curtail and redefine" land rights even after they have been assigned and granted to owners, users and lessees. "Taken together, these limitations and uncertainties make it impossible to say, with assurance, that the person holding land rights today will continue to hold the same rights tomorrow or into the medium and long term future". (Valletta, 2002)

Some hurdles also continue to obstruct the free transferability of land. A number of countries have placed moratoria on the selling of privatized land for a certain period; in Ukraine, for example, agricultural land cannot be sold before 2005, reflecting a fear of speculation, and a concern that new landholders will easily be tricked into relinquishing their land. The Ukraine Land Code also requires that agricultural land only be sold to persons certified by the government as having agricultural education or experience. In this and other ways, the government retains a strong presence in private land transactions in Ukraine, posing potentially significant constraints on the emergence of a vigorous and efficient market. (Valletta, 2002, and Rolfes, 2002)

A number of the restrictions described above may in fact be rooted in exaggerated fears, ideological ambivalence, a lack of legal sophistication or the vested interests of government agencies. From a broader perspective, however, they can also be seen as expressions (albeit frequently ill-considered ones) of the perennial attempt to balance the economic and social functions of land in a way that is appropriate for a particular society at particular point in history. (McAuslan, 2000a) There are sporadic indications that countries within the region are continuing to examine and chip away at such constraints. Most recently, for example, the lower house of the Parliament of the Russian Federation passed a bill on 24 June 2002, allowing the sale of agricultural land, after an extensive and often bitter debate. In one form or another, however, concerns over the potential social effects of the commoditization of land have played a role in the design of land law in all parts of the world throughout history, and will continue to influence efforts for the foreseeable future.

3.1.4. Improving Land Administration

Earlier sections have focused on the substantive content of land rights in national laws. By contrast, land administration, as that term is used here, refers to the institutions and processes that are required in order for a system of land rights to operate in practice. As such, land administration covers a broad range of subjects, including:

- procedures by which land rights are allocated or recognized;
- the definition and delimitation of boundaries between parcels;
- the recording of information about land rights, rights holders and parcels;
- procedures governing transactions in land, including sales, mortgages, leases and dispositions;
- the resolution of uncertainty or adjudication of disputes concerning land rights and boundaries;
- institutions and processes for the planning, controlling and monitoring of land use; and
- land valuation and taxation procedures.

There are a wide variety of approaches to these various land administration functions in different parts of the world. With respect to recording land rights, for example, some countries may use highly sophisticated, computerized registration systems, with each parcel professionally surveyed. In some customary settings, on the other hand, information about who has what rights to what land may not be documented at all or documented only very simply, with the community's collective memory serving effectively as the repository of information. In between these two extremes, there are countless variations.

Whatever the context, it is increasingly recognized that poorly designed or malfunctioning land administration systems can undermine the value of land, reduce security of tenure and exacerbate conflicts. However strong a land right may be in terms of substantive law, it is severely weakened in practice if there is not a functioning institutional and legal apparatus that allows it to be exercised and enforced. In this respect, many of the land administration systems around the world are seriously flawed, in one or more of the following ways:

- Procedures are often cumbersome, complicated and difficult to understand and use. Key institutions, such as registries and courts, are frequently located far from many users. Factors such as these contribute to systems that are expensive and inaccessible, and that people seek to avoid, for example, through informal, off-the-record transactions.
- Some systems are "over-designed", by including technical standards and requirements for precision that exceed the needs of users, are difficult to implement in practice and, again, add to costs.

- Some approaches to land administration functions may be poorly adapted to specific social contexts, such as adjudication and recording techniques that fail to reflect various secondary or derived rights to land (see section 3.2.1.).
- Unclear allocation of authority between different agencies within the system creates confusion, overlap, duplication of effort and conflict.
- Many land administration agencies suffer from insufficient financing and human capacity, with the result that cadastral maps lie unfinished, transactions go unrecorded, information is unreliable and disputes are unresolved.

The shift towards enhanced private land rights described earlier has necessarily been accompanied by attention to its administrative implications, and to a number of the above problems. Conspicuous evidence of this attention can be found in the large number of land titling programmes that governments have initiated (or in some cases continued) over the last decade, almost always with donor assistance. Large-scale or pilot titling programmes are under way in most of the former Soviet Republics and in a number of former communist countries of Central and Eastern Europe; throughout Southeast Asia; in Sri Lanka and Bangladesh; in a number of Latin American countries; and in projects at various stages of design and implementation in Ghana and elsewhere in Africa.

There are a wide variety of approaches, outcomes and controversies associated with these different titling efforts. Reduced to their most basic elements, they share the premise that some sort of formal recognition and systematic clarification of land rights is essential for making those rights secure and operational. In some cases, however, critics have questioned whether the benefits of titling programmes justify the costs, and whether the systems being put in place will be sustainable in the future. Others have also questioned whether the formalization of land rights is necessarily desirable in all contexts, particularly where the approach used may strengthen the position of more privileged land users vis-à-vis those with weaker interests. Nevertheless, without denying the shortcomings that exist, these programmes are proving to be useful arenas in which to design and test new techniques for lowering costs, for streamlining procedures and for enhancing institutional coherence. There is also a more nuanced view emerging about how to design formalization strategies that better meet the specific needs of particular groups (a topic discussed in more detail in section 3.2., below).

In terms of legal reforms in support of improved land administration, much of the activity in the European and Asian transition economies has centred on the issue of land registration. The 1997 registration law of the Russian Federation is a particularly impressive example. Among other things, this law:

- establishes a parcel-based registration system;
- clearly identifies the rights that are to be included in the register, and makes registration of those rights mandatory;
- protects registered interests, except in the case of certain types of fraud;
- makes information in the system accessible to interested parties;
- unifies the registration of land and buildings within one system;
- provides for some institutional variation between local registration entities, within the framework of national rules administered by the Ministry of Justice. (Rolfes, 2002)

A number of other transition countries have been less successful in drafting coherent registration laws. Frequent shortcomings, found in different combinations in recent laws, include: failure to provide clear institutional mandates, and to reduce the number of institutions involved in various parts of the process; unsound provisions for the registration of land and buildings in separate systems; failure to define procedures clearly; failure to put in place a parcel-based system; uncertainty about the treatment of easements and pre-existing rights; and ambiguity as to the legal effect of registering or failure to register. (RDI, 1999)

In other parts of the world, there has been scattered legislative attention to registration issues, mostly at the level of modification to details within existing registration legal frameworks (see, for example, Trackman, et al., 1999, concerning Central American experiences). There are several examples of more comprehensive legislative reforms. Sri Lanka's Registration of Titles Act in 1998, for example, lays the foundation for the replacement of Sri Lanka's current deeds registration system with a registration of title system.[2] It provides for the systematic adjudication of parcels in declared districts, the compilation and maintenance of a register that is conclusive evidence as to the interests affecting each registered

---

[2] A deeds system records only transactions, without purporting to guarantee that the person transferring the land actually holds the interest in question. A title system, by contrast, registers title to an interest in land. The official title register keeps a conclusive record of all interests affecting a particular parcel, with the goal of making transactions easier and more secure.

parcel and indemnification by the state in the event of certain types of fraud or mistake. The act is, in its basic form and substance, well within a tradition of title registration laws that can be found in a number of former British colonies, and hence does not in itself represent an innovation in terms of legal technique. Its implementation, however, could provide important lessons about the practicality, costs and benefits of replacing long-established (if malfunctioning) documentation and conveyancing systems with a significantly new system in a developing country context.

Land administration in all its facets is undergoing rapid change in many countries. Consequently, this will be an area requiring sustained attention from lawmakers in order to consolidate institutional reform, to update procedures and standards and to reflect the introduction of new technology. Experience over the last decade has also reinforced the need to tailor administrative tools better to specific cultural and economic contexts. Some of the more interesting experiments to emerge along these lines are discussed in the next section.

3.2 Accommodating Customary and Indigenous Rights Within National Legal Frameworks

The past decade, while notable for the liberalization and increased market orientation of land laws in a number of countries, also witnessed significant advances in the legal recognition of indigenous land rights and customary land tenure arrangements. These developments have taken different forms, reflecting the widely varying contexts in which they have occurred. In Latin America, Australia, Cambodia, Canada, the Philippines, the Russian Federation and several other countries, important new laws recognize, or provide mechanisms for the recognition of, long-standing land claims by ethnically distinct indigenous groups. In Africa, the main focus has not been on the rights of indigenous peoples *per se*, in part because of the difficulty of applying that term in the African context; instead, the debate has revolved around how to strengthen the rights of people holding land within the customary sector, which in many African countries is a substantial majority of the population.

A review of some of the more noteworthy legal innovations that have emerged will help illustrate some common themes that arise, as well as some shortcomings and dilemmas that will continue to require attention in the coming years. At the outset, it is important to note that these efforts have many points in common with those described in the previous section. In both instances, the focus has largely been on securing and strengthening private rights over land, and on limiting the ability of the state or other outsiders to interfere with those rights. Where differences lie is in how and by whom rights are held, and in the origin of the rules that govern those rights. In contrast to section 3.1., the emphasis in this section is on private rights that are held by community-based groups or by individuals within such groups, and that are regulated in large part by rules that emerge locally.

3.2.1. Legal Recognition of Customary Rights, with Special Reference to Africa

Until relatively recently, the dominant policy approach to customary land issues in Africa presumed that any meaningful strengthening of land rights for customary landholders would entail the progressive replacement of customary systems with systems of individual private ownership, under titling and registration programmes initiated by the state and governed by uniform national property laws. Advocates of private, individual title typically assert that customary land systems depress agricultural productivity and efficiency. In the absence of individual, tradeable interests in land, they argue, cultivators lack the incentive or the security to make necessary capital improvements or to obtain credit.

Criticism of this approach was well under way by the end of the 1980s; the criticism has deepened and entered the policy and legal "mainstream" during the decade since Rio. Customary tenure, the criticism goes, often provides a high sense of security to individual cultivators. Despite the absence of written titles, individuals operating within customary systems frequently have well-defined rights to land and a realistic expectation that those rights will be secure over time. Moreover, the argument runs, customary systems can be adaptable, and where conditions have warranted, markets for land rights within such systems have emerged. These critics also point out that there is as yet little empirical evidence that individual titling results either in increased productivity or better access to credit. Titling might itself contribute to insecurity of tenure, by raising the spectre of land being lost to outsiders and creditors, and by disrupting locally recognized systems without replacing them with other institutions that can or will effectively protect the newly delineated rights. Indeed, typically the main sense of insecurity experienced within strong customary systems is caused by the behaviour of the state and external market forces (Bouderbala, et al., 1996), in part because the legal status of customary areas is so poorly or weakly defined by state law that some governments have tended to treat such areas as reserves of "empty" land, open to discretionary allocation and re-allocation.

Such concerns have led to the emergence of a pragmatic approach to the issue of tenure reform. Bruce and Migot-Adholla (1994) identify a move away from a "replacement paradigm" – in which customary tenures are to be replaced by tenure provided by the state – toward an "adaptation paradigm", focused on creating the appropriate legal and administrative environment to permit evolutionary change within community-based systems. This approach calls for a more incremental programme of change. It advocates titling activities that are more narrowly focused on particular localities with particular needs, where, for example, conflicts are endemic and customary institutions are failing to cope with them, where land is increasingly subject to competition and where the commercialization of agriculture is relatively advanced. And it calls for creating "space" within national land law systems for local tenure arrangements to function.

It is premature to say that this approach has substantially reshaped the legal treatment of customary tenure in Africa. Some laws have continued to move in the direction of unitary, individualized tenure regimes, based on the argument that existing customary tenure practices are inherently insecure (see, for example, the Eritrea Land Proclamation, 1994). However, the move toward greater accommodation of local diversity and decisionmaking is a powerful force within ongoing land policy debates in many African countries. It has inspired a large number of project-based experiments throughout the continent and, in a few very important instances, it has found expression in new national land laws. Amongst the latter are laws from Mozambique, the United Republic of Tanzania and Uganda, and from several countries in West Africa.

The Mozambique Land Law of 1997, as noted in section 3.1.2. above, retains the principle that land itself is owned by the state, but recognizes within that context a "right of use and benefit" over land, which is a private property right that is not subject to the discretionary will of the state as owner. (Garvey, 1998) Such a right may be acquired in a number of ways, most notably: (a) by occupation in accordance with customary norms and practices, or (b) through good faith occupation for more than ten years. While provision is made for issuing title documents, the issuance of a title is *not* a prerequisite for claiming protection under the law: in other words, the right exists; it is not created by state action.

One of the most interesting innovations under the Mozambique law is its recognition of "Local Communities" as entities potentially capable of holding rights over land, and of obtaining title to land in their name. Thus legal recognition may in effect be given to existing local systems of land-holding and resource access within which individual holdings are nested. Within a community area demarcated under the law, customary rules (or, perhaps more accurately, rules generated by and deemed legitimate by the community, whether based on long-standing custom or not) would govern the allocation of land. Thus, effectively the law provides legal recognition to local customary rules, without "freezing" those rules in place by attempting to codify them. This approach leaves flexibility for such rules to evolve over time.

At the same time, this device allows communities for the first time to gain legally recognized rights over areas used in common that are integral parts of their livelihood strategies and farming systems. Where land rights have been limited to the individual farming and homestead plots of individual households, it is precisely these common areas – grazing land, wood lots, bodies of water, etc. – that are most vulnerable to exploitation and encroachment from outside, based on the legal fiction that such areas are "empty". Under the 1997 Land Law, communities will now have a formal say in how such areas are used, developed and allocated.

Implementing the new Mozambique law necessarily requires coming to grips with questions such as how a community is to be defined, both in terms of its social makeup and the area over which it may legitimately assert control. The definition of "community" provided in the law is worth quoting, in part because it demonstrates the difficulties of capturing this complex and elusive concept in legal terms:

> "A grouping of families and individuals, living in a circumscribed territorial area at the level of a locality [the lowest official unit of local government in Mozambique] or below, which has as its objective the safeguarding of common interests through the protection of areas of habitation, agricultural areas, whether cultivated or in fallow, forests, sites of socio-cultural importance, grazing lands, water sources and areas for expansion". (Art. 1, unofficial translation)

There is, in essence, no predefined social or physical unit that automatically comprises a community for purposes of the Land Law. Regulations issued under the Law, in particular a so-called Technical Annex, make it clear that the definition is intended to provide only the broadest guidance for what is in fact a case-by-case process of community self-identification. This process includes participatory delimitation and mapping of community boundaries, and negotiations regarding the management of shared resources with neighbouring communities. (Tanner, 2002)

The United Republic of Tanzania's Village Land Act of 1999 is broadly similar in many of its main features to the Mozambique Land Law, though it differs at the level of detail. Again within a context where the state still holds radical title, the Act recognizes so-called "rights of occupancy" which can be of two types: granted (i.e., rights of occupancy allocated formally by the government), or customary (i.e., rights of occupancy arising by operation of custom). The Act makes clear its intention to provide recognition for "existing rights in and recognised long-standing occupation or use of land". Customary rights are, as in the case of Mozambique, to be protected whether registered or not. However, the Act contemplates a process for the adjudication, recording, registering and issuing of titles for customary rights. On village land, land allocation is to be governed by rules drawn up by the community itself. Unlike Mozambique, however, the "community" is an already defined entity in the form of a village which is recognized under Tanzanian law as being the lowest level of local government. Hence, while there will be in many cases a need to define the land over which a particular village has jurisdiction, the governing entity is already in place. The Village Council is, under the Act, the Village Land Manager, responsible for making decisions concerning the allocation of village land, the issuance of Certificates of Customary Rights of Occupancy and the maintenance of a Village Land Register. (Wily and Mbaya, 2001)

Ugandan land legislation offers yet more variations on these themes. The Constitution of 1995 and the 1998 Land Act recognize customary rights over land, and customary occupants of land are endowed with secure tenure even in the absence of registration. Within customary land areas, tenure relations are to be governed by local customary laws as administered by local Land Committees. Certificates of Customary Ownership are available, and may be issued by the Land Committees after adjudication, boundary demarcation and other decisionmaking processes are carried out in accordance with customary law. The certificate shall be considered conclusive evidence of title over the land, and provided conditions in the certificate allow, the land covered by the certificate may be sold, leased, mortgaged or otherwise disposed of. There is also a mechanism for the conversion of customary ownership into freehold. Finally, the Act also provides for the possibility that land may be held in communal ownership, a device that enables group ownership of farm and homestead land if desired, and allows for community assertions of ownership over resources used in common.

Mozambique, Tanzania and Uganda were not alone in pursuing legal reform designed to provide space within national land laws for the operation of diverse local arrangements. A number of other important African legislative examples from the past decade warrant mention:

- The *Code rural* in the Niger, passed in 1993 after a lengthy process of consultation, provides for giving legal recognition to customary rights through issuance of certificates attesting those rights by Land Commissions (*Commissions foncières*) established at *arrondissement* level. Customary use rights over pastures (which are typically state-owned) are both recognized and given priority. Attempts at conciliation before a competent traditional authority are mandatory before land disputes may be brought to courts. (Cavérivière, et al., 1991)
- South Africa's Communal Property Associations Act, 1996, while not specifically providing for the recognition of customary tenure regimes, provides a new tool by which groups may assert joint ownership of land. Internal arrangements within a group are governed by a self-designed constitution, which provides flexibility for the accommodation of existing community-based tenure regimes to the extent the group chooses.
- The 2001 *Charte pastorale* in Mali provides a new framework for addressing increasing conflicts between the users of pastoral lands, and for putting in place participatory joint management approaches that combine the efforts of local government institutions and pastoral associations. The drafting of the law was innovative because it was based on an in-depth inventory of diverse local practices affecting the use and management of pastoral lands. (FAO, 1999)

There are ongoing processes of land policy formulation in a number of African countries, such as Botswana, Kenya, Lesotho, Malawi and Swaziland, as well as an intense debate about the appropriate legal framework for land rights in the former South African homelands. These suggest that further law reforms addressing similar issues are likely to be proposed in the near future.

3.2.2. Strengthening the Land Rights of Indigenous Peoples

Laws recognizing the land rights of indigenous people in other parts of the world have emerged from a somewhat different policy context than legal reforms seeking to accommodate customary rights in Africa. They represent a response to efforts by distinct ethnic groups to maintain their cultural identities in the face of threats by majority populations or colonists. However, in substance, the laws that have emerged are concerned with many of the same issues as those in the recent African laws summarized above.

The region with the longest history of widespread, if wavering, attention to indigenous land issues is Latin America. The estimated indigenous population in the region was 40 million as of 1995, and is characterized by high concentrations of poverty and land insecurity. Throughout recent history, indigenous lands have been especially vulnerable to colonial and non-indigenous expansion, a trend exacerbated by a widespread failure of state legal regimes effectively to recognize indigenous forms of landholding. Throughout the twentieth century in a number of countries, there were periods of reform during which protectionist measures were put in place. In some countries, serious legislative attention has been paid over a number of decades to securing indigenous lands rights, even if implementation has been problematic. In general, however, the prevailing pattern has been one of "dispossession, displacement, marginalisation and assimilation". (Colchester, 2001)

The last decade and a half has witnessed renewed and heightened attention to the problem of indigenous peoples and lands. Rejecting previous policies that tended to favour the integration of indigenous groups, the new generation of Latin American constitutions adopted since 1985 have for the most part embraced a multicultural approach. In the case of land, this has resulted in a number of significant constitutional and legislative reforms that recognize the collective rights of indigenous peoples to own, use and manage their lands.

A few examples will illustrate some of the approaches that have been tried and the problems that persist. The 1999 Constitution of Venezuela, for instance, guarantees indigenous peoples the right to their lands and habitats as their "inalienable, un-leasable, un-mortgageable, untransferable collective property". A Demarcation Law passed in 2000 establishes a process by which indigenous peoples can demarcate their own lands and have those boundaries recognized. Although some ambiguity remains, the recent reforms and several others under consideration appear to consolidate a move towards a conception of indigenous landholdings as including wider areas used for hunting, fishing, gathering and rotational farming. (Colchester, 2001)

Ecuador's 1998 Constitution provides for the recognition of territorial rights of ethnic groups through the device of "Indigenous Territorial Circumscriptions". In addition to retaining preexisting restrictions on the sale or division of ancestral lands, it also provides that any decisions concerning resource exploitation or conservation in such territories must be undertaken with the full participation of indigenous peoples. Colombia's 1991 Constitution similarly vests rights in indigenous populations to participate in natural resource management decisions, and recognizes the authority of Indigenous Councils established and governed by traditional custom. (Plant and Hvalkof, 1999)

The 1996 Agrarian Reform Law in Bolivia gives legal recognition to *Tierras comunitarias de origen* (TCOs), and through this device vests in indigenous communities a collective, inalienable right over land and the resources located thereon. The law has run into considerable difficulty in terms of implementation, however. The procedures for demarcation of TCOs have triggered complaints about their complexity and the resulting slowness with which they can be applied. Moreover, preexisting concessions for timber, oil and minerals cover substantial areas within prospective TCOs, and the law is unclear about how, if at all, these earlier concessions are to be treated.

Not all Latin American laws on indigenous land rights from the past decade have similarly sought to protect identified territories from the incursions of the market. Peru's Land Law of 1995 provides mechanisms for the sale by the state of various types of land within indigenous territories to private investors. This law and a subsequent law on Coastal Peasant Communities have eased the conditions for the privatization of communal land tenure regimes, sparking criticism among many indigenous groups that such laws have the potential to accelerate the unravelling of indigenous tenure regimes. (Plant and Hvalkof, 1999) Similarly, Mexico's Constitution and Agrarian Law of 1992 allow for the first time the alienation of *ejido* (communal) land.

Outside of Latin America, important laws on indigenous land rights were adopted in a number of countries over the last decade, including Australia, Cambodia, Canada, the Philippines and the Russian Federation.

The adoption of a new Native Title Act in Australia in 1993 was prompted by an Australian High Court decision the year before. In *Mabo and others v. Queensland (No. 2)*, 170 CLR 1 (1992), the court held for the first time that native title of aboriginal communities had survived the assertion of radical title by the Crown over the territories that now comprise Australia. The Native Title Act gives legislative backing to the *Mabo* decision, and provides a framework for recognizing and settling native title claims. Although most of the Australian states already had various forms of aboriginal land rights legislation in place, *Mabo* and the Native Title Act were revolutionary in recognizing that native title arises from the continued validity of preexisting customary law, not from legislative grants from state governments to native groups. (Fingleton, 1998)

In the Philippines, passage of the Indigenous Peoples Rights Act (IPRA) in 1997 represented an important milestone in the efforts by advocates for the country's more than six million indigenous peoples to gain recognition of their ownership of ancestral lands. Indigenous people had long been subject to dispossession by government and outsiders. Despite the existence of case law supporting indigenous rights on the basis of "immemorial possession", in practice these rights were substantially disregarded. The 1992 Constitution affirmed the right of indigenous peoples to ancestral domains, a right that was given some operational substance in subsequent years, first in a series of important administrative orders and ultimately in the IPRA. The IPRA establishes procedures for the recognition of individual and communal ownership of "ancestral domains" and "ancestral lands". The Act:

- recognizes the principle of indigenous ownership and control over defined territories;
- describes a process for identifying and delineating the boundaries of ancestral domains and lands;
- accepts the application of customary law for the adjudication of disputes and for community decisions over resource management and land allocations within the territory;
- establishes the principle of "free and informed consent" before lands can be alienated or communities relocated; and
- puts in place a number of regulatory deterrents against the exploitation of indigenous land by outsiders.

In 2000, the IPRA survived an important challenge to its constitutionality in the Philippine Supreme Court, eliminating one of the obstacles to its implementation.

3.2.3. Common Threads and Common Concerns

The above examples of legal innovations relating to customary and indigenous rights come from a wide variety of different contexts. Nevertheless, it is possible to extract from these developments some common threads and to identify some common problems that will need attention in the years ahead. Broadly speaking, these laws share some of the following characteristics and reflect some of the following aspirations:

- They share a recognition that land has a social value, and that in some contexts that value is best realized by allowing land relations to be governed to a significant extent by the rules of the community in which the land is located, rather than by uniform systems of property law set by the state.
- They reflect a conviction that, in certain settings, community-based rules may be better at providing security of tenure to individual cultivators than are state systems. Often what individual cultivators fear is dispossession at the hands of government or outsiders, rather than by others within the community. In such contexts, the most appropriate role of legislation may be to enhance the security of the community system as a whole, rather than seeking to define and document the individual arrangements within that system.
- They acknowledge that community-based systems can often be better at reflecting the complex rights that individuals, families and groups have over land, including secondary rights of access and use – rights that might be distorted or lost by titling according to a standardized format that is not adapted to local realities.
- They recognize that a community's relationship with land is more than just an aggregate of individually occupied and used plots; it is a system that includes land-based resources used in common, such as pastures, water and forests. The need for legal protection does not stop at the border of cultivated parcels, but extends into other components of the system as well.

At the same time, the drafting of laws that recognize community-based rights and that can coherently accommodate a number of tenure regimes within a national legal framework is a complex task. While experience with the operation of many of these laws is slender so far, it is possible to identify a number of problems and challenges that are likely to require attention from law drafters, administrators and advocates of local rights:

Weak, ambiguous or inconsistent laws. In many cases, relevant laws define local rights vaguely or weakly, leaving those rights difficult to enforce and vulnerable to the interpretive discretion of officials. Overly broad definitions of "national interest" and unclear descriptions of community powers can serve as a pretext for governments overriding local rights when it serves their needs or the needs of their allies. Vague statements in land laws regarding local control over common resources may be inconsistent with more specific powers given to officials or concessionaires under forestry, mining or wildlife laws and may thus be ignored in practice.

Complexities in defining the communities, rules and institutions being recognized. State recognition of customary or community-based tenure regimes does not usually require the codification of customary law; indeed, it is widely argued that codification could have the undesirable effect of undermining the flexibility and adaptability of local systems. But formal recognition does require identifying, with some degree of precision, the community whose rights are being recognized, the area over which it has legitimate claims and the local institutions or decision-making processes that are entitled to respect by formal legal institutions. If carelessly done, formal recognition may unduly privilege one of several competing local visions of what constitutes the community, and what rules or authorities are legitimate. This is exacerbated where outsiders automatically make a connection between a community and certain conspicuous symbols of the community – for example, by attributing greater power to chiefs than would be considered legitimate by the community itself.

Balancing respect for local decisionmaking with the promotion of human rights, democracy and accountability. In some contexts, custom may run counter to a vision of human rights enshrined in a national constitution or other national laws, particularly where it comes to the treatment of women and minorities. Laws such as the Mozambique Land Law therefore require courts to apply customary law only to the extent it is consistent with the constitution. While unexceptional as a principle of constitutional law, in practice its implementation may prove difficult. A similar dilemma arises when it comes to ensuring minimum levels of accountability and transparency within local structures. In many rural communities, traditional checks and balances on the exercise of power may be eroding and rules may be undergoing reinterpretation in ways that favour the elite. In such instances, calls for some degree of formalization of individual holdings and for a clearer legal definition of the powers and responsibilities of traditional leaders may come from within communities themselves. Again, the challenge lies in identifying the right level of intervention to address such concerns while still promoting local processes. How far should government law intervene in this respect? How far *can* it intervene without fundamentally altering the very institutions it purports to empower?

Protecting community-based rights while enhancing economic opportunities. There is no inherent contradiction between giving increased legal recognition to customary or indigenous tenure systems and promoting economic growth – indeed, in some contexts it is argued that the former is a prerequisite for the latter. But the choice of legal techniques may have the effect of skewing the balance between protection on the one hand and the ability to adapt to new opportunities or challenges on the other. Protecting the integrity of local systems against the incursions of richer and more sophisticated outsiders may, as a starting point, justify restrictions on the alienability of land, which are found in many of the laws referred to above. The question is whether an emphasis on protection reflects the needs and aspirations of local people, particularly in rapidly changing economic environments. Some of the laws above provide avenues by which communities or individuals may seek to attract outside investment on their land, subject to an internal process of approval. There are in some cases opportunities for individuals or groups to "opt out" of local tenure systems in favour of acquiring individualized titles under a state-sponsored scheme (e.g., Uganda's Land Act of 1998). To a great extent, these techniques are still untested, and it remains an open question how they will function over time.

The challenge of capacity. The trend towards devolving greater authority to local institutions – whether traditional bodies or local governments – has many strong justifications. These approaches are not, however, necessarily cheap, either in financial or human terms. The process of delimiting ancestral domains in the Philippines, for example, has suffered from insufficient allocation of financial and human resources. It is estimated that the ambitious and innovative decentralization of land administration set forth in Uganda's Land Act would, if fully implemented, exceed considerably the financial capacity of the responsible ministry. The impressive example of some traditional chieftaincy areas (stools) in Ghana that have established land secretariats is not one that is necessarily replicable on a wide scale within the country, due to widely differing capacities, circumstances and interests of traditional authorities. These are obviously not reasons for abandoning devolution strategies. They do suggest, however, a need for more systematic reflection on the part of institutional reformers and lawmakers about the demands that new innovations will put on capacity, both within government and local communities, and how those capacity demands can be met.

3.3 Facilitating Access to Land

Over the last decade, a great deal of research and analysis has reinforced the importance of enabling the landless or the land-poor to acquire land. As a general aspiration, this has been widely embraced by policymakers at both national and international levels. Similarly, significant policy attention has focused on the special disadvantages faced by women with respect to land access. However, compared to the issues discussed in the preceding sections, efforts to address access problems through legislative reform have been modest at best.

3.3.1. Privatization, Restitution and Other Redistributive Mechanisms

Most of the more famous land reforms undertaken in the decades after World War II (in jurisdictions such as Japan, Korea, Taiwan, Brazil and elsewhere in Latin America, India, etc.) focused primarily on redistributive issues. They were directly concerned with reducing land concentration and transferring land rights to existing tenants, sharecroppers or labourers on large estates or to the landless. Today, in many parts of the world, the problem of inequitable distribution of land ownership remains acute, exacerbating the problems of landlessness, social tension and unsustainable use of marginal or environmentally sensitive lands.

In the past decade, new policies and legal initiatives directly focusing on redistribution of land are conspicuous for their relative absence. There are several major exceptions, but these largely emerged in particular parts of the world in response to unique historical moments – the end of communism, the demise of apartheid, the cessation of hostilities that had resulted in massive long-term displacement. They cannot therefore be classified as legislative efforts to deal systematically with the chronic inequality of land distribution that exists in many countries.

The most intensive redistribution of land that occurred during this period involved the redistribution of state land to private persons in the form of land privatization in Central and Eastern Europe and the former Soviet Union. The new types of private land rights that have emerged in these countries have been discussed already in section 3.1. To get lands into private hands in the first place, however, required a separate legislative step. Several privatization mechanisms were legislated across the region, ranging from the auctioning of land owned by state enterprises to the restructuring of collective farms. One frequent type of privatization in the case of agricultural land has been the "land share" approach, found in the Russian Federation, Ukraine and elsewhere. Under this approach, members of collective or state farms have been issued shares representing ownership of a portion of the farm. These shares may be transferred through sale or otherwise, and may in theory be converted into a specific parcel of land for individual farming purposes (though in practice this conversion may be difficult to accomplish). (Valletta & Nosick, 2002)

Another type of privatization involves the restitution of land to persons or the descendants of persons who owned the land prior to its nationalization under communist regimes. This process has been the centrepiece of reforms in much of Central and Eastern Europe, and has been the subject of numerous constitutional provisions and laws. Lithuania's Law on Restitution, for example, provides for the return of land to individuals (or their children or grandchildren) who had ownership rights in 1940, if the land has remained substantially unchanged in character during the intervening years. If the land has been altered, the claimant is entitled to choose another available parcel or compensation in the form of vouchers or money.

Restitution has also played important roles, unrelated to privatization, in a number of other countries. In South Africa, for example, restitution was one of three pillars in the country's post-apartheid land reform programme. In post-conflict societies such as Cambodia, Burundi and Rwanda, recent laws have had to accommodate the return of large numbers of internally displaced persons or exiles to land that is frequently occupied by new families or communities.

Outside the context of privatization and restitution programmes, only a few countries have adopted new legislation during the past decade in support of redistribution. Namibia adopted in 1995 an Agricultural (Commercial) Land Reform Act, which provides for the imposition of size limits on commercial farms based on agro-ecological zoning and other criteria. Land made surplus through the application of these limits is to be used for resettlement. (McAuslan, et al., 1995) More famous has been Zimbabwe's policy of acquiring primarily white-owned commercial farms for resettlement purposes. A legislative framework for this acquisition was provided by the Land Acquisition Act, 1992, which has been amended a number of times with the effect of dramatically increasing the powers of the President to acquire land, by reducing various procedural safeguards and compensation requirements.

More generally, measures aimed directly at redistributing land or preventing the accumulation of large landholdings have not been high on the political agenda in most parts of the world during the last decade. In large part this is because there simply has not been sufficient political will to push such measures given their highly sensitive and potentially explosive nature and their financial costs. Many countries continue to have on the books various methods of imposing size limitations on landholdings (and in several cases these have been enacted or re-enacted in laws passed during the 1990s, in Africa, Central and Eastern Europe, the former Soviet Republics and elsewhere), but these are seldom invoked and often easily circumvented. India's experience over the last few decades with laws that place ceilings on the allowable size of land-holdings has led some observers to conclude that they primarily create distortions and impose regulatory costs on the operation of land markets.

Discouragement with standard approaches to redistributive reform led during the past decade to several important attempts to design and test alternative approaches. One is an approach referred to as "negotiated land reform", which focuses on facilitating voluntary transfers from buyers to sellers, with the government providing monetary grants to qualified beneficiaries. Variations of this basic approach have been tried in Brazil, Colombia, South Africa and several other countries. In some cases, these approaches found expression in new laws, such as the 1994 Land Reform Law in Colombia which provides a framework for the allocation of land purchase grants. Early implementation of the Colombian grant scheme ran into trouble because of restrictions in the law that limited the use of funds to the acquisition of land alone, and disallowed their use for complementary investments. This contributed, among other things, to collusion between buyers and sellers with respect to the sales price, a problem which subsequent adjustments attempted to address. (Deininger, 1999) Variations and refinements on these themes have more recently been grouped under the rubric "community managed agrarian reform", and described as "models of demand-driven reform with strong involvement by local communities and beneficiaries that aims to link the land reform process more closely to development at the local levels". (Deininger, 2002)

The effectiveness of these approaches in terms of what they can achieve on the ground remains to be seen, and their implications for the further evolution of land law are similarly unclear. What is clear, however, is that the profound economic and social costs of inequitable land distribution are increasingly well understood by donors, researchers and governments, and pressure to address those costs more aggressively is likely to grow in the future.

3.3.2. Rethinking Restrictions on Leasing

Particularly given the difficulties associated with redistributive land reforms, new attention has focused in recent years on the potential of other regulatory reforms to enhance the ability of the rural poor to gain access to land. One subject receiving particular scrutiny is the tendency of governments to discourage the leasing of private agricultural land.

Traditionally, governments have considered leasing an *obstacle* to land reform. Inspired by a desire to eliminate absentee landlordism and exploitative landlord-tenant relations, a number of governments have imposed significant restrictions on the private leasing of agricultural land. In some cases, leasing has essentially been prohibited, as in a number of Indian states. In other cases, laws may provide for the ripening of a leasehold into ownership after a short time, and/or may impose strict controls on the amount of rent that can be charged.

There has been a serious rethinking of these approaches in recent years. This has been prompted in part by a growing appreciation of the importance of tenancy to the livelihood strategies of the rural poor in many countries notwithstanding attempts to curtail it, particularly in contexts where access through purchase or government redistribution is difficult or unlikely. Where attempts have been made to severely restrict leasing of agricultural land, one of the effects has been to drive the practice underground, where it continues to flourish outside the pale of the law. Studies in India, for example, show that far from eliminating leasing and sharecropping, legal restrictions have arguably increased the lack of security experienced by tenants and significantly reduced the amount of land to which poor farmers could otherwise have access. Eager to avoid the operation of the law, landlords may shift tenants frequently from area to area. Tenants are subjected to threats of eviction or physical intimidation to ensure that tenancies go unreported (Lindsay, et al., 2001), and the state is in a weak position to mediate a relationship it no longer recognizes as existing (FAO, 2001).

As of yet, there are few examples from developing countries of laws designed to strike a new, more appropriate balance between liberalization and tenant protection, an objective that is likely to require different techniques in different contexts. Nevertheless, a number of policy proposals have been put forth, in regions as diverse as South Asia and the Caribbean, and it is likely that this will be an area to which increasing legislative attention is devoted in the coming years.

3.3.3. Improving Women's Access to Land

Not all segments of a rural society confront similar obstacles in gaining access to land. As is well known, women often face especially profound constraints in acquiring secure rights to land and other natural resources, in retaining land over time and in accessing credit markets and other inputs. In many instances, laws and local practices effectively preclude women from obtaining title to land in their own names, and inheritance laws frequently discriminate against female offspring. Married women frequently find that, with divorce or widowhood, they retain few rights over household land. "In many countries ... cultural if not legal norms dictate that men are the owners of land and that women have access to land only through their relationship with a male relative, be it father, husband, brother, or even brother-in-law". (Lastarria-Cornhiel, 2002) Many of these factors are examined in more detail in the next chapter.

These problems have increasing significance in rapidly changing rural societies. Women play a major role – in some cases the predominant role – in the provision of agricultural labour, and current trends suggest that this role is growing. In many areas of the world, there has been a steep rise in the number of female-headed households, due to a range of factors, including increasing migration of males to urban areas in search of off-farm employment, and changing male-female population ratios because of chronic armed conflict and HIV/AIDS. Changing social structures and norms mean that some of the social safety nets that women might have been able to rely upon in the past have weakened or disappeared.

As already noted, women's land issues have gained high visibility in international fora, and have been the focus of intense advocacy work both locally and worldwide. One of the outcomes has been increasing reference to women's land rights in national constitutions and legislation. Frequently such references are in the form of general statements establishing the principle of gender equity in land rights. In a few cases, laws have gone further towards putting in place mechanisms for implementing the principle. These and other issues relating to enhancing women's rights to land are explored in greater detail in Chapter 9.

IV. CONCLUSION

The record of the last decade with respect to land law reform is a mixed one. In some parts of the world, there has been substantial legislative progress towards strengthening the rights and clarifying the responsibilities of individuals and communities, and rationalizing the role of government. New legal space for local initiatives and local institutions has been created, and important conceptual advances have been made in terms of designing laws that attempt to accommodate and coordinate diverse tenure regimes, rather than standardize them.

At the same time, in many countries much remains unfinished or even not yet begun. Some important laws that have been passed are riddled with ambiguities, apparent contradictions and excessive complexities. In other cases, promising reform initiatives have stalled altogether. In part, these outcomes simply reflect the fact that the process of land law reform is usually a slow one, subject to fits and starts and diversions. More significantly, it is also often a highly contentious process, in which "'objective' considerations of what is best for economic or social or sustainable development" are frequently sidetracked by politics. (McAuslan, 2000b) Even when it comes to such "objective" considerations, land laws often reflect the interplay of a number of agendas which are prone to push in different directions.

Finally, as in many areas of law, some of the more promising innovations in land law from this decade lie largely un-implemented – victims, in some cases, of over-ambition on the part of their drafters; in many cases, of governmental failure to muster the resources or sustained commitment needed for implementation and of constraints on civil society's ability to mobilize and demand action.

In short, the developments reported on here are perhaps less significant as a measure of what has been accomplished, then they are as harbingers of things to come: they provide rough road maps to the issues and complexities that are likely to consume the attention of policymakers, lawyers and advocates for land rights in the years ahead.

REFERENCES

Bouderbala, N., Cavérivière, M. & Ouédraogo, H. 1996. *Tendances d'évolution des législations agrofoncières en Afrique francophone.* Legislative Study No. 56, FAO, Rome.

Bruce, J.W. & Migot-Adholla, S. (eds.). 1994. *Searching for Land Tenure Security in Africa.* Kendall/Hunt, Dubuque.

Cavérivière M., Debene, M. & Mouddour, B. 1991. *Niger. Appui à l'élaboration du code rural.* FAO, Rome.

Convention on Biological Diversity (CBD). 1997. *Traditional Knowledge and Biological Diversity,* UNEP/CBD/ TKBD/1/2.

Colchester, M. (ed.). 2001. *A Survey of Indigenous Land Tenure: A Report for the Land Tenure Service of the Food and Agriculture Organization.* FAO, Rome.

Deininger, K. 1999. *Making Negotiated Land Reform Work: Initial Experience from Colombia, Brazil and South Africa.* World Bank, Washington, D.C.

Deininger, K. 2002. *Land Institutions and Policy: Key Messages of the Policy Research Report.* In *World Bank Regional Workshop on Land Policy Issues in Asia,* World Bank, Phnom Penh.

FAO. 1999. *Mali. Appui à l'inventaire des normes et coutumes en matière de foncier pastoral,* Rome.

FAO. 2001. *Good Practice Guidelines for Agricultural Leasing Arrangements,* Rome.

Fingleton, J. 1998. *Legal Recognition of Indigenous Groups.* FAO Legal Paper Online 1 (www.fao.org/Legal).

Garvey, J. 1998. *The Nature of Rights under Mozambique's Reform Land Law.* In *International Conference on Land Tenure in the Developing World, with a Focus on Southern Africa,* GTZ, Capetown.

Giovarelli, R. & Bledsoe, D. 2001. *Land Reform in Eastern Europe.* FAO, Rome.

Hendrix, S. 1993. *Property Law Innovations in Latin America, with Recommendations,* Land Tenure Center Working Paper, Madison.

Lastarria-Cornhiel, S. 2002. *Integrating Gender in Land Tenure Programmes: Findings and Lessons from Country Case Studies.* FAO, Rome.

Lindsay, J.M. 1997. *Creating a Legal Framework for Land Registration in Eritrea.* FAO, Rome.

Lindsay, J.M., Palmer, D. & Rekhi, V.S. 2001. *Land Administration and Management in Madhya Pradesh.* FAO/World Bank, Rome.

McAuslan, P. 2000a. *From Greenland's Icy Mountains, From India's Coral Strand: The Globalisation of Land Markets and its Impact on National Land Law.* In *1° Congresso Brasileiro de Direito Urbanístico, Ordem dos Advogados do Brasil, Seção Belo Horizonte.*

McAuslan, P. 2000b. *Only the Name of the Country Changes: The Diaspora of 'European' Land Law in Commonwealth Africa.* In C. Toulmin & J. Quan (eds.), *Evolving Land Rights, Policy and Tenure in Africa,* IIED, London.

McAuslan, P., Behnke, R.H. & Howard, J. 1995. *Namibia. Assistance in Implementation of Agricultural (Commercial) Land Reform.* FAO, Rome.

Plant, R. & Hvalkof, S. 2000. *Land Titling and Indigenous Peoples.* Inter-American Development Bank, Washington, D.C.

Rolfes, Jr., L. 2002. *Making the Legal Basis for Private Land Rights Operational and Effective.* In *World Bank Regional Workshop on Land Policy Issues: Central Europe and the CIS,* World Bank, Budapest.

Rural Development Institute (RDI). 1999. *Legal Impediments to Effective Rural Land Relations in ECA Countries: A Comparative Perspective.* RDI, Seattle.

Tanner, C. 2002. *Law Making in an African Context: The 1997 Mozambican Land Law.* FAO Legal Paper Online No. 26 (www.fao.org/Legal).

Trackman, B., Fisher, W. & Salas, L. 1999. *The Reform of Property Registration Systems in Costa Rica: A Status Report.* Harvard Law School, Cambridge.

Valletta, W. 2000. *Completing the Transition: Lithuania Nears the End of its Land Restitution and Reform Programme.* FAO Legal Paper Online No. 11 (www.fao.org/Legal).

Valletta, W. & Nosick, V. 2002. *Ukraine: The Continuing Dilemma of Land Rights of the People.* FAO Legal Paper Online No. 25 (www.fao.org/Legal).

Valletta, W. & Venable, H. 1998. *China's New Land Administration Law.* (unpublished manuscript).

Wily, L.A. & Mbaya, S. 2001. *Land, People and Forest in Eastern and Southern Africa at the Beginning of the 21ˢᵗ Century.* IUCN, Nairobi.

9

GENDER

Contents

I. INTRODUCTION

As noted in the previous chapter, in many countries, women constitute a large portion of the economically active population engaged in agriculture. However, in many parts of the world, women have little or no access to resources such as land, credit and extension services. Moreover, women tend to remain concentrated in the informal sector of the economy. In plantations, they often provide labour without employment contracts, on a temporary or seasonal basis or as wives or daughters of male farm workers.

Women's rights are affected by a great variety of norms, including international instruments and national legislation. Moreover, women's rights are affected by customary law, which is widely applied in the rural areas of Africa, the Asia-Pacific region and Latin America, especially in those regions inhabited by indigenous communities. Finally, the exercise of women's rights is affected by entrenched cultural attitudes and perceptions, often internalized by women themselves.

The post-Rio decade has witnessed a major change in that there is much greater attention paid to gender, at both international and national levels. Recent international treaties and conferences have stressed the importance of women's rights and gender equality. At the national level, many countries have adopted comprehensive plans of action, and have taken steps to improve women's rights in general legislation (e.g., family and succession laws) and in sectoral laws (on land, agrarian reform, cooperatives, etc.). Courts have also played an important role, developing case law on women's rights concerning inheritance, land and labour.

This chapter reviews some of the main developments concerning women's rights in agriculture since the Rio Conference. While these issues are dealt with separately for reasons of clarity, they are in reality intertwined. For instance, land rights are determined both by land legislation and by family and succession law, and the borderline between these may be blurred in legislation (with land laws addressing women's inheritance rights), case law (with cases involving both types of norms) and customary law. Similarly, access to credit partly depends on land ownership, as land titles can be used as collateral to secure loans. Some important aspects of women's rights are not covered in this chapter, due to their only indirect bearing on agriculture (e.g., reproductive health).

II.   INTERNATIONAL DEVELOPMENTS

2.1. International Gender-related Conferences

Recent international conferences have adopted soft law declarations and plans of action revealing increased attention in the international community to gender issues. Particularly important are the 1994 Cairo Plan of Action on Population and Development, the 1995 Beijing Platform for Action adopted by the Fourth World Conference on Women and the 1996 World Food Summit Plan of Action. Some provisions of these documents relate directly to environment and agriculture. For instance, the Beijing Platform for Action envisages legislative and administrative reforms to ensure gender equality in access to natural resources, including inheritance rights (para. 61(b)). The World Food Summit Plan of Action also envisages measures to enhance women's access to natural resources (para. 16(b)), and affirms the goal of ensuring gender equality and women's empowerment (objective 1.3).

2.2. International Human Rights Instruments

The main global instrument dealing with women's rights is the Convention on the Elimination of All Forms of Discrimination Against Women (CEDAW, 1979), which prohibits sex discrimination and provides for affirmative action (arts. 2 and 4). The principle of non-discrimination is stated in a very broad way, applying not only to state-enacted laws and regulations, but also to the behaviour of private individuals. Women's rights under the CEDAW include the right to a legal capacity identical to that of men, including equal rights to conclude contracts and administer property (art. 15); gender equality in relation to marriage and family (art. 16); and non-discrimination in employment and training (arts. 11 and 12). Article 14 specifically protects the rights of rural women, including the right to "equal treatment in land and agrarian reform".

A major development in relation to the CEDAW has been the adoption of an Optional Protocol (1999) allowing individuals and groups claiming violations to submit complaints to the Committee on the Elimination of All Forms of Discrimination Against Women. After hearing such complaints, the Committee communicates to the parties its views and recommendations, and states are to "give due consideration" to these and provide a written response. (Protocol, arts. 1, 2 and 7). Moreover, the Committee may on its own initiative start confidential inquiries on "grave or systematic violations", although states may opt out of this procedure (arts. 8–10).

Soft law instruments have also been adopted by United Nations human rights institutions. For instance, Resolution 15 (1998) of the Sub-Commission on the Promotion and Protection of Human Rights states that discrimination against women with respect to acquiring and securing land constitutes a violation of human rights law. The Resolution urges governments to amend or repeal discriminatory laws and policies and to encourage the transformation of discriminatory customs and traditions.

Women's rights are also protected by regional human rights treaties, such as the European Convention for the Protection of Human Rights and Fundamental Freedoms (1950, as amended), the American Convention on Human Rights (1969), the African Charter on Human and Peoples' Rights (1981) and the Arab Charter on Human Rights (adopted in 1994 but not yet in force).

2.3. International Environmental Instruments

Some Rio and post-Rio international environmental instruments contain provisions specifically addressing gender. The preamble of the Convention on Biological Diversity recognizes women's "vital role" in the conservation and sustainable use of biodiversity, and affirms the need for their participation in policies concerning these issues. Among Rio soft law instruments, principle 20 of the Rio Declaration states that "women have a vital role in environmental management and development", and "their full participation is therefore essential to achieve sustainable development". The Non-Legally Binding Authoritative Statement of Principles on Forests calls for women's participation in the planning, development and implementation of national forest policies and in the management, conservation and sustainable development of forests (principles 2(d) and 5(b)). Moreover, Chapter 24 of Agenda 21 is specifically devoted to gender.

An example of a gender-sensitive post-Rio instrument is the 1994 Convention to Combat Desertification, which provides for the facilitation of women's participation in efforts to combat desertification at all levels, and specifically for their effective participation in national action programmes (arts. 5 and 10). Women's participation in national action programmes is also required by article 8 of the Regional Implementation Annex for Africa, an associated instrument to the Convention.

2.4. International Labour Conventions and Declarations

The rights of women agricultural workers are addressed in several conventions adopted by the International Labour Organization (ILO), particularly the Equal Remuneration Convention 100 of 1951, the Maternity Protection (Revised) Convention 103 of 1952, the Discrimination (Employment and Occupation) Convention 111 of 1958 and the Plantations Convention 110 of 1958 with its 1982 Protocol.

A major recent development in this field has been the adoption of the 1998 ILO Declaration on the Fundamental Principles and Rights at Work, which reaffirms some principles and rights to which all ILO member states must adhere by the very fact of their ILO membership, regardless of their ratification of the relevant conventions. The principles include the elimination of discrimination in employment and occupation, which encompasses sex discrimination.

III. NATIONAL LAW

3.1. Impact of International Instruments on National Legal Systems

The international developments cited above have had reverberations at national level. Most countries have adopted comprehensive plans of action and established specific institutions to follow up the Beijing Platform for Action. In some cases, discriminatory norms have been repealed under the direct pressure of international instruments. For instance, in *Morales de Sierra v. Guatemala*, a woman filed a complaint with the Inter-American Commission on Human Rights concerning some provisions of the Guatemalan Civil Code. These empowered the husband to administer family property and allowed married women to undertake an occupation only where consistent with their role as housewives. In 1998, after a positive preliminary decision on the admissibility of the complaint, the Guatemalan Government repealed most of the challenged norms. (Inter-American Commission on Human Rights, Case 11625, Report No. 28/98, 6 March 1998, and Report No. 4/01, 19 January 2001)

In some cases, international law has an even more direct bearing on national legal systems, for example where it provides guidance in the interpretation of domestic law, including law affecting women's legal status. For instance, the 1996 Constitution of South Africa states that international law must be considered when interpreting the human rights recognized in the Constitution, and that interpretations of national legislation consistent with international law must be preferred. In some countries, self-executing treaty provisions, including those on women's rights, are enforceable before courts. Human rights treaties have been relied upon by national courts to strike down discriminatory domestic norms.

3.2. Gender Equality in Constitutions

Most pre-Rio constitutions prohibit sex discrimination (1988 Constitution of Brazil; 1949 Constitution of India; 1948 Constitution of Italy; 1917 Constitution of Mexico), or state the principle of equality without specifying any ground of discrimination (1959 Constitution of Tunisia). The constitutions of the 1990s tend to place greater emphasis on human rights in general and on women's rights in particular. Most prohibit sex discrimination (1990 Constitution of Namibia; 1992 Constitutions of Ghana, Paraguay and Uzbekistan; 1995 Constitutions of Malawi and Uganda; 1997 Constitutions of Burkina Faso and Thailand). The Constitution of South Africa (1996) prohibits discrimination on the basis of sex, gender, pregnancy and marital status, and lists "non-sexism" among the fundamental values of the state. On the basis of the constitutional principle of non-discrimination, courts may invalidate norms discriminating against women. Some earlier constitutions have been amended to address gender equality: in Kenya, a 1997 constitutional amendment included "sex" among the prohibited grounds of discrimination. In some cases, however, the principle of non-discrimination remains qualified by exceptions for family and succession law and for customary law (Fiji, Ghana, Kenya).

Besides prohibiting sex / gender discrimination, some constitutions contain an affirmative action clause allowing special measures in favour of women (Ghana, Paraguay, Uganda). Similar clauses may be included among principles guiding state policies. Thus, the Constitution of Ghana requires the government to take steps to fully integrate women "into the mainstream of the economic development of Ghana". The Namibian Constitution requires legislation ensuring equality of opportunities for women "to enable them to participate fully in all spheres of Namibian society".

Some recent constitutions have addressed the issue of discrimination embodied in customary norms. The Constitution of Uganda specifically prohibits "laws, cultures, customs or traditions which are against the dignity, welfare or interest of women or which undermine their status".

The Constitution of South Africa, although it recognizes the role of customary law and institutions, requires respect for the Constitution and statutory legislation.

3.3. Family and Succession Law

3.3.1. Legal Capacity

Several legal systems envisage limits on the capacity of married women to perform acts with legal effect, including signing contracts and filing legal cases. Some states have norms subjecting a woman's taking up of employment to her household responsibilities or to the husband's authorization (the Civil Code of Indonesia; the Personal Status Act of the Syrian Arab Republic; the Civil Code of some Mexican states, e.g., Oaxaca). Their ability to carry out business transactions may also be limited. For instance, the Civil Code of the Dominican Republic prohibits a married woman from entering into contractual obligations without the authorization of her husband. (Galán, 1998) Under the Commercial Code of Chile, a woman married under certain marital property regimes must obtain her husband's authorization to sign contracts establishing companies.

The last decades have witnessed a trend toward the gradual repeal of these norms. For instance, in Brazil, the original text of the Civil Code of 1916 made married women incapable of performing certain acts without their husband's authorization; Law 4121 (1962) reduced the number of acts requiring the husband's consent; and finally the Constitution of 1988 and the Civil Code of 2002 affirmed the equality of rights and duties of both spouses. In South Africa, the inferior status of women married under customary law envisaged by the Black Administration Act of 1927 was repealed by the Recognition of Customary Marriages Act of 1998. In Tunisia, provisions of the Code of Obligations and Contracts requiring the husband's authorization for married women to sign service contracts were repealed by Law 17 (2000). In Malawi, the 1995 Constitution grants women equal legal capacity to enter into contracts and to acquire and maintain property rights.

In some cases, these changes have been prompted by complaints brought before international institutions (as noted above for Guatemala) or domestic courts. For instance, in Turkey, article 159 of the 1926 Civil Code, requiring the husband's consent for married women to enter into labour contracts, was set aside by the Constitutional Court (Judgement 30/31, 29 November 1990); the Civil Code 2001 abolishes the spousal authorization, although the welfare of the family is to be taken into account in the choice and pursuit of occupation.

In a few cases, provisions on legal capacity are contained in gender-specific legislation. For instance, the Philippines' Women in Development and Nation Building Act of 1992 grants women full legal capacity to act and to enter into contracts, regardless of their marital status.

3.3.2. Rights in Family Property

Norms concerning the internal organization of the family and the conduct of family affairs may affect the ability of women to acquire and control property, including land. The legislation of some countries recognizes the husband as household head or representative (the Civil Codes of Dominican Republic, Honduras and Nicaragua), and grants him exclusive administrative rights over family property (Dominican Republic, Honduras) and even over the personal property of the wife (Dominican Republic). (Galán, 1998) In the Philippines, the Family Code provides for community property, with joint administration by both spouses, although in case of disagreement, the decision of the husband prevails.

In several countries, the last decade has witnessed some positive changes, particularly in relation to the adoption of community property as the default marital property regime. The Family Code of Ethiopia (2000) grants spouses equal rights in the management of the family; provides for community property in relation to property acquired after marriage, with some exceptions; creates a presumption of common property for goods registered in the name of one spouse; requires the consent of both spouses for transfers of common property; and envisages joint administration of family property. The Code also envisages community property for *de facto* unions lasting not less than three years. The Brazilian Civil Code of 2002 provides for the equality of rights and duties of the spouses and for the application, in the absence of prenuptial agreements, of a regime of partial community property, with each spouse having equal rights to administer common property and to administer his or her separate property.

Under Turkey's Civil Code of 2001, the husband is no longer the household head, and men and women have equal status within marriage. The Code also introduced a community property regime with equal shares for the spouses. In Tunisia, a 1993 amendment to the 1956 Personal Status Code replaced the duty of the wife to obey her husband with the principle of mutual assistance: while the husband remains the household head, both spouses are to cooperate in the management of family affairs. Moreover, Law 98-91 (1998) allows spouses to opt for a community property regime.

Rights in family property may also be determined by customary law. In some customary systems of the Philippines, for instance, both spouses have exclusive management rights over their individual property (e.g., among the Ilocano); where the husband administers family property, he must acquire the consent of the wife for land transfers (e.g., among the Pangasinense). (Judd and Dulnuan, 2001)

3.3.3. Inheritance Rights

Succession law affects women's access to land rights, particularly in countries where land sales are rare and inheritance is the primary form of land acquisition. Problems can arise where testamentary freedom is very broad, as testators may leave land to male relatives, following socio-cultural practices. Some legal systems recognize a nearly absolute testamentary freedom, providing only for the maintenance of the surviving spouse. The Mexican Agrarian Law 1992, for instance, which created institutional arrangements for holding and managing land redistributed under agrarian reform (*ejidos*), allows *ejidatarios* (individual right-holders) to freely choose one heir (*ejido* rights cannot be subdivided) among the spouse, a child or "any other person". The *ejidatario* may exclude the spouse from succession, and field studies reveal that in many Mexican states land is usually left to the eldest son. (Katz, 1999)

In rural areas where customary law is applied, women's inheritance rights are often severely limited, not only within patrilineal systems (where property devolves along the male line, to the exclusion of women), but also in matrilineal systems (where, although property traces through the mother's line, land control usually rests with male family members). For instance, among the Mossi of Burkina Faso, wives and daughters usually do not inherit land, and even Muslim women, who under *Shari'a* law are generally entitled to half the share of men, tend to waive their rights in favour of their brothers. Similar patterns are found in India. (Agarwal, 1994) On the other hand, in the bilateral inheritance systems of the Philippines, where inheritance follows both the male and the female line, succession norms adopt either the primogeniture system (whereby land is inherited by the eldest male or female child) or the equal sharing system (whereby all male and female heirs inherit equally). The surviving spouse, male or female, may not inherit, but holds land as a trustee for the children. (Judd and Dulnuan, 2001)

In relation to succession, judicial decisions may annul or limit customary norms. In Nigeria, the Enugu Court of Appeal invalidated norms providing for inheritance by male family members only (*Mojekwu v. Mojekwu*, 1997, 7 NWLR 283) and subjecting inheritance by daughters to their undertaking to remain unmarried and raise their brothers (*Mojekwu v. Ejikeme*, 2000, 5 NWLR 402). On the other hand, the courts of some countries have upheld rigid and discriminatory interpretations of customary law. For instance, the Supreme Court of Zimbabwe upheld a customary norm excluding women from intestate succession, naming as the heir the second male child instead of the eldest female child. (*Magaya v. Magaya*, 1998)

In yet other cases, courts have only partially invalidated customary norms. In the Nepali case *Dhungana v. Law, Justice and Parliamentary Affairs Ministry* (4 S.Ct. Bull. 1), the petitioner challenged the provisions of Nepal's National Civil Code limiting daughters' inheritance rights (entitling them to an inheritance share only after they reached the age of 35 unmarried, and providing for land restitution to the family if they subsequently married). The Supreme Court, while recognizing that the norm discriminated against women, did not invalidate it, but directed the government to amend it in the light of the equality provision enshrined in the Constitution. After years of intense lobbying and debates, a Civil Code Amendment Bill was passed by Parliament in March 2002, recognizing women's equal right to inherit parental property but confirming the norm whereby women lose the land they inherit if they subsequently marry.

In the Indian case *Kishwar v. Bihar* (1996, 5 SCC 125), the Supreme Court held that the provisions of the 1908 Chotanagpur Tenancy Act of Bihar, limiting succession in tenancy relationships to the male line, violated women's right to livelihood recognized in the Constitution. While not striking down the provisions, the court declared that female heirs of the tenant have a remedy under the Constitution to continue holding the land so long as they are dependent on it, and called on the State of Bihar to amend the law.

3.4. Rights to Land and Other Natural Resources

Rights to natural resources are extremely important for rural women. Firstly, women's livelihoods in rural areas crucially depend upon them, especially in developing countries. Secondly, the nature and extent of these rights affect women's bargaining power within the household (vis-à-vis husbands and male family members), as well as within the community and society at large. Yet women's rights to natural resources are often curtailed. Beyond the family and succession law norms examined in the previous section, this may be caused by norms specifically concerning natural resources. While in most cases these are gender-neutral in formulation, their practical implementation or their interaction with other social norms and practices (particularly customary law) may lead to inequitable outcomes. As a result, in many parts of the world women have few independent rights to natural resources. Some interesting developments of the 1990s have attempted to address this issue.

3.4.1. Women and Land Law

While land legislation long made no reference to gender, laws adopted since the 1990s have paid greater attention to gender equity, by embracing the principle of non-discrimination, abrogating customary norms, presuming joint ownership of family land, outlawing land sales without consent of both spouses and providing for women's representation in land management bodies.

For instance, the Eritrean Land Proclamation of 1994 explicitly states the principle of non-discrimination in land rights, and regulates women's land rights with regard to succession, marriage and divorce. The Niger's Rural Code of 1993 recognizes the equal right of citizens to access natural resources without sex discrimination. In Burkina Faso, Law 14 (1996), confirming previous legislation, provides for the allocation of state-owned land without distinction based on sex or marital status, and under the Mozambican Land Act of 1997, both men and women may have rights in state-owned land.

The Tanzanian Land Act of 1999 explicitly affirms the equality of men's and women's land rights. Spousal co-ownership of family land is presumed. Consent of both spouses is required to mortgage the matrimonial home, and in case of borrower default, the lender must serve a notice on the borrower's spouse before selling mortgaged land. Moreover, a "fair balance" of men and women is to be ensured in the appointment of the National Land Advisory Council. Under the Ugandan Land Act of 1998, specific provisions ensure women's representation in the Uganda Land Commission, in Land District Boards and in parish-level Land Committees. Although selling, leasing or giving away land requires the consent of the spouse, a clause introducing the presumption of spousal co-ownership, initially included in the Bill passed by the Parliament, was excluded by the President from the gazetted text.

Customary land tenure remains widespread in Africa and Asia. While these elements are extremely diverse, in most cases rights in arable land are allocated by the lineage authority to the (male) household head; women have "secondary" rights, i.e., cultivation rights, obtained through the relationship with male family members (husbands and male relatives). With population pressures, cultural change and agricultural intensification and commercialization, many customary systems have evolved towards greater individualization, extending the rights vested in (male) household heads and eroding women's secondary rights. (Mackenzie, 1998; Gray and Kevane, 1999)

On the other hand, women may hold important rights under customary law. In the bilateral systems of the Philippines, for instance, both men and women can hold land. (Judd and Dulnuan, 2001) Customary law may also grant women rights additional to those envisaged by statutory law. A typical example is where a land titling programme issues freehold titles to male household heads without mentioning women's secondary rights, which continue to be recognized only under customary law. Field studies show that women and men rely on different norms of both statutory and customary law to support their land claims, and that the extent of women's land rights is in practice determined by the interplay of these norms (e.g., on Kenya, Mackenzie, 1998).

Judicial decisions have also played an important role in determining women's land rights, particularly by invalidating discriminatory norms on constitutional grounds. A landmark case is *Ephrahim v. Pastory and Another*, decided by the High Court of the United Republic of Tanzania. (Mwanza PC, Civil Appeal No. 70 of 1989) There, a Haya woman who had inherited land from her father sold it outside the clan. A male clan member brought an action to declare the sale void, as women could not sell land under Haya customary law (as codified in the Declaration of Customary Law of 1963). The Tanzanian High Court invalidated the norm on the basis of the principle of non-discrimination (affirmed in the amended Tanzanian Constitution and in international human rights treaties ratified by the United Republic of Tanzania). The court stated therefore that Haya women could sell land on the same conditions as Haya men, and held the disputed land sale valid.

3.4.2. Women's Rights Within Agrarian Reform Programmes

Traditionally, very little attention was paid to gender within agrarian reform programmes, ranging from land titling to land redistribution. For instance, in the Kenyan land registration programme (1954 onwards), registration was usually made to the male household head, thereby undermining women's unregistered secondary rights. (Shipton, 1988; Mackenzie, 1998) In India, state-level land tenancy reforms and land redistribution programmes mainly benefited male household heads. (Agarwal, 1994) Most Latin American agrarian reforms have targeted household heads and permanent agricultural workers in formal employment; both groups consist predominantly of men.

In some cases, agrarian reform laws explicitly discriminated against women. In Mexico, for instance, up to 1971 only men over 18 were eligible for the reform programme, while women were eligible only if household heads. As a result, only a very small percentage of women benefited from Latin American land redistribution programmes (between 4 and 15 percent in Chile, Colombia, Costa Rica, El Salvador, Honduras, Mexico, Nicaragua and Peru). (Katz, 1999)

In the 1990s, agrarian reforms have paid greater attention to gender. Nicaragua's land titling legislation (Laws 209 of 1995 and 278 of 1997) grants men and women equal rights to obtain land titles, and provides for joint titling for couples, whether married or not. In Paraguay, the 1992 Constitution includes among the fundamental principles of the agrarian reform women's participation in reform plans on an equal basis with men. In Brazil, the 1988 Constitution and Law 8629 (1993) state that both men and women, regardless of their marital status, can be allocated property rights or concessions under the agrarian reform, either individually or jointly. Ordinance 33 (2001), adopted by the Minister for Agrarian Development, institutionalizes an affirmative action programme to facilitate rural women's access to land.

Under the Ugandan Land Act of 1998, customary land right certificates are to be issued recording all interests in land not amounting to ownership, including customary use rights (usually enjoyed by women in their husband's land). Moreover, while decisions on land adjudication are to be made according to customary law, decisions denying women access to ownership, occupation or use are null and void.

In South African land reform, gender equity is one of the fundamental principles of the White Paper on Land Policy, and a specific Land Reform Gender Policy was adopted in 1997. The policy has been implemented in a variety of ways. First, legislation must be formulated in non-discriminatory terms. For example, right holders are referred to as "he or she" in the Extension of Security of Tenure Act of 1997 (sec. 6(1)) and in the Interim Protection of Informal Rights Act of 1996 (sec. 2(1)). Second, non-discrimination is in some cases explicitly referred to. For instance, the Communal Property Associations Act of 1996 empowers communities to own and manage property through associations complying with several requirements, including non-discrimination on the basis of sex and gender. Third, relevant case law has been developed under agrarian reform legislation. In *Hadebe v. Hadebe and Another* (LCC 138/99, 14 June 2000), a black woman had purchased land but registered it to her son as a nominee because the Black Administration Act and the Natal Code of Bantu Law prevented black women married under customary law from holding property. She brought an action before the Land Claims Court under the Restitution of Land Rights Act of 1994, in order to transfer the property into her name. The court held that the discriminatory statutory provisions were inconsistent with the principle of equality stated in the Constitution, and ordered the property transfer in favour of the woman.

In the Philippines, the Comprehensive Agrarian Reform Law of 1988 grants women rural labourers equal rights to own land and to participate in advisory and decisionmaking bodies. Women's right to "equal treat-ment in agrarian reform and land resettlement programmes" is confirmed by the Women in Development and Nation Building Act of 1992. The implementation of these provisions has been improved by administrative guidelines adopted by the Department of Agrarian Reform, namely Memorandum Circular 18 of 1996 and Administrative Order 1 of 2001. Under these guidelines, no sex discrimination can be made in beneficiary selection, and land titles are to be issued in the name of both spouses (whether legally married or not) "when both spouses are jointly working and cultivating common tillage". Moreover, the consent of both spouses is required for land sales, mortgages and "all other transactions involving waiver of rights". (Judd and Dulnuan, 2001) Administrative Order 96-29 (1996) provides that contracts concluded with persons occupying forest lands must be signed by both spouses.

It is hard to assess the overall effectiveness of these norms in increasing women's participation in reform programmes. The Nicaraguan titling programme has led to a substantial increase in the number of women land owners. On the other hand, in Brazil land is still usually registered with the husband and joint registration remains rare, also because many rural women lack the documents required to obtain land titles. The 1996 Agrarian Reform Census revealed that only 12.6 percent of land reform beneficiaries were women, although there was considerable variation by state. (Guivant, 2001)

In any case, even in programmes granting titles to women, attention should be paid to the extent to which women effectively control land, especially in the case of joint titles. In Mexico, the 1992 Agrarian Law grants equal rights to male and female *ejido* members. However, in practice women *ejido* members usually obtain their status through succession from their husbands rather than through direct land allocation under the land reform. (FAO, 1994) Only a small number of *ejido* members are women (16.3 percent in 283 *ejidos* surveyed by Katz, 1999), and the percentage of women in *ejido* leadership positions is even lower (4.9 percent of *comisariados ejidales* surveyed by Katz, 1999). Decisions on the alienation of allocated plots are taken exclusively by (usually male) *ejido* right-holders, without the need for spousal consent.

Finally, many agrarian reform programmes still largely ignore gender. Law 98-750 (1998) of Côte d'Ivoire, outlining a titling programme, states that "every person" may access land but contains no provisions on gender. The situation is the same for most agrarian reforms adopted in Central Asia. For instance, under the 1994 Regulations on land use rights of Kyrgyzstan, land titles are registered in the name of the household head; the registration must indicate the number of family members but not their names or sexes. (Giovarelli and Duncan, 1999)

3.4.3. Rights to Other Natural Resources

Legislation concerning natural resources other than land rarely refers to gender, but there are some recent exceptions. These laws take into account gender, mainly by providing for:

- *inclusion of gender equity among the objectives of the law.* For instance, the South African National Water Act of 1998 includes among its explicit purposes the promotion of "equitable access to water", redressing the results of past gender discrimination and ensuring "appropriate" gender representation in the competent institutions.
- *requiring consideration of gender in natural resource management.* The South African Water Act, for instance, requires the authority to take into account "the need to redress the results of past ... gender discrimination" in the issuance of licences, in the allocation of financial assistance and in the performance of the functions of the catchment management agencies. In the Philippines, Administrative Order 98-55 (1998, as amended), integrates gender into natural resource policies, programmes and activities.
- *granting special support to women users of natural resources.* In the Philippines, the Fisheries Code of 1998 includes support for women fishers among its policy directions and among the functions of the Bureau of Fisheries and Aquatic Resources.
- *mechanisms ensuring women's representation in natural resource management bodies.* For example, the Nepali Irrigation Regulation of 2000 requires that executive committees of water user associations include at least two women (out of nine members). Under the Water Act of South Africa, the responsible minister may appoint members of the governing board of catchment management agencies to achieve "sufficient" gender representation. Under the Fisheries Code of the Philippines, representatives of women fishers are included in fisheries management councils.

3.5. Rights of Women Agricultural Workers

In many countries, women farm workers face hard working conditions. While respect for labour rights in plantations varies immensely from estate to estate, field studies reveal widespread discriminatory practices, including:

- discrimination in access to employment, with women concentrated in subordinate and lower-paid jobs in the fields and men in higher positions, particularly as supervisors and headmen;
- wage differentials, with higher wages for typically men's positions (e.g., sugar cane cutters) than for women's positions (e.g., weeders);
- discrimination in access to training and vocational courses;
- discrimination in allocation of benefits, such as housing;
- sexual harassment; and

- discrimination within trade unions (regarding participation and access to leadership positions). (Mbilinyi, 1995, sugar cane plantation in Tanzania; Bob, 1996, coffee plantation in South Africa)

In many countries, legislators have recently paid greater attention to gender in the labour legislation applicable to agriculture. An example is provided by South Africa, where women farm workers had until recently very little protection. In 1993, legislation on minimum labour standards was extended to agricultural workers. Moreover, the Employment Equity Act of 1998 prohibits direct and indirect unfair discrimination in access and treatment on grounds of gender, sex, pregnancy, marital status and family responsibility. Where discrimination is alleged, the burden of proof is placed on the employer. The Act also provides for affirmative action, including preferential treatment and numerical goals, with regard to establishments employing 50 or more workers (including agricultural employers).

Some countries have tackled specific issues typically concerning women workers, especially on plantations. Brazilian Laws 9029 (1995) and 9799 (1999) prohibit employers from requiring sterilization or pregnancy certifications or examinations as a condition for employment, and bar employers from conducting intimate examinations of employees. Several countries have adopted specific norms on sexual harassment in the workplace (e.g., the 1995 Anti-Sexual Harassment Act of the Philippines), which apply equally to farms and plantations.

Developments have also come through judicial decisions. In India, guidelines on sexual harassment on the workplace were developed by the Supreme Court in *Vishaka v. Rajasthan and Others* (AIR 1997 SC 3011), building on the Indian Constitution and the CEDAW. Lawsuits have also been brought by women agricultural workers, although the overall number of these cases remains low. In South Africa, case law has been developed under the Extension of Security of Tenure Act of 1997, which protects from eviction persons occupying land with the consent of the land owner, including farm workers. A particularly important case is *Conradie v. Hanekom and Another* (1999 (4) SA 491 (LCC)), in which the South African Land Claims Court set aside an eviction order against two farm workers, husband and wife, employed on the same farm. Having dismissed the husband, the land owner had sought to evict both. The court held that the wife, as employee, had a right not to be evicted under the Act, and her eviction order was set aside. The court also held that the Act guaranteed to her the right to family life, so that her husband (who after his dismissal was no longer a protected "occupier") had a right to reside on the land as a family member.

3.6. Women in Rural Cooperatives

Notwithstanding the important role of women in agricultural production, women's participation in rural cooperatives and producer associations is very limited throughout the world, although with great variation. In Africa, the percentage of women members of cooperatives ranges from 6 percent in Burkina Faso to 11 percent in Benin and 15 percent in Sudan, and the percentage of women officers is even lower; however, a substantial growth of women's involvement in rural organizations has taken place on the continent during the last two decades. (FAO, 1995) The causes of this limited participation are primarily socio-cultural (taboos, etc.). Moreover, cooperative by-laws may contain direct or indirect discriminatory provisions; a common example is requiring land ownership as a condition for membership, which *de facto* excludes women where land distribution is gender-biased. Family law norms on the legal capacity of married women may also hinder women's involvement.

Traditionally, legislation on cooperatives contains no provisions on gender. The Philippines' 1990 Cooperative Code and the Niger's 1996 Ordinance on Cooperatives, for example, are worded in gender-neutral terms. However, some more recent laws explicitly address gender issues. Nicaragua's Law on Agricultural and Agro-industrial Cooperatives (1990) prohibits cooperatives from discriminating on the basis of sex and provides for the full integration of women in cooperatives on the basis of equality of rights and obligations. Mexico's General Law on Cooperatives of 1994 also states the principle of gender equality.

In the United Republic of Tanzania, the Co-operative Societies Act of 1991, as amended in 1997, prohibits gender discrimination in access to membership, states that both men and women can be elected as cooperative representatives and affirms the principle of equality of all members in the activities of cooperatives. Burkina Faso's 1999 law on cooperatives prohibits discrimination on the basis of sex. In Ethiopia, Co-operative Societies Proclamation 147 (1998) includes among the "Guiding Principles of Co-operative Societies" the prohibition of gender discrimination. Namibia's Co-operatives Act of 1996 contains a similar provision, and provides for women's representation in the managing boards of cooperatives having a minimum number of women members.

In the Philippines, women have equal access to membership in social, civic and other organizations (Women in Development and Nation-Building Act of 1992), and both spouses have the right to join cooperatives (Administrative Order No. 1 of 2001). In India, some state-level laws on cooperatives have been amended to reserve for women seats in managing committees (Kerala in 1985; Andhra Pradesh in 1991). Some of these laws have been challenged before courts on grounds of (reverse) sex discrimination. In *Toguru Sudhakar Reddy and Another v. The Government of Andhra Pradesh and Others*, the Supreme Court dismissed such a challenge with regard to the legislation of Andhra Pradesh (AIR, 1994, SC, 544). In *K.R. Gopinathan Nair v. The Senior Inspector-cum Spl. Sales Officer of Co-operative Societies and Others* (AIR 1989, Kerala, 167), a similar challenge relating to the legislation of Kerala was dismissed by the High Court of Kerala.

Some legal systems envisage special forms of associations for rural women. Within Mexican *ejidos*, women over the age of 16 (either *ejidatarias* or spouses or relatives of *ejidatarios*) may exercise crop, livestock and rural industry activities through a specific form of association (*Unidades agrícolas industriales de la mujer*, UAIMs). The functioning of UAIMs is regulated by a 1998 regulation adopted under the Agrarian Law of 1992. Under the Law, *ejido* assemblies may allocate land to UAIMs, although in practice only a limited number of *ejidos* have done so (12 percent of the *ejidos* surveyed by Katz, 1999).

3.7. Credit, Extension and Training

3.7.1. Access to Credit

Rural women face more difficulties than men in gaining access to credit for agricultural purposes. In Africa, the percentage of rural credit directly benefiting women ranges from 5 percent (Burkina Faso's National Fund for Agricultural Credit) to 32 percent (Zimbabwe's Agricultural Finance Corporation). Moreover, women obtained only 2.8 percent of the loans from Turkey's Agricultural Bank, 5 percent from Jamaica's Bank of Agricultural Credit, 6 percent from the Agricultural Credit Corporation in Jordan and 15 percent from the Agricultural Bank in Iran. (FAO, 1995 and 1996) This limited access to credit is mainly caused by high illiteracy rates, limited access to formal employment, transport costs, fear of indebtedness, lack of information, cumbersome procedures and exclusion from cooperatives through which credit is provided.

As noted in Chapter 8, women's access to credit may also be curtailed by their limited land rights, preventing them from offering land as collateral to secure a loan. Even where this is not the case, rural financial institutions may in practice require the husband's authorization on women's applications for credit. Moreover, in the rural areas of many developing countries, credit is obtained informally through "interlinked contracts", whereby two persons are bound by several contractual relations simultaneously (e.g., a landlord or employer lending money to the tenant or farm worker); therefore, women's access to credit may be affected by the fact that tenancy or employment contracts are mainly held by men.

Credit laws usually do not make explicit reference to gender, and on paper women have rights equal to men. However, in the last decade, some countries have taken measures to address the reality of restrictions on women's access to credit, mainly in two ways. First, sex/gender discrimination in access to credit may be explicitly prohibited. In South Africa, the Promotion of Equality and Prevention of Unfair Discrimination Act of 2000 prohibits unfair discrimination against women by the state and by all persons, including in access to credit. In the Philippines, the Women in Development Act of 1992 grants women equal access to government and private sector programmes granting agricultural credit, and the Social Reform and Poverty Alleviation Act of 1997 provides *inter alia* for a gender-responsive approach to poverty alleviation and for credit programmes benefiting rural women.

Second, affirmative action may be envisaged. In Nicaragua, Law 209 of 1995 grants priority for women in access to credit. (Galán, 1998) In Brazil, Ordinance 121 (2001) of the Minister for Agrarian Development reserves "preferentially" to women 30 percent of credit granted under the National Programme to Support Family Agriculture (PRONAF) and by the Land Bank (established in 1998 to provide credit for land purchases and for basic agricultural infrastructure). Under the 1997 Agriculture and Fisheries Modernization Act of the Philippines, the state must promote access to credit for farmers and fishers, "particularly the women involved in the production, processing and trading of agriculture and fisheries products".

The 1990s have also witnessed a massive expansion of women-targeted micro-credit programmes. These were pioneered by the Grameen Bank in Bangladesh, and include innovative institutional arrangements overcoming women's problems in accessing credit, namely: group responsibility, with borrowers organized in groups and responsible for loans contracted by other group members; self-selection, with borrowers themselves choosing the members of their group; sequential lending, with loans granted in turn to group members; and accessibility, with bank branches and officers assigned to rural areas. Women-targeted credit programmes are also carried out by governments. An example is Fiji's Women's Social and Economic Development Programme, established by the Ministry for Women and Culture in 1993 to promote and support women's income-generating activities, including through subsidized credit. About 70 percent of the loans requested under this programme are for agriculture-related activities.

3.7.2. Agricultural Extension and Vocational Training

Similar developments have taken place with regard to agricultural extension and vocational training. As in the case of credit, women face much greater difficulties than men in accessing these services. Sociocultural factors, particularly taboos relating to interactions between men and women and to women's attendance at meetings outside the home, are among the major causes.

Laws and regulations are usually silent on gender with regard to extension and training. However, some recent laws include gender-specific provisions and institutions. In South Africa, gender concerns have been integrated into education and training programmes (National Education Policy Act of 1996 and Further Education and Training Act of 1998). In Brazil, Ordinance 121 (2001) reserves "preferentially" to women 30 percent of training and extension services provided under the PRONAF. Under the Philippines' Agriculture and Fisheries Modernization Act of 1997, the status of women is among the "special concerns" of the Department of Agriculture, and special training programmes for women are provided for.

In other cases, gender is integrated through institutional reforms in competent ministries. For instance, the Tunisian Decree 420 (2001) on the organization of the Ministry of Agriculture establishes within the Ministry a bureau for the support of rural women, responsible among other things for promoting women's training and integration in agricultural production activities. In Italy, a 1997 decree of the Minister responsible for agriculture established a unit to monitor women's economic activities, collect data and formulate policies and strategies. In Burkina Faso, Decree 97-428 (1997) establishes within the Ministry for Animal Resources a directorate on extension service and technology transfer, which is responsible for promoting awareness among "new actors", including women. Legislation may also add women's representatives to training-related institutions (Vanuatu's National Training Council Act of 1999; South Africa's Further Education and Training Act of 1998 and Skills Development Act of 1998). Some countries have made efforts to increase the number of female extension and training officers. For example, in Tanzania, one village extension officer out of three is a woman. (Due, et al., 1997)

3.8. Means of Implementation

Norms advancing women's legal status are often scarcely implemented in rural areas, due to the persistence of discriminatory socio-cultural norms and practices, often internalized by women themselves. Indeed, while law often reflects and follows social change, gender-equality provisions promote social change, and their implementation is therefore much more difficult, as the process of social and cultural change is inevitably slow. Other major factors affecting implementation of gender-related norms include:

- *rural women's lack of awareness of their statutory rights.* Where illiteracy rates are high and access to documents problematic, publication of laws in official bulletins is unlikely to reach rural women.
- *rural women's lack of resources to enforce their rights.* Often, legal aid funds are mainly allocated to criminal law cases, rather than to family law disputes (where women's rights issues mainly arise). Also, while the Beijing Platform for Action calls for the provision of free or low-cost legal services designed to reach women living in poverty, many countries have not paid attention to gender in their legal aid schemes. One exception is India's Legal Services Authorities Act of 1987, as amended in 1994, which explicitly lists women among possible legal aid beneficiaries.
- *lack of resources for the implementation of gender-related legislation.* Few resources may be allocated by government to implement gender-sensitive legislation, ranging from gender-sensitive agrarian reforms to women-targeted credit programmes and to gender-specific institutions.
- *women's scarce representation in decisionmaking positions.* Women may not be represented on policymaking bodies, whether agriculture-related ministries or elected political office.

Some of these constraints may mean that provisions on gender equality often have no real impact on women's everyday lives. Nonetheless, there are several avenues for enforcement of women's rights, and these means of implementation are explored below.

3.8.1. Courts

Women's access to courts is in many countries severely limited. Practices like female seclusion hinder the possibilities for women to claim their rights. Moreover, in many rural areas, it would be shameful for a woman to claim before courts her rights vis-à-vis her male family members (as documented in India by Agarwal, 1994). In many countries, women are under-represented in the judiciary, and prejudices about the credibility of female witnesses are widespread. Court fees may also constitute an obstacle for rural women, who tend to have less access to cash than men.

Women's access to courts may also be constrained by norms limiting their legal capacity and preventing them from bringing judicial disputes autonomously. (See section 3.3.1.) In most countries, these norms have been repealed (e.g., South Africa's Recognition of Customary Marriages Act of 1998). Some countries have affirmatively granted to women equal access to legal remedies. For example, in the Philippines, Administrative Order 1 of 2001 states that either spouse may bring claims relating to the agrarian reform. (Judd and Dulnuan, 2001)

The case law examined in this chapter shows that although women's access to justice may be constrained, courts constitute a fundamental institution for the enforcement of women's rights. Moreover, courts are a crucial agent of legal change, invalidating discriminatory norms on constitutional grounds (*Pastory* case in Tanzania), "amending" the application of norms in the light of constitutional principles (*Kishwar* case in India) and directing governments to amend discriminatory legislation (*Dhungana* case in Nepal).

3.8.2. Human Rights Commissions and Gender-specific Institutions

A clear trend that emerged in the last decade is the establishment of human rights or gender-specific commissions. These are independent authorities competent to investigate human rights violations, both upon complaint and on their own motion. Compared to courts, they provide more accessible and speedy mechanisms of redress, and are less costly and cumbersome. Another advantage is that where violations may be investigated on the court's own initiative, discriminatory situations may be redressed even where the victims have no access to justice.

Human rights commissions usually do not issue binding decisions, but rather recommendations; an exception is the Human Rights Commission of Uganda, whose decisions are as binding and enforceable as court judgments. More often, when their recommendations are not complied with, human rights commissions may report to Parliament or, in a few cases, bring an action before courts (as in the case of Ghana's Commission on Human Rights and Administrative Justice). In federal jurisdictions, human rights commissions may be established at both federal and state level (e.g., India and Mexico).

An example of a gender-specific institution is India's National Commission for Women (established under the National Commission for Women Act of 1990), which may investigate violations both upon complaint and on its own motion. The South African Commission on Gender Equality has the same dual mandate, and may resolve disputes by negotiation, mediation or conciliation, and may refer matters to the Human Rights Commission (Commission on Gender Equality Act of 1996).

Human rights and gender commissions can contribute to the implementation of women's rights. However, their effectiveness may be limited by resource constraints and by factors similar to those relating to courts, such as geographical inaccessibility and cultural norms preventing women from claiming their rights.

3.8.3. Customary Dispute Resolution Authorities

The last decade has witnessed a renewed interest in the dispute settlement role of customary institutions. To mention just an example, the Niger's 1993 Rural Code provides for a mandatory conciliation procedure before customary authorities as a condition for initiating judicial proceedings.

For women, customary institutions have advantages and disadvantages. On the one hand, compared to courts, customary institutions may provide more easily accessible (both geographically and economically) and speedier fora for rural women, and may enjoy greater social legitimacy. On the other hand, while their nature varies considerably from place to place, customary institutions are often gender-biased in composition and in orientation. In most places, they are constituted by male elders, and apply a male-biased interpretation of customary law. Women may be discriminated against even procedurally, as they may need a male intermediary to bring a dispute and to appear before the authority.

Some countries have attempted to improve the gender outlook of customary institutions. In India, the Constitution, as amended in 1993, provides for direct election of members of *panchayats* (local government institutions rooted in tradition), and reserves to women one-third of the seats. In South Africa, the Constitution recognizes the role and status of traditional institutions, although subject to the principles of the Constitution. Similar norms are contained in the Constitution of Uganda. It is difficult to assess whether this type of norm is effective in reforming deeply rooted institutions. In both India and South Africa, there are reports that most customary institutions continue to be dominated by male elites, and to favour a gender-biased interpretation of the law. While guaranteeing women's representation through quotas is an important tool, women sitting in councils may in practice not speak, may act merely as spokespersons for their male relatives or may otherwise face resistance to their role.

IV. CONCLUSION

In the last decade, gender has received considerable attention. At the international level, the Beijing Platform for Action has provided comprehensive policy directives, the Optional Protocol to the CEDAW has strengthened international human rights mechanisms and international environmental instruments have addressed gender issues. Domestic measures have also been adopted in various forms. At the policy level, plans of action have been adopted by most countries to follow up the Beijing Platform for Action. In the legislative arena, efforts have been made to eliminate discrimination and to improve women's legal position, e.g., by reforming family and succession law, by revising agrarian law, by protecting women's labour rights and by prohibiting discrimination and providing affirmative action in certain contexts. Judicially, discriminatory norms have been declared unconstitutional, and women's rights have been enforced.

Notwithstanding these improvements, much remains to be done. Many countries still have discriminatory norms, including succession law limiting women's right to inherit land, family law granting the husband greater rights in family property, agrarian reforms allocating land to (male) household heads and norms subjecting women's employment and other contracts to the husband's authorization. Where legislation is not discriminatory, its gender-neutral formulation may not be enough to overcome inequalities entrenched in society. Finally, gender-sensitive legislation may not be implemented due to socio-cultural factors.

In these cases, action needs to be taken in two directions: legal reform and implementation. Legal reform is needed to eliminate directly or indirectly discriminatory norms and to address gender issues where gender-neutral legislation is inadequate to counter existing practice. In some cases, special measures to advance the position of women may be necessary to redress past and existing discrimination (e.g., granting priority to women in land distribution or in access to public agricultural credit programmes). Other sector-specific measures may also be needed (e.g., joint titling in the context of land redistribution or registration).

As women's rights are determined by a complex system of rules, legal reform needs to be comprehensive. For instance, where family and succession laws restrict women's legal capacity and inheritance rights, a reform of land legislation to redress gender inequality in land rights can only be effective if accompanied by a reform of these other laws.

Where appropriate legislation is already in place, efforts must be made to effectively implement it, addressing the factors constraining implementation. These include educating rural women regarding their rights, increasing women's representation in decisionmaking bodies, providing legal assistance and addressing legal and cultural barriers to women's access to the courts and other enforcement mechanisms.

REFERENCES

Agarwal, B. 1994. *A Field of One's Own: Gender and Land Rights in South Asia.* Cambridge University Press, Cambridge.

Bob, U. 1996. *Gender Struggles and Social Differentiation.* In R. Levin & D. Weiner (eds.), *"No More Tears...." - Struggles for Land in Mpumalanga, South Africa,* Africa World Press, Trenton.

Cotula, L. (forthcoming). *Women's Rights in Agriculture.* Legislative Study. FAO, Rome.

Due, J.M., Magayane, F. & Temu, A.A. 1997. *Gender Again - Views of Female Agricultural Extension Officers by Smallholder Farmers in Tanzania,* World Development 5.

FAO. 1994. *The Legal Status of Rural Women in Nineteen Latin American Countries,* Rome.

FAO. 1995. *Women, Agriculture and Rural Development - A Synthesis Report of the Africa Region,* Rome.

Galán, B.B. 1998. *Aspectos jurídicos en el acceso de la mujer rural a la tierra en Cuba, Honduras, Nicaragua y República Dominicana.* FAO, Rome.

Giovarelli, R. & Duncan, J. 1999. *Women and Land in Eastern Europe and Central Asia, Paper submitted to the Conference on "Women Farmers: Enhancing Rights and Productivity", Bonn, Germany, 26-27 August 1999.*

Gray, L. & Kevane, M. 1999. *Diminished Access, Diverted Exclusion: Women and Land Tenure in Sub-Saharan Africa,* African Studies Review 42(2).

Guivant, J.S. 2001. *Gender and Land Rights in Brazil. Paper prepared for the UNRISD Project on Agrarian Change, Gender and Land Rights, Geneva.*

Judd, M. & Dulnuan, J. 2001. *Women's Legal and Customary Access to Land in the Philippines.* World Bank, Washington, D.C.

Katz, E. 1999. *Mexico: Gender and Ejido Reform.* World Bank, Washington, D.C.

Mackenzie, F. 1998. *Land, Ecology and Resistance in Kenya, 1880-1952.* Edinburgh University Press, Edinburgh.

Mbilinyi, M. 1995. *Gender and Employment on Sugar Cane Plantations in Tanzania.* Sectoral Activities Programme Working Papers, ILO, Geneva.

Shipton, P. 1988. *The Kenyan Land Tenure Reform: Misunderstandings in the Public Creation of Private Property.* In R.E. Downs & S.P. Reyna (eds.), *Land and Society in Contemporary Africa,* University Press of New England, Hanover.

10

FORESTRY

Contents

I. INTRODUCTION

Over the past decades, FAO has been collecting, analysing and disseminating forestry data. Its latest worldwide forest evaluation, the Global Forest Resources Assessment 2000, provided information on the status and trends in forest cover, as well as parameters on productive, environmental and socio-economic benefits of forests. The total forest area in 2000 was 3 860 million hectares, of which 95 percent was natural forest and 5 percent was forest plantation. About half of that area was located in tropical and subtropical regions, mostly in developing countries, and the other half in temperate and boreal regions, predominantly in industrialized countries. More precisely, about 47 percent of the world's forests were tropical, 9 percent subtropical, 11 percent temperate and 33 percent boreal.

While forests covered 27 percent of the globe's total land area, or nearly 0.6 hectares per capita, their distribution among regions and countries was highly unequal. Europe and South America had almost half of their area under forest, whereas Africa, Asia and Oceania had less than 20 percent. More than 70 countries had less than 10 percent of their land area forested, whereas seven countries had forest on more than 60 percent of their land area. The four countries with the largest forest cover, namely the Russian Federation, Brazil, Canada and the United States, accounted for no less than half the world's forests.

Between 1990 and 2000, deforestation continued to be high, although at a lower rate than that in the pre-Rio decade. In developing countries, mainly in tropical and subtropical regions, the estimated annual net loss of forest cover was, for the decades before and after Rio, respectively 12.7 and 10.7 million hectares, i.e., a decrease of 10 percent over the 1980–90 period. By contrast, in industrialized countries the temperate and boreal forest cover has stabilized after Rio and is even slightly increasing overall.[1] Gains in forest area are primarily due to forest plantation and natural regeneration, whereas deforestation is largely the consequence of the conversion of forest to other uses such as agriculture, pasture and infrastructure, as well as timber harvesting, severe wildfires and devastating windstorms. (FAO, 2000 and 2001a)

---

[1] These figures are also partly due to the fact that, for the first time, a uniform definition of forest was used in the 2000 assessment. As a result, for some countries the forest cover was higher than in previous assessments.

Parallel to this loss in the planet's forests, the post-Rio decade has witnessed numerous endeavours towards the strengthening of forest laws and institutions, both globally and nationally. In the international arena, while attempts to develop a world forest convention have remained unconsummated during and after Rio, other significant initiatives have fostered multilateral forestry cooperation, mainly through forestry-related fora and non-binding instruments.

More importantly, legal reforms have been carried out in a multitude of countries, bringing about major changes in national forestry legislation worldwide. Overall, contemporary forest law now appears to place less emphasis on the role of forests as economic assets but a much greater focus on their multifunctional nature, with sustainability concerns, ecological values and social interests clearly achieving more and more prominence. This more balanced approach is reflected in many recently developed national forestry laws.

The present chapter will describe this post-Rio evolution of forest law, first addressing international developments, then discussing national trends.

II.   INTERNATIONAL FRAMEWORK: KEY DEVELOPMENTS

The current international forest regime is a composite and complex one. (Amilien, 1995; Humphreys, 1996; Tarasofsky, 1999) Although no world treaty on forests has yet been adopted, a number of international initiatives, including non-governmental and private sector ones, have been taken since Rio, such as the development of new forest policies by various international institutions (FAO, the United Nations Development Programme, the World Bank, Greenpeace, the World Conservation Union, the World Wildlife Fund, etc.). In addition, there were statements on forests by the G8 Summits; establishment of an advocacy international NGO, the World Commission on Forests and Sustainable Development; and creation of an accreditor of certification bodies, the Forest Stewardship Council. Another development has been forest industry involvement in the World Business Council for Sustainable Development.

At the regional level, one post-Rio treaty that specifically deals with forests was adopted in 1993 in Guatemala City: the Central American Convention for the Management and Conservation of Natural Forest Ecosystems and the Development of Forest Plantations. Similarly, a draft

Forestry Protocol is being developed for the Southern African Development Community region.

In addition, numerous international instruments which affect forestry, both binding and non-binding, are already in place and were largely built up in the years since Rio. Together with trade-related instruments, these are briefly described, as they represent a guiding legal and policy frame of reference for domestic lawmaking, one which has frequently inspired national forest law reforms over the last decade.

2.1. Instruments Derived from Rio

At the Rio Conference and during its preparations, forests were among the most contentious and hotly debated issues, with North and South polarized over tropical deforestation. This divide did not permit agreement on a global forest convention, although it had been advocated by a number of countries. Instead, states decided to devote a specific chapter of Agenda 21 to forests – Chapter 11, "Combating Deforestation" – and to adopt a "Non-Legally Binding Authoritative Statement of Principles for a Global Consensus on the Management, Conservation and Sustainable Development of All Types of Forests" (Forest Principles). Other instruments with a bearing on forests, developed in anticipation of or subsequent to Rio, include the 1992 Convention on Biological Diversity (CBD), the 1992 UN Framework Convention on Climate Change (FCCC) and the 1994 UN Convention to Combat Desertification (CCD).

2.1.1. Agenda 21 and the Forest Principles

Focusing on deforestation, Chapter 11 of Agenda 21 highlights four programme areas: sustaining the multiple roles and functions of forests; promoting efficient resource utilization and evaluation techniques that incorporate all forest values; strengthening capacities for planning assessments of forestry activities; and enhancing conservation and management of degraded forest areas. The chapter urges countries to develop national forest strategies and plans addressing these policy areas. It also calls for the formulation of criteria and guidelines to help sustainably manage, conserve and utilize forests.

Acknowledging national sovereignty over forest resources, the Forest Principles provide a policy platform aimed at directing country efforts to maintain and increase forest cover and productivity in economically, ecologically, socially and culturally sound ways. National forest policies that balance environmental and development concerns and are supported by appropriate institutional arrangements, are to be designed and implemented in a participatory manner, with the involvement of all interested stakeholders, including forest dwellers and indigenous peoples. Additionally, the costs of forest conservation and development actions should be equitably shared by the international community, and trade in forest products should not be unduly restricted.

These two major forest-specific UNCED documents, though not legally binding, have greatly inspired post-Rio developments, nationally as well as internationally, both in the policy arena and in the legal sphere. In particular, in light of Chapter 11 and the Forest Principles, some 120 national forest programmes have been developed and/or updated in recent years. The formulation process of these programmes has, in turn, brought about considerable legislative change in the forestry sector (discussed in Part III below).

2.1.2. Convention on Biological Diversity and Forests

In force since December 1993 and ratified by 183 parties as of June 2002, the CBD seeks to promote the conservation and sustainable use of biodiversity, while ensuring equitable distribution of the benefits derived from the use of genetic resources. Beyond species diversity, it holistically addresses biodiversity in natural habitats, including forest ecosystems. Hence it has significant potential effects on forest resource management, preservation and use. (Tarasofsky, 1995)

Specific discussions on forest biodiversity started at the third Conference of Parties (COP-3) in 1996 and continued at COP-4 in 1998 and COP-6 in 2000. Subsequently, an action-based work programme on forest bio-diversity was drafted by CBD's Subsidiary Body for Scientific, Technical and Technological Advice in 2001, and eventually adopted at COP-6 in April 2002. It consists of 130 activities clustered in three groups: conservation, sustainable use and benefit sharing; the institutional and socio-economic enabling environment; and knowledge, assessment and monitoring. Parties are requested to report on programme implementation in their national reports, and an *ad hoc* technical expert group is to be established to advise in this respect. When and how parties will translate this programme into action remains to be seen. However, due to the CBD's influence, greater emphasis is already being placed in recent forest legislation on the biological values of forests. (See section 3.2.)

2.1.3. Framework Convention on Climate Change and Forests

The FCCC has been in force since March 1994 and had 186 parties by June 2002. FCCC's objective is to stabilize the concentration of greenhouse gases (GHGs) in the atmosphere, in particular carbon dioxide (CO_2). This general commitment was later made more specific in the 1997 Kyoto Protocol (KP), which set GHG emission reduction targets for developed countries and countries in transition to market economies, but has yet to come into force. Forests can help to slow down climate change, acting as reservoirs by storing carbon, and functioning as carbon sinks when their area or productivity is increased, resulting in greater uptake of CO_2. Conversely, forests become a source of GHGs when their biomass burns or decays.

Under the KP, afforestation, reforestation and improved forest conservation and management practices are to be used to offset emission targets. On the other hand, activities which deplete forest carbon sinks, such as deforestation, are to be subtracted from the amounts of allowed GHG emissions. Operational details for measuring and assessing the contribution of forests to cuts in emissions (among other issues) have been the subject of long negotiations, and were only agreed upon in November 2001 at FCCC's COP-7 – an agreement that could clear the way for the KP's entry into force. So far, however, the FCCC and the KP have not yet had significant impacts on national forest laws.

2.1.4. Convention to Combat Desertification and Forests

The Convention to Combat Desertification (CCD) became legally binding in December 1996 and had 179 parties by June 2002. It aims to combat desertification and to mitigate the effects of drought in an integrated manner, through the adoption of national action programmes. These are to address the underlying causes of desertification and drought – which include deforestation – as well as preventive and remedial measures. Conservation and regeneration of the vegetation cover is part and parcel of these, hence the significant role that forestry can play in desertification control policies and strategies. Yet, although forest laws generally cover various issues related to desertification, such as land clearing, over-logging, over-grazing and over-cultivation, desertification is rarely explicitly addressed.

2.2. Post-UNCED International Processes

After the "spirit of confrontation" over forests that prevailed at the Rio Conference, there was a need for confidence building through international dialogue. Intergovernmental deliberations continued mainly through the Commission on Sustainable Development, in the course of its own sessions and under two ad hoc groups that were created under its aegis, the Intergovernmental Panel on Forests (IPF) and the Intergovernmental Forum on Forests (IFF). They met from 1995 to 1997 (IPF) and from 1997 to 2000 (IFF), and considered a vast range of forestry issues on which progress was made to varying degrees, but without final agreement on the idea of a possible forest convention. To further advance this effort, in October 2000, the UN Economic and Social Council established, as its subsidiary body, the United Nations Forum on Forests (UNFF) for a term of five years. Drawing on IPF/IFF's 270 proposals for action, UNFF has taken up outstanding matters and should eventually consider, by 2005, a "mandate for developing a legal framework on all types of forests". (ECOSOC Resolution 2000/35)

Among the topics on which significant progress was made through these and other processes, the area of Criteria and Indicators for Sustainable Forest Management (C&I) is particularly noteworthy. Building on the proposals for action on C&I that were made by IPF and IFF, several eco-regional initiatives, involving some 150 countries, led to the development of nine major series of specific C&I for all types of forests worldwide.[2] With these C&I in place, sustainable forest management can now be better defined conceptually and progress towards achieving it measured more

---

[2] While the "criteria" define the principles against which sustainability is judged, the "indicators" help monitor the effects of management over time, considering the productive, protective and social roles of forests. The main eco-regional initiatives on C&I are: (i) *Helsinki Process*: 6 criteria and 27 indicators for boreal, temperate and Mediterranean forests in 37 European countries; (ii) *Montreal Process*: 7 criteria and 67 indicators for boreal and temperate forests in 12 non-European countries; (iii) *Tarapoto Proposal*: 13 criteria and 76 indicators for the forests of the 8 state parties to the Amazon Cooperation Treaty; (iv) *Dry-Zone Africa Process*: 7 criteria and 47 indicators for dry forests in 28 countries; (v) *Near East Process*: 7 criteria and 65 indicators for dry forests in 30 countries; (vi) *Lepaterique Process*: 12 criteria and 93 indicators for the forests of the 7 states of Central America; (vi) *Dry-Zone Asia Initiative*: 8 criteria and 49 indicators for dry forests in 9 Asian countries; (viii) *ITTO Initiative*: 6 criteria and 27 indicators for tropical forests of the 12 International Tropical Timber Organization member states; (ix) *African Timber Organization Initiative*: 28 criteria and 60 indicators for tropical forests of the 13 member states.

precisely, both nationally and at the forest unit level. However, as they are relatively recent, such C&I have, to date, only been reflected in a handful of forest laws.

2.3. Trade-related Agreements

Trade has been a key issue in the international debate on forests, both at and since the Rio Conference. Trade in forest products was specifically addressed in Chapter 11 of Agenda 21 and in the Forest Principles, and has been a major topic of IPF and IFF deliberations. Trade in timber is also dealt with by two pre-UNCED accords: the International Tropical Timber Agreement (ITTA) and, to a lesser extent, the Convention on International Trade in Endangered Species of Wild Fauna and Flora (CITES). The WTO mandate includes forest-related issues, although it has not yet specifically considered timber matters.

Initially adopted in 1983, ITTA was renegotiated after UNCED. Like its predecessor, the new agreement, brought into force in 1997, seeks to foster cooperation in trade and utilization of tropical timber, with a greater focus on sustainability. It promotes timber trade that is based on sound management and sustainable exploitation of tropical forests. In April 2002, ITTO had a membership of 57 parties, which accounted for 76 percent of the world's natural tropical forests and 90 percent of international trade in tropical timber. Under its "Year 2000 Objective" (adopted in 1990), ITTO members committed to having all traded timber come from sustainably managed forests by the year 2000. To this end, ITTO published in 1992 the first set of C&I for sustainable forest management, which broke new ground at the time and are now being updated and improved, particularly in terms of increased efficiency in processing and marketing. (Cirelli, et al., 2001)

Under CITES, several tree species have been listed for many years in the three appendices, with various levels of control on their trade. In the years since Rio, attempts to list some other major commercial tree species generated controversy, particularly with the listing in Appendix III of big-leaf mahogany in 1995; a Timber Trade Group was therefore created to look into these issues. (FAO, 1997) Subsequent proposals were made to move this species to Appendix II in view of its stricter trade restrictions, but no agreement could be reached by either CITES' 10th Conference of Parties (COP-10) in 1997 or COP-11 in 2000. A Mahogany Working Group was thus established to further study the matter and to report to COP-12 in 2002.

On the other hand, COP-11 decided to uplist two tree species to Appendix I: the monkey puzzle tree and lignum vitae. By and large, CITES is believed to provide a useful forum where trade and conservation concerns are in general fairly balanced, and whose decisions are usually well implemented through national legislation in its 158 member countries (as of June 2002).

Within WTO, the Committee on Trade and the Environment's mandate includes forest-related issues. In 1998, the Committee briefly discussed forestry in connection with trade restrictions and distortions. (WTO, 1997) Since then, WTO has had no timber dispute to resolve and has not developed a forest policy. And although environmental matters figured prominently in the 2001 Doha Declaration of the WTO Ministerial Conference, forestry was not explicitly mentioned in the related work programme. WTO's role in timber trade is therefore yet to be clearly defined, with persistent uncertainties lingering on whether or not environment-related measures such as certification, eco-labelling, export bans or export quotas could be considered barriers to trade. As a result, national forest policies and laws will likely continue to take divergent approaches to trade in forest products.

III. MAJOR TRENDS IN NATIONAL LEGISLATION

In the aftermath of Rio, steady efforts at forest law design and reform have been taking place throughout the world. As can be seen in the Annex, some 90 countries have enacted new laws or amended existing legislation on forests over the last decade. These developments have occurred in very diverse political, institutional and legal contexts, as well as under extremely different economic, social, cultural and environmental conditions, including differences in the nature and significance of forest resources. As a result, the legal issues at stake in the forestry sector varied dramatically from place to place. Notwithstanding this great diversity, several common trends in recent legislation are noticeable worldwide, which may be clustered in the following interrelated categories: management, conservation, utilization, privatization, devolution and decentralization.

Other areas of recent development in forest laws, which are not specifically addressed in this chapter, include such debated and evolving issues as the definition of forests and forestry concepts, forest tenure and tree tenure, forestry-related activities (sylvo-pastoralism, agro-forestry), urban forestry, logging bans and log export bans, institutional and financial aspects, corrupt practices and compliance and enforcement issues.[3]

3.1. Forest Management

New forestry legislation tends to promote, in more and more explicit terms, the integration of sustainability principles into forest management, in particular through the use of planning tools.

3.1.1. Sustainability Concerns

Adherence to the concept of sustainable development is clearly one of the emerging trends in legislation, one that pre-UNCED forest laws rarely echoed. This concept is understood to embrace the notion of multiple forest uses and benefits as enshrined in the Rio Forest Principles, i.e., timber, food and fuel, as well as biological diversity and resources, protection of ecosystems and watersheds and recreation and tourism. It is now reflected in several recent laws, such as Bolivia's 1996 Forest Act, which aims to regulate the conservation and sustainable use of woodlands and forest resources for the benefit of present and future generations, reconciling the country's social, economic and ecological interests. Referring to the precautionary principle, it stipulates that where there is evidence that a practice in forest management is likely to cause serious or irreversible damage to the ecosystem, responsible officials must take appropriate measures to prevent or mitigate its effects. The law also states that exemption from liability may not be claimed on the grounds of lack of scientific certainty, or the fact that an authorization has been granted by the competent authority. Similarly, Solomon Islands' Forests Act of 1999 provides for the precautionary principle to be applied "in order to protect forest resources and preserve the forest environment". The same principle is also explicitly embodied in Mozambique's Forest Law of 1999.

In the same vein, the 1996 Forest Law of Portugal expressly refers to sustainability among its basic principles, providing that sustainable forest development must be the main objective of the country's forest policy. Forests are to be managed sustainably, in the broader framework of

---

[3] For a discussion of some of these subject matters, see in the references, in particular: Contreras, 2002; Kern, et al., 1998; FAO, 2001b; FAO, 2001c; Fingleton, 2002; Lindsay, Mekouar and Christy, 2002; Prieur and Doumbé-Billé, 1996; Rosenbaum, 2002; Rosenbaum and Lindsay, 2001.

integrated rural development, so as to meet the needs of present and future generations. Likewise, Estonia's Forest Act of 1998 provides for the management of forests as a renewable natural resource with a view to satisfying economic and other needs of the population without causing unnecessary damage to the environment. The same objective is spelled out in similar terms in the Georgian Forest Code of 1999. In Africa, various recent forest acts or bills also aim to achieve sustainability. For example, the forest laws of the Republic of Congo and Mozambique as well as the forest bills of the Niger and Togo define the concepts of sustainable development and integrated management as they apply to the forestry sector. (Kern, et al., 1998; Cirelli, et al., 2001)

As to the criteria and indicators aimed at improving forest management, while most states are currently involved in C&I-related international initiatives (see section 2.2. above), to date only a small number of laws contain specific requirements to comply with such processes domestically. One is Costa Rica, whose legislation is quite specific in this regard. It requires management plans to be prepared in accordance with officially approved C&I for sustainable forest management (1997 Regulations). A detailed set of national C&I were developed accordingly, binding for natural forests and voluntarily applicable to forest plantations (1998 Regulations). Further C&I were later specially produced for "secondary forests", taking into account their particular features (1999 Regulations).

Another illustration is South Africa's Forests Act of 1998. With a view to promoting sustainability in forest management, it directs the competent minister to set criteria to determine whether a forest is managed sustainably; establish indicators to measure the state of forests and forestry activities; and formulate appropriate standards in relation to those indicators, the breach of which is an offence. Under Peru's Forest Law of 2000, forest concessions may only be granted on the basis of management plans, which must comply with C&I approved by regulation.

3.1.2. Planning Tools

Management plans, the most significant forestry planning tool,[4] have long

---

[4] Other important management planning instruments, not discussed here, include forest inventories, which are often required by law to periodically assess forest resources quantitatively and qualitatively, both country-wide and at the forest level (e.g., 1999 Forest Law of Mozambique).

been a common characteristic of forest legislation. During the last decade, however, they have acquired more prominence in forest laws, with a marked trend towards a widening of their objectives and an extension of their coverage. Beyond timber extraction, legislation now requires planners to pay greater attention to a broader array of social, cultural and environmental interests that have been, in the past, overlooked or neglected in conventional planning. Moreover, management plans are more and more often made a legal prerequisite for the exploitation of all categories of forests, whether public or private. In addition, provision is increasingly made for stakeholders' involvement in the formulation and implementation of management plans.

Illustrations of this widespread trend are found in recent legislation throughout the world. In Africa, almost all recent laws require a forest management plan, with a varying degree of coverage and detail. Under Mali's Forest Law of 1995, a plan must be produced for all government forests, whether gazetted or not. In other countries, such as South Africa (1998 Forest Act), even privately owned forests are subject to management planning. However, where forests are under community management, the law may be less demanding and only require "simple" plans, as is the case in Cameroon (1994 Forest Law). In Europe, too, the preparation of management plans is frequently made compulsory by law, although the nature and scope of the plan may vary significantly, depending in particular on the form of forest ownership. Occasionally, management plans are not required; instead, innovative management techniques not involving the development of plans for every parcel of forest may be put in place, such as in Sweden. (Cirelli, et al., 2001)

In most countries experiencing a shift from centrally controlled to market-driven forestry, management planning has taken on a particular meaning. Owing to the tendency towards central planning under former systems, forestry planning is often still focused on the determination of timber demand and production quotas, even in recent forest laws such as China's Forestry Act of 1998. However, legislative changes reflecting the transition to a market economy are progressively discernible in the provisions dealing with management planning, for example in Cuba's Forest Law of 1998.

Establishment of a hierarchy among a country's forest management plans is not uncommon in post-Rio forest laws. Quite often, legislators take a staged approach to forestry planning, providing for the development of various plans at different government levels, and requiring local plans (or plans developed at the forest unit level) to be consistent with broader regional or national plans. This is the case with Papua New Guinea's Forestry Act, which calls for the preparation of a national forest plan, provincial forest plans, five year working plans and annual logging plans. Guinea's Forest Law, too, provides for a multi-layer planning system. In addition to a national plan spelling out the country's forest policy, lower-level plans must be produced for the regions and the *préfectures*, as well as for each management unit. Similarly, under the United States' forestry legislation, the Forest Service is required to prepare national renewable resources assessments and programmes, regional plans for the forest system and land and management plans for the forest units. (Kern, et al., 1998) By contrast, Vanuatu's Forest Act of 2001 provides for a unique Forestry Sector Plan that acknowledges the limited size of the country and requires its application in the conduct of all forestry operations within the whole national territory. (Fingleton, 2002)

Regarding the legal status accorded to forest management plans, in particular whether or not their prescriptions are legally binding, there seems to be no distinct trend in recent legislation. In some instances, the law expressly requires that forestry operations be consistent with approved management plans (e.g., Burkina Faso's Forest Code of 1997, Guinea's Forest Act of 1999), occasionally providing that non-compliance is an administrative offence (e.g., Senegal's Forest Regulations of 1999) or even a criminal offence (e.g., the Republic of Congo's Forest Code of 2000). In other situations, forest officials are legally required to abide by the prescriptions of the plans in the exercise of their licensing powers, for example to grant – or refuse the award of – cutting permits in accordance with specified allowable cuts (South Africa's Forest Act of 1998, Zanzibar's Forest Act of 1996). More frequently, the conclusion of a forestry contract or the granting of a timber concession is made conditional upon prior approval of a management plan for the relevant forest, in which case the plan itself is part of the overall contractual arrangement (Bolivia's Forest Act of 1996, Cameroon's Forest Act of 1994, Guatemala's Forest Act of 1996).

Greater public involvement and inter-institutional consultation in the design of management plans is another trend in recent legislation, though not yet fully established in all regions of the world. Many forest laws now provide for public meetings and hearings, access to available information – including draft plans – and opportunities to comment throughout the planning process (Estonia's Forest Act of 1998, Finland's Forest Act of 1996, Nicaragua's Forest Regulations of 1993). Further, the public is sometimes allowed to participate even in the implementation, monitoring, assessment and revision of the plans, as is the case for provincial forest plans in the Canadian provinces of Ontario (Crown Forest Sustainability Act of 1994) and Saskatchewan (1996 Forest Resources Management Act). The involvement of stakeholders may also be promoted through advisory or coordinating forestry bodies, where interested parties, whether public or private, can be represented and voice their concerns. Illustrations of this type of forum are found in many forest laws, such as those of Bulgaria (1994), Mexico (1997), Peru (2000) and Portugal (1996), as well as in forest bills from Honduras (2001) and Paraguay (2002).

The growing prominence given to management plans in forestry legislation, however, is not necessarily matched in actual practice. In many countries, the ambitious objectives of lawmakers in terms of management planning do not accurately reflect the realities on the ground. This is due in part to the lack of capacities and resources needed to produce and implement management plans, both in government agencies and the private sector. Recent statistics indicate that, while forest areas under management plans are on the rise globally, in developing countries only 6 percent of the total forest area is covered by officially approved plans. This can be contrasted with the situation in industrialized countries, where some 89 percent of the forests are managed according to formal or informal plans. (FAO, 2000)[5]

3.2. Forest Conservation

Forest lawmaking has always been relatively receptive to conservation concerns. Since Rio, however, forest laws have become even more broadly inclusive of the environmental values of forest ecosystems. Besides confirming traditional protection measures – deforestation control, fire fighting, creation of protected areas, etc. – legislators are now placing greater emphasis on forest ecological functions in terms of biological processes and environmental services.

3.2.1. Environmental Values

Many recent laws now consistently refer to the goals of forestry as including the need to manage sustainably the country's environment and

---

[5] Similarly, only a handful of developing countries regularly carry out national forest inventories. About half of the countries have had only one forest inventory and one-fifth of them have never carried out an inventory. (FAO, 2000)

biological diversity, as well as to comply with international obligations deriving from applicable conservation treaties. This tendency is notable in preambles or objective statements introducing forestry laws. For example, the stated purpose of the 1996 Forestry Law of the Lao People's Democratic Republic is to set the "fundamental principles, regulations and measures for the management, preservation and use of forest resources and forest land ... with a view of ensuring the balance of nature ..., preserving water resources, preventing land erosion, preserving seeds, trees, aquatic animals, wildlife and the environment in a contribution to the national socio-economic development". Similar objectives are spelled out in the initial provisions of Papua New Guinea's Forestry Act and the Forests Act of the Solomon Islands.

The specific legal content given to these general goals varies greatly from country to country, and the goals themselves are achieved using several techniques. Typically, the legal provisions relating to forest policies and inventories, or to the classification and management of forests, take explicit account of environmental considerations. For example, Burkina Faso's Forest Code of 1997 states that the conservation of biodiversity is one of main pillars upon which the country's forest policy must be shaped.

Current forest legislation also tends to be more specific in requiring that environmental criteria be considered in the formulation and implementation of management plans (e.g., Guinea's Forest Law of 1999). Such a requirement often applies to both production and protection forests (e.g., Benin's Forest Regulations of 1996). The collection of environ-mental and biodiversity information is also increasingly prescribed as part of legally mandated forest inventories (e.g., 1999 Forest Law of Mozambique). In addition, laws frequently establish forest categories that embody specific environmental objectives, requiring that each type of classified forest be managed according to a distinctive conservation regime. Illustrations of these include forest nature reserves, watershed forests, coastal area protection forests or other categories designed to protect certain indigenous forests from commercial logging (1996 Forest Act of Zanzibar, 1998 Forest Law of Cuba, 1999 Forest Code of the Dominican Republic, 2000 Forest Law of Peru).

Environmental impact assessments (EIAs) and audits are increasingly becoming common tools of forest management, either by explicit reference in forest laws or more often through general environmental legislation. EIAs are mandated in different ways. They may be required as part of the approval process of forest management plans, forest concessions and other development projects (Cameroon's Forest Law of 1994, Senegal's Forest Regulations of 1999). They may also be prescribed as a precondition to the declassification of gazetted forests (Cape Verde's Forest Law of 1998, Guinea's Forest Act of 1999). Sometimes, EIAs must be carried out prior to major land clearing (Burkina Faso's Forest Code of 1997, the Republic of Congo's Forest Code of 2000) or the introduction of alien species (1999 Forest Law of Mozambique, 2001 Forest Regulations of Peru).

Occasionally, EIAs may also involve the consideration of social impacts of forestry programmes or development projects occurring in forest areas, for instance their effects on the livelihoods of forest-dependent people (Bhutan's Forest Act of 1995, Chad and Comoros Forest Bills). In general, EIA processes include the design of solutions to mitigate the likely negative impacts of proposed actions (2001 Forest Law of Guinea-Bissau, 1997 Forest Law of Mauritania). Less frequently, some laws provide for the evaluation of ongoing projects to update or revise the initial assessments. Under Bolivia's Forest Act of 1996, for example, forest inspections and audits must periodically assess the environmental and social effects of forestry activities. With a similar goal, "environmental forest audits" are also foreseen in Nepal's Forest Act (1993) and Regulations (1995).

Finally, forest environmental services tend to figure more and more prominently in most post-Rio forest laws. Thanks to the impact of CBD's work, greater emphasis is being placed in recent forest laws on the biological values and functions of forest ecosystems. New ecological services have recently begun to surface in forest legislation, adding to their traditionally stated watershed, soil and water conservation functions, as well as their increasingly recognized roles in maintaining biological diversity, processes and resources. (Kern, et al., 1998; Cirelli, et al., 2001)

In conjunction with the opportunities expected to arise from the implementation of the Kyoto Protocol, attempts to reflect the potential of forests to fix carbon are becoming discernible in a few laws. So far, however, the FCCC and the KP have barely influenced domestic forest laws, and climate-related provisions remain scarce and unspecific in forest legislation – although some examples exist. The Forest Acts of China (1998) and of Peru (2001) contain brief statements in this regard, tying forestry to climate in general terms. Under the 1999 Forest Law of the Dominican Republic, regulations may be made to create incentives for managing forests for environmental services such as carbon sequestration. The Australian state of New South Wales, through a 1998 amendment to its property legislation, recognized a separate legal interest in the carbon sequestration potential of forest land.

Costa Rica's Forest Law and Regulations of 1996 offer a unique illustration of a relatively detailed set of provisions in this area. A third of the national tax on hydrocarbons is dedicated to the conservation of forests to compensate for the environmental services they provide, including mitigation of gas emissions. Forest land owners can receive certificates for forest conservation representing payment for environmental services, which they can use to pay taxes and other fees owed to the government. Furthermore, "greenhouse gas mitigation certificates" were created as a tradeable security. They represent specific levels of gas reduction or mitigation, expressed as equivalent amounts of carbon removed from the atmosphere. Through a reforestation and forest conservation project, the first certificates, issued in 1997, represented credit for 200 000 metric tonnes of carbon offset. (Rosenbaum, 2001)

3.2.2. Protection Measures

Control of deforestation, pests, fires and pollution, as well as the protection of tree species or the creation of forest protected areas, are among the traditional conservation measures most commonly found in legislation. They remain present in post-Rio forest laws apparently without significant changes, the only novel area being that of forest certification. Forest certification has lately emerged as an instrument with the potential to promote forest protection, though it is also widely viewed as a primarily market-based tool, the assumption being that products certified as coming from sustainably managed forests would have the preference of consumers. (Bourque, 2002) Whatever the logic behind it, certification was hardly mentioned in forest legislation until recently, although more than 50 certification schemes have already been developed since Rio.

Some legal developments suggest that certification is beginning to find its way into law, essentially as a voluntary scheme for certifying forest management standards or products from managed forests. South Africa's Forests Act of 1998, for instance, requires the Minister responsible for forestry to "create or promote a certification programme ... to encourage sustainable forest management". Likewise, Georgia's Forest Code of 1999 states that regulations shall be made for the voluntary certification "of forests, forest resources and management techniques". In Peru's Forest Law of 2000, voluntary certification of products from managed forests is encouraged through the reduction of concession fees. By contrast, the 1997 Forest Code of the Russian Federation is probably unique in making certification mandatory for "wood supplies and secondary forest resources", specifying that their certification must be organized and carried out by the forestry agency, in the manner determined by the government.

Other conservation mechanisms include placing forests under some protected area status, which continues to be the most frequently used tool in legislation. Today, about 10 percent of the world's forests are estimated to be under a formal protected area category. (FAO, 2000) For example, Zanzibar's Forest Act of 1996 provides for the designation of "nature forest reserves". In some countries, such as Burkina Faso, Mozambique and Peru, protected areas and wildlife are mainly governed by forest legislation. In most cases, however, the creation of protected forests is separate from the establishment of national parks and other protected areas, both institutionally and legislatively. Moreover, rare or endangered forest tree species are often listed for partial or full protection, owing to their socio-economic, medical or cultural values, as well as their ecological, botanical or scientific interest. Where the exploitation of such species is allowed, it is usually subject to a special permit (e.g., Guinea's Forest Law of 1999, Mali's Forest Law of 1995).

Protecting forests against clearing – a major deforestation cause in many countries – may be achieved in law through different techniques. One way is to restrict or prohibit the clearing of specified categories of land, such as forest areas situated on river banks or on steep slopes (e.g, 2001 Forest Law of Guinea-Bissau). Another is to allow land clearing only in cases where it is undeniably in the public interest (Madagascar's Forest Law of 1997) or when development projects for which clearing is needed may not be located outside the forest (Mauritania's Forest Law of 1997, Forest Bills of Chad and Comoros). In addition, some laws require the plantation or reforestation of a piece of land to compensate for an authorized clearing. This may be achieved either directly through an obligation to replant or indirectly through clearing taxes, the proceeds of which are used to finance compensatory reforestation (1998 Forest Law of Cape Verde, 1999 Forest Law of Guinea). A less common and more recent method to limit major land clearing is to make it subject to a formal EIA procedure, as indicated earlier.

Forest laws often contain a chapter on protection against fires. Sometimes, forest fires are the subject of specific regulations (e.g., Brazil 1999, Indonesia 1995, Italy 1997, Portugal 2001, Viet Nam 1998) or even separate parliamentary acts in a few countries (e.g., Ontario in Canada 1996, South Africa 1998). Fire fighting measures typically include prohibitions and restrictions. Forest fires are systematically forbidden for hunting purposes and frequently prohibited for agricultural or grazing purposes. Controlled fires, however, are quite commonly allowed for management and prevention, provided the necessary precautions are taken to avoid fires spreading. Not infrequently, such fires are only permitted in specified seasons or periods (e.g., Mali's Forest Law of 1995, Mauritania's Forest Law of 1997). Preventive measures generally include the creation of firebreaks, the erection of observation posts in areas susceptible to fire or in critical periods of the year or the setting up of fire fighting units. In a number of laws, local authorities and people are required to help fighters control fires that break out in nearby forests (the Republic of Congo's Forest Code of 2000, Guinea's Forest Law of 1999). In some cases, fire-induced damage must be covered by special insurance (1996 Forest Law of Portugal).

3.3. Forest Utilization

Forest laws traditionally embody licensing requirements and contractual arrangements for forest resource exploitation in its various forms. Since Rio, the apparent trend here is that, although lawmakers have been rather creative with respect to forestry contracts, they have not significantly deviated from well-established approaches to licensing of forestry operations.

3.3.1. Licensing Requirements

In general, forest laws continue to require licences for forest harvesting of all kinds, from both public and private stands. Licences are also imposed on most forest market operators, be they transporters, charcoal producers, sawmill owners, importers or exporters. Under the Gambia's legislation, for example, separate licences are mandated for forest harvesting and milling and for wood merchants. The possession of a licence only allows the undertaking of the corresponding category of activity; however; a licensee may still be required to obtain specific permits for particular actions. Similarly, in Ghana, chainsaw owners must register with the relevant local authority, and further obtain a permit whenever the chainsaw is used to fell any tree. (Cirelli, et al., 2001)

While licensing is needed to control illegal behaviour, it may represent an oppressive burden on both government and private actors, particularly on poorly equipped forestry services and small entrepreneurs, without necessarily providing noteworthy benefits in terms of improved forest management or quality of market outputs. Hence the emerging trend, in recent forest legislation, to ease some licensing requirements. For example, in Guinea, instead of a permit, a simple declaration by the owner or operator may suffice for the harvesting of forest trees planted on private land (1999 Forest Law). In such cases, the selection and marking of trees to be logged, which would otherwise usually be required by law, may also be waived.

A different approach to prior licensing is taken in some European countries. In Sweden, a permit is required for logging on forest land that is protected or difficult to regenerate; otherwise, forest owners must simply give notice of logging operations, specifying how they intend to satisfy the objectives of conservation (Forest Act of 1994). In Finland, interested owners may issue a felling declaration, following which the competent authorities may wish to negotiate conditions if the operation is likely to have undesirable effects. If any are found, the activity may be prohibited (Forest Act of 1996). Other limited innovations have been introduced in the licensing schemes of a few post-Rio laws, either by establishing auctions for the awarding of harvesting licences, or by allowing the possibility of extending the duration of licences, and modifying applicable fees if the holders have made investments on the concerned lands (e.g., 1992 Forest Law of Albania, 1994 Forest Law of Armenia, 2000 Forest Code of the Republic of Congo).

3.3.2. Contractual Arrangements

Besides licences, forest resources are also exploited, in numerous countries, by means of concessions, leases and other contractual arrangements. (FAO, 2001c) Older forest laws were generally imprecise, if not silent, regarding the conditions and procedures governing the award of forestry contracts. As a result, most concessions were granted in secretive ways, often regardless of technical criteria and without ensuring fair competition among potential concessionaires. Over the years, this brought about not only widespread corrupt practices, but also severe economic loss and serious environmental damage in the forestry sector. In an effort to remedy this situation, lawmakers tend nowadays to set forth in some detail the procedures by which forestry contracts are to be awarded in a more transparent manner.

In particular, new forest laws now seek to specify the basic elements of an auction and bidding system, including the content of a call for bids, the form and content of submissions, the professional qualifications and independence of auctioneers and decisionmaking timeframes. Sometimes they also specify when non-economic criteria can be used to distinguish between competing bids. For example, under Bolivia's 1996 Forest Act, special weight may be conferred on non-quantifiable characteristics of the bidding entity where preference in concession awards is given to neighbouring indigenous communities. Moreover, concessions may be publicly registered and must be granted in a continuous and uninterrupted area. The logging area must also be protected, together with its natural resources and biodiversity.

In Ghana, the Timber Resources Management Act of 1997 supplanted prior concession arrangements and established "timber utilization contracts" which must be concluded through a process involving, *inter alia*: open competition among eligible candidates; consultation of the land owner community regarding the area under contract and the forest operations to be conducted; and local people's participation in determining the social responsibilities of the contractor. Land owners and farmers whose land is within the contract area have a specific right to oppose harvesting on that land or to claim compensation for damage caused thereby. A number of other recent laws have similar provisions on forest concession or lease arrangements, such as the forest acts of Malawi (1997), the Russian Federation (1997), South Africa (1998), Peru (2000) and the Republic of Congo (2000).

Spelling out the process of awarding forestry contracts not only promotes greater openness and accountability in decisionmaking, but also helps provide a level playing field for interested competitors. Furthermore, with a well-ordered process of granting, evaluating and recording such contracts, conflicts generated by overlapping concessions may be substantially reduced, existing rights within concession areas may be more easily settled and respected, interests of third parties may be better protected and illegal activities may be prevented and tracked more efficiently.

3.4. Privatization in Forestry

With the role of private owners and operators attracting growing attention in law reforms, privatization in forestry is another clearly observable trend. The common orientation is undoubtedly towards greater promotion of private initiatives and investments in the forest sector worldwide. In several countries, this tendency extends to include the transfer of government forest land to private hands.

3.4.1. Private Forests

Since Rio, privatization of forests has emerged as one of the most complex issues of legal reform in various regions of the world. This was especially the case in the former centrally planned economies, where the transition to market economies brought about comprehensive reassessments of forest policies. As a result of structural adjustment undergone through the last decade, the roles assumed by the states needed to be redefined away from being rigid command-and-control authorities and forest owners and managers. In addition, the legal provisions governing the ownership of forest lands and assets were the subject of significant debate and key change.

This process was carried out in a variety of ways and involved several interconnected issues. Among the apprehensions raised by privatization, a central concern was: is private ownership of forest land desirable in view of the overall national interests and in terms of sustainable forest management? In the face of growing privatization of forest lands, in recent years the fear has been expressed that: (i) proper management will become impossible if the extent of small holdings falls below a certain minimum (which is frequently the case in the countries in transition – thus the 1994 Forest Act of Lithuania prohibits dividing properties into parcels smaller than a minimum size in order to prevent excessive fragmentation); (ii) for lack of means, capacity or oversight, private owners will over-exploit their forests, will not provide adequate wood supplies for industries and will not sufficiently invest in the equipment required for sustainable resource management.

Other thorny questions included: How far and how fast should established forms of forest ownership be transformed? How can the forest assets to be privatized be properly valued? What efficient and equitable tools should be better used for transferring forest ownership – restitution, distribution or sale; priority to employees; nationals only or also foreigners? (FAO, 1994) Different approaches were taken in national laws, but in essence they involved some common features, namely: (i) the transformation of state enterprises carrying out forestry and related activities (mainly through administrative reforms); (ii) the partial restitution, sale or distribution of forest lands to former owners or to other private entities; and (iii) the definition of the legal regime applicable to privatized forests (e.g.,

Albania's Law of 1998 on "giving ownership in agricultural lands, forests, pastures and meadows").

In many instances, privatization extended to the ownership of forest resources and holdings. Countries where forest lands may now be privately held include Croatia, the Czech Republic, Estonia, Georgia, Hungary, Latvia, Lithuania, Poland, Romania, Slovakia and Slovenia. (FAO, 2001a) In other cases, governments decided to retain ownership of forest lands even where agricultural holdings may have been handed out to former owners. As a result, the numbers of small private forest holdings have rapidly grown in certain countries, especially in those that used to have many forest owners in the past (e.g., Estonia, Latvia, the Czech Republic, Hungary, Poland). Notwithstanding these legal changes, in actual fact most forest lands in the majority of countries in transition to market economies still remain in state hands, and are expected to be retained by the government for the foreseeable future. In exceptional cases, as in Armenia, the law does not yet allow the privatization of state forest land.

A similar move away from the monopolistic approach to forest ownership is also noticeable in other parts of the world, where the forest estate used to be mostly or entirely state-owned in colonial times, particularly in Africa and Asia. In these regions, private ownership of forests is now permitted in recent legislation, although often in limited ways. This trend is evidenced in Africa by the laws of Benin (1993), Guinea (1999), Madagascar (1997) and Mauritania (1997), and in Asia by the laws of Bhutan (1995), China (1998), Myanmar (1992) and Nepal. For example, under the 1996 Forest Law of the Lao People's Democratic Republic, individuals may own and inherit forests planted by them under specified conditions. Likewise, pursuant to the legislation of Senegal (1998–99), where individuals plant forest stands in the national domain, they acquire ownership of the forest stands but not the land itself.

3.4.2. Private Forestry

More generally, fostering private management is a common feature in new forest laws, even in the rare instances where forest lands remain wholly owned or controlled by the state. Provision is more frequently made in most countries for some form of privatization in the forestry sector, such us allowing individuals or private companies to engage in forestry (planning, planting, harvesting, etc.), with reduced involvement of state agencies in logging, processing, marketing and pricing, and with growing openness to foreign competition. (Kern, et al., 1998; Cirelli, et al., 2001)

Moreover, private rights in government-owned forests are increasingly given in various legal forms, such as leaseholds, concessions and other contractual use rights. Quite often such rights are now granted for longer periods of time (forestry generally requiring a long turnaround on investment activity), which makes them more secure and sometimes akin to ownership. The forest laws of Cameroon (1994), the Republic of Congo (2000) and Gabon (2001) offer examples of this trend.

In many countries, other legal tools designed to promote private forestry include financial incentives to private operators, on the one hand, and some degree of deregulation of private forest management, on the other. Forestation and afforestation of private lands, for example, are increasingly encouraged in legislation through tax exemptions (1993 Law of Benin, 1997 Law of Madagascar), as well as through subsidies and low interest rate loans (1998 Law of Cape Verde, 1997 Law of Equatorial Guinea).

Liberalization in the forest sector, in the sense of reduced regulation and control of private activities, is also used as an incentive in a growing number of countries. For instance, throughout Western Europe, normal licensing requirements are generally less stringent for private forest owners and operators. However, where particular restrictions on the use of private forests are imposed, the affected owners are entitled to compensation. In Great Britain, where a licence to fell trees on private land is denied, the owner may claim and obtain damages. Similarly, in Norway, reparation must be paid to the owner of a forest who cannot take wood from it for reasons of environmental protection. (Cirelli, et al., 2001)

3.5. Devolution and Decentralization

In recent forest law reforms, local forest management has received a great deal of attention, especially with respect to community-based activities and the realignment of powers and responsibilities between central and local governments. Local management of forests is now increasingly promoted in various ways, though it is still subject to numerous limitations.

3.5.1. Promotion of Local Management

Since Rio, community-based forest management was promoted not only as a way of improving local livelihoods and of recognizing local claims to rights over forest resources, but also as part of a worldwide move towards devolving or decentralizing various governance functions. It is now broadly recognized that without local people having a significant stake in the management of local forest resources, the efforts of under-staffed and poorly financed forest officials to protect forests will often be futile. (Lindsay, Mekouar and Christy, 2002)

Historically, forestry legislation has generally been unfriendly to local management. In most parts of the world, the overall trend was toward an assertion of central government control over forests, at the expense of local practices, perceptions and values. It is true, however, that forest usage rights have been given some recognition in most countries' legislation – particularly in developing countries – thereby allowing local people to meet their household needs in forest products. Nevertheless, forest laws have traditionally provided little scope for local people to play a meaningful part in the planning, management and allocation of forest resources on which they have depended for centuries – and which they may have actively managed and protected. Typically, the state itself has taken on this role, giving very weak or no legal protection to existing community-based systems, and providing no alternative mechanisms by which local groups or individuals might assert effective control. (Bruce, 1999) Efforts to address these shortcomings in recent forest law reform have taken various forms, with the common aim of improving the legal environment for local participation in forest management.

First, various mechanisms for the devolution of forest management to local communities, villages, user groups or households have been created through site-specific arrangements such as co-management agreements, community forestry leases, village forest reserves and related devices. An illustration of this approach is Nepal's 1993 Forest Act, which provides for the "turning over" of portions of national forest to local user groups who agree to manage the areas in accordance with an approved plan. A broad range of variations on this approach may be found in a growing number of forest laws, including those of Benin (1993 Forest Law), Bolivia (1996 Forest Law), Burkina Faso (1997 Forest Code), Cameroon (1994 Forest Law), Costa Rica (1996 Forest Law), the Gambia (1998 Forest Act), Guinea-Bissau (2001 Forest Law), India (1992 Joint Forest Management Regulations), the Lao People's Democratic Republic (1996 Forest Law),

Madagascar (1996 Law on Local Management of Natural Resources), Mozambique (1999 Forest Law) and South Africa (1998 Forests Act).

Second, several countries have accorded increasing recognition to the historical land or the territorial claims of local peoples. A notable example of this trend is the 1997 Indigenous Peoples' Rights Act in the Philippines. Similarly, the rights of indigenous communities figure prominently in the legislation of several Latin American countries, such as Bolivia (1996 Forest Law), Mexico (1997 Forest Law) and Nicaragua (1993 Forest Regulations). A number of other countries, including Australia, Canada, South Africa, the United States and several countries in Central and Eastern Europe, are engaged in restoring the lands of dispossessed communities and individuals, some of which lands include natural forests or commercial plantations. (FAO, 1994; Kern, et al., 1998; Cirelli, et al., 2001)

Third, many countries have moved to decentralize various aspects of forest administration to local government bodies. This may be carried out either specifically within forest legislation, or more generally as part of an overall revision of local government law. Again, examples can be found in all regions, from Latin America (Guatemala, Honduras, Mexico, Peru), to the Sahel (Guinea, Mali, Senegal) and Asia (China, Fiji, India, the Lao People's Democratic Republic, Mongolia, Viet Nam). (Kern, et al., 1998; Cirelli, et al., 2001)

These three categories are only indicative of a wider variety of approaches that are being tried throughout the world. Moreover, they are not mutually exclusive, and often overlap or operate concurrently. For instance, under some West African laws (e.g., Burkina Faso, Guinea, Mali, Senegal), where management of certain forests has been decentralized to the level of the *commune,* the local government may have the opportunity further to devolve management over specific sub-areas through a contract with local users. (Cirelli, et al., 2001)

3.5.2. Limitations on Local Management

Despite the higher profile given to local forest management in recent legislation, many of the reforms are characterized by significant limitations and ambivalence, both on paper and in practice. Quite frequently, government forest departments continue to hold most of the important decisionmaking powers, including the power to draft and approve management plans, and to decide about the selection of species, the marketing of harvested products and the use of benefits by local groups. Furthermore, the strength of the rights granted or recognized under local arrangements may be unclear or insecure, either because the terms of the agreements are too short, or because governments tend to retain wide powers to terminate agreements or to cancel legal recognition for poorly defined reasons. In addition, legal provisions that appear to protect the traditional rights of indigenous peoples are sometimes so weakly or ambiguously drafted as to be unusable.

In truth, in a number of countries forest authorities have embraced the concept of community-based management mainly in areas where forest resources are already depleted. There is frequently a reluctance to share control over richer, more intact areas, even where there is evidence that the health of the resource is due in large part to the long-established informal stewardship of local people. There is therefore a continuing need to find workable legal arrangements that provide or recognize meaningful and secure rights for local forest managers, while allowing a flexible response to vastly different local conditions as well as an appropriate balance between various interests. This is an area of forest law that will surely continue to experience significant evolution in the years ahead. (Lindsay, 1999)

IV. CONCLUSION

After a sharp political divide on forest issues at UNCED, which did not allow agreement on a world forest treaty, the post-Rio decade witnessed numerous efforts at fostering dialogues and strengthening laws and institutions, both globally and nationally. Significant initiatives have been taken to advance multilateral cooperation, through non-legally binding instruments – Forest Principles, Agenda 21 – as well as forestry and forestry-related international fora – IPF, IFF, UNFF, CBD, FCCC, CCD, CITES, ITTO, in particular.

Stirred and inspired by these intergovernmental endeavours and other non-governmental undertakings, domestic legal reforms have been carried out worldwide, bringing about major changes in contemporary forest law. Although the legal issues addressed varied profoundly from place to place, several common trends in recent statutes are clearly noticeable. Overall, forest legislation has been steadily reoriented towards a more balanced, integrated approach to forest management, conservation and development. With sustainability concerns, ecological values and social interests increasingly achieving more prominence, less emphasis is now being put on the role of forests as economic assets, and greater focus is being placed on their multifunctional nature.

The concept of sustainable development is central to modern forest law. It translates into the notion of multiple forest uses and benefits, which embrace not only timber, fuel, food and other forest products, but also biological diversity and resources, protection of ecosystems and water-sheds, recreation and tourism, as well as other environmental services, including carbon sequestration. Planning tools, especially management plans, are more visibly present in forest laws, with wider objectives and extended coverage. There is also growing provision for forest concessions and contracts to be more precise and transparent, to provide greater accountability and to prevent corruption. Further, with the worldwide drive towards the privatization of forests and forestry, private owners and operators have become key players in most recent forest laws. Likewise, as decentralization of responsibilities and devolu-tion of powers gain ground in the forestry sector, local actors are given more important stakes and better defined roles in forest planning, use and management, including through community-based arrangements.

REFERENCES

Amilien, C. 1995. *Droit international et gestion durable des forêts tropicales,* Thèse pour le doctorat en droit, Faculté de droit et de science politique, Aix-Marseilles.

Bruce, J.W. 1999. *Legal Bases for the Management of Forest Resources as Common Property.* Community Forestry Paper 14, FAO, Rome.

Bourque, I.J. 2002. *Forest Certification and Forest Law Compliance, FAO Meeting on Policy Options for Improving Forest Law Compliance, Rome, 14–16 January 2002.*

Cirelli, M.T., Schmithüsen, F., Texier, J. & Young, T. 2001. *Trends in Forestry Law in Europe and Africa.* Legislative Study No. 72, FAO, Rome.

Contreras, A. 2002. *Policy and Legal Options to Improve Law Compliance in the Forest Sector, FAO Meeting on Policy Options for Improving Forest Law Compliance, Rome, 14–16 January 2002.*

FAO. 1994. *Forestry in Countries with Economies in Transition,* UNASYLVA, 179, Vol. 45, Rome.

FAO. 1997. *State of the World's Forests 1997,* Rome.

FAO. 1999. *State of the World's Forests 1999*, Rome.

FAO. 2000. *Global Forest Resources Assessment 2000*, Forestry Paper 140, Rome.

FAO. 2001a. *State of the World's Forests 2001*, Rome.

FAO. 2001b. *Forests Out of Bounds: Impacts and Effectiveness of Logging Bans in Natural Forests in Asia-Pacific*, Asia-Pacific Forestry Commission, Bangkok.

FAO. 2001c. *Governance Principles for Concessions and Contracts in Public Forests*, Forestry Paper 139, Rome.

Fingleton, J. 2002. *Regional Study on Pacific Islands Forestry Legislation*. FAO Legal Paper Online No. 30 (www.fao.org/Legal).

Humphreys, D. 1996. *Forest Politics. The Evolution of International Cooperation*. Earthscan, London.

Kern, E., Rosenbaum, K.L., Silva Repetto, R. & Young, T. 1998. *Trends in Forestry Law in America and Asia.* Legislative Study No. 66, FAO, Rome.

Lindsay, J.M. 1999. *Creating a Legal Framework for Community-Based Management: Principles and Dilemmas*, UNASYLVA, Vol. 50, No. 4, FAO, Rome.

Lindsay, J., Mekouar, A. & Christy, L. 2002. *Why Law Matters: Design Principles for Strengthening the Role of Forestry Legislation in Reducing Illegal Activities and Corrupt Practices.* FAO Legal Paper Online No. 27 (www.fao.org/Legal).

Prieur, M. & Doumbé-Billé, S. (eds.). 1996. *Droit, forêts et développement durable.* AUPELF-UREF, Bruylant, Brussels.

Rosenbaum, K.L. 2001. *Climate Change and the Forestry Sector: Possible Legislative Responses for National and Subnational Governments.* FAO Legal Paper Online No. 14 (www.fao.org/Legal).

Rosenbaum, K.L. 2002. *Illegal Actions and the Forest Sector: A Legal Perspective, FAO Meeting on Policy Options for Improving Forest Law Compliance, Rome, 14– 16 January 2002.*

Rosenbaum, K.L. & Lindsay, J.M. 2001. *An Overview of National Forest Funds: Current Approaches and Future Opportunities.* FAO Legal Paper Online No. 15 (www.fao.org/Legal).

Tarasofsky, R.G. 1995. *The International Forest Regime. Legal and Policy Options.* IUCN/WWF, Gland.

Tarasofsky, R.G. (ed.). 1999. *Assessing the International Forest Regime*, IUCN Environmental Law Paper 37, Bonn.

WTO. 1997. *Environmental Benefits of Removing Trade Restrictions and Distortions.* Committee on Trade and Environment, WT/CTE/W/67, Geneva.

Annex - Post-Rio Forest Legislation at the Domestic Level:
New Enactments and Major Amendments

Date	Laws	Regulations
1992	*Albania, Mexico, Myanmar, Switzerland*	Belize, Brazil, Canada, Equatorial Guinea, Fiji, France, Gabon, Nicaragua, Peru, Poland, Viet Nam
1993	*Benin*, Croatia, *Cuba, Estonia, Kazakhstan, Nepal*, New Zealand, Russia, *Senegal, Slovenia, Tajikistan*	Albania, Australia, Belgium, Bhutan, Brazil, Cuba, Finland, France, Gabon, Guinea, Indonesia, Lao PDR, Malaysia, Niger, Russia, Uruguay
1994	*Armenia, Bulgaria, Cameroon*, Colombia, Hungary, *Latvia, Lithuania, Norway, Panama*, Paraguay, *Sweden, Syria, Ukraine*	Brazil, Colombia, Costa Rica, Ecuador, Gabon, Indonesia, Italy, Lao PDR, Madagascar, Mexico, New Zealand, Portugal, United Kingdom
1995	Austria, *Bhutan, Mali, Mongolia*, New Zealand, Paraguay, Turkey	Cameroon, Ecuador, France, Indonesia, Luxembourg, Mali, Nepal, Paraguay, Senegal, Tanzania, Turkey
1996	Austria, *Bolivia*, Canada, *Costa Rica, Czech Republic, Denmark, Finland, Guatemala, Hungary, Jamaica, Lao PDR*, Lebanon, Mali, *Portugal, Romania, Tanzania (Zanzibar)*	Albania, Australia, Belize, Benin, Bolivia, Brazil, Cameroon, Colombia, Costa Rica, Ecuador, Finland, France, Gambia, Guinea-Bissau, Indonesia, Mali, New Zealand, Niger, Peru, Senegal, Tanzania, Tunisia
1997	Bulgaria, *Burkina Faso, Equatorial Guinea, Madagascar, Malawi, Mauritania, Mexico*, Norway, *Poland, Russia*	Belgium, Bolivia, Colombia, Costa Rica, Hungary, Italy, Kyrgyzstan, Lithuania, Mali, Mexico, Russia, Turkey, Zambia
1998	Albania, *Cape Verde*, Chile, *China*, Costa Rica, Croatia, *Cuba, Estonia*, Finland, France, *Gambia*, Georgia, Ghana, *Lesotho*, Norway, *Senegal, South Africa*	Albania, Belgium, Brazil, Chile, Costa Rica, Ecuador, Finland, Georgia, Hungary, Indonesia, Mexico, Nicaragua, Portugal, Russia, Viet Nam
1999	Argentina, *Dominican Republic, Georgia, Guinea, Kyrgyzstan, Mozambique, Solomon Islands, Zambia*	Argentina, Belgium, Brazil, Cameroon, Costa Rica, Cuba, Guatemala, Indonesia, Peru, Portugal, Russia, Senegal, United Kingdom, Viet Nam, Zambia
2000	*China (Taiwan), France, Peru, Republic of Congo*	Argentina, Canada, China, Costa Rica, Cuba, Ecuador, France, Georgia, Peru, Portugal, Russia, Spain
2001	*Gabon, Guinea-Bissau*	Argentina, Bolivia, Cameroon, Malta, Peru, Viet Nam

* In the left-hand column, states that have enacted new laws or substantially amended existing laws since Rio are in bold italics (the other states listed in that column only slightly amended their laws), while the right-hand column lists the countries where major subsidiary legislation was adopted during the same period.

11

WILDLIFE

Contents

I. INTRODUCTION

The post-Rio decade has witnessed important developments in wildlife legislation. Traditionally, legislation on wildlife focused on protected areas and hunting restrictions (e.g., protection of listed species), and rarely adopted a comprehensive approach to wildlife management. While retaining some of these features, recent wildlife laws also contain important innovations.

First, well-established wildlife protection instruments, such as hunting regulations and the protection of particular species or habitats, tend to be reinterpreted in a new light. For instance, protected areas are increasingly established as parts of national systems rather than in a "patchwork" way. Moreover, within hunting regulations, greater attention is paid to the subsistence needs of traditional hunting communities.

Second, recent wildlife laws address new issues and envisage new means to protect and manage wildlife. In particular, they tend to give greater consideration to the interdependence among species, by providing for the protection of biodiversity. While extinction of species is part of a natural process in geological time, extinction rates have increased dramatically in recent eras. It is estimated that 24 percent of mammal species and 12 percent of bird species are currently threatened with extinction. (CBD/UNEP, 2001) This raises concerns not only because these particular species may not survive, but also because of the importance that biodiversity has for human life. For that reason, wildlife protection is seen as a part of biodiversity protection, calling for a comprehensive approach.

Similarly, rather than focusing on hunting alone, recent laws consider broader threats to wildlife, for instance by requiring an assessment of the impact of all activities potentially harmful to wildlife. They also place greater emphasis on management planning, requiring monitoring of the state of wildlife and envisaging management plans for the sustainable use of wildlife resources. Finally, in some cases they create mechanisms for the involvement of concerned persons in wildlife-related decisionmaking and for the participation of local communities in the economic benefits deriving from wildlife.

This chapter discusses the major trends emerging in national wildlife legislation. Brief mention is first made of developments at the international level.

II.   INTERNATIONAL FRAMEWORK: KEY DEVELOPMENTS

2.1. Overview of the Main International Agreements

International wildlife law includes both species-based treaties, protecting particular species, and area-based treaties, protecting specific habitats, with the borderline between the two sometimes blurred (e.g., the Bonn Convention protects migratory species of wild animals, through means that include conservation and restoration of their habitats). The Convention on Biological Diversity adopts a more comprehensive approach, protecting biodiversity as a whole.

2.1.1. Species-based Treaties

One of the early species-based treaties is the Convention on International Trade in Endangered Species of Wild Flora and Fauna (CITES, Washington, 1973), which protects endangered species by restricting and regulating their international trade through export permit systems. For species threatened with extinction which are or may be affected by trade (listed in Appendix I to the Convention), export permits may be granted only in exceptional circumstances and subject to strict requirements; the importation of these species also requires a permit, while trade for primarily commercial purposes is not allowed. For species which may become endangered if their trade is not subject to strict regulation (listed in Appendix II), export permits (including for commercial trade) can only be granted if export is not detrimental to the survival of that species and if other requirements are met. For species subject to national regulation and needing international co-operation for trade control (listed in Appendix III), export permits may be granted for specimens not obtained illegally.

Additions and deletions of species from Appendices I and II are made by the Conference of Parties (COP), according to established criteria. In 1994, the COP adopted new criteria, repealing those long in force. The new criteria encompass general principles such as the precautionary principle, and detailed biological and other requirements.

The Convention requires states to adopt legislation that penalizes trade in and possession of covered species, and to provide for the confiscation or return to the state of illegal exports. In the last decade, the COP has adopted several resolutions on enforcement and compliance, such as Resolution 9.9 (1994), recommending confiscation of specimens exported illegally; Resolution 9.10 (Rev.) (1994), on disposal of confiscated specimens or parts or derivatives thereof; and Resolution 11.3 (2000), recommending greater coordination between competent authorities, and outlining measures to promote enforcement, such as creating appropriate incentives for local and rural communities. The COP has also adopted resolutions on trade in specified species, and on ranching and breeding of protected species.

The Convention on the Conservation of Migratory Species of Wild Animals (Bonn, 1979) requires cooperation among "range" states host to migratory species regularly crossing international boundaries. With regard to species considered as endangered (listed in Appendix I), states must conserve and restore their habitats; prevent, remove or minimize impediments to their migration; prevent, reduce and control factors endangering them; and prohibit their taking. With regard to other species which have an unfavourable conservation status (listed in Appendix II), range states undertake to conclude agreements to maintain or restore concerned species in a favourable conservation status.

The concept of conservation status, relating to population, range and habitats of migratory species, is an important feature of the Convention, and is used in other wildlife instruments (e.g., the EU Habitats Directive). For state parties, the concept requires that species or populations be maintained in a favourable status, which entails a number of *obligations de moyen* (obligations of process, as contrasted with *obligations de résultats* or obligations of results), such as controlling potentially harmful activities. (De Klemm, 1999) One post-Rio agreement adopted under the Convention is the Agreement on the Conservation of African-Eurasian Migratory Waterbirds (1995), which provides for concerted actions to be taken by the range states (117 countries, from the northern reaches of Canada and the Russian Federation to the southernmost tip of Africa) throughout the migration systems of the 172 species of water birds to which it applies.

A "Strategy for the Future Development of the Convention" was adopted by the COP in 1997, prioritizing objectives for the triennium 1998-2000. In 1999, the COP adopted the Strategic Plan for 2000-2005, whose objectives include prioritizing conservation actions for migratory species (*inter alia* by integrating consideration for migratory species in government policies, by mitigating obstacles to migration, and by identifying priority Appendix II species for the conclusion of agreements under the Convention); promoting accession of targeted countries to the Convention; and facilitating and improving implementation of the Convention, by mobilizing financial resources, rationalizing institutional arrangements and strengthening linkages with other international biodiversity-related arrangements.

2.1.2. Area-based Treaties

The main area-based treaties are the Convention on Wetlands of
International Importance Especially as Waterfowl Habitat (Ramsar
Convention, 1971), and the Convention Concerning the Protection of the
World Cultural and Natural Heritage (World Heritage Convention, Paris,
1972). As noted, these treaties protect habitats rather than particular
species.

Parties to the Ramsar Convention must designate wetlands in their
territory for inclusion in a List of Wetlands of International Importance,
and promote their conservation and wise use, for example by establishing
nature reserves. "Criteria for Identifying Wetlands of International Importance" were adopted at the 4th, 6th and 7th meetings of the COP in 1990, 1996
and 1999, respectively. A Strategic Plan 1997-2002 was adopted by the
COP in 1996, emphasizing the need to integrate wetland protection with
sustainable development (considered as synonymous with "wise use"[1]) to
promote participation of local communities and involvement of the
private sector, and to mobilize resources at the international level.

The World Heritage Convention provides for the identification and
conservation of sites of outstanding universal value from a natural or
cultural point of view, which are published in the World Heritage List.
While responsibility for conservation is primarily vested in the state
where the site is located, the Convention also provides for international
assistance funded by the World Heritage Fund. At the time of writing, 721
properties were listed, including 144 natural and 23 mixed (cultural and
natural).

2.1.3. Convention on Biological Diversity

The 1992 Convention on Biological Diversity (CBD) reflects the increased
awareness worldwide of the interdependence among species. The Convention is not limited to particular species or habitats, but provides for the
conservation and sustainable use of biodiversity, defined as "the variability
among living organisms", including "diversity within species, between
species and of ecosystems" (art. 2).

---

[1] As early as 1980, recommendation 1.5 of the Conference of Parties stated that "wise
use of wetlands involves maintenance of their ecological character, as a basis not only
for nature conservation, but for sustainable development" (preamble).

Biodiversity conservation and sustainable use are to be pursued by adopting specific strategies, plans and programmes and by incorporating relevant concerns into any plans, programmes and policies. Sustainable use of biodiversity must also be a consideration in national decisionmaking. Parties must establish a system of protected areas, rehabilitate and restore degraded ecosystems and promote recovery of threatened species. The threats to biodiversity are not limited to deliberate killing (e.g., hunting): parties are required to identify and control all potential sources of adverse impacts on biodiversity, and to carry out environmental impact assessments of projects likely to have "significant adverse effects" on biological diversity (art. 14).

The COP has adopted a large number of decisions on the implementation of the CBD. Decision V/6 (2000), in particular, calls on parties to apply an ecosystem approach, while not precluding other conservation approaches, whether area-based or species-based. Ecosystem in this context is defined as "a dynamic complex of plant, animal and micro-organism communities and their non-living environment interacting as a functional unit", without determining the spatial scale of that unit. The Decision also formulates guiding principles in this regard, including decentralization, consideration of adjacent and other ecosystems, long-term objectives and integration of use and conservation.

2.2. A Regional System: European Union Law

In addition to international agreements, wildlife is also protected by treaties adopted at the regional level. A particularly developed example of regional arrangements is the legal system of the European Union. In the EU system, some forms of legislation are directly applicable in member states (regulations), while others are not (as a general rule, directives). Moreover, implementation of EU legislation is strengthened by the presence of the European Court of Justice (ECJ), which interprets states' choices under the various directives, and in so doing creates a corpus of judicially created law in the EU. In the years since Rio, the ECJ has interpreted EU wildlife legislation in a number of cases.

The most significant instruments of EU wildlife legislation are the 1979 Birds Directive and the 1992 Habitats Directive. The former requires member states to take measures to maintain or restore wild bird populations to levels corresponding to ecological, scientific and cultural requirements, while taking into account economic and recreational requirements. Moreover, member states must take special conservation measures for species listed in Annex I, and in particular designate as special protection areas the most suitable territories for the conservation of those species. The Habitats Directive aims to promote the maintenance of biodiversity, while taking into account economic, social, cultural and regional needs. The directive provides for the designation of special areas of conservation (through a procedure contained in the directive), in order to ensure the favourable conservation status of listed habitats and species of Union interest, thereby creating a European ecological network ("Natura 2000").

The ECJ has developed case law on the implementation of EU wildlife legislation, focusing on two key aspects:

- Member states' violations of EU law, concerning either the lack of adequate domestic implementing legislation or member states' implementation choices under EU law; and
- interpretation of controversial provisions of EU wildlife legislation.

As for the first category, in *Commission v. France* (Case C-166/97, 18 March 1999), the French government was found in violation of the Habitats Directive, as it had not adopted specific legislation for the assessment of plans and projects likely to have a significant impact on special areas of conservation. The provisions of French law on environmental impact assessment in general were considered inadequate in this regard because they did not include consideration of the specific conservation objectives of the site, as required by the directive. In *Commission v. France* (Case C-256/98, 6 April 2000), the ECJ considered that French provisions merely maintaining an area under the status of public domain, or as a hunting reserve, were inadequate to meet the requirements of the Birds Directive, in the absence of concrete measures regarding sectors other than hunting.

Moreover, in several cases the ECJ reviewed the criteria followed by member states in the selection of protected sites, thus limiting the extent of state discretion. For instance, in *Commission v. Netherlands* (Case C-3/96, 19 May 1998), the ECJ clarified that it may find violations of the Birds Directive if a member state classifies as special protected areas sites whose number and total area are "manifestly less" than the number and area considered as "suitable" (e.g., on the basis of the Inventory of Important Bird Areas in the European Union, a list of areas important for the conservation of wild birds in the EU). In *Marismas de Santoña* (*Commission v. Spain*, Case C-355/90, 2 August 1993), the court held that member states' discretion as to the identification of appropriate sites is limited by the ornithological criteria determined in the Birds Directive. In *Commission v. France* (Case C-220/99, 11 September 2001), the ECJ held that, in selecting protected areas under the

Habitats Directive, member states must adhere to scientific criteria, reflect the ecological diversity of habitats and species in their territory and adequately represent habitats and species listed in the annexes to the directive. In addition, in *Commission v. Germany* (Case C-57/89, 28 February 1991), the Court held that the discretionary power enjoyed by states in reducing the size of existing protection areas is more limited than their discretion in selecting sites.

In the second category, in *Association pour la protection des animaux sauvages et al. v. Préfet de Maine-et-Loire and Préfet de la Loire Atlantique* (Case C-435/92, 9 January 1994), the court clarified that hunting seasons for migratory species and waterfowl must be determined with a view to protecting these species during pre-mating migration. In *Criminal Proceedings against Didier Vergy* (Case C-149/94, 8 February 1996), the court held that member states are required to forbid trade in naturally occurring birds in their wild state, even if such birds are not listed in the annexes to the Birds Directive. In *Criminal Proceedings against Godefridus van der Feesten* (Case C-202/94, 8 February 1996), the ECJ affirmed the applicability of the Birds Directive to bird subspecies that naturally occur in the wild only outside the territory of member states, provided that the species they belong to do occur within such territory.

Two other cases addressed states' interpretations of the Birds Directive. In *Italian Association for the World Wildlife Fund et al. v. Veneto Region* (Case C-118/94, 7 March 1996), the ECJ held that derogations from the Birds Directive are permissible only on the grounds and under the circumstances specified in the directive itself. Finally, in the *Lappel Bank* case (*Regina v. Secretary of State for the Environment*, Case C-44/95, 11 July 1996), the ECJ held that economic requirements may not be considered in connection with the declaration or delimitation of special protection areas.

III. MAJOR TRENDS IN NATIONAL LEGISLATION

3.1. Wildlife Protection and Management

Some evolutions of international environmental law are reflected in developments in national legislation. While originally focusing on listed species or protected areas, and on specific threats thereto (particularly hunting), wildlife legislation in several states has evolved towards a broader consideration of ecosystems and of interactions between species, and towards a broader consideration of activities potentially having an impact on wildlife. As for the latter, it has been argued that emphasis has switched from management of species to management of activities and processes that may potentially harm them. (De Klemm, 1999)

3.1.1. Hunting Regulations

Hunting regulations are a common and well-established form of wildlife protection. They include: (i) limits on the number of animals that may be hunted (e.g., through licence systems), usually fixed in subsidiary rather than in principal legislation; (ii) limits on the time of hunting, both by the day (most laws prohibit hunting between sunset and sunrise) and by the year (the fixing of open and closed hunting seasons is also common, especially under subsidiary legislation); (iii) limits on the places where hunting is allowed; (iv) limits on the species that may be hunted; and (v) limits regarding hunting methods and weapons (e.g., on the use of drugs, poison, explosives, etc.).

For their licence systems, most countries require some kind of authorization for hunting, and in some cases different kinds of hunting licences are set out in the legislation.[2] Some are based on different degrees of protection granted to the animals concerned or on different types and size of animals. There may also be different licences depending on the purpose of hunting (whether for recreation or tradition/subsistence), and different licences for visitors and residents. For instance, Guinea's law on wildlife and hunting of 1997 distinguishes between "small hunting permits", which are required for recreational and traditional hunting, and "big hunting permits", which must be obtained to hunt partly protected animals. Similarly, Botswana's Wildlife Conservation and National Parks Act of 1992, as amended, distinguishes between "bird licences", "single game licences", "small game licences" and "special game licences", the last to be issued to citizens "who are principally dependent on hunting and gathering veld produce for their food".

As with all licensing schemes, public policy can be taken into account in the issuance of hunting licences, by giving discretion to the administration to take into account certain criteria in granting or denying licences. One example is the 1992 law of Malawi, which provides that the administration's discretion is to be guided by "the interests of wildlife management". The law allows the Chief Parks and Wildlife Officer to refuse a licence if he/she is

---

[2] Most countries also require some permit or licence to carry hunting weapons; rules and conditions for such licences are rarely included in wildlife legislation, but the possession of these licences is usually a prerequisite for the issuance of hunting licences.

satisfied that such interests "will be better served by a temporary freeze in issuing licences of that class".

Licensing may also facilitate enforcement of the legislation, by permitting the identification of hunters and providing effective sanctions for offences (licence suspension or cancellation), and constitutes a source of revenue, as a fee is usually charged for their issuance or renewal. Appropriate definitions of hunting, including wandering with firearms, as in the law of Guinea and the 1997 wildlife and hunting law of Mauritania, may also help enforcement.

In countries where hunting continues to contribute to subsistence, recent legislation has taken into account the subsistence needs of local communities by exempting traditional hunting practices from hunting prohibitions. These exemptions are generally limited to specified species (usually small game) and to the areas where hunters live, and exclude hunting for commercial purposes. For example, the 1997 Forestry Code of Burkina Faso expressly allows subsistence or traditional hunting by local communities. Under Cameroon's forest law of 1994, traditional hunting is "free" on any land except within private properties, although within protected areas it may be subject to regulation; animals obtained from traditional hunting may not be used for commercial purposes.

The issue of whether and to what extent particular methods of hunting should be authorized because they are traditional, even though more destructive than other practices, is also debated in Europe. For example, the 1992 Italian legislation chose to specify permitted hunting methods, phasing out other methods until then traditionally practised.

3.1.2. Management Planning

Early wildlife management provisions were usually limited to hunting, as hunting was the most common focus of wildlife protection in legislation. Recent wildlife laws (e.g., Albania, Cameroon, Guinea, Malawi and Portugal) contain provisions on management planning, spelling out the basic dynamics of the management process and addressing protection as well as sustainable exploitation. Management planning is intended to guide administrations to adopt relevant decisions in a rational and transparent manner. The optimal process of management planning is first to assess the state of the resources, then to adopt management plans based on up-to-date findings, and finally to manage, subject to these plans.

Under the Italian wildlife and hunting legislation (1992), the National Wildlife Institute, a statutory body with research, training and advisory functions, is responsible for surveying the state of wild fauna and its evolution and relations with other environmental components. All agro-sylvo-pastoral lands are subject to wildlife/hunting management planning, to be carried out by local authorities. However, planning is not expressly required to be linked to the results of the surveys, and its scope is limited by the fact that hunting seasons are determined directly by principal legislation (although regional laws may modify them subject to specific conditions). The Spanish Law on Nature and Wildlife of 1989 (amended in 1997) also includes basic principles for the management of natural resources and biodiversity. It requires administrations to formulate natural resource management plans, with specified contents, which are to prevail over any other planning instruments which may apply to the same areas.

Hunting licence schemes can contribute to management where they are effectively used to limit the number of animals that may be taken under a single licence, based on a periodic assessment of sustainable levels of exploitation and adequate plans. However, provisions which clearly relate the number of permitted animals to actual surveys or management plans are rare. The Spanish law is one exception, where hunting is subject to a "technical plan" for the protection of game, to be adopted in accordance with regional legislation.

In some countries, legislation requires surveying and monitoring the state of wildlife (e.g., China, Lithuania, Tajikistan). In others, the law requires the Minister to ensure that measures taken are based on the results of scientific investigations (e.g., Malawi).

3.1.3. Species-based Protection

In many countries, legislation grants special protection to more valuable or endangered species, stating the fundamental principles in the basic law and listing the protected species in subsidiary legislation. For example, the law of Guinea provides for fauna conservation through favourable environment conservation and management as well as for maintenance or restoration of sufficiently diverse habitats, and requires lists of totally and partially protected species to be set out by implementing decrees. Similar approaches are taken for instance in Burkina Faso, Chile, China and Tajikistan.

In other countries, the lists of protected species are set out in the principal legislation itself. Examples of this approach may be found in Benin, Botswana, Cameroon and Mauritania. In Cameroon, an implementing decree of 1995 requires the classification set out in the 1994 law to be updated at least every five years.

In yet other cases, legislation allows more flexibility, by stating fundamental conservation principles and allowing (rather than mandating) the declaration of protected species. This is the case in Malawi (1992 Act) and Uganda (Wildlife Statute of 1996). Among the purposes expressly stated in the law of Malawi is the conservation of wildlife so that the abundance and diversity of species are maintained at optimum levels, in order to support sustainable utilization.

Focusing protection rules on more valuable species often means that species other than mammals receive little or no protection. In the United Kingdom, protection for insects, fish, amphibians and reptiles is only envisaged for endangered or threatened species, with a few exceptions for some common reptiles. (Harrop, 2000) By contrast, the 1997 Law on Wildlife of Lithuania defines wildlife as including both vertebrate and invertebrate species, while some regions of Italy, such as Emilia Romagna, have adopted specific laws for the protection of "lesser fauna". Prohibitions could also be strengthened by forbidding the possession (rather than only the taking) of specimens or parts of prohibited species.

Rules on endangered species may also regulate international trade in these species. In countries that are parties to CITES, import and export permit systems are frequently found in specific legislation for the implementation of the Convention. The law of Guinea prohibits the export of totally protected species, except for scientific or conservation purposes, and refers to regulations regarding import and export of partly protected animals. The taking of protected animals for scientific or educational purposes is usually subject to authorization, referred to as "special licence" in Malawi and "scientific permit" in Guinea. Conditions for these licences are very strict; in Guinea, scientific permits may be issued only to people belonging to scientific institutions, and no hunting must be involved, unless related to the objective of the research and duly authorized under a permit.

3.1.4. Area-based Protection

A traditional form of wildlife conservation is the establishment of protected areas, where human activities are prohibited or controlled with a view to safeguarding particular species or their habitats. In recent legislation, as required under the Convention on Biological Diversity, the creation of protected areas is conceived as part of a national system, or even of an international network, rather than a patchwork of protected areas, so that objectives of overall biodiversity protection can more effectively be pursued. Examples of provisions which require the setting up of a national system are found in Bulgaria, Peru, the Philippines, Portugal and Romania.

Whether or not a system is set up, relevant legislation usually envisages different types of protected areas. Thus, the law of Botswana envisages game reserves or sanctuaries for specified species, as well as "private game reserves" created upon a request of the owner. Hunting or capturing of animals may be practised in "wildlife management areas" and "controlled hunting areas" – in the latter case only under a specific endorsement on a hunting licence and upon payment of a fee. Burkina Faso has whole or partial "fauna reserves" (where the hunting of all or some species is prohibited), "local refuges" (which may be reserved by local authorities to facilitate reproduction and exploitation of wild animals) and village hunting areas. Cameroon's law envisages "fauna reserves" and "hunting reserves" (*zones cynégétiques*) among protected areas. The former are slated for conservation, management and reproduction of fauna and its habitats, and hunting may only be authorized by the Minister in the framework of authorized management operations. The latter are reserved for hunting, and may be managed by the wildlife administration or a local authority or any person, and hunting within them is subject to the payment of a fee. The law also envisages *territoires de chasse* (any area where hunting is allowed and regulated) and *territoires de chasse communautaire* (areas of state land managed by a local community under a management agreement).

Some countries specifically require environmental impact assessments of actions which may affect protected areas (e.g., Cameroon, Guinea). The EU Habitats Directive requires a specific evaluation of the implications of relevant activities on sites slated for protection under the directive. This assessment must be made specifically in view of the site's conservation objectives; therefore, this process differs from the general environmental impact assessment process, as regulated in separate legislation.

In the declaration and management of protected areas, attention should be paid to the relationship of wildlife management to other forms of land use within protected areas and in neighbouring areas, and more generally to land use policies and planning. In Africa, the creation of protected areas has had a strong impact on human activities, particularly with increasing population pressure and land scarcity. These have led to increased competition and encroachments between different land uses (protected areas, agriculture, livestock grazing). (KWFT/UNEP, 1988) Thus, decisions regarding protected areas may have important implications for the development and livelihoods of local communities.

Land use policies sometimes conflict with wildlife protection. Subdivision of pastures into fenced sub-units has often led to overgrazing and created impediments on wildlife migration routes and on herd mobility, which is a survival strategy. (KWFT/UNEP, 1988) Sometimes, conflicts have been caused by contradictory policies encouraging competing land uses, for example between expanding cultivated plots on the one hand and establishing protected areas for wildlife conservation on the other.

One solution is to consider wildlife management as a form of land use, as in Uganda, where wildlife legislation is intended to maintain optimum levels of diversity "commensurate with other forms of land use, in order to support sustainable utilization of wildlife". The Kenyan wildlife legislation also requires taking into account the different forms of land use and the interrelationship between wildlife conservation and management and other forms of land use. The Italian legislation, mainly in an attempt to limit hunting, fixes percentages of land areas to be devoted to the different uses: 20 percent to 30 percent of the agro-sylvo-pastoral land area in every region must be devoted to wildlife protection, while the rest of the land area is open for hunting under management plans.

A number of policies and laws reflect a recognition that protecting wildlife through a focus on restricted geographical areas has its limitations. "Agenda 2000", an EU plan of action, specifically refers to the protection of biodiversity in non-protected areas. Switzerland's 1996 legislation on nature and landscape also goes beyond protection of selected areas by requiring, if possible, the protection of indigenous flora and fauna by an "appropriate agricultural and sylvicultural exploitation of their vital space (biotope)". For this purpose, it requires cooperation among authorities responsible for agriculture, forestry and protection of nature and landscape. In addition, a 2000 regional law of Tuscany (Italy), in implementing the EU Birds and Habitats Directives, takes into consideration ecological corridors between "sites of Community importance" with "sites of Regional importance".

3.1.5. Protection of Biodiversity

In international law, there is a trend toward a comprehensive protection and management of biodiversity rather than limiting protection to listed species or areas. This trend is also beginning to appear in national legal systems, either through the incorporation of relevant objectives in environmental or wildlife management legislation or through the adoption of separate legislation on biodiversity. This acknowledges the weaknesses of laws concentrating protection exclusively on specific species, as species should not be considered in isolation from related species and their habitats.

Costa Rica is among the countries that adopted a specific law on biodiversity in 1998. The law requires that any central or local institution issuing plans and authorizations relating to natural resources, including fauna, must take into account the conservation of biodiversity. The law sets out general principles and provides for the creation of a national commission responsible mainly for policymaking and coordination among agencies. It also provides for the creation of a national system of conservation areas and for the related administrative structures. Access to genetic and biochemical components of biodiversity is regulated with a view to safeguarding the rights of local communities to be adequately informed and, if they wish, object to the operations.

The 1999 Australian Environment Protection and Biodiversity Conservation Act encourages the identification and monitoring of biodiversity. The law focuses particularly on planning, setting out various types of plans that must or may be adopted: bioregional plans, recovery plans and wildlife conservation plans. Other countries have incorporated obligations to protect biodiversity into legislation on environmental protection, wildlife or protected areas (e.g., Cameroon, Spain, Ireland).

3.1.6. Game Ranching and Breeding

Game ranching and game breeding can be important contributors to food availability and revenues in rural areas. They may also have a significant impact on the environment. It is therefore important for the applicable legal framework to strike a balance between the encouragement of these initiatives and conservation concerns. A common approach is to make game ranching and breeding subject to authorizations/permissions/licences (Albania, Botswana, Burkina Faso, Cameroon). Specific permits may also be required for the sale of animals or meat and for breeding of protected species (Botswana).

Other forms of regulation include fencing requirements for areas utilized for breeding of wild animals. Fencing may be mandatory (Burkina Faso) or not, in which case it may affect the applicable rules (e.g., in Botswana, if the area is fenced there is no limit on the number of animals that may be taken, otherwise culling is subject to a permit). Legislation may also subject ranching and breeding to the more general condition that they do not endanger surrounding areas (Mauritania).

The 2000 law of Colombia regarding wildlife management concentrates mainly on the creation and operation of "*zoocriaderos*", whether "open" (where animals are periodically taken from the wild and introduced with a view to their exploitation), "closed" (where only an initial couple is introduced) or "mixed" (where both techniques may be combined). Numerous rules ensure that such structures have adequate conditions for the reproduction of animals from both the technical and the environmental points of view, with details on licensing and enforcement. Under the hunting and wildlife law of Albania (1994), there is an obligation to provide 10 percent of the ranches' annual production of animals for the repopulation of forest areas, without compensation.

Appropriate exemptions with regard to licensing requirements may have to be set out for animals obtained from ranching and breeding, as making them subject to the same rules as those found in the wild may result in disincentives for ranchers and breeders. The legislation may also create incentives to promote these activities. Among the rare examples of such supportive provisions, the law of Burkina Faso exempts animals obtained from ranching and breeding from the restrictions established for hunting and makes them the property of the breeder. Similar provisions are found in Botswana.

3.1.7. Assessment of Processes Harmful to Wildlife

Reflecting recent developments in international law, a number of domestic laws have started to require the assessment and mitigation of any processes that may be potentially harmful to wildlife. The law of Malawi, for example, requires "wildlife impact assessments" for any "process or activity" which may have an adverse effect on wildlife. Although only the Minister may undertake the assessment, any person who has reason to believe that such an adverse effect will be produced may make a request to undertake it. The process leads to the submission of a report with recommendations regarding subsequent government action. In Uganda, persons wishing to undertake projects which may have a significant effect on any wildlife species or community must undertake an environmental impact assessment.

The 1999 Australian law requires listing of key threatening processes. The Minister must ensure that a "recovery plan" is in force for each listed threatened species and ecological community, and that a "threat abatement plan" is adopted for key threatening processes where appropriate. Lithuania's law of 1997 requires that in planning and implementing any economic activity, measures must be taken to mitigate impacts on habitats, breeding conditions and migration routes of wildlife. Any development that may have a significant effect on wildlife species or communities is subject to an environmental impact assessment.

3.2. Ownership of Wildlife and Related Rights and Obligations

3.2.1. Legislative Approaches to Ownership of Wildlife

Most legal systems address the issue of ownership of wildlife, which entails benefits (such as hunting rights and entitlements to revenue from wildlife viewing or hunting tourism) and obligations (such as management responsibilities and liability for damage caused by animals). The approaches taken are diverse, and there is no clear trend toward harmonization. However, wildlife is generally regarded either as a part of the rights of ownership of land or as state property. There is also a tendency to extend the prerogatives of private land owners by reducing limitations regarding wildlife found on their land. The following are the main approaches followed.

(a) Wildlife as State Property

In many countries, ownership of wild animals is vested in the state on behalf of and for the benefit of the people (e.g., China, Malawi, Tajikistan, Uganda). However, in some countries, although ownership of wildlife is vested in the state, hunting rights on private land are reserved for land owners. In Burkina Faso, for example, forests, fauna and fish are declared to be part of the national estate, but owners have the exclusive right to hunt on their own land. In Botswana, land owners and other specified lawful occupiers have the right to hunt without a licence on their land, subject to restrictions on the number of animals hunted and to the payment of fees. Land owners also have the right to authorize third parties to hunt on their land upon approval of the administration. A right of ownership in animals, however, is expressly recognized in the owner of land only in the case of animals kept or confined within a game-proof fence.

In other legal systems, even where wildlife is state property, the rights of private land owners are significantly limited, in that hunters are allowed access into any private land. For instance, in Italy wildlife is state property and hunters have free access to any land, including private lands, for hunting purposes. This free-access rule has two exceptions: first, access to cultivated or fenced land is prohibited; second, exemptions may be granted to land owners submitting specific reasons, and on the basis of regional legislation.

(b)   Wildlife as Property of Land Owners

In the majority of Western European countries, wildlife ownership is vested in the owners of the land where the animals are found. In some cases ownership entails the automatic right to hunt (e.g., the United Kingdom and Norway), whereas in others such right is not automatic (France and Spain) (Bouckaert, 1999). A consequence of these arrangements is that owners are generally responsible for wildlife management within their land. As this is inappropriate where holdings are very small, various countries require a minimum size of land as a condition for their owners to exercise hunting rights, such as Belgium, France, Germany and Norway. (Burhenne, 1999)

In France, the "Verdeille Law" of 1964 envisaged the compulsory grouping of owners of land areas smaller than 20 hectares, with devolution of hunting rights to the Communal Hunting Association thus created. Within the concerned areas, all specified hunters, such as land owners and other local residents, may hunt. In 1999, the European Court of Human Rights stated that the provisions making it compulsory for land owners to join hunting associations and to allow hunting on the concerned land violated the European Convention on Human Rights, namely article 11, on freedom of association, and article 1 of protocol 1, on the right of ownership (Decision of 29 April 1999, *Chassagnou et al. v. France*). A provision allowing individual owners to exempt their lands from Communal Hunting Associations was introduced in 2000.

An interesting example of legislation vesting ownership of wildlife in land owners is the Parks and Wildlife Act 1975 of Zimbabwe. Originally, ownership of wildlife was granted only to private land owners (i.e., white commercial farmers). In 1982, an amendment to the Act extended it to communal lands (inhabited by black farmers), although as communal farmers did not have formal land titles, ownership and management responsibilities were given to district councils rather than to customary land holders. This provided the basis for the Communal Areas Management

Programme for Indigenous Resources (CAMPFIRE). While in theory embracing all natural resources, CAMPFIRE focuses on wildlife, as this provides quick and direct financial returns through safari hunting, photographic tourism, lodges, etc. Revenues from the sale of hunting quotas mainly go to the district council and rural community where the animal is shot. (Kalèn and Trägårdh, 1998) Problems reported include lack of authority of local communities and lack of competence in wildlife management by some district councils. Further evolution towards resource management as common property remains one of the objectives of CAMPFIRE.

(c)   Wildlife as *Res Nullius*

In some countries, wildlife is considered as *res nullius*, as in Morocco (Mekouar, 1999), meaning that it belongs neither to state nor individual. Also under Lithuania's wildlife law of 1997, although wild animals found within fenced areas belong to the owner of the area, animals in the wild may not be considered the property of any natural or legal person. Moreover, land owners may make personal use of wild animals found on their land, although subject to obligations not to upset the balance of natural communities and to adopt protection measures.

3.2.2.   Compensation and Protection of Persons and Property

Ownership of wildlife usually entails the obligation to compensate for damage caused by it. Countries take different approaches to compensation, depending on the owner of wildlife (state or land owners), and they sometimes limit compensation depending on whether or not the persons who have suffered damage have taken adequate action to prevent or limit it.

Where wildlife ownership is vested in the state, it is the state that must bear the costs of compensating for damages caused by wild animals. Several solutions have been adopted in this regard. In China, for instance, compensation is envisaged only for damage caused by protected species, and people have an obligation to adopt appropriate precautionary measures to prevent such damage (1992 Wildlife Regulations). In other cases, an exemption from liability is envisaged. In Botswana, loss of life or property caused by non-captive animals, whether or not within protected areas, is exempted from liability; however, damage caused to livestock by specified animals (such as lions and leopards) may be compensated if the predators have escaped into a national park before they could be killed. Due *inter alia* to difficulties in addressing increasing demands for compensation, some countries have undertaken a transfer of wildlife ownership from the state to land owners (e.g., Zimbabwe).

Countries also take different approaches regarding permissible action against wild animals that may threaten people or property. Killing of wild animals for this purpose is allowed more widely in defence of people than of property, but in any case various conditions are usually specified to prevent abuses (e.g., requiring notification to an officer prior to killing animals or promptly afterwards). In Uganda, for example, killing of animals is generally allowed in defence of people, whereas in defence of property, killing is allowed as a last resort, only if it does not endanger the survival of a species, and only following notification to an officer, who must determine the necessary action. In Botswana, land owners or occupiers have the right to kill animals that threaten persons, crops or other property on their land; circumstances must be reported as soon as possible to the wildlife administration. In Mauritania, hunting for defence of people or for protection of cultivated fields or livestock is allowed without need for authorization, but immediate notice of any action taken must be given to authorized officials.

It is less common to expressly authorize organized actions by the administration against animals that cause damage, although to prevent vigilantism this approach may be preferable to action by individuals. Under the law of Guinea, specially organized hunting of noxious animals (*battues de destruction*) may be exceptionally authorized and must be reported in detail to the national Director of Fauna, and resulting meat must be left to the local people who have suffered damage. However, provisions authorizing the indiscriminate killing of "noxious" animals are increasingly being abandoned. For instance, even the law of Guinea limits the destruction of noxious animals to dangerous species (e.g., poisonous snakes) and prohibits it within national parks and nature reserves.

3.3. Institutions, People and Wildlife

It is widely recognized that where opportunities for public participation in wildlife utilization are increased, and resulting benefits are made available to participants, the public is likely to be more willing to support adopted measures and to contribute to the costs of controlling wildlife. In line with these considerations, most recent laws envisage some involvement of the concerned people in wildlife management and in the creation or management of protected areas.

3.3.1. Information, Consultation and Advisory Bodies

A basic prerequisite for public participation is that relevant information must be made available. The law of Tajikistan, for example, establishes that citizens have a right to obtain complete information "on the conditions of the animal world", and that the administration must arrange for the periodic publication of such information.

In many countries the law specifically requires some form of consultation with the public or with specified stakeholders in wildlife-related decision-making, such as the adoption of plans or the declaration of protected areas. In these cases, requirements include adequate publicizing of proposals, sufficient time to allow comments, and specific consideration of these comments by the authorities. In some cases the law requires the administration to take into account the interests of concerned people, without specifying how such interests should be identified and interpreted. The 1994 regulations of China on nature reserves, for example, require that local economic activities and the "everyday life" of residents be properly considered in the creation and management of nature reserves.

In Australia, in adopting threat abatement plans, or recovery plans for listed threatened species and ecological communities, regard must be given to the role and interests of indigenous people in the conservation of the country's biodiversity. Draft plans must be publicized in a number of specified ways, and comments received must be considered. Similar provisions apply to wildlife conservation plans.

In Botswana, public notice of proposals and subsequent confirmation by Parliament must be given for the declaration of national parks. Consultation with the public or even concerned owners does not seem to be required for the creation of other types of protected areas, regardless of the fact that "any" lands (and therefore not only public lands) may be affected. The administration is however required to consult with land boards and district councils in the management of wildlife management areas. In Uganda, public participation in wildlife management is an objective expressly stated in the law. Management plans for each wildlife protected area must be prepared following consultation with the public and the concerned district.

In other cases, consultation is envisaged through the creation of advisory bodies including representation of interested associations and people (e.g., Australia, Mexico, Romania). Under the Portuguese hunting legislation of

1999, the state must consult with the various interest groups and local authorities for the formulation of the national policy on hunting and of hunting management plans. Local hunting and fauna conservation councils are created to advise municipal authorities with a view to balancing hunting interests with agriculture, forestry, grazing and nature conservation, and enhancing the contribution of hunting to rural development. A General Council for Hunting and the Conservation of Nature is also in place, with advisory functions. These councils include representatives of environmental, hunters' and farmers' associations.

In some countries, people-centred bodies with responsibilities for wildlife management have been created. In Mauritania, wildlife management associations are established in each *commune* in order to enable people's participation in wildlife management. These associations participate in policy definition, wildlife monitoring and surveillance and establishment of hunting seasons and of allowed species and quotas. For their funding, they are entitled to a share (20 percent) of the moneys earned under the law.

In Italy, collective management of hunting areas was introduced by the law of 1992 and has been successful. Hunting areas within every region are divided into a number of units, where bodies including representatives of hunters' and farmers' associations (60 percent), of environmental associations (20 percent) and of local authorities (20 percent) are responsible for a number of activities, such as monitoring the state of the resources and planning habitat improvement.

3.3.2. Agreements Between Individuals or Communities and the Public Administration

Several laws envisage the possibility for interested individuals or communities to enter into agreements for the management of areas or resources for wildlife-related purposes which may or may not include economic exploitation. For example, under the Albanian law, the state promotes private investments aiming at the preservation and management of fauna, and the administration may enter into agreements with any persons concerning wild animal breeding, hunting, tourism or other activities related to the implementation of the law. In Romania, the law refers to "contracts" for the management of hunting areas, specifying their minimum contents.

The law of Guinea envisages the possibility for the administration to enter into management agreements for protected areas, particularly with local communities and associations. The Ugandan legislation also recognizes a role for local or private initiatives through "Community Wildlife Areas", i.e., areas in which holders of property rights in land may carry out activities for the sustainable management of wildlife, subject to land use measures which may be prescribed. In Australia, "conservation agreements" may be signed between the Minister and indigenous peoples regarding protection, conservation and management of any listed species or ecological communities, or their habitats, and addressing mitigation or avoidance of actions that might adversely affect biodiversity.

A concern sometimes shown in legislation is to ensure that equal opportunities and fair distribution of benefits are offered to all community members. For example, in Cameroon, free technical assistance is offered by the wildlife administration to local communities for the formulation of agreements for the management of community hunting areas. A meeting of the community, supervised by the concerned technical administration, must be held for the designation of a person responsible for the initiative. All participants must sign the report of the meeting. In Burkina Faso, local authorities may benefit from the technical assistance of local wildlife services, and all possible measures must be adopted to ensure the participation of representatives of local communities in the management of "local refuges". Revenue and taxes deriving from local refuges and village hunting areas must be distributed between local budgets and village wildlife management organizations.

3.3.3. Devolution of Authority

There are numerous examples of countries with a federal or similarly decentralized structure which have delegated some legislative powers in the wildlife management sector to local authorities. This has happened for example with *Länder* of Austria and Germany, cantons of Switzerland, *comunidades autónomas* of Spain and regions of Italy. The 2000 wildlife law of Mexico makes wildlife a shared responsibility of the federal government, states and communes. In most cases, local authorities are empowered to legislate within the framework set out by national legislation.

Sometimes powers given for the adoption of legislation at the local level are mainly for the regulation of local initiatives. The law of Burkina Faso, for example, charges local administrations (*collectivités territoriales décentralisées*) with determining the activities allowed within "local refuges", while it charges local communities (*communautés de base*) with determining activities allowed in "village hunting areas". In Zimbabwe the adoption of by-laws by district councils, enabled by legislation of 1988, has enhanced the implementation of the CAMPFIRE programme by revamping traditional wildlife management rules. (Kalèn and Trägårdh, 1998)

Some recent laws allow the definition of the respective responsibilities of the central government and local governments through agreements between them. In Australia, the Commonwealth and the states or self-governing territories may enter into agreements concerning environmental protection, sustainable use of natural resources and environmental impact assessment processes. In Mexico, after setting out the respective responsibilities of the various levels of government, the law similarly allows certain agreements for better coordination.

Even where local by-laws have an unclear legal status, they may still significantly contribute to wildlife management by creating local support for it. In Zanzibar, for example, antelope protection by-laws in some cases simply reinstated existing laws, but whereas these laws were poorly enforced, local by-laws had much better implementation, by shifting the perception of antelope from an open-access resource to a resource belonging to the villages. (Williams, Masoud and Othman, 1998) The uncertain legal status of by-laws under the legislation of Zanzibar, however, undermines the stability of these arrangements.

3.3.4. Socio-cultural Issues

Within wildlife management, an increasing number of laws show a concern for social and cultural issues. The law of Burkina Faso, for example, expressly aims at harmonizing the protection of natural resources with the need to meet economic, social and cultural requirements. Respect for cultural diversity generally tends to be emphasized in legislation on biodiversity (e.g., in Costa Rica). In France, hunting is defined as an "environmental, cultural, social and economic activity". In the law of Mauritania, classification of land into some category of protected area or declassification is authorized only if the advantages from the ecological, social, economic and cultural points of view exceed possible disadvantages.
Consideration of cultural aspects may add value to opportunities for sustainable economic development offered by wildlife and protected areas. Some laws conceive protected areas as places where the whole local heritage is to be enhanced, in its natural, historical, cultural or anthropological dimensions. These objectives are pursued, for example, in the 1998 revisions to Italy's law on protected areas. Pursuant to these revisions, management of protected areas is expected to bring out the value of local agro-sylvo-pastoral

uses and traditions. Rather than as a series of prohibitions, regulations for each park are to be conceived as a means of focusing on local characteristics and values and sustainably managing them. With a similar approach, under the 1998 Bulgarian law on protected areas, national parks are to be managed for purposes of sustainable use of renewable natural resources, but the state must preserve "traditional forms of livelihood".

IV. CONCLUSION

Post-Rio wildlife legislation reveals some important innovations. These are mainly related to biodiversity, management planning and impact assessment, while other aspects have witnessed less remarkable change (e.g., licence systems and wildlife ownership). Some "traditional" instruments have been reinterpreted in order to pursue broader objectives. Thus, protected areas tend to be placed within national systems rather than established in a "patchwork" way, and in some (still rare) cases attention is paid to neighbouring areas; this allows for more rational and comprehensive protection.

More generally, post-Rio laws tend to go beyond protecting specified species, taking greater account of the interdependence between species and increasingly providing for the protection of biodiversity. They tend to require an assessment of the impact of all activities potentially harmful to wildlife, for example, rather than limiting attention to the dangers of hunting. Modern laws devote greater attention to management planning, making management processes and their basic objectives increasingly guided by the law rather than by the changing initiatives of administrations. Finally, recent laws tend to create rules, institutions and procedures to involve affected persons in wildlife-related decision-making, to allow local communities to participate in the economic benefits deriving from wildlife use and to consider socio-cultural dimensions of wildlife management. Stakeholder involvement may be not only envisaged in legislation but actually promoted by it.

Nonetheless, much remains to be done. For instance, few laws address issues of competing land uses and integration of wildlife management with other activities in rural areas. Existing management planning can be further improved by regulating planning processes in a more systematic and coherent way, and by explicitly linking management planning and measures to scientific research. Where protection is granted to particular species, other important, albeit less spectacular, biodiversity elements should not be neglected. For countries that still need to revise their wildlife legislation, the challenge is to catch up with the important developments witnessed in the post-Rio decade.

REFERENCES

Bouckaert, J. 1999. *Les territoires de chasse et les habitats.* In Société Française pour le Droit de l'Environnement, *La chasse en droit comparé. Actes du Colloque organisé au Palais de l'Europe, à Strasbourg, les 9 et 10 novembre 1995,* L'Harmattan, Paris.

Burhenne, W.E. 1999. *Le droit de la chasse en Allemagne et en Autriche.* In Société Française pour le Droit de l'Environnement, *La chasse en droit comparé. Actes du Colloque organisé au Palais de l'Europe, à Strasbourg, les 9 et 10 novembre 1995,* L'Harmattan, Paris.

Convention on Biological Diversity and United Nations Environment Programme (CBD/UNEP). 2001. *Global Diversity Outlook,* Secretariat for the Convention on Biological Diversity and United Nations Environment Programme, Montreal.

Chardonnet, P. (ed.). 1995. *Faune sauvage africaine - La ressource oubliée.* Fondation internationale pour la sauvegarde de la faune/Département d'élevage et de médecine vétérinaire. CIRAD-EMVT, Commission européenne, Brussels.

De Klemm, C. 1999. *Les sources internationales du droit de la chasse.* In Société Française pour le Droit de l'Environnement, *La chasse en droit comparé. Actes du Colloque organisé au Palais de l'Europe, à Strasbourg, les 9 et 10 novembre 1995,* L'Harmattan, Paris.

Harrop, S.R. 2000. *The UK's Implementation of EU Legislation on Wildlife Management.* In *Provincia di Pesaro e Urbino, Proceedings of the Workshop A Consultative Process on Wildlife Management Legislation, Pesaro-Urbino, Italy, 28–30 September 2000.*

Kalèn, C. & Trägårdh, N. 1998. *Sustainable Use of Wildlife - A Case Study from the Campfire Programme in Zimbabwe.* Swedish University of Agricultural Sciences, Minor Field Studies No. 40, Uppsala.

Kenya Wildlife Fund Trustees and United Nations Environment Programme (KWFT/UNEP). 1988. *People, Parks and Wildlife.* Kenya Wildlife Fund Trustees and United Nations Environment Programme, Nairobi.

Mekouar, M.A. 1999. *Le droit de la chasse au Maroc.* In Société Française pour le Droit de l'Environnement, *La chasse en droit comparé. Actes du Colloque organisé au Palais de l'Europe, à Strasbourg, les 9 et 10 novembre 1995,* L'Harmattan, Paris.

Overseas Development Administration. 1996. *African Wildlife Policy Consultation - Final Report of the Consultation. Sunningdale Park, Berkshire, UK, 18 and 19 April 1996.*

Provincia di Pesaro e Urbino. 2000. *A Consultative Process on Wildlife Management Legislation, Proceedings of a Workshop held in Pesaro and Urbino, Italy, 28–30 September 2000.*

Williams, A., Masoud, T.S. & Othman, W.J. 1998. *Community-based Conservation: Experiences from Zanzibar.* International Institute for Environment and Development, Gatekeeper Series No. 80, London.

12

MOUNTAINS

Contents

I.   INTRODUCTION

Covering one quarter of the Earth's surface, home to at least one in ten people and as fragile as they often are, mountain ecosystems are unique islands of cultural diversity and precious reservoirs of biological diversity, as well as the source of the world's great rivers and the providers of much-needed fresh water. However, mountain people are among the poorest and the hungriest, and mountain regions are among the most vulnerable to environmental degradation, urban development and climate change.

Despite their importance throughout human history and their wealth of resources, mountains have only recently begun to attract the attention of political decisionmakers and economic planners. National and inter-national lawmakers similarly failed, until recently, to take an interest in mountain areas. It was not until 1991 that the Alpine Convention, the first transnational agreement relating to a mountain range, came into being, and the first national laws in this area were passed only a few years before that. Mountain law is, thus, still in its infancy: only a few mountain-specific legal instruments, national and international, are currently in place.

The present chapter looks at the development of this type of legislation. It broadly describes mountain-specific legal texts, first in the international sphere, then at the domestic level. Although there are many other laws which also affect the legal status of mountains, such as agricultural, forestry, soil, watershed, land use planning and environmental laws, this chapter focuses only on those legal frameworks that are specific to mountains.[1]

II.   MAJOR INTERNATIONAL INSTRUMENTS ON MOUNTAINS

Because mountain ranges often cross national borders, the issues involving them are inherently transnational. Legislation supporting international cooperation or action may be required to take account of transnational or regional dimensions of mountain protection and develop-ment. However, with the exception of the Alpine Convention, this need

---

[1] This chapter is based on an earlier paper published in *UNASYLVA* 208 (2002).

has not prompted the shaping of legally binding, mountain-specific international instruments, either globally or regionally.

2.1. Treaty Law

2.1.1. Absence of a Worldwide Mountain-focused Convention

The fact that so far no global treaty has been created for mountain ecosystems is partly due to the existence of numerous conventions which, though not dealing directly with mountains as such, do have some bearing on mountain peoples and resources. Post-Rio examples include the Convention to Combat Desertification, whose preamble acknowledges the impacts of desertification on arid regions with mountain ecosystems in Africa, Central Asia and the Transcaucasus; the Convention on Biological Diversity, whose relevance stems from the fact that mountain ecosystems are frequently home to biodiversity-rich areas; and the Framework Convention on Climate Change, whose preamble notes the special vulnerability of "fragile mountain ecosystems" to climate change.[2] Other earlier conventions are also relevant to mountains in some respects, such as the 1972 World Heritage Convention, as many natural sites included in the World Heritage List are mountain areas of outstanding importance, or the 1968 African Convention on the Conservation of Nature and Natural Resources, which addresses some mountain-related issues such as soil erosion in connection with agriculture, and land use planning. The potential contribution of such conventions to sustainable mountain management is, however, limited to the specific aspects they cover in relation to mountain protection or development.

In addition to the mountain-related provisions of those conventions, there are some general principles of international environmental law which are applicable to mountain ecosystems. One is the obligation of states to manage their natural resources so as not to "cause damage to the environment of other States or of areas beyond the limits of national juris-diction". (Principle 2 of the Rio Declaration on Environment and Develop-ment) Another is the duty to cooperate in a spirit of partnership (principle 7 of the same Declaration), which may apply to the management of transborder mountain ranges shared by two or more states. More broadly, the principle of sustainability, although not precisely defined in this context, is key to the management of mountain ecosystems. It implies a

---

[2] For a discussion of these and other conventions with mountain relevance, see Fodella and Pineschi (2000) and Lynch and Maggio (2000).

wise and equitable use of mountain resources in environmental, economic, social and cultural terms, taking due account of the interests of both present and future generations. (Fodella and Pineschi, 2000)

2.1.2. A Regional Mountain-specific Accord: The Alpine Convention

The principles of sustainability are reflected in the only legally binding instrument in existence that specifically deals with a mountain range: the Convention on the Protection of the Alps. Adopted in Salzburg, Austria, in 1991, it entered into force in 1995. Its initial signatories – Austria, France, the European Union, Germany, Italy, Liechtenstein and Switzerland – were later joined by Slovenia and Monaco. All nine parties had ratified the Convention by 1999.

The Convention provides for the protection and sustainable development of the Alps in their entirety as a uniform regional ecosystem. Parties agree to establish a comprehensive policy towards this end, and endeavour to cooperate in several areas of common interest, including agriculture, forestry, land use planning, protection of landscapes, culture and population, leisure activities and air pollution control. The Convention is designed as a framework-type agreement: its substantive provisions are set out in general terms, which need, for their effective implementation, to be specified through additional protocols.

Nine such protocols were concluded: (i) in 1994 three protocols: on mountain agriculture; nature protection and landscape conservation; and land use planning and sustainable development; (ii) in 1996 two protocols: on mountain forests; and tourism; (iii) in 1998 two protocols: on soil conservation; and energy; and (iv) in 2000 two protocols: on transport; and dispute settlement. Four other protocols are foreseen by the Convention but have not yet been prepared: on population and culture; water; air quality; and waste management. Some of the protocols, especially the one on transport, have been hard to negotiate and to agree upon. Although they were signed by most parties, only Liechtenstein had ratified them as of June 2002, but other parties are now taking steps toward their ratification. The Alpine Convention is therefore yet to be fully implemented.

Nonetheless, as a good basis for transboundary collaboration, this convention is viewed as a model for the development of mountain accords in other regions of the world. Similar range-wide agreements are currently in the making, at varying stages of preparation or design. They include proposed conventions for: (i) the Altai Range, involving China, Kazakhstan, Mongolia and the Russian Federation; (ii) the Caucasus Range, involving Armenia, Azerbaijan, Georgia and the Russian Federation; and (iii) the Carpathian Range, involving the Czech Republic, Hungary, Moldova, Poland, Romania, Slovakia, Ukraine and the Federal Republic of Yugoslavia.

Similarly, in the framework of the Council of Europe (CE), a draft European Convention of Mountain Regions, covering most aspects of mountain development and protection, was developed in 2000 based on an earlier draft European Charter of Mountain Regions. The proposed convention was recently considered by the CE Committee of Ministers but has not yet been endorsed.

2.2. Soft Law

Soft law instruments – declarations or resolutions, plans of action and codes of conduct – generally shaped and adopted through international fora and conferences, have often been used in the recent past to promote norm-creating processes that, in turn, help lead to the development of hard law agreements. A number of such instruments concern mountain peoples and ecosystems, such as Chapter 13 of Agenda 21 and various other post-Rio declaratory documents, some of which are briefly outlined below.

2.2.1. A Global Mountain Platform: Chapter 13 of Agenda 21

"Managing fragile ecosystems: sustainable mountain development" is the title of the Chapter that was devoted to mountains under Agenda 21. Endorsing this chapter at the highest political level in such a global forum – the Rio Conference, which assembled 180 UN member countries – the international community, for the first time, clearly and formally signaled its common concern for the world's mountains as essential preserves of natural and human resources, which need to be protected, restored and developed.

Chapter 13 is a policy tool geared towards action at the national and international levels. It identifies rural development, food security, fresh water, biological diversity, forests, climate change, culture, traditional knowledge and tourism, among others, as the main mountain issues. Sustainable mountain development can be achieved notably through: (i) raising the awareness and supporting the efforts of mountain peoples to reverse the trend of degradation; and (ii) creating effective mountain constituencies and building networks of national, regional and global mountain institutions.

Assessing the progress made in implementing Chapter 13 since Rio, the Commission on Sustainable Development concluded in 2001 that the level of economic development in most mountain regions of the world "remains unacceptably low". However, it also found that significant results have been achieved, particularly in the creation of innovative mechanisms that foster collaboration among the sectors involved in mountain issues, as well as in the adoption of approaches that increasingly balance development needs and environmental concerns.

2.2.2. A Draft World Charter for Mountain Populations

In the final declaration of the World Mountain Forum, held in June 2000, more than 800 persons representing 70 mountain countries endorsed a draft world charter designed to represent the needs and aspirations of mountain peoples. (WMF, 2000a and 2000b) According to the draft, three conditions are crucial to meeting mountain populations' requirements: (i) mountain peoples must find a place in society while retaining their identity; (ii) mountain peoples must face economic competition while changing the conditions of trade to their advantage; and (iii) mountain peoples need to retain control of their environment and the development of their natural resources, managing them for their own needs as well as on behalf of the national and world community.

The draft charter foresees the establishment of a worldwide organization to be called "Mountains of the World", which would speak for mountain areas, and whose membership would be open to local authorities, associations and groups representing mountain dwellers. Alongside this organization, there should be a financial mechanism, possibly in the form of a foundation, which would mobilize the resources needed to strengthen cooperation and build partnerships among mountain regions and countries.

The draft charter is undergoing a review and revision process with a view to its adoption at the second World Meeting of Mountain Populations in Quito, Ecuador, in September 2002. A new version of the text was issued in May 2002, with additional inputs from a recently established non-governmental organization, the Association of Mountain Populations of the World. It should be further discussed and amended at six regional preparatory meetings prior to its finalization for the Quito event.

2.2.3. Other Non-binding Instruments: Some Illustrations

In the aftermath of Rio, a flurry of soft law instruments on mountain ecosystems, often inspired by Chapter 13, were developed in governmental and non-governmental fora in many regions of the world. Some are:

- The Cusco Declaration on Sustainable Development of Mountain Ecosystems, drawn up by representatives of 18 countries from various continents gathered in Cusco, Peru, in 2001, identifies the environmental, social and economic measures most widely recognized as essential to the sustainable management of mountain areas.
- The draft Central Asian Charter for the Sustainable Development of Mountain Regions covers the mountainous areas of Kazakhstan, Kyrgyzstan, Tajikistan, Turkmenistan and Uzbekistan. Interministerial consultations among concerned countries are being carried out with the aim of adopting the charter at the Global Mountain Summit to take place in November 2002 in Bishkek, Kyrgyzstan.
- The Euromontana Final Declaration was the product of the second continent-wide conference of Euromontana – an association of 36 mountain organizations from 15 countries of Central, Eastern and Western Europe – held in Trento, Italy, in 2000. Its central message is that the comparative advantage of mountain regions, as preserves of environmental and cultural diversity, is quality. In the face of globalization, the sustainability of economic activities in mountain zones can only be ensured by high quality, value-added products.
- The African Mountains and Highlands Declaration, adopted at the International Workshop of the African Mountains Association held in Antananarivo, Madagascar, in 1997, highlights the major problems affecting Africa's mountain ecosystems and provides policy recommendations to address them.
- The UIAA Kathmandu Declaration, adopted by the International Union of Alpinist Associations (UIAA) meeting in Kathmandu, Nepal, in 1997, calls for the effective protection of the mountain environment, respect for the culture and dignity of mountain peoples and the promotion of contacts between mountaineers in a spirit of friendship, respect and peace.

- The Charter for the Protection of the Pyrénées, developed in 1995 by the International Associated Council for the Protection of the Pyrénées, has three objectives: preservation of the range's ecological values; access for visitors without altering access points; and economic development that respects the environment.

III. MAIN FEATURES OF DOMESTIC MOUNTAIN LAW

The international instruments reviewed above reflect states' common concerns for the protection and development of major mountain ecosystems at regional and sub-regional levels. As noted, because many mountain areas cross national borders, international agreements and actions are often required to articulate and formalize international mountain policy goals. However, practical mountain conservation and development measures take place mainly within state borders through national legislation.

So far, a dozen or so states have passed exhaustive or sectoral mountain-specific laws, including Cuba, France, Georgia, Greece, Italy, Switzerland and Ukraine. Other states, such as the Russian Federation (including Siberia), Kyrgyzstan, Morocco and Romania, are about to draw up or to enact similar laws. For instance, Bulgaria has fully completed the preparation of a bill on mountain areas. Furthermore, in some countries mountain legislation has been developed at the sub-national level. An example is the Republic of North Ossetia-Alania in the Russian Federation, with its Act of 30 December 1998 relating to mountain territories. In Italy, most mountainous regions enacted mountain laws between 1996 and 2000. The main examples of national and sub-national legislation are listed in the Annex.

An analysis of these domestic legal texts dealing with mountains reveals a number of similarities: in their objectives and scope; in their institutional frameworks; and in the economic, social and environmental policies they reflect.

3.1. Scope and Objectives

National laws generally define "mountains" in order to delineate the scope of the law. Of the currently used definition criteria, altitude is the most meaningful, for at certain altitudes living conditions become much more difficult and precarious than in the lowlands. Thus it is often the altitude factor that makes it necessary to adopt specific laws. Other specific natural characteristics such as climate, vegetation and topography are also used to determine a mountain's boundaries. Box 1 gives some examples of legal definitions.

Promoting the protection and sustainable development of mountain areas is the first aim of most laws relating to mountains. Within this general objective, the emphasis is adjusted to fit national contexts. Respecting the cultural identity of mountain communities is a further aim pursued by a number of laws. Insofar as locally enacted laws meet the special needs of the mountain peoples and the mountain areas they cover, they are best suited to fulfil their regulatory role efficiently. (Lynch and Maggio, 2000) For example, in the Georgian law, a stated objective is to meet the needs of today's mountain peoples as well as those of future generations. Likewise, one of the aims of the Swiss law on aid to investment is the promotion of sustainable development of mountain regions through the allocation of funding for infrastructure development.

Box 1 – Examples of Criteria Used in the Definition of Mountain Areas

France – 1985 Act
- altitude and the presence of steep slopes indicating significant handicaps are the general criteria used to describe a mountain area
- the country's various mountain ranges are specifically identified and, to some extent, come under different regimes

Georgia – 1999 Act
- areas located at altitudes above 1 500 m are considered mountainous
- certain areas located between 800 m and 1 000 m may also be described as mountain areas, with additional factors taken into account (gradient, soil quality, economic and ecological condition, demographic situation, etc.)

Italy – 1971 Act, amended in 1990
- initially, altitude (600 m), adjusted according to socio-economic factors, was the main criterion
- the 1990 amendment removed definition criteria, which practically implied a confirmation of previously identified mountain areas (Maglia and Santoloci, 1998)

Switzerland – 1998 Ordinance on Cadastral Surveys
- mountain regions are defined on the basis of three criteria which are, in declining order of importance, climate, transport links and topography

---

3.2. Institutional Frameworks

The administrative organization of mountain areas usually leads to the creation of specialized institutions with support, advisory, coordination or management powers. For example, in France, the 1985 Act established such structures at two levels: at the central level, the National Board for Mountain Development, Management and Protection coordinates government action in mountain areas; and for each mountain range – there are seven altogether – a committee provides advice and makes proposals on management, protection and development measures. In addition, local inhabitants are involved in decisionmaking processes. (Decree 85-994) In Cuba, an interministerial commission was established to promote socio-economic development in mountain areas. (1995 Decree) The Bulgarian bill makes provision for the establishment of a National Board for Mountain Regions whose role will be to supervise the implementation of the law and to coordinate actions taken by the state, by mountain district authorities and by mountain commune associations.

Some countries, on the other hand, have not found it appropriate to establish institutions to deal specifically with mountains. Nevertheless, they have mechanisms to ensure that central and local bodies which exercise some authority with respect to mountains can consult and share responsibilities. This is the situation in Switzerland, a federal state where powers are shared between the Confederation and the cantons. The law on aid to investment in mountain regions sets out their respective powers, namely, that the cantons are responsible for implementing the law, whereas the Confederation monitors the actions they take; and whereas funding is provided by the Confederation, the cantons determine the loan allocations.

3.3. Economic Incentives

3.3.1. Mountain Funds

Because of the characteristically harsh conditions of mountain areas, legislators have often seen the necessity of designing economic measures to meet some of the law's objectives. In particular, special funds are often set up to support investment and development in mountain regions, with the accrued resources being used or redistributed in the form of subsidies, investment loans, research funding and other support. Examples of such funds are given in Box 2.

Box 2 - Examples of Mountain Funds

Bulgaria

Chapter V of the 1993 Bill, which deals with the development fund for mountain regions, states that its accrued resources will be redistributed in the form of subsidies, investment loans, research funding, etc.

France

Initially, section 80 of the 1985 Act made provision for an intervention fund for mountain self-development. This fund was later absorbed by the national land use planning and development fund, designed to pool credits earmarked, *inter alia*, for mountain development. (1995 Act)

Italy

The national mountain fund established under the 1994 Act is funded by contributions from the state and the municipalities. The funds are distributed between the regions and the autonomous provinces. The latter establish their own regional mountain funds and decide how they are to be allocated.

Switzerland

Section 14 of the 1997 Act provides for a fund designed to finance aid to investment in mountain areas, including loans for the establishment of new mountain infrastructure.

3.3.2. Mountain Agriculture

Many mountain people depend on agriculture, which not only meets their food requirements directly, but also helps to create jobs and contributes to economic development. Hence the pride of place that agriculture occupies in many mountain laws. In France, agriculture is acknowledged as being of public interest inasmuch as it is essential for mountain peoples. (Sec. 18, 1985 Act, incorporated in sec. L.113-1, Rural Code) In Georgia, agri-food industries are considered to be one of the cornerstones for the socio-economic development of mountain regions. In Switzerland, general legislation dealing with agricultural development (the 1998 Federal Law on Agriculture and the 1998 Ordinance on Direct Payments to Agriculture) contains provisions for the promotion of mountain agriculture. An example is financial aid for crops grown on sloping land (sec. 75, 1998 Ordinance).

3.3.3. Mountain Tourism

The growing attraction of mountain areas as tourist destinations has led to an expansion of leisure activities, with an increase in accommodation facilities, amenities and infrastructures that can undermine the natural and cultural environment of mountain ecosystems. In an effort to remedy this situation, legislators have placed certain restrictions on mountain tourism. In France, the 1985 Act devotes an entire chapter to the running of tourism facilities and the management of ski lifts and ski runs, which must be operated under the supervision of the local authorities. For all new operations, contracts must be drawn up between the promoters and the local authorities, thereby allowing for some control over tourism development. The Georgian law provides for aid to investment and subsidized loans for mountain tourism that respects historical monuments and nature sites. The Ukrainian law also makes provision for subsidies and loans for tourism development.

3.3.4. Local Products

Some laws deal with local products, usually crafts, from mountain areas. France awards a special label to such products as a guarantee of their quality and to promote local production (1985 Act). Awarding of the "mountain" label is subject to conditions set out in Decree 2000-1231. In Italy, a similar label is awarded to products made in mountain areas (1994 Act). The Georgian law, too, promotes local crafts by providing loans on preferential terms.

3.4. Social Policies

National and sub-national laws seek to improve the living standards of mountain communities. The Northern Ossetia law, for example, states that mountain peoples can expect the same socio-economic benefits as lowland inhabitants. Recommended measures include the improvement and development of infrastructure and the enhancement of public services in mountain areas.

3.4.1. Infrastructure and Communications

The isolation of mountain populations is often due to the lack or weakness of means of communication – hence the measures put in place by legislators. Switzerland's 1997 Act on aid to investment makes provision for loans for mountain infrastructure development. To be eligible for these loans, projects must aim at enhancing living standards, economic potential and industrial competitiveness in the region. The Georgian law provides for a change in mountain road construction standards. In Ukraine, subsidies and loans may be granted for the development of public transport, roads and telecommunication and broadcasting facilities. In France, the 1985 Act provides for improving the efficiency of radio and television broadcasting techniques. In Italy, local public services in mountain communities must open information offices to remedy communication shortcomings and must give their inhabitants free access to non-confidential information (1994 Act).

3.4.2. Culture, Education and Health

Mountain people have an unrivaled knowledge of their environment. However, they must be in a position to capitalize on and transmit that knowledge using the appropriate tools. To this end, Northern Ossetia's law states that mountain people have priority rights to use the natural resources in the mountain area, and the law also makes provision for public financing of scientific research and teaching activities in mountainous regions. The Ukraine law provides for state loans and subsidies for health and education in mountain areas. In France, school and university education and teaching programmes must take into consideration the specific environmental, economic and social conditions of mountain ranges (1985 Act).

3.5. Environmental Protection

Fragile mountain ecosystems need to be protected against damage from forest clearing and soil erosion. Thus, provisions to protect the environment are commonly included in laws pertaining to mountains, as well as in related texts (laws governing forests, water, soils, the environment, land use planning, etc.). The Northern Ossetia law prescribes rational use of mountain natural resources, with provision for liability of users who damage those resources (secs. 15 and 16). In Italy, water management, reforestation and erosion control measures may be adopted for environmental protection purposes, including expropriation of lands for which conservation is necessary (1971 and 1994 Acts). Likewise, mountain soil improvement is one of the priorities of the Ukrainian law, while the Georgian law seeks more broadly to provide protection for mountain ecosystems, including adequate management of their natural resources and rehabilitation of their arid areas (sec. 1).

IV. CONCLUSION

After nearly a decade of implementation of Chapter 13 of Agenda 21, only a few countries, such as France, Georgia, Italy, Switzerland and Ukraine, have adopted legal instruments focusing specifically on mountain areas.

In most countries, there are no laws to address the particular conditions and needs of mountain regions and peoples. Existing legislation tends to have a bias towards lowland priorities, thereby undermining the interests of mountain ecosystems and inhabitants.

It is therefore desirable to develop mountain-specific laws, as well as appropriate institutional structures such as national mountain committees, in order to provide normative tools that are supportive of sustainable mountain development, as well as to facilitate coordination with other mountain-related laws and institutions. To be effective and efficient, mountain-specific legal frameworks should:

- address in a coordinated, integrated, balanced and coherent manner the various aspects of sustainable mountain development such as forestry, agriculture, transportation, culture, education, health, economy, environment, biodiversity, tourism and mining;
- respect the cultures, protect the rights, promote the well-being and ensure the participation of local communities in mountain areas;
- establish institutional settings that promote and facilitate dialogue and consensus among various stakeholders and interests in a multisectoral context;
- provide suitable mechanisms for conflict resolution and dispute settlement in mountain regions; and
- promote and facilitate bilateral and multilateral cooperation, particularly in transboundary mountain regions, taking account of relevant international instruments.

Such legal frameworks should be based on and supported by comprehensive national policies and strategies for the sustainable management of mountain ecosystems. They should also be supplemented, where appropriate, by regional agreements such as the Alpine Convention, which provide for transfrontier collaboration among countries sharing mountain ranges.

REFERENCES

African Mountains Association. 1997. *African Mountains and Highlands - Declaration of Antananarivo, International Workshop of the African Mountains Association, 26 May – 1 June 1997, Antananarivo, Madagascar* (www. mtnforum.org/resources/mpl/73africanmtns.htm).

Commission on Sustainable Development. 2001. *Sustainable Mountain Development, Report of the Secretary-General.* E/CN.17/2001/PC/14.

Conseil International Associatif pour la Protection des Pyrénées. 1995. *Charter for the Protection of the Pyrénées.* English Summary (www. mtnforum.org/resources/library/ciapp95a.htm).

Euromontana. 2000. *Final Declaration for the Second European Mountain Conference, Trento, Italy, 17 and 18 March 2000* (www.mtnforum.org/ resources/library/eurom00c.htm).

Fodella, A. & Pineschi, L. 2000. *Environment Protection and Sustainable Development of Mountain Areas - Preliminary Report, Mountains and the Environment: Ten Years after Rio, Courmayeur, 16 and 17 June 2000.*

Fourth International Conference on Sustainable Mountain Development. 2001. *Proceedings of the Fourth International Conference on Sustainable Mountain Development: Regional and Transboundary Cooperation and Policy Issues, Vladikavkaz, Russian Federation, 23–26 September 2001.*

International Union of Alpinist Associations (UIAA). 1997. *UIAA Kathmandu Declaration* (www.mtnforum.org/resources/library/uiaa97c.htm).

International Workshop on Sustainable Mountain Development. 2001. *Cusco Declaration. International Workshop on Mountain Ecosystems: A Vision of the Future, Cusco, Peru, 25–27 April 2001* (www.mtnforum.org/resources/ library/iwsmd01b.htm).

Lynch, O. & Maggio, G. 2000. *Mountain Laws and Peoples: Moving Towards Sustainable Development and Recognition of Community-based Property Rights.* Center for International Environmental Law, Washington, D.C.

Maglia, S. & Santoloci, M. 1998. *Il codice dell'ambiente (9th ed.).* Editrice La Tribuna, Piacenza.

Servon, F. 1997. *La Convention alpine (la montagne et la souris).* Revue Juridique de l'Environnement, No. 3.

United Nations. 1997. *Natural Resource Aspects of Sustainable Development in Greece.* Agenda 21 - National Information (www.un.org/esa/agenda21/ natlinfo/countr/greece/natur.htm).

UNEP. 2001. *European Mountain Initiative - News* (www.unep.ch/ roe/emi.htm).

Villeneuve, A., Talla P. & Mekouar M.A. 2002. *The Legal Framework for Sustainable Mountain Management: An Overview of Mountain-specific Instruments.* UNASYLVA 208.

World Mountain Forum (WMF). 2000a. *Draft World Charter for Mountain Populations* (www.forum-mondial-montagne.org/ouvangl.html).

World Mountain Forum (WMF). 2000b. *Final Declaration* (www.forum-mondial-montagne.org/ouvangl.html).

Zakrevsky, A. 1995. *Status of Mountain Human Settlements [Ukraine].* Letter to Mountain Forum (www.mtnforum.org/resources/library/zakra95a.htm).

Annex - Main Examples of Domestic Legislation Specific to Mountains

Country	Mountain-specific Legal Texts
Bulgaria	· Bill on the development of mountain regions, 1993
Cuba	· Decree No. 197 of 17 January 1995 on the Commissions of the Turquino-Manati Plan
France	· Act No. 85-30 of 9 January 1985 on mountain development and protection · Framework Law No. 95-115 of 4 February 1995 on land use planning and development · Framework Law No. 99-533 of 25 June 1999 on sustainable land use planning and development, amending Law No. 95-115 · Decree No. 85-994 of 20 September 1985 on the membership and the operation of the National Mountain Board · Decrees Nos. 85-995 to 85-1001 of 20 September 1985 on the membership and the operation of the committees covering the seven mountain ranges in France (Central Range, Northern Alps, Southern Alps, Corsica, Pyrénées, Jura, Vosges) · Decree No. 2000-1231 of 15 December 2000 on the use of the term "mountain"
Georgia	· Act of 8 June 1999 on the socio-economic and cultural development of mountain regions
Greece	· Act No. 1892/90 encouraging the economy and development of mountain regions, amended by Act 2234/94
Italy	· Act 991 of 25 July 1952 on woods, forests and mountain areas · Act 1102 of 3 December 1971 on woods, forests and mountain areas (amended by Act 142 of 6 June 1990 on Local Autonomous Authorities) · Act 97 of 31 January 1994 on woods, forests and mountain areas · Regional Laws of Abruzzi, Basilicata, Calabria, Friuli-Venezia-Giulia, Latium, Liguria, Lombardy, Marches, Molise, Piedmont, Tuscany and Umbria · Law of the Autonomous Province of Bolzano
Russian Federation	· Act of 30 December 1998 on mountain territories of the Republic of North Ossetia-Alania
Switzerland	· Federal Act of 21 March 1997 on aid to investment in mountain regions · Ordinance of 7 December 1998 on the cadastral survey of agricultural production and area demarcation
Ukraine	· 1995 Act on the status of human mountain settlements

AFTERWORD

The decade since Rio has been a momentous one, reflecting dramatic political, economic, philosophical and legislative change. A greater sophistication on the part of citizens regarding the environment, an increasing recognition of the importance of stakeholder participation and community involvement and a growing appreciation of the need to respond to the effects of globalization – these are only a few of the converging worldwide trends that have had an impact on the goals and processes of legislative change. In this context, sharing international experiences is increasingly important.

The Legal Office of FAO has developed some tools over the years that can be helpful to governments seeking to review and revise their legislation in light of international developments and new national concerns, as well as to those seeking to advocate or influence such processes. Perhaps the most important is FAOLEX, an online database of food and agricultural law from around the world. It contains over 20 000 full texts of treaties, laws and regulations dealing with most of the issues of agriculture, natural resources management and sustainable development. It can be accessed in English, French and Spanish at www.fao.org/Legal. Another tool is the series of printed publications on current legal issues available from the FAO Legal Office, which has now been augmented by the Legal Papers Online series, also accessible at www.fao.org/Legal. Recent papers deal in detail with legal aspects of forestry, fisheries, wildlife, animal health, land, plant genetic resources and other subjects that are covered in the present study.

It is hoped that this book will also be a useful resource for lawyers, government officials, researchers and others interested in trends in the law on sustainable development – trends that have crystallized in the decade since the Rio Conference, and trends that can be expected to further evolve in the coming years. The fact that the book has been divided into individual chapters organized around the subject areas addressed by the Legal Office in the course of its technical assistance work should not obscure the many links and cross-connections among them.

One of these is the movement toward the harmonization of international standards and national legislation in accordance with international models. The amalgamation of food safety, animal health and plant health concerns in the WTO's Agreement on Sanitary and Phytosanitary Measures most clearly reflects this trend. It is now axiomatic that national sovereignty does not justify the creation of local standards that impinge on internationally agreed environmental, trade or other concerns. International sources are to be consulted, and where necessary international advice obtained, to develop national standards and laws that are in harmony not only with international obligations but that are also regionally consistent and tailored to national concerns.

The formalization of international standards as binding on WTO members under the SPS Agreement mirrors another development over the course of the last decade: a significant number of informal arrangements have become binding agreements or have led to the development of formal treaties, after sustained international negotiations. The International Undertaking on Plant Genetics Resources has become an international treaty; UNCED's call for effective implementation of the 1982 UN Convention on the Law of the Sea led to adoption of the FAO Compliance Agreement and UN Fish Stocks Agreement; the PIC Convention arose from the earlier non-binding FAO Code of Conduct and the UNEP London Guidelines. Other examples abound.

In many of the fields addressed in this book, there has also been a conceptual shift toward cross-sectoral cooperation and organization and away from compartmentalized approaches. Whether in considering ecosystems in water resources management; whether in recognizing the intersection between sanitary and phytosanitary standards and food safety; or in acknowledging the special problems of mountain areas – problems that cross-cut land, water, forestry and environmental issues – policy-makers, legislators and government officials can no longer afford to focus solely on their own concerns. For example, ministries of health monitoring water quality for human consumption, ministries of agriculture regulating water quality for irrigation and ministries of energy and environment assessing water quantity must devise cross-sectoral strategies and solutions. Similarly, standard-setting bodies charged with promoting food safety cannot ignore plant protection effects on agricultural produce or the human health risks arising from certain animal diseases.

The goal of recognizing all implicated actors is mirrored by a desire to take into account the interests of those who may not have received equal attention before. For example, evolving attitudes on gender have triggered policy and legal efforts to remove constraints to women's full participation and to rectify the effects of past discrimination in land, property and a variety of other areas. Equally, the protection of indigenous communities with regard to plant breeding, land rights and forestry, among others, has gained increasing attention, as have the benefits of community management in such contexts as forestry, irrigation schemes and fishing. This concept can be expressed as the desire not to forget any organization or stakeholder in the revision of legislation: all must be at the negotiating table, whether at international conferences or at rural meetings of citizens and groups affected by proposed legislative amendments.

Finally, the most important trend must be toward incorporation of the concept of sustainable development itself into legislation. Forest laws, fisheries laws, wildlife laws, laws on genetics resources – in all of these the concept of sustainable management has gained primacy in recent years. In land law, strengthening security of tenure for individuals and groups is an important step towards the sustainable use of land, whereas in water resources management, the shift toward greater government control reflects concerns about unregulated access to limited resources which are subject to competing uses; in fisheries law, the focus has shifted from exploitation to conservation and sustainable utilization. In these and the other contexts addressed in this book, the use of law to achieve sustainable development has assumed primary importance since Rio.

REPORTS AND PUBLICATIONS

Contents

INTRODUCTION

The following is a selected list of reports and publications of the FAO Legal Office relating to the subjects addressed by this book, covering the years 1992 to mid-2002: the post-Rio decade. It includes final technical reports prepared by FAO staff and consultants in the context of technical assistance or advisory projects, entries in the Legislative Studies and Legal Papers Online series and a number of additional documents of interest.

References have been thematically grouped according to the system of subject classification used within the Legal Office. Thus, earlier chapters on the cross-cutting subjects of agrobiodiversity, gender and mountains do not have specific corresponding sections in this list. The last two categories in the list – agriculture and environment – are intended to include the outputs both of projects that covered a large number of related subjects simultaneously, and of projects that focused on specific subjects that do not fit comfortably in one of the other categories.

I.   FOOD

Aziz Bin Mangkat, A. 1995. *Laos. Meat Inspection Legislation.*

Banklerova, A. 1996. *Slovakian Standards and Food Legislation.*

Barthomeuf, R. 1994. *Burkina Faso. Rapport d'expertise en normalisation.*

Blomberg, B. 1994. *Food Legislation in Albania.*

Brouwer, O. & Chiaradia-Bousquet, J.-P. 1992. *Hungary. Food Quality Control Legislation.*

Chiaradia-Bousquet, J.-P. 1995. *Legislation Governing Food Control and Quality Certification.* Legislative Study No. 54.

Doussin, J.P. 1996. *Liban. Consultation en législation et organisation du contrôle des denrées alimentaires.*

El Kazem, W. 1992. *Liban. Contrôle de qualité des denrées alimentaires.*

FAO. 1998. *The Right to Food in Theory and Practice.*

FAO. 1999. *Extracts from International and Regional Instruments and Declarations and other Authoritative Texts Addressing the Right to Food.* Legislative Study No. 68.

Féral, M.F. 1992. *Guinée. Renforcement du service de contrôle de qualité des denrées alimentaires.*

Féral, M.F. 1995. *Cambodge. Avant-projet de loi sur la qualité et la sécurité des produits et des services.*

Féral, M.F. 1995. *Cambodge. Réhabilitation de Camcontrol dans ses activités de contrôle alimentaire.*

Féral, M.F. 1996. *Contrôle et normalisation de la qualité des productions horticoles en République du Sénégal.*

Féral, M.F. 1997. *Roumanie. Renforcement de la législation et des contrôles de l'alimentation.*

Féral, M.F. 2000. *Sénégal. Stratégie pour la réorganisation du secteur de l'alimentation de rue à Dakar.*

Féral, M.F. & Castang, C. 1998. *Maroc. Contrôle, législation et réglementation des denrées alimentaires et de la fraude sur les marchandises.*

Frainchard, S. 1994. *Burkina Faso. Renforcement du contrôle de la qualité des denrées alimentaires.*

Galán, B.B. 1997. *Venezuela. Asistencia en la revisión del anteproyecto de ley orgánica de desarrollo agropecuario y seguridad alimentaria y en la formulación de los respectivos reglamentos de aplicación.*

Gardeñes, M. 1994. *Food Law in Estonia: Actual Problems and Future Perspectives.*

Glowka, L. 2002. *The Role of Law in Realising the Potential and Avoiding the Risks of Modern Biotechnology. Selected Issues of Relevance to Food and Agriculture.*

Heugas, J.F. 1996. *Gabon. Appui à la restructuration des activités de contrôle de la qualité des denrées alimentaires.*

Kasobwa, K. 1994. *Zaïre. Stratégies pour promouvoir et contrôler le secteur informel de l'alimentation.*

Macher, H. 1995. *Strengthening Food Control in Poland.*

Pardo Leal, M. 1998. *Legislación alimentaria de Bolivia.*

Pincus, G. 1995. *Improving the Legal and Administrative Framework of the Food Control System (Food Law) in Indonesia.*

Shick, B.A. 1993. *Strategy Proposals for Strengthening Food Control in Estonia.*

Schick, B.A. 1995. *Strategy Proposals for Strengthening Food Control in Lithuania.*

Sheridan, B. 1996. *Malta. Assistance in Strengthening the Food Control System.*

Temple, H. 1995. *Food Legislation in Lithuania.*

Vapnek, J.C. 1996. *Latvia. Strengthening Food Quality Control.*

Vapnek, J.C. 1998. *Armenia. Strengthening Food Quality Control.*

Vapnek, J.C. 2001. *Bhutan. Strengthening National Capacities for Food Control and Effective Participation in Codex.*

Vapnek, J.C. 2001. *Swaziland. Strengthening the National Food Control System.*

Vapnek, J.C. & Martinière, P. 1995. *Food Control Administration in Albania.*

II. ANIMALS

Chiaradia-Bousquet, J.-P. 1992. *Algérie. Santé animale: contrôle régional de la lucilie bouchère.*

Christy, L.C. 1992. *Report to the Government of Myanmar on Animal Health and Legislation.*

Féral, M.F. 1994. *Côte d'Ivoire. Appui aux services d'inspection sanitaire des denrées d'origine animale.*

Féral, M.F. 1995. *Laos. Mise en place des bases législatives et réglementaires du contrôle des denrées animales.*

Fiadjoe, A.K. 2000. *Guyana. Updating Veterinary Legislation.*

Fiadjoe, A.K. 2002. *Barbados. Legislation for Veterinary Drugs Control.*

Fingleton, J.S. 2001. *Mozambique. Veterinary Pharmacology Legislation.*

Lodge, M.W. 1996. *Tonga. Review of Legislation Relating to Plant and Animal Quarantine and Plant Export.*

Ntambirweki, J. 1994. *Tick and Tick-borne Disease Control Legislation and Related Matters in the United Republic of Tanzania, Uganda, Malawi and Zimbabwe.*

Ouédraogo, H. & Cavérivière, M. 2001. *Plan d'action et programme d'investissement pour le secteur de l'élevage au Burkina Faso. Le cadre juridique: avant-projet de code pastoral.*

Silva Repetto, R. 1999. *Kyrgyz Republic. Review of Agricultural Legislation: Veterinary Legislation Component.*

Temple, H. 1996. *CEBV. Revue technique et opérationnelle de la Communauté économique du bétail et de la viande.*

Vapnek, J.C. 1999. *Enhancing Prevention Capacities for Emergency Intervention against African Swine Fever in West Africa.*

Vapnek, J.C. 1999. *Institutional and Legal Measures to Combat African Swine Fever.* FAO Legal Paper Online No. 3.

Yacouba, M. 2001. Niger. *Relance du secteur de l'élevage. Aspects juridiques et institutionnels.*

III.   PLANTS

Balasubramaniam, A. 1994. *Mongolia. Proposed Pesticide Regulation.*

Banklerova, A. 1996. *Slovakian Plant Legislation.*

Barberis, G. 1995. *Albania. Strengthening Seed Legislation.*

Barberis, G. & Chiaradia-Bousquet, J.-P. 1995. *Pesticide Registration Legislation.* Legislative Study No. 51.

Barberis, G. & Simonnau, F. 1992. *Mali. Renforcement du service de la protection des végétaux.*

Bombín, L.M. 1993. *Technical Report to the Government of Antigua and Barbuda on Plant Protection Legislation.*

Bombín, L.M. 1993. *Technical Report to the Government of Saint Kitts and Nevis on Plant Protection Legislation.*

Bombín, L.M. 1993. *Technical Report to the Government of Saint Vincent and the Grenadines on Plant Protection Legislation.*

Bombín, L.M. & Silva Repetto, R. 1994. *República Dominicana. Informe sobre la legislación de semillas.*

Bombín, L.M. & Silva-Repetto, R. 1997. *Plant Variety Protection in Malaysia: Legal Implications of Article 27.3(b) of the TRIPS Agreement.*

Canal-Forgues, E. 1992. *CEPGL. Contrôle des échanges semenciers dans les pays membres de la CEPGL.*

Canal-Forgues, E. 1996. *Lithuania. Seed and Plant Breeders' Rights Legislation.*

Canal-Forgues, E. 1997. *Palestine. Seed Legislation.*

Canal-Forgues, E. 2000. *Madagascar. Renforcement des capacités techniques du service officiel de contrôle des semences.*

Cantarella, C. 2001. *Seychelles. Plant Genetic Resources.*

Cantarella, C. & Cooper, H.D. 2002. *Formulation of Draft Legislation on Plant Genetic Resources for Syria.*

Chaplin, G.R. 1996. *Tonga. Legislative Control of Pesticides.*

Chiaradia-Bousquet, J.-P. 1992. *Final Report on the Establishment of Pakistan Cotton Standards Institute.*

Chiaradia-Bousquet, J.-P. 1994. *Mongolia. Improvement of Pesticides Application and Control.*

Chiaradia-Bousquet, J.-P. 1995. *Liban. Législation des pesticides.*

Chiaradia-Bousquet, J.-P. 1997. *Strengthening Plant Protection Capabilities in India.*

Chiaradia-Bousquet, J.-P. 1997. *Nepal. Proceedings of the First National Workshop: Plant Quarantine Programme Improvement.*

Cruz Ramirez, T. 1995. *El Salvador. Sinopsis sobre la legislación de plaguicidas: variación media de requisitos.*

Cullinan, C. 1994. *Malta. Strengthening Plant Quarantine Capabilities.*

Cullinan, C. 1997. *Malawi. Introduction of a Pesticides Registration and Control Scheme.*

Doumbé-Billé, S. 2002. *Harmonisation des législations semencières en Afrique de l'Ouest et du Centre.*

Durand, S. 1998. *Seed Legislation and Plant Variety Protection in the Republic of Georgia.*

Durand, S. & Chiaradia-Bousquet, J.-P. 1999. *New Principles of Phytosanitary Legislation.* Legislative Study No. 62.

Fecteau, J. & Dale, P. 1994. *Seychelles. Strengthening Plant Protection Capacities: Legislation and Training.*

Fiadjoe, A.K. 1998. *Gambia. Strengthening Plant Quarantine Capabilities.*

Gaiger, M.C. 1992. *Pakistan. Pesticides Registration.*

Gaiger, M.C. 1992. *Swaziland. Strengthening Plant Protection Services.*

Galán, B.B. 1992. *Paraguay. Ley de semillas.*

Helfer, L.R. 2002. *Intellectual Property Rights in Plant Varieties: An Overview of Options for National Governments.* FAO Legal Paper Online No. 31.

Kern, E. 2000. *Report to the Government of the Republic of Tajikistan on Seed Legislation.*

Lodge, M.W. 1996. *Tonga. Review of Legislation Relating to Plant and Animal Quarantine and Plant Export.*

McCalla, W. 1993. *Caribbean. Assistance in Legislative Drafting and Enactment of Amblyomma variegatum Tick Eradication Programme.*

McCalla, W. 1993. *CARICOM. Legal Aspects of Harmonization in Plant Quarantine.*

Mekouar, M.A. 2002. *A Global Instrument on Agrobiodiversity : the International Treaty on Plant Genetic Resources.* FAO Legal Paper Online No. 24.

Müller, Y. 1992. *Rapport sur l'harmonisation des législations nationales en matière de pesticides au sein de la CEDEAO.*

Ntambirweki, J. 1992. *Gambia. Implementation of a National Pesticide Registration and Control Scheme.*

Ntambirweki, J. 1993. *Gambia. Final Report on Pesticides Legislation.*

Ould Bouboutt, S.M. 1994. *Législation semencière en Mauritanie.*

Ould Bouboutt, S.M. 1994. *Mauritanie. Rapport sur la législation relative aux banques de céréales.*

Pardo Leal, M. 1999. *Révision de la réglementation sur l'homologation des pesticides commune aux Etats membres du CILSS et des législations nationales sur les pesticides.*

Pardo Leal, M. 2001. *Sudan. Strengthening Phytosanitary Legislation.*

Razafiarijaona, J. 2000. *Madagascar. Législation semencière.*

Salazar Mejía, M.A. 1996. *Análisis comparativo de la legislación sobre plaguicidas para uso en la agricultura de Costa Rica, El Salvador, Guatemala, Honduras, Nicaragua y Panamá, con relación al Código internacional de conducta para la distribución de plaguicidas.*

Silva Repetto, R. 1995. *El Salvador. Legislación de semillas.*

Silva Repetto, R. 1997. *Plant Protection and Pesticides Legislation in Eritrea.*

Silva Repetto, R. 1997. *Kyrgyz Republic. Seed Legislation and Quality Control.*

Silva Repetto, R. 1998. *Ecuador. Reestructuración del Programa nacional de semillas.*

Silva Repetto, R. 1998. *Namibia. Seed Legislation.*

Temple, H. 1993. *Tchad. Renforcement du service national de la protection des végétaux.*

Vandevenne, R. 1994. *Mauritanie. Réglementation de la production, du contrôle et de la certification des semences des plantes de grande culture.*

Vapnek, J.C. 1996. *Improved Seed Production: CARICOM Countries and Suriname. Model Seed Act for the Caribbean Region.*

Vapnek, J.C. 1996. *Cyprus. Strengthening Plant Quarantine Capabilities: Legislation and Training.*

Vapnek, J.C. 1997. *Ghana. Strengthening Plant Quarantine Capabilities.*

Vapnek, J.C. 1997. *Jamaica. Establishment of a Mandatory Health Certification Scheme for Citrus.*

Vapnek, J.C. 1997. *Namibia. Strengthening Plant Protection Capabilities and Legislation.*

Vapnek, J.C. 1998. *Belize. Establishment of a Mandatory Health Certification Scheme for Citrus.*

Vapnek, J.C. 1998. *Suriname. Development of a National Seed Programme.*

Vapnek, J.C. 2001. *CARICOM. Strengthening Phytosanitary Capabilities.*

Vapnek, J.C. 2001. *Plant Quarantine Law for the Co-operation Council for the Arab Countries of the Gulf.*

Vapnek, J.C. 2002. *Oman. Citrus Certification Programme.*

Young, T.R. 1995. *Plant Breeders' Rights in Tanzania.*

Zweigert, M., Ostermann, H., Djibrilla, S. & Djateng, F. 1999. *Cameroun. Amélioration de la gestion des produits phytosanitaires.*

IV. WATER

Betlem, I. 1997. *National Water Resources Laws and Institutions in Tanzania.*

Bichara, D. & Burchi, S. 1999. *Elaboration des réglementations nationales de gestion des ressources en eau.* Legislative Study No. 69.

Bouderbala, N., Nanni, M. & Mekouar, M.A. 1993. *Législation foncière, forestière et hydraulique en RDP Lao.*

Burchi, S. 1993. *Treaties Concerning the Non-navigational Uses of International Watercourses - Europe.* Legislative Study No. 50.

Burchi, S. 1994. *Preparing National Regulations for Water Resources Management.* Legislative Study No. 52.

Burchi, S. 1998. *Report on Selected Aspects of Irrigation Development in Saint Lucia.*

Burchi, S. 1999. *National Regulations for Groundwater: Options, Issues and Best Practices.* FAO Legal Paper Online No. 5.

Burchi, S. & Harris, R. 1998. *Report on Selected Legal Aspects of Irrigation Development in Dominica.*

De Silva, S. 1997. *Sri Lanka. Review of Laws and Regulations Relating to Water Resources Management.*

Dezfouli, I.B. 1996. *Iran. Land and Water Law and Institutions.*

Ecaat, J. 1997. *Uganda. Final Report on Linkages between Water Use Permits and EIA Procedures for Uganda.*

FAO. 1995. *Treaties Concerning the Non-navigational Uses of International Watercourses - Asia.* Legislative Study No. 55.

FAO. 1998. *Política y legislación de aguas en el Istmo centroamericano - El Salvador, Guatemala, Honduras.* Estudio legislativo 64.

FAO. 1998. *Sources of International Water Law.* Legislative Study No. 65.

FAO. 1999. *Issues in Water Law Reform.* Legislative Study No. 67.

FAO. 1999. *Treaties Concerning the Non-navigational Uses of International Watercourses - Africa.* Legislative Study No. 61.

Garduño Velasco, H. 1998. *Assistance to the Government of the Republic of South Africa in Water Rights Administration.*

Garduño Velasco, H. 1999. *Assistance to the Government of Sri Lanka in the Implementation of a Water Rights System.*

Garduño Velasco, H. 2000. *Assistance to the Government of Namibia in the Drafting of a New Water Resources Bill and the Implementation of a Water Rights Administration System.*

Garduño Velasco, H. 2001. *Water Rights Administration - Experiences, Issues and Guidelines.* Legislative Study No. 70.

Herrera, O. 1998. *Uganda. Assistance to the Government on the Implementation of a Water Right System.*

Hodgson, S. 1997. *Albania. Review of the Water Sector Legislation.*

Hodgson, S. & Pilt, T. 1998. *Estonia. Analysis of the Legal Framework for Land Drainage and Water Resources Management.*

Kiari, K. & Nanni, M. 1998. *Niger. Avant-projets d'arrêtés d'application de l'Ordonnance 93-014 du 2 mars 1993 portant régime de l'eau et du décret 97-368 du 2 octobre 1997.*

Magnani, C. 1997. *Bolivia. Aspectos legales vinculados con el Plan nacional de manejo de cuencas hidrográficas.*

Manríquez Lobos, G. 1996. *El Salvador. Revisión del anteproyecto de Ley de Aguas.*

Manríquez Lobos, G. 1996. *Guatemala. Análisis de la legislación vigente y propuesta de modernización.*

Manríquez Lobos, G. 1996. *Honduras. Análisis de la legislación vigente y propuesta de modernización.*

Nanni, M. 1994. *Lithuania. Agricultural and Environmental Legislation: Water Law and Institutions.*

Nanni, M. 1994. *Water Laws and Institutions in Belize.*

Nanni, M. 1998. *Lao PDR. Regulations on the Use of Water for Irrigation Purposes.*

Nanni, M. 1998. *Lao PDR. The Law on Water and Aquatic Resources: Gaps and Remedies.*

Nanni, M. & Betlem, I. 1997. *Sri Lanka. Discussion Paper on Water Allocation and Water Rights.*

Nanni, M., Betlem , I., De Silva, S. & Nanayakkara, A. 1998. *Sri Lanka. Draft Water Resources Legislation.*

Ntambirweki, J. 1997. *Uganda. Improvement of Regulations under the Water Statute relating to Water Rights.*

Ntambirweki, J. 1998. *Uganda. Report on the Proposed Water (Environmental Impact Assessment) Regulations.*

Ramazzotti, M. 1996. *Readings in African Customary Water Law.* Legislative Study No. 58.

Sarpong, G.A. 1998. *Ghana. Development of Support Structure for Irrigated Agriculture.*

Shauri, V. & Betlem, I. 1998. *Tanzania. Water Resources Act and Regulations.*

Sironneau, J. 1992. *Burundi. Projet de loi sur l'eau.*

Sironneau, J. 1996. *Guinée. Elaboration des textes d'application du code de l'eau.*

Vapnek, J.C. 1999. *Dominica. Pre-feasibility Study for Irrigation Development: Final Report on Legal Issues.*

Vapnek, J.C. 2000. *Establishing a Water Abstraction Scheme: Issues and Options.* FAO Legal Paper Online No. 9.

Wilkinson, G.K. & Ramadas, K. 1996. *Malaysia. Final Draft: Irrigation and Drainage Act.*

V.   FISHERIES

Betlem, I. 2000. *Malaysia. High Seas Fishing Legislation.*

Betlem, I. 2002. *Barbados. High Seas Fishing Legislation.*

Bombín, L.M., *et al.* 1992. *Perú. La ordenación y planificación pesquera y la reactivación del sector pesquero en el Perú.*

Bombín, L.M. & García Mesinas, A. 1992. *América Central. Legislación pesquera en el Istmo centroamericano.*

Bonucci, N. 1992. *La législation des pêches à Madagascar. Propositions pour de nouveaux instruments juridiques en matière de pêche et d'aquaculture.*

Bonucci, N., Edeson, W.R. & Van Houtte, A. 1993. *Analyse préliminaire de certains textes législatifs régissant l'aquaculture.* Legislative Study No. 49.

Bonucci, N. & Roest, F. 1992. *Burundi. Une nouvelle législation sur la pêche et l'aquaculture : propositions et projets de textes.*

Breuil, C., Cacaud, P. & Nugent, C. 1995. *République Centrafricaine. Contribution à la préparation d'une revue et des orientations stratégiques de développement du secteur des pêches et de la pisciculture.*

Breuil, C., Charles-Dominique, E. & Van Houtte, A. 1995. *Côte d'Ivoire. Amélioration du cadre juridique pour la coopération, l'aménagement et le développement halieutique des Etats côtiers de l'Afrique de l'Ouest. Assistance à la préparation d'un plan d'aménagement des pêches en lagune Aby-Tendo-Ehy.*

Cacaud, P. 1995. *Burkina Faso. Avant-projet de lois sur la pêche et l'aquaculture.*

Cacaud, P. 1995. *Togo. Analyse du cadre juridique de la pêche et l'aquaculture.*

Cacaud, P. 1996. *Report Prepared for the Governments of Burundi, Tanzania, Zaire and Zambia on Institutional Choices for Co-operation on Fisheries Management and Conservation on Lake Tanganyika.*

Cacaud, P. 1996. *Guinée. Schéma directeur pêche et pisciculture : aspects institutionnels et juridiques.*

Cacaud, P. 1996. *République Centrafricaine. Avant-projets de loi sur la pêche et la pisciculture.*

Cacaud, P. 1998. *Malaysia. Legal Issues Relating to Vessel Monitoring Systems.*

Cacaud, P. 1998. *Palestine. Preliminary Draft Fisheries Bill.*

Cacaud, P. 1999. *Projet de loi sur la pêche continentale et la pisciculture au Gabon.*

Cacaud, P. 2000. *Maroc. Considérations d'ordre juridique relatives à l'introduction d'un système de quota de pêche pour la pêcherie de la pieuvre commune.*

Canal-Forgues, E. 1995. *Législation des pêches à Madagascar.*

Canal-Forgues, E. 1997. *Côte d'Ivoire. La Législation des pêches : proposition de nouveaux textes juridiques.*

Christy, L.C. 1996. *Namibia. Review of the Sea Fisheries Act.*

Cirelli, M.T. 1992. *Fisheries legislation. Report to the Government of Belize.*

Cirelli, M.T. 1993. *Albania. Review of the Draft Law on the Protection of Wildlife, Hunting and Fisheries in Inland Waters.*

Cirelli, M.T. 1996. *Legal Aspects of Cooperation in Monitoring, Control and Surveillance in the Southwest Indian Ocean and the Maldives.*

Cysne, M. & Pereira, E. 1997. *Projectos de lei e de regulamento das pescas para São Tomé e Principe.*

Dioh, B., Kelleher, M.K. & Roberts, K. 1997. *Fisheries Access Agreements in West Africa.*

Djalal, H. 2001. *Assistance in Marine Fisheries Legislation: Indonesia and International Fisheries Agreements.*

Edeson, W.R. 1992. *Trinidad and Tobago. The Need for Revision of Fisheries Legislation.*

Edeson, W.R. 1996. *Guyana. New Fisheries Laws.*

Elferink, A.G.O. 1999. *The Impact of Article 7(2) of the Fish Stocks Agreement on the Formulation of Conservation and Management Measures for Straddling and Highly Migratory Fish Stocks.* FAO Legal Paper Online No. 4.

FAO. 1992. *Report to the Government of the People's Republic of China on Legal Issues Associated with Fisheries Management.*

FAO. 1998. *Malaysia. Draft Inland Fisheries Rules (Aquaculture).*

FAO. 1999. *Tchad. Projet de loi portant régime des forêts, de la faune et de la pêche.*

Flewelling, P., Bonucci, N. & Christy, L.C. 1992. *Revision of Fisheries Legislation in Seychelles.*

Franckx, E. 1995. *Report Prepared for the Government of Lithuania on the Elaboration of Appropriate Fisheries Legislation.*

Franckx, E. 1999. *Rapport préparé pour le Gouvernement de la République algérienne démocratique et populaire concernant l'analyse et l'élaboration de l'ensemble du dispositif législatif relatif à la pêche.*

Franckx, E. 2000. Pacta Tertiis *and the Agreement for the Implementation of the Provisions of the United Nations Convention on the Law of the Sea of 10 December 1982 Relating to the Conservation and Management of Straddling Fish Stocks and Highly Migratory Fish Stocks.* FAO Legal Paper Online No. 8.

Franckx, E. 2001. *Fisheries Enforcement – Related Legal and Institutional Issues: National, Subregional or Regional Perspectives.* Legislative Study No. 71.

Freestone, D. 1998. *The Burden of Proof in Natural Resources Legislation: Some Critical Issues for Fisheries Law.* Legislative Study No. 63.

Gaiger, M.C. 1992. *Report to the Government of Malta on Fisheries Legislation.*

Gaiger, M.C. 1994. *Report to the Government of the Kingdom of Lesotho on Fisheries Legislation.*

Galache Valiente, P.J. 1996. *Ecuador. Análisis de la legislación y propuesta de modernización (Anteproyecto de Ley de pesca y acuicultura).*

Gueye, B. 1992. *Report on Harmonization of Fisheries Legislation with Regard to MCS in ECOWAS Member Countries.*

Hey, E. 1992. *Fisheries Legislation in Suriname.*

Hodgson, S. 1998. *Ethiopia. Regional Fisheries Regulations.*

Hodgson, S. 1998. *Sudan. Inland Fisheries Legislation.*

Howarth, W., Hernandez, A.R. & Van Houtte, A. 2001. *Legislation Governing Shrimp Aquaculture: Legal Issues, National Experiences and Options.* FAO Legal Paper Online No. 18.

Jesus, J.L. 2002. *Projecto de assistencia jurídica para a revisao da legislaçao das pescas de Moçambique.*

Juste Ruiz, J. 1998. *República Dominicana. Revisión de la legislación pesquera.*

Lima do Santos, C.A. 2002. *Namibia. Safety and Quality Aspects of Products of Aquaculture.*

Kandé, J.M. 1996. *Une loi-cadre sur la pêche et l'aquaculture continentales en Guinée.*

Kern, E. 1996. *Estonia. Fisheries Legislation.*

Konaté, F. 1994. *La répression des infractions de pêche en Guinée.*

Kuemlangan, B. 2000. *Report on Assistance to Tonga in Fisheries Legislation.*

Lería, C. 1996. *El Salvador. Reglamento al anteproyecto de Ley de pesca y acuicultura.*

Lobach, T. 2002. *Port State Control of Foreign Fishing Vessels,* FAO Legal Paper Online No. 29.

Maga-pa-Maga. 1995. *Analyse comparative des législations des pêches de quelques Etats du Golfe de Guinée.*

Maga-pa-Maga & Tavares de Pinho, A. 1997. *Révision de la législation des pêches du Gabon.*

Mangatalle, D. 1996. *Coastal State Requirements for Foreign Fishing.* Legislative Study No. 57.

McDorman, T. 1992. *Myanmar. Fisheries Legislation.*

McManus, R. 1992. *A Proposal for a Convention on the Establishment of the Lake Victoria Fisheries Commission.*

Mekouar, M.A. 1993. *Législation sur les forêts, la faune et la pêche au Burkina Faso.*

Molenaar, E.J. & Tsamenyi, M. 2000. *Satellite Based Vessel Monitoring Systems (VMSs) for Fisheries Management – International Legal Aspects and Developments in State Practice.* FAO Legal Paper Online No. 7.

N'Diaye, B. 1994. *Synopsis des législations des pêches du Cap Vert, de la Gambie, de la Guinée, de la Guinée-Bissau, de la Mauritanie et du Sénégal.*

Ngoubili, A. 1996. *Propositions préliminaires pour la réglementation des affrètements de navires de pêche au Congo.*

Ouédraogo, H. 1996. *Burkina Faso. Avant-projet de code des forêts, de la faune et de la pêche.*

Pereira, E. 1996. *Projecto de lei das pescas para São Tomé e Principe.*

Pires Filho d'Almeida, I. 1996. *Mozambique. Aquaculture Legislation. Report on Legal Assistance.*

Pires Filho d'Almeida, I. 1996. *Mozambique. Legal Framework Governing Shrimpculture.*

Rackowe, R., Roberts, K. & Tandstad, M. 1996. *Cooperation Between Angola and Namibia on the Management of Transboundary Stocks.*

Roberts, K. 1995. *Legal Aspects of Monitoring, Control, and Surveillance of Fisheries and Prosecution of Offences.*

Samb, A. 1999. *Haïti. Définition d'une politique générale et élaboration d'un plan d'action pour la pêche et l'aquaculture. Rapport de la consultation sur les institutions et la législation des pêches.*

Sané, M. 1996. *Proposta de regulamento geral do exercício da pesca para a Guiné-Bissau.*

Scovazzi, T. & Reynolds, J.E. 1992. *Eritrea. Initial Considerations and Proposals for an Eritrean Fisheries Legal Framework.*

Silly, D.G. 1995. *Les accords bilatéraux de pêche conclus par la Mauritanie.*

Talla, P. 2002. *Projet de rédaction finale des textes législatifs sur la pêche et sur l'aquaculture au Gabon.*

Tavares de Pinho, A. 1994. *Moçambique. Projecto de Regulamento da pesca maritima.*

Tavares de Pinho, A. 1996. *Propostas para a regulamentação da pesca artesanal na Guiné-Bissau.*

Van Houtte, A. 1992. *Cyprus. Preliminary Report on Legal Aspects of Environmental Management of Aquaculture Development.*

Van Houtte, A. 1993. *Malaysia, Sri Lanka, Korea, Indonesia. Legal Research Work on Legislation Governing Interaction between Aquaculture and the Environment.*

Van Houtte, A. 1996. *Mauritius. Implementation of Recent International Fisheries Agreements: A Few Issues for Discussion.*

VI. LAND

Barrière, O. 1997. *Rwanda. Cadre juridique de la réforme foncière. Analyses et propositions préliminaires.*

Barrière, O. & Barrière C. 1997. *Le foncier-environnement. Fondements juridico-institutionnels pour une gestion viable des ressources naturelles renouvelables au Sahel.* Legislative Study No. 60.

Bouderbala, N. 1992. *Burundi. Appui à l'élaboration d'un code rural.*

Bouderbala, N. 1993. *Législation foncière rurale en RDP Lao. Avant-projets de textes annotés.*

Bouderbala, N. 1995. *Burundi. Appui à la conception d'un code rural.*

Bouderbala, N. 1995. *Guinée. Réglementation foncière rurale.*

Bouderbala, N. 1998. *Niger. Réglementation foncière rurale.*

Bouderbala, N. 2000. *Les voies possibles d'évolution des terres domaniales en Algérie.*

Bouderbala, N., Arzika, S., Ari Lawan, G. & Yacouba, M. 1999. *Niger. Réglementation foncière rurale. Projets de textes complémentaires du code rural.*

Bouderbala, N., Cavérivière, M., Dérouiche, M., Mangatalle, D. & Ratiaray, R. 1992. *Les périmètres irrigués en droit comparé africain (Madagascar, Maroc, Niger, Sénégal, Tunisie).* Legislative Study No. 48.

Bouderbala, N., Cavérivière, M. & Ouédraogo, H. 1996. *Tendances d'évolution des législations agrofoncières en Afrique francophone.* Legislative Study No. 56.

Bouderbala, N. & Mekouar, M.A. 1992. *Législation foncière et forestière au Laos.*

Bouderbala, N., Nanni, M. & Mekouar, M.A. 1993. *Législation foncière, forestière et hydraulique en RDP Lao.*

Bouderbala, N., Sow, B.S. & Sy, M.A. 1996. *Guinée. Réglementation foncière rurale.*

Breton, J. M. 1994. *Réforme de la législation agro-foncière au Congo.*

Christy, L.C. & Riddell, J.C. 1994. *Mongolia. Land Regularization Policies for Sustainable Agriculture.*

Cliffe, L. & McAuslan, P. 1998. *Swaziland. Legal and Institutional Assistance to the Land Resettlement Programme.*

Dezfouli, I.B. 1996. *Iran. Land and Water Law and Institutions.*

Fingleton, J.S. 1998. *Legal Recognition of Indigenous Groups.* FAO Legal Paper Online No. 1.

Hernández, A.R. 1992. *Normas jurídicas relativas a la reforma agraria en Nicaragua.*

Hernández, A.R. 1994. *Bolivia. Legislación agraria. Informe de misión.*

Hodgson, S., Cullinan, C. & Campbell, K. 1999. *Land Ownership and Foreigners: A Comparative Analysis of Regulatory Approaches to the Acquisition and Use of Land by Foreigners.* FAO Legal Paper Online No. 6.

Kern, E. 1992. *Final Report to the Government of the Cook Islands on the Legislative Framework for Conservation and Restoration in Land Use.*

Lamb, A.J. & Lindsay, J.M. 2000. *FAO Legal Assistance to the Government of Sri Lanka in Connection with the World Bank Land Titling and Related Services Project.*

Leonen, M. & Lindsay, J.M. 1997. *Philippines: Support Activities for Indigenous Groups in Agrarian Reform Communities - Report on the Legal Framework.*

Lindsay, J.M. 1997. *Creating a Legal Framework for Land Registration in Eritrea.*

Lindsay, J.M., Palmer, D. & Rekhi, V.S. 2001. *Land Administration and Management in Madhya Pradesh.*

Lindsay, J.M. & Trenchard, R.J. 1995. *Guyana: Land Policy and Administration - Identifying Constraints to Agrarian Reform.*

Lindsay, J.M. & Trenchard, R.J. 1997. *Swaziland. Legal and Institutional Assistance to the Land Resettlement Programme.*

Machado, P.A.L. 1992. *Legislação agraria da República de Cabo Verde. Anteprojecto de Lei Rural.*

Madureira, S. 1996. *Venezuela. Aspectos institucionales de la tenencia de la tierra y desarrollo rural.*

McAuslan, P., Behnke, R.H. & Howard, J. 1995. *Namibia. Assistance in Implementation of Agricultural (Commercial) Land Reform.*

Marong, A.B.M. 1999. *The Legal Framework for Participatory Planning: Final Report on Legal Aspects of Land Tenure, Planning and Management in The Gambia.*

Mekouar, M.A. 1993. *Laos. Gestion durable des ressources foncières: aspects juridiques et institutionnels.*

Mekouar, M.A. 1994. *Laos. Espaces villageois et transactions foncières: aspects juridiques.*

Mekouar, M.A. 1998. *Niger. Réglementation foncière rurale.*

Okoth-Ogendo, H.W.O. 1995. *Reform of Land Tenure and Land Use Legislation in Tanzania.*

Pires, I. 1996. *Mozambique. Support to the Land Commission.*

Pires, I. 1998. *Anteprojecto de Revisão do Regulamento da Lei de Terras de Moçambique: Comentários e recomendações.*

Sarpong, G.A. 1999. *The Legal Framework for Participatory Planning: Final Report on Legal Aspects of Land Tenure, Planning and Management in Ghana.*

Tanner, C. 2002. *Law Making in an African Context: The 1997 Mozambican Land Law.* FAO Legal Paper Online No. 26.

Toppin-Allahar, C. 2002. *Land Law and Agricultural Diversification in the Eastern Caribbean: A Regional Overview of Issues and Options in OECS Countries.*

Valletta, W. 1994. *Lithuania. Agricultural and Environmental Legislation: Report on Land Property Legislation.*

Valletta, W. 2000. *Completing the Transition: Lithuania Nears the End of its Land Restitution and Reform Programme.* FAO Legal Paper Online No. 11.

Valletta, W. & Keith, S. 1998. *The Introduction of Agricultural Land Leasing into Estonia: Agricultural Land Leases as Part of Continuing Land Reform.*

Valletta, W. & Keith, S. 1998. *The Introduction of Agricultural Land Leasing into Estonia: Considerations for Agricultural Land Leasehold.*

Valletta, W. & Nosick, V. 2002. *Ukraine: The Continuing Dilemma of Land Rights of the People.* FAO Legal Paper Online No. 25.

Viesca de la Garza, E. & Martínez, R. 1994. *Colombia. Propuesta de decreto con el cual se reglamenta la Ley de adecuación de tierras.*

VII. FORESTRY

Bellongini, P. & Cirelli, M.T. 1999. *Albania. Technical Assistance to the Forestry Project. Institutional and Legal Issues.*

Bouderbala, N. & Mekouar, M.A. 1992. *Législation foncière et forestière au Laos.*

Bouderbala, N., Nanni, M. & Mekouar, M.A. 1993. *Législation foncière, forestière et hydraulique en RDP Lao.*

Burchi, S. 1992. *Myanmar. Draft Forestry Act.*

Canal-Forgues, E. 1999. *Niger. Législation forestière. Projets de loi et de décret portant code forestier.*

Cavérivière, M. 1995. *Burkina Faso. Avant-projet de loi relative aux forêts.*

Christy, L.C. 1993. *Report to the Royal Government of Bhutan on Forestry Legislation.*

Christy, L.C. 2001. *Report to the United Nations Interim Administration in Kosovo on Forestry Legislation.*

Christy, L.C. & Morell, M. 1995. *Namibia. Issues in Forestry Legislation.*

Cirelli, M.T. 1995. *Armenia. Forestry Legislation.*

Cirelli, M.T. 1997. *Romania. Forestry Legislation.*

Cirelli, M.T. & Christy, L.C. 1992. *Fiji. Forestry Legislation.*

Cirelli, M.T. & Uliescu, M. 1998. *Romania. Forestry Legislation: Review, Issues and Recommendations for Reform.*

Cullinan, C. 1996. *Suriname. Strengthening National Capacity for Sustainable Development of Forests on Public Lands.*

Djibril, L., Fall, A., Doumbé-Billé, S. & Mekouar, M.A. 1996. *Mauritanie. Réactualisation des législations forestière et faunique.*

Doumbé-Billé, S. 1998. *Madagascar. Contrôle de la production et assistance à l'exportation des produits forestiers.*

Doumbé-Billé, S. 1999. *République du Tchad. Appui à la révision du code forestier.*

Du Saussay, C. 1992. *Législation forestière cap-verdienne. Projet de décret portant réglementation du régime forestier.*

Du Saussay, C. 1992. *La législation forestière marocaine.*

Du Saussay, C. 1997. *Congo. Appui à l'élaboration d'une nouvelle législation forestière.*

Du Saussay, C. & Zaki, A. 1995. *Comores. Politique et législation forestières.*

Edens, J. 1999. *Suriname. Elaboration of Regulations for the Forest Management Act.*

FAO. 1999. *Tchad. Projet de loi portant régime des forêts, de la faune et de la pêche.*

Fingleton, J.S. 1994. *Tonga. Review of Agriculture and Forestry Legislation.*

Fingleton, J.S. 2001. *Vanuatu. Assistance in Forestry Legislation.*

Fingleton, J.S. 2002. *Regional Study on Pacific Islands Forestry Legislation.* FAO Legal Paper Online No. 30.

García Váldez, O. 1993. *Bolivia. Revisión de la Ley general forestal.*

Garea Alonso, J.M. 2001. *La Ley Forestal de Cuba: su importancia y repercusión.* FAO Legal Paper Online No. 17.

Grandbois, M. & Pereira Raposo, C. 1996. *Assistance to Mozambique on Forestry and Wildlife Law.*

Hilmi, H.A. & Blatch, C. 2000. *Development of the Private Forestry Sector in Lithuania.*

Hilmi, H.A., Jerrold, R.M. & Rosenbaum, K.L. 1997. *Bangladesh: Support to Master Plan for the Forestry Sector.*

Kamara, C.S.B., Djibril, L., Fall, A. & Doumbé-Billé, S. 1995. *Mauritanie. Réactualisation des législations forestière et faunique.*

Kamto, M. 2001. *Cameroun. Examen critique des textes sur l'aménagement forestier et propositions.*

Lindsay, J.M. 1995. *Community Forestry Rules for Myanmar.*

Lindsay, J.M. 1996. *Recommendations for Revised Forestry Legislation for Zanzibar.*

Lindsay, J.M. 2001. *India. Improving the Legal Framework for Sustainable Forest Management in Himachal Pradesh: Issues and Options in the Light of International Experience (IIED).*

Lindsay, J.M., Mekouar, M.A. & Christy, L.C. 2002. *Why Law Matters: Design Principles for Strengthening the Role of Forestry Legislation in Reducing Illegal Activities and Corrupt Practices.* FAO Legal Paper Online No. 27.

Lindsay, J.M. & Rosenbaum, K. 2001. *An Overview of National Forest Funds: Current Approaches and Future Opportunities.* FAO Legal Paper Online No. 15.

Maidoka, A. 2001. *Appui à la relance de la production et de la commercialisation de la gomme arabique au Niger.*

Mekouar, M.A. 1992. *Guinée. Réglementation forestière.*

Mekouar, M.A. 1993. *Législation sur les forêts, la faune et la pêche au Burkina Faso.*

Mekouar, M.A. 1993. *Législation forestière en RDP Lao. Avant-projets de textes annotés.*

Mekouar, M.A. 1993. *Mission Report on Forestry Legislation in Jordan.*

Mekouar, M.A. 1993. *Mission Report on Forestry Legislation in Syria.*

Mekouar, M.A. 1996. *Bénin. Législation forestière et faunique.*

Mekouar, M.A. 1996. *Cambodge. Législation forestière. Projets de textes juridiques annotés.*

Mekouar, M.A. 1998. *Haïti. Avant-projets de lois sur les forêts et les aires protégées.*

Mekouar, M.A. 1998. *Maroc. Avant-projet de code forestier.*

Ouédraogo, H. 1996. *Burkina Faso. Avant-projet de code des forêts, de la faune et de la pêche.*

Paveri-Anziani, M. & Mekouar, M.A. 1996. *Cuba. Formulación de una nueva ley forestal.*

Pires, I. 1999. *Mozambique: Forestry and Wildlife Regulations – Mission Report on Legal Assistance.*

Riveros Rey, F.E. 2001. *Paraguay. Apoyo a la Mesa forestal nacional.*

Rosenbaum, K. 2001. *Climate Change and the Forestry Sector: Possible Legislative Responses for National and Subnational Governments.* FAO Legal Paper Online No. 14.

Rosenbaum, K. 2001. *Forest Law in Kosovo.*

Rosenbaum, K. 2002. *Forest Law in Kosovo. Follow-Up.*

Saastamoinen, O., Silima, P.A., Lischi, M. & Lindsay, J.M. 1995. *Tanzania. Formulation of a National Forest Policy for Zanzibar.*

Young, T.R. 1995. *Tonga. Review of Forestry and Related Legislation and Proposals for its Revision.*

Young, T.R. 1995. *Evaluation of Commercial Forest Plantation Resources of Trinidad and Tobago.*

Young, T.R. 1996. *Indonesia. Legal Issues Relating to Strengthening National Forest Fire Management Capacity.*

Young, T.R. 1997. *Bhutan. Forestry Legislaton.*

Young, T.R. 1998. *China, Mongolia, Myanmar, Viet Nam – Recommendations Regarding Legislation in Support of the Transition of Forestry Activities to Market Economic Operation.*

Young, T.R. 1999. *Slovak Republic. Harmonization of Legislation and Strategy for Development of the Forestry Sector.*

VIII. WILDLIFE AND PROTECTED AREAS

Cirelli, M.T. 1993. *Albania. Review of the Draft Law on the Protection of Wildlife, Hunting and Fisheries in Inland Waters.*

Doumbé-Billé, S. 2001. *Droit international de la faune et des aires protégées: importance et implications pour l'Afrique.* FAO Legal Paper Online No. 20.

FAO. 1999. *Tchad. Projet de loi portant régime des forêts, de la faune et de la pêche.*

Grandbois, M. & Pereira Raposo, C. 1996. *Assistance to Mozambique on Forestry and Wildlife Law.*

Hitchcock, L. 1996. *Tanzania. Proceedings and Materials from Workshop on Revision of National Parks Legislation.*

Hitchcock, L. 1997. *Tanzania. Annotated Discussion Draft of Proposed National Parks Act.*

Hitchcock, L. & Shauri, V. 1998. *Tanzania. Revised Annotated Discussion Draft of Proposed National Parks Act.*

Konate, A. 2001. *Tendances d'évolution du droit de la faune et des aires protégées en Afrique centrale.* FAO Legal Paper Online No. 21.

Lería, C. 1998. *Malaysia. Marine Parks and Reserves: A Brief Overview.*

Ly, D. 2000. *Congo. Révision de la législation relative à la faune et aux aires protégées.*

Ly, D., Fall, A., Doumbé-Billé, S. & Mekouar, M.A. 1996. *Mauritanie. Réactualisation des législations forestière et faunique.*

Ly, I. 2001. *Tendances d'évolution du droit de la faune et des aires protégées en Afrique occidentale.* FAO Legal Paper Online No. 13.

Mekouar, M.A. 1993. *Législation sur les forêts, la faune et la pêche au Burkina Faso.*

Mekouar, M.A. 1994. *Guinée. Mise en oeuvre du code de la protection de la faune et de la réglementation de la chasse.*

Mekouar, M.A. 1996. *Bénin. Législation forestière et faunique.*

Mekouar, M.A. 1998. *Bénin. Révision de la législation relative à la faune.*

Mekouar, M.A. 1998. *Haïti. Avant-projets de lois sur les forêts et les aires protégées.*

Ouédraogo, H. 1995. *Burkina Faso. Avant-projet de loi relative à la faune.*

Ouédraogo, H. 1996. *Burkina Faso. Avant-projet de code des forêts, de la faune et de la pêche.*

Pires, I. 1999. *Mozambique: Forestry and Wildlife Regulations - Mission Report on Legal Assistance.*

Wilkinson, P.F. & Young, T.R. 1993. *Environmental Legislation in the Seychelles. Conservation and National Parks Laws and Regulations. Review of Legislation Regarding Nature Conservation and the Establishment and Management of Protected Areas and Recommendations Regarding Revision or Additional Legislation.*

Young, T.R. 1992. *Tanzania. Marine Parks and Reserves Act and Regulations: Legislative Proposal regarding the Management of Marine Resources in the Proposed Mafia Island Marine Reserve and Provision for Future Additional Reserves.*

IX. AGRICULTURE

Banklerova, A. 1996. *Strategy for Agricultural and Rural Development in Slovakia.*

Bisson, J.M. & Cavérivière, M. 1994. *République Centrafricaine. Investissements privés dans le secteur agricole.*

Bouderbala, N. 1997. *Haïti. Appui à la définition d'une politique de réforme agro-foncière.*

Bouderbala, N. & Zirari, M. 1995. *Maroc. Etude pour la mise à jour du code des investissements agricoles.*

Canal-Forgues, E. 1997. *Palestine. Review of Agricultural Legislation.*

Cavérivière, M., Dyemkouma, D. & Zampou, J. 1999. *Burkina Faso. Appui à l'élaboration du code des investissements agricoles.*

Chiaradia-Bousquet, J.-P. 1992. *Indonesia. Agricultural Legislation.*

Diallo, C. 1994. *Mali. Etude de redéfinition du cadre juridique et institutionnel de la radio rurale.*

Diallo, C. 2000. *Mali. Etude de définition du cadre juridique des services privés de diffusion sonore par voie hertzienne terrestre en modulation de fréquence.*

Doumbé-Billé, S. 1996. *Mauritanie. Législation des oasis.*

FAO. 1999. *Mali. Appui à l'inventaire des normes et coutumes en matière de foncier pastoral.*

FAO. 2000. *Legal Framework Analysis for Rural and Agricultural Investment Projects: Concepts and Guidelines.* FAO Legal Paper Online No. 12.

Fingleton, J.S. 1994. *Tonga. Review of Agriculture and Forestry Legislation. Report of Formulation Mission.*

Fingleton, J.S. 1999. *Bahamas. Assistance to Review Agricultural Policies and Legislation.*

Fingleton, J.S. 2000. *Papua New Guinea. Assistance in Agriculture Legislation in Support of Food Security.*

Galán, B.B. 1996. *Venezuela. Consultoría en legislación agraria.*

Galán, B.B. 1997. *Venezuela. Asistencia en la revisión del anteproyecto de ley orgánica de desarrollo agropecuario y seguridad alimentaria y en la formulación de los respectivos reglamentos de aplicación.*

Garea Alonso, J.M. & Sosa, M.O. 2001. *Reforma agraria: la experiencia cubana.* FAO Legal Paper Online No. 22.

Glowka, L. 2002. *The Role of Law in Realising the Potential and Avoiding the Risks of Modern Biotechnology. Selected Issues of Relevance to Food and Agriculture.*

Henry, H. 1994. *Viet Nam. Review of Proposed Cooperatives Legislation.*

Hernández, A.R. 1996. *Paraguay. Apoyo a la reestructuración del Instituto de Bienestar Rural.*

Heugas, J.F. & Makon, P.H. 1995. *Guinée. Promotion des organisations paysannes.*

Makon, P.H. 1996. *Cameroun. Formulation d'un programme sectoriel de promotion des PME agricoles, agro-alimentaires et rurales. Aspects juridiques.*

McCalla, W. 1993. *Grenada. Final Mission Report to the Government on Legislation for Farmers and Growers Associations.*

Mekouar, M.A. 2002. *A Global Instrument on Agrobiodiversity: The International Treaty on Plant Genetic Resources for Food and Agriculture.* FAO Legal Paper Online No. 24.

Ouédraogo, H. & Cavérivière, M. 2001. *Plan d'action et programme d'investissement pour le secteur de l'élevage au Burkina Faso. Le cadre juridique: avant-projet de code pastoral.*

Ouédraogo, H. & Diallo, M. 1992. *Guinée. Elaboration du code pastoral.*

Oz, G. & Von Zebinsky, M. 1997. *Assistance for Agricultural Policy Reform in Turkey Relating to GATT and EU Agreements.*

X. ENVIRONMENT

Awogbade, S. 2000. *Nigeria. Streamlining Environmental Law and Agricultural Practices for Sustainable Development.*

Barrière, O. & Barrière, C. 1997. *Le foncier-environnement. Fondements juridico-institutionnels pour une gestion viable des ressources naturelles renouvelables au Sahel.* Legislative Study No. 60.

Bensted-Smith, R. 1995. *Tanzania. Environmental Legislation for Zanzibar.*

Boelaert-Suominen, S. & Cullinan, C. 1994. *Legal and Institutional Aspects of Integrated Coastal Zone Management.*

Cullinan, C. 1999. *Malawi. Environmental and Natural Resources Management.*

Ecaat, J. 1997. *Uganda. Final Report on Linkages between Water Use Permits and EIA Procedures for Uganda.*

FAO. 1994. *Kingdom of Cambodia. Draft Natural Resource and Environmental Management Law. Review and Comments.*

FAO. 1999. *Maroc. Projets de lois relatives à l'environnement et aux déchets. Observations et suggestions.*

Filali Meknassi, R. 2002. *Maroc. Etude sur la loi montagne - Rapport préliminaire.*

Kern, E. 1992. *Final Report to the Government of the Cook Islands on the Legislative Framework for Conservation and Restoration in Land Use.*

Kern, E. 1994. *Nigeria. In-depth Study of Federal and State Legislation related to Environmental Protection and Natural Resources Conservation and Management.*

Kern, E. 1995. *Tanzania. Final Report for Zanzibar. Annotated Draft Environmental Legislation.*

Kern, E. 1996. *Laos. Environmental Policy and Planning for Sustainable Agriculture and Rural Development.*

Loulidi, S. 1999. *Burundi. Appui à l'élaboration d'une législation des marais.*

Loulidi, S. & Mekouar, M.A. 2001. *Projet de loi sur les marais au Burundi.* FAO Legal Paper Online No. 19.

Mekouar, M.A. 1992. *Gestion durable de l'environnement à Djibouti: aperçu sur quelques aspects juridiques et institutionnels.*

Mekouar, M.A. 1995. *Cameroun. Législation de l'environnement: cadre institutionnel.*

Mekouar, M.A. 2001. *Le droit à l'environnement dans la charte africaine des droits de l'homme et des peuples.* FAO Legal Paper Online No. 14.

Nimpagaritse, D., Ndayishimiye, P. & Hakizimana, C. 1999. *Burundi. Législation des marais. Aspects juridiques, contexte socio-économique et dimensions techniques: état des lieux et premières propositions.*

Ntambirweki, J. 1998. *Uganda. Report on the Proposed Water (Environmental Impact Assessment) Regulations.*

Ouédraogo, H. 1994. *Les coutumes relatives à la gestion des ressources naturelles au Burkina Faso.*

Ouédraogo, H. 2002. *Rép. dém. du Congo. Appui à la formulation d'un cadre juridique de gestion de l'environnement.*

Prieur, M. 1994. *Evaluation des impacts sur l'environnement pour un développement rural durable: étude juridique.* Legislative Study No. 53.

Van Houtte, A. 1992. *Cyprus. Preliminary Report on Legal Aspects of Environmental Management of Aquaculture Development.*

Van Houtte, A. 1993. *Comoros. Integrated Coastal Zone Management Legislation.*

Van Houtte, A. 1993. *Malaysia, Sri Lanka, Korea, Indonesia. Legal Research Work on Legislation Governing Interaction between Aquaculture and the Environment.*

Wilkinson, P.F. & Young, T.R. 1993. *Environmental Legislation in the Seychelles. Conservation and National Parks Laws and Regulations. Review of Legislation Regarding Nature Conservation and the Establishment and Management of Protected Areas and Recommendations Regarding Revision or Additional Legislation.*

Young, T.R. 1995. *Tanzania. Institutional Support for the Protection of East African Biodiversity.*

Young, T.R. 1996. *Cyprus. Legal Framework and Monitoring Measures for the Protection and Management of Nature.*

1. Wildlife and national park legislation in Asia, 1971 (E*)
2. Wildlife and national park legislation in Latin America, 1971 (E* S*)
3. Vicuña conservation legislation, 1971 (E* S*)
4. Legal systems for environment protection: Japan, Sweden, United States, 1973 (E*)
5. Agrarian law and judicial systems, 1975 (E* F* S*)
6. Agricultural credit legislation in selected developing countries, 1974 (E*)
7. An outline of food law, 1983 (E* F S*)
8. Legislación de aguas en América Central, Caribe y México – Vol. I, 1983 (S)
9. A legal and institutional framework for natural resources management, 1983 (E S)
10. Water law in selected European countries (Belgium, England and Wales, France, Israel, Italy, Spain, Turkey) – Vol. I, 1979 (E* F S*)
11. Fundamentos teóricos para una legislación tributaria en el sector agropecuario, 1976 (S*)
12. International food standards and national laws, 1976 (E F*)
13. Derecho agrario y desarrollo agrícola: estado actual y perspectivas en América Latina, 1978 (S*)
14. Legal and institutional responses to growing water demand, 1977 (E* F* S*)
15. Systematic index of international water resources treaties, declarations, acts and cases by basin – Vol. I, 1978 (E/F/S*)
16. Seed legislation, 1980 (E F* S)
17. Water law in selected African countries, 1980 (E* F S)
18. Reforma agraria y desarrollo rural integrado, 1979 (S*)
19. Water legislation in South American countries, 1983 (E* F S*)
20. Legislation on wildlife, hunting and protected areas in some European countries, 1980 (E* F* S*)
21. Coastal state requirements for foreign fishing has been replaced by FISHLEX database published in the FAO Legal Office home page: www.fao.org/Legal
22. Agricultural insurance legislation, 1981 (E* S*)
23. The law of international water resources, 1980 (E* F S)
24. Irrigation users' organizations in the legislation and administration of certain Latin American countries, 1983 (E S)

25. Legislation on wildlife and protected areas in Africa, 1984 (E F)
26. The UN Convention on the Law of the Sea: impacts on tuna regulation, 1982 (E F)
27. Regional compendium of fisheries legislation – West Africa (CECAF Region), 1983 (E/F*)
28. Plant protection legislation, 1984 (E* F S)
29. Legislation on foods for infants and small children, 1983 (E*)
30. Water law in selected European countries (Cyprus, Finland, the Netherlands, Union of Soviet Socialist Republics, Yugoslavia) – Vol. II, 1983 (E)
31. The role of legislation in land use planning for developing countries, 1985 (E)
32. Agricultural census legislation, 1984 (E*)
33. Legislation on productivity in agriculture: a comparative outline, 1985 (E F S)
34. Systematic index of international water resources treaties, declarations, acts and cases by basin – Vol. II, 1984 (E/F/S*)
35. Regional compendium of fisheries legislation (Western Pacific Region) – Vols. I and II, 1984 (E)
36. Legislation controlling the international beef and veal trade, 1985 (E* F S)
37. La législation forestière au Cap-Vert, en Ethiopie, en Gambie, au Mali et en Mauritanie, au Niger, au Rwanda et au Sénégal, 1986 (F)
38. The environmental impact of economic incentives for agricultural production: a comparative law study, 1990 (E F S)
39. Propiedad, tenencia y redistribución de tierras en la legislación de América Central y México, 1986 (S)
40. International groundwater resources law, 1986 (E F S)
41. Land tenure systems and forest policy, 1987 (E F)
42. Regional compendium of fisheries legislation (Indian Ocean Region) – Vols I and II, 1987 (E)
43. Pesticide labelling legislation, 1988 (E F S)
44. La réforme du droit de la terre dans certains pays d'Afrique francophone, 1987 (F)
45. Legal aspects of international joint ventures in agriculture, 1990 (E)
46. The freshwater-maritime interface: legal and institutional aspects, 1990 (E)
47. The regulation of driftnet fishing on the high seas: legal issues, 1991 (E F)

48. Les périmètres irrigués en droit comparé africain (Madagascar, Maroc, Niger, Sénégal, Tunisie), 1992 (F)
49. Analyse préliminaire de certains textes législatifs régissant l'aquaculture, 1993 (F S)
50. Treaties concerning the non-navigational uses of international watercourses – Europe, 1993 (E/F/S)
51. Pesticide registration legislation, 1995 (E F)
52. Preparating national regulations for water resources management, 1994 (E)
53. Evaluation des impacts sur l'environnement pour un développement rural durable: étude juridique, 1994 (F)
54. Legislation governing food control and quality certification – The authorities and procedures, 1995 (E F)
55. Treaties concerning the non-navigational uses of international watercourses – Asia, 1995 (E/F)
56. Tendances d'évolution des législations agrofroncières en Afrique francophone, 1996 (F)
57. Coastal State requirements for foreign fishing, 1996 (E), has been replaced by FISHLEX database published in the FAO Legal Office home page:www.fao.org/Legal
58. Readings in African customary water law, 1996 (E/F)
59. Cadre juridique de la sécurité alimentaire, 1996 (F)
60. Le foncier-environnement – Fondements juridico-institutionnels pour une gestion viable des ressources naturelles renouvelables au Sahel, 1997 (F)
61. Treaties concerning the non-navigational uses of international watercourses – Africa, 1997 (E/F)
62. New principles of phytosanitary legislation, 1999 (E F S)
63. The burden of proof in natural resources legislation – Some critical issues for fisheries law, 1998 (E)
64. Política y legislación de aguas en el Istmo centroamericano – El Salvador, Guatemala, Honduras, 1998 (S)
65. Sources of international water law, 1998 (E)
66. Trends in Forestry Law in America and Asia, 1998 (E F S)
67. Issues in water law reform, 1999 (E)
68. Extracts from international and regional instruments and declarations, and other authoritative texts addressing the right to food, 1999 (E/F/S)

69. Élaboration des réglementations nationales de gestion des ressources en eau – Principes et pratiques, 1999 (F)
70. Water rights administration – Experience, issues and guidelines, 2001 (E)
71. Fisheries enforcement – Related legal and institutional issues: national, subregional or regional perspectives, 2001 (E)
72. Trends in forestry law in Europe and Africa, 2001 (E)
73. Law and sustainable development since Rio – Legal trends in agriculture and natural resource management, 2002 (E)
74. Legal trends in wildlife management, 2002 (E S)
75. Mountains and the law – Emerging trends, 2002 (E F)

ANNUAL PUBLICATION

Food and Agricultural Legislation (E/F/S) - A selection of significant and illustrative laws and regulations governing food and agriculture in FAO Member Nations has been replaced by FAOLEX database published in the FAO Legal Office Web site: www.fao.org or directly at http://faolex.fao.org/faolex/

Availability: November 2002

Ar	– Arabic	Multil	– Multilingual
C	– Chinese	*	Out of print
E	– English	**	In preparation
F	– French		
P	– Portuguese		
S	– Spanish		

The FAO Technical Papers are available through the authorized FAO Sales Agents or directly from Sales and Marketing Group, FAO, Viale delle Terme di Caracalla, 00100 Rome, Italy.